Shetland's Boats

Shetland's Boats: origin, evolution and use

by Marc Chivers

The Shetland Times Ltd.
Lerwick
2022

First published by The Shetland Times Ltd., 2022.

ISBN 978-1-910997-41-3

A catalogue record for this book
is available from the British Library.

Printed and published by
The Shetland Times Ltd.,
Gremista, Lerwick,
Shetland ZE1 0PX

Dedication

To all those, past and present, who set
forth upon the sea in small open boats.

Contents

List of illustrations

Foreword

I t is testimony to the enduring place of the open boat in the culture of
Shetland that 150 years after the islands' renowned working boats were
said to have reached their apogee, it has still been possible for Marc
Chivers to recover previously unrecorded information about the building and
operation of these watercraft (and their direct descendants) from oral sources
and artisanal practices that live on in the islands. And, although it might
be held that the radical economic and social changes which impacted the
islands during the late 20th and early 21st centuries meant that the centrality
of the wooden boat to "the Shetland way of life" shrank in people's everyday
experience, this book is a welcome reminder that, beneath the surface of the
many changes that have taken place, the cultural imprint of the open boat
has – like traditional fiddle music – come to exemplify one of the strong and
reviving currents within the islanders' perceptions of who and what they are,
and where they have come from. Prospective readers would be misled however
if they thought that this book was of interest to Shetland folk alone, for its
appeal is far wider than that.

True, for the intellectually curious readership within the islands themselves,
Shetland historians and the archipelago's many boat enthusiasts, it will
provide the first rigorous, geographically comprehensive, and graphically
detailed work on the origins, inter-island distribution and many-faceted
typology of "their" vernacular open boats. Quite simply, the author's research
has exponentially enlarged the meaningful, but regrettably incomplete,
descriptive coverage of the subject provided by earlier writers. This critical
mass of "new knowledge" is the informed result of sympathetic, island-wide
fieldwork carried out over recent years, perceptive examination of archival
and printed sources in Scotland and Norway, and the special understanding
that is afforded by hands-on boat usage and construction.

Beyond Shetland's shores the factual content and constructs embraced
in this book earns the author a place within the purview of that respected
national discipline, Scottish ethnology, itself the successor to an extraordinary school of formal (and amateur) "folk life" practitioners whose work
ranges back to the late 1800s when, by no coincidence, the first serious
antiquarian writings about Shetland's unique boat culture emerged. Indeed,
Marc's approach reflects not just that of the modern university-based ethnological disciplines, but encouragingly retains much of the eclectic spirit of the
older folk life canon too. Moreover, when surveyed in the rather specialised
context of British maritime history, it makes a significant contribution to
what may sketchily be termed the archaeology of the British vernacular boat

– its technology, empirical design, and socio-economic functions. Arguably, it might be claimed that his work provides the most extensive in-depth study of a regionally significant British open boat type yet published, carrying surveys of this kind to a commendable new level. Beyond which, it displays an international dimension in conveying new evidence and ideas on the type's transition from pure Norwegian break-bulk import to independent, home-produced "Shetland Model".

At its heart, the book tells the story of the Shetland boat with an authority that requires no help from the writer of this foreword, except perhaps to gently underscore an intrinsic theme. In former times the old Nordic adage, "Bound is the Boatless Man", undoubtedly held true in Hjaltland (Shetland) as well. But all too often a boat might also bind a man and his dependents to a life which comprised little more than survival at sea, bare subsistence on land, and economic servitude to others. Existential conditions that, in retrospect, we can offset just a little today by pursuing an understanding not only of the complex, easily lost, seafaring skills acquired by so many individuals over so many generations, but also by continuing to value the craft of those artisans whose collective labours expressed a unique regional identity when working with that peerless natural material – wood.

It has been a pleasure and a privilege to see Marc's work grow, from "makkin the keel" up ...

Dr Adrian G. Osler
Lesbury, 2021

Preface

This book is the culmination of research for a PhD jointly funded by Lerwick Port Authority and Shetland Amenity Trust. This resulted in a thesis, completed in 2017, titled "Shetland Vernacular Boats 1500-2000", and this is an edited version of that work. Included is new information that recently came to light relating to the early eighteenth century import of boats from Norway to Shetland. The accidental uncovering of this Shetland Museum and Archives' (SMA) document illustrates that there is still much to learn about the development and use of Shetland's small open boats, and this book is just another stage on that journey of discovery.

Research by its nature builds upon the previous work of other people. Prior to beginning this research, during the preliminary review of the literature, it became evident that the majority of authors had generally, sometimes romantically, focused upon particular types of nineteenth century commercial fishing boats. The habit of historians to approach this subject in a romantic way was noted by academics Robb Robinson and David J. Starkey during their review of British fisheries research literature (Robinson and Starkey 1996: 121-122).

From a Shetland perspective there were notable exceptions to this romantic and narrow commercial fishing focus. The earliest of these authors was Norwegian maritime historian Atle Thowsen who, in 1969, wrote a chapter in the *Norwegian Yearbook of Maritime History* titled "The Export of Boats to Shetland, and its Influence Upon Shetland Boat Building and Usage". Thowsen analysed Norwegian export documents and undertook a comparative analysis between Norwegian and Shetland boat nomenclature which he then used to identify the probable Norwegian regional influence on Shetland's own types of boats.

One year later, in 1970, Edgar March published his two-volume *Inshore Craft of Britain in the Days of Sail and Oar.* March described and discussed Shetland vernacular boats using letter evidence obtained from John Smith, a fisherman and boatbuilder from Yell. March also discussed information obtained from eighteenth century documents he had been given by Shetland antiquarian Robert Stuart Bruce who was the last of the land-owning Bruces of Symbister, Whalsay.

The final notable work was the research undertaken by Adrian Osler during the 1970s that resulted in the publication, in 1983, of a monograph titled *The Shetland Boat: South Mainland and Fair Isle.* Osler was the first Shetland vernacular-boat author to seriously use folklife source material combining information obtained from artefacts, verbal testimony, and documents. This resulted in an all-round analysis of Shetland's indigenous boats. For me personally the most important elements of Osler's research was that on hull-form, oars and rowing, sailing configuration, and the detailed ethnographic account of the processes used by the well-known Shetland boatbuilder Walter Duncan senior to construct a 12 foot of keel boat.

Even with the contributions these authors have made to compiling the story of Shetland's small open boats there remained a somewhat fragmented picture of the development of indigenous boatbuilding, and the purposes for which these boats were used. The purpose of my research was therefore to simply provide a more complete narrative about the origin, development and uses of Shetland's vernacular boats. The approach was similar to the one adopted by the curator of Shetland Museum and Archives, Dr Ian Tait, in his book *Shetland Vernacular Buildings 1600-1900*.

The situation in regard to Shetland's native buildings is analogous with Shetland's native boats: the examination of this topic had been limited and large gaps were left in the knowledge of their nature, origin and evolution. The sources of evidence used to try to address these gaps in knowledge include representative examples of surviving boats from the nineteenth century forward to the present day, linguistic evidence found within the remains of Shetland's native language Norn which was replaced by Scottish/English during the latter part of the eighteenth century (Barnes, 1998:2), archive documents, historic images and oral history.

Acknowledgements

The person to whom I owe everything is Rachel, or Rae as she is known by her friends. The PhD and this book would have foundered at the start had it not been for Rae's tireless patience, support, encouragement, advice and her willingness to leave Devon and move to Shetland. Next are my sons Tom and Matt, their mum Rachael, and my extended family whose forbearance has been constant, thank you.

Thank you to the funders of the PhD, Shetland Amenity Trust (SAT) and Lerwick Port Authority, and in particular Jimmy Moncrieff, who died prematurely in 2017. Special thanks go to my director of studies, Dr Andrew Jennings, Institute for Northern Studies (INS), University of the Highlands & Islands (UHI) for his guidance, support and friendship. I am enormously thankful to my supervisor Brian Smith, along with Emeritus Professor Arne Emil Christensen, Dr Ian Tait and Dr Adrian Osler for sharing their expertise and knowledge. Thanks also to Dr Simon Clarke, Archaeology Institute, UHI; Dr David J. Starkey, Professor of Maritime History, University of Hull; Professor Donna Heddle INS, UHI; and Professor Tom McKean, Elphinstone Institute, University of Aberdeen. I am very grateful to Dr Michael Stratigos and Ian Tait for getting me involved in their wonderful project to document Shetland's oldest boat, *Mary* LK 981.

People have been exceptionally generous in sharing their knowledge, giving hours, and in some cases days, of their time. In particular Brian Wishart who has been generous in the extreme and who taught me the technique of sailing a traditional Shetland boat. Brian, along with Jim Tait and Robert Wishart, has been instrumental in reviving traditional sailing skills and training the enthusiastic crew of Shetland Museum's replica sixareen *Vaila Mae*. Others who have generously given their time and shared their expertise are: Leslie Moncrieff, Malcolm Hutchison, Angus McNeil, Tommy Isbister, Willie Mouat, Alan Moncrieff, Robbie Tait, Jack Duncan, Stuart Williamson, Ian Best, Charlie Simpson, Allister Rendall, Davy Leask, George Peterson, Maurice Henderson, Andrew Holt, Dr Angela Watt, Lisa Watt, Davy Cooper (SAT), Eileen Brooke Freeman (SAT), Dr Val Turner (County Archaeologist, SAT), Dr Viveka Velupillai (Professor of Linguistics, University of Giessen), Ronnie Eunson, Linda Sutherland, Bobby Johnson, Dr Esther Renwick (Archaeology Shetland, and director of Moder Dy CIC), Dr Claire Christie, the SCAPE Trust (in particular Dr Jo Hambly, Dr Tom Dawson, and Ellie Graham), Archaeology Shetland's Steven Jennings and Caroline Henderson, Robbie Simpson, George Johnson, Gordon Johnson, Robbie Williamson, George Hutchison, Joe Kay, Davy Johnson, Emma Miller (organiser of

Shetland Boat Week) Dr Jonathan Wills, Allister Rendall, Davy Leask, peerie Walter Duncan, George Peterson, Andrew Holt, Dr Silke Reepleog, Roberto Getto, and the Trondra yoal rowing team.

Enormous thanks to Duncan Sandison who passed away on 24th October, 2020, aged 93. Duncan's contribution to competitive sailing in Shetland and the preservation of its maritime heritage in the form of the Unst Boat Haven museum is immense. Special thanks also to the staff at the boat haven. The support provided by Shetland Museum and Archives has been unwavering, and I am particularly grateful to the museum's curator, Ian Tait, and archivist and historian Brian Smith and the staff in the archives, Angus Johnson, Dr Mark Smith, and Blair Bruce. Thank you to Jenny Murray, Laurie Goodlad and Carol Christiansen who pointed me in the direction of artefacts in the museum store, and Trevor Jamieson for his practical boat advice. I would like to say a special thank you to John and Wendy Scott of Gardie House, Bressay, who generously permitted me access to their private archive, and archive assistant Jane Manson who located documents that yielded information that underpins this book, and to Bressay History Group. Thanks also to historian John Ballantyne who has generously pointed out sources that have led to new insights. Thanks also to Ruth Priest and Susan Davy the librarians at the North Atlantic Fisheries College Marine Centre, and Shetland College.

Thanks to Grieg and Jo Anderson who invited Rae and me to Whalsay soon after we arrived in Shetland and introduced us to the Whalsay History Group. Thank you to George Lamont Williamson, Laurina Herculson (who sadly died on the same day as Duncan Sandison) and her husband Tony who provided me with insight into life in Burra before the bridge came. Thanks also to the other members of Burra History Group and in particular Adalene Fullerton and Douglas Sinclair. Other Burra residents I would like to thank are Davy Inkster, Susan Inkster, Geordie Duncan, George and Barbara Tait, Ewen and Kim Tait, Elaine Tait, Peter and Joan Eunson and their daughter Emma, Michael Pottinger and Bobby Hunter.

The Norwegian input into this research has been generous in the extreme. I would again like to thank Arne Emil Christensen, who welcomed me into his Oslo home and who shared, amongst many things, his knowledge and expertise in documenting boats. I would like to thank Kjell Magnus Økland, whose knowledge of the Oselvar boat is phenomenal, and who, with his family, welcomed me into their Bergen home. Thanks also goes to a friend sorely missed, and his family, Oselvar boatbuilder Hallgeir Forstrønen Bjørnevik, who tragically died in 2016 leaving his wife Kari, and four wonderful children.

Finally, I would like to thank The Shetland Times publishing team and in particular Robert Wishart for his no-nonsense support in publishing this book.

Glossary

Shetland and Norwegian boat terms

This is not a complete list of Shetland dialect or Norwegian boat terminology but is a guide to words used in this book, with some additions. There is no standard spelling of dialect words and correspondents, publishers and authors have at times adopted different spellings, sometimes to try to replicate usage in a specific locality. The first word in each entry is generally the spelling if the word is used in this volume, with some variations given for interest. An explanation has generally been given in the text when a term is first used. By necessity, definitions given here are somewhat simplified.

Air, ar, remak, remek, or rimmek. Oar.

Andoo or andu. By help of oars to keep a boat from drifting with wind and tide. To keep the boat in the same spot by rowing slightly against wind or tide.

Åttring. A west Norwegian eight-oared boat.

Auskerry, owskerri or austkerrie. Bailer carved from a single piece of wood.

Ayre. Beach.

Band, baand, or baund. Timber or frame.

Bark. An early modern period version of skuda, sometimes referred to as a bark during the sixteenth and seventeenth centuries.

Bete. A west Norwegian term for cross-tie beam, in Shetland called a bekk, fastiband, or haddabaund.

Bowline. System of ropes used for tensioning the luff of a dipping asymmetric square sail.

Bught. Fishing lines that when combined formed a pakki (a set of fishing lines). Each crew member had two pakkis of lines. When all crew members' pakkis were joined together they formed one great longline called a fleet of tows.

Deal boat. Shetland boats constructed from imported deal timber.

Deal. Standard size fir or pine boards.

Eela. A term used to describe the close-to-shore non-commercial fishery.

Færing. A Norwegian four-oared boat.

Fastiband, hadiband, haddabaund, or bekk. A cross-tie beam affixed to the band which holds the band in shape and permits the taft (thwart) to be removable.

First garbuird. Garboard strake.

Fiskavils. Upright slats fixed under the fastiband that stops the catch of fish sliding fore and aft in the boat.

Fitlin. A stretcher in a boat supporting the feet in rowing.

Flattie. A term used to describe a flat-bottomed dinghy.

Fourareen, fourern. Four-oared boat Shetland boat.

Haaf. The eighteenth and nineteenth century commercial deep ocean fishery.

Hals, halsane. Norwegian term for the axe-carved fore (fram hals) and aft end (bak hals) boards of the garboard strake.

Halsins, hassins. Fore and aft strake sections joined in the middle by a board called the slot. Commonly the second strake run up from the keel, although this does vary regionally.

Halv yoal, peerie yoal. A smaller version of a full sized yoal.

Hinnispot, hunnispot or honeyspot. Breasthook.

Hjaltabåt/Hjeltebåt. Norwegian, from Old Norse meaning "Shetland boat".

Hjalta-skantar. Norwegian, derived from Old Norse meaning "Shetland template" used to pattern the boards/strakes for Shetland boats.

Homliband, humlaband, or humliband. A grommet made originally of rawhide for fixing the oar to the thole pin, or kabe.

Horn. Stem head.

Jekt. A small Norwegian cargo vessel.

Kabe, kaeb or keb. Wooden thole pin.

Kappi. A stone fishing weight used to hold a longline in position on the seabed.

Kirkebåt. A west Norwegian church boat. Usually owned by the community and used for going to church.

Kjølrenne. Norwegian word which roughly translates to keel trench, meaning a double garboard. Created a deeper underwater section which enabled boats to perform better when sailing to windward.

Knar. A large medieval Scandinavian trading vessel which in Shetland was called a knorrin.

Linns. Commonly whale rib bones, or pieces of wood, laid down at a landing place over which a boat is drawn.

Longline. A fishing line constructed of smaller lines (bughts) tied together that lay on the seabed, held in position at either end by stone sinkers attached to surface marker buoys.

Nigler. Bung for the nile.

Nile. Drainage hole in the bottom of a boat.

Noost. A shelter for a boat.

Owse. To bail.

Pakki. A set of fishing lines (each fisherman had a set of two pakkis) which when joined together formed a bught of line. When all the crews bughts of lines were joined together this formed a longline called a fleet of tows.

Pram. A type of small clinker constructed dinghy with transom stern and a transom bow.

Quillie or whillie. A small fourareen of 10 feet of keel or less.

Rae. The yard.

Rakkie. Curved piece of hardwood, bone, or cow horn which acts to hold the rae (yard) against the stong (mast).

Reebing, reebin, ribin or neebeen. Sheer strake.

Remek, remak. Oar

Rimwol. The rubbing strake of the gunwale.

Rong. Norwegian word for the frames nearest the bow and stern, in Shetland stameron.

Roost. Tidal race.

Rum, room. The divisions within a boat.

Ruth. A piece of wood upon which the oar rests and pivots against the kabe.

Säi, säien or si. Tarred strip of cloth laid between two overlapping strakes on a clinker boat.

Second garbuird. Next strake from garboard.

Segel. Sail.

Sem. An iron nail.

Set-up. A term used to describe a completely built boat.

Shott, run, waderum. The rum or room within the boat where the catch of fish was kept.

Sixareen. Shetland boat developed for the haaf fishing. Can be defined as a six-oared boat with a keel length greater than 17.5ft and usually rowed by six men.

Skair or sker. A scarph or scarf joint.

Sklette. The protective hardwood pieces (traditionally oak) that were nailed to the loom of the oar that had wearing contact with the ruth and the kabe.

Skúda/skuda. A medieval small general purpose Scandinavian ship. Early modern period versions of these vessels are sometimes referred to as barks during the sixteenth and seventeenth centuries.

Snikk. Bead moulding

Soolbuird or sulbuird. The strakes above the waterline.

Stameron, stammeron, stamron, stammering. The bands nearest the bow and the stern.

Steed. A place where a boat is drawn along to or from its noost.

Stockfish. Salted air-dried white fish.

Stong. Mast.

Strood. Shroud.

Taft. Thwart.

Tilfer. Sole board.

Tows. Halyard.

Unset-up. A term used to describe a boat in boards that comprised its roughly cut component parts.

Voe. A relatively long and narrow sea inlet.

Wearing or wairin. Stringer running fore and aft upon which the taft (thwart) rest.

Yoal. A type of six-oared boat that typically (due to its narrow hull form) was suited for use in the notorious seas surrounding the southern part of Shetland's mainland and Fair Isle.

General boat terms

Athwartships. Across the boat from one side to the other.

Ballast. A weight, usually of iron, lead or in Shetland often beach stones, sometimes a cargo, such as salt placed low down to improve a boat or vessel's stability.

Beam. The maximum width of a boat.

Beur away. To put the helm over in order to turn away from another vessel or the wind.

Beating. To sail close-hauled to windward on alternate tacks.

Bermuda rig. Triangular mainsail, generally of high aspect ratio.

Bevel. An angle cut into a piece of wood, usually to facilitate the joining of that piece to another. For example: a clinker strake is bevelled on the outside upper edge to permit the next strake to overlap if for a watertight fit.

Bilge. On the outside it is curved underpart of the hull of a boat where it curves towards the keel. Inside it is the lowest part of the boat or vessel.

Boltrope. A rope sewn into the edge of a sail to strengthen it and take the strain of halyards and sheets.

Broach-to. With the wind astern a boat may sometimes swing broadside into the troughs of waves – a dangerous position in an open boat in breaking seas.

Broad reach. Sailing with the wind just aft of the beam.

Carvel-built. When the strakes are laid edge to edge, thus making a smooth hull surface.

Cleat. A specially shaped piece of wood to which a rope can be made fast.

Clinker-built. The opposite of carvel. The strakes are laid slightly overlapping each other.

Close-hauled. Sailing to windward as close to the wind as possible.

Crook. A naturally grown branch or root of a tree in a shape suitable for a structural member.

Draught. The minimum depth of water a vessel requires to float freely.

Feather. When rowing the oar, after leaving the water at the end of the stroke, is turned horizontally as it comes forward. This lessens its resistance to wind and spray.

Freeboard. The height of the gunwhale above the waterline.

Garboard strake. The planks next to the keel. In Shetland called the boddam runner.

Gudgeon. A fitting that takes a pintle to create a hinge upon which the rudder swings.

Gunter. A triangular mainsail with its head fixed to a yard, which when hauled up extends above the masthead.

Gunwale. Pronounced "gunnel". The top edge of a boat's side.

Gybe. To alter course when the wind is astern to bring the wind from one side of the boat to the other, bringing the stern through the wind.

Halyard. A rope used for hoisting; in Shetland called the tows.

Horse. Metal rod on which the mainsheet traveller is mounted.

Jib. Triangular sail attached to a forestay.

Knee. A brace or bracket between two adjoining members used to strengthen the hull.

Laid-up. Not in commission.

Lee. The side away from the wind.

Leech. The trailing edge of a sail.

Leeward. Away from the wind.

Loom. The shaft of an oar.

Luff. Leading edge of a sail

Neap tide. Those that occur between spring tides, having the least rise and fall.

Neck of an oar. The narrow outboard part next to the blade.

Pintle. Fits into the gudgeon to form a hinge on which the rudder swings.

Planing. To move over the water at high speed with hull supported by hydrodynamic lift and thus exceeding normal displacement hull-speed.

Point of sailing. Course relative to the wind. For example: close-hauled, reaching, running.

Port. The left-hand side of the vessel facing forward.

Quarter. Between amidships and the stern, referred to as the port or starboard quarter.

Reach. To sail across the wind.

Reef. (v) To shorten sail. (n) The part of the sail so reduced.

Rig. The general arrangement of a vessel's sails and masts.

Rove. Iron or copper washer used to form a rivet on a clinker boat.

Rubbing strake. A protective strip of wood fitted all round the boat just below the gunwale preventing chafing when moored alongside another vessel, jetty or quay.

Run. Sail with the wind astern.

Scarph. A bevelled joint between two short pieces of wood to make a long one. In Shetland called a sker.

Sheer. The uppermost visible line of the hull in profile view.

Sheet. Rope attached to and controlling the angle of the sail to the wind.

Shroud. Rope or wire supporting a mast athwartships.

Spring tide. Those that occur between neap tides, which have greatest rise and fall of tide.

Starboard. The right-hand side of a vessel facing forward.

Stay. Rigging supporting the mast fore and aft.

Strakes. The side planks in the hull.

Stringer. A longitudinal strengthening member fastened inside the frames.

Tack. Forward lower corner of a sail.

Tacking. In sailing to windward, putting the boat through the wind to take the wind from one side to the other. Also referred to as going about or staying.

Thimble. A grooved metal ring generally heart-shaped around which a wire or rope is spliced to make an eye.

Thwart. Seat running across the boat, in Shetland called a taft.

Transom. The transverse structure at the aft end of the boat on which the strakes are fastened.

Trenel. A wooden dowel fastening, partially cut across the grain, driven into a pre-bored hole. A wedge is driven into the cross grain cut to hold it in place, the end of which is then trimmed.

Trim. The balance of the boat either athwartships or fore-and-aft.

Windward. The direction from which the wind is blowing. Sailing to windward: beating, close-hauled.

Yard. A spar hoisted on the mast to hold or spread a sail, in Shetland called a rae.

Abbreviations, references and conventions

Abbreviated references are given in brackets in the text. For example: (Pålsson and Edwards 1978: 132). The full reference is given in the list of references at the end of the book: Pålsson, H. and Edwards, P. (1978) *Orkneyinga Saga: The history of the earls of Orkney.* London, Penguin Books.

INS	Institute for Northern Studies.
NLS	National Library of Scotland.
NRO	National Records Office.
OA	Orkney Archives.
SAT	Shetland Amenity Trust.
SMA	Shetland Museum and Archives.
UHI	University of the Highlands and Islands.
PC	Personal communication with the author.
PI	Personal interview with the author.

Distances at sea are in nautical miles and on land in statute miles unless otherwise stated (a nautical mile is approximately 1.15 statute miles).

Boat names can confuse or be duplicated so where available the registered number is also given. For example: *Mary* LK981.

It is normal practice to give boat lengths "overall" – over the stems. However, throughout this publication the term "length of keel" is used. This was, and remains, the normal measurement of length of Shetland boats. The length of keel is the distance between the forward and aft stem scarf joints as measured from inside the boat.

Chapter 1

'Bound is a boatless man'

T his is the story of the origin and evolution of Shetland's unique small boat heritage. It is an investigation into how Shetlanders developed and used boats for their subsistence living, for commercial fishing and, latterly, for recreational purposes.

Documentary evidence commences in the sixteenth century and the analytical narrative of boat development continues until the latter part of the twentieth century, which is when Shetland's vernacular boat culture declined. The term "vernacular" is used to describe boats whose development and construction relied on local knowledge and available materials. Shetland's vernacular craft are defined as being of clinker construction, open, double-ended and were four or six-oared rowing/sailing boats. These craft were originally square sail rigged which by the mid-nineteenth century had evolved into the widely adopted and more efficient higher peaked asymmetric dipping square sail (Osler 1983: 15, 38). During the latter part of the nineteenth century the standing lug rig also became popular, although in some parts of Shetland, notably Fair Isle, the square sail remained the preferred rig until the early 1900s (Osler 1983: 38). The standing lug, along with the fore-and-aft sliding gunter, were adopted for recreational racing which began around 1880, and these rigs were later followed in the twentieth century by the Bermudan rig (Osler 1983: 15, 28, 38; PC, Wishart, R. 2020).

The origin of Shetland's vernacular boatbuilding tradition was western Norway. The nomenclature of Shetland's four- and six-oared boats followed the naming conventions of that region, where boats were generally named by the number of oars they used. Therefore, a boat with four oars was called a færing and in Shetland it was known as a fourareen or fourern (Fig.1). Similarly, the six-oared boat in western Norway was called a seksæring and in Shetland a sixareen or sixern (Fig. 2) (Thowsen 1969: 166). Early twentieth century Faroese etymologist Jakob Jakobsen studied the surviving remnants of Shetland's variant of Old Norse called Norn. Jakobsen identified that Shetland's boat nomenclature was Norn in origin, this means that these naming conventions date from the medieval period (Jakobsen 1928: 197, 747).

Within these Shetland six- and four-oared boat categories was another boat type called the yoal. The yoal did not follow this naming convention. Instead it was broadly named after the districts where these boats were commonly used – Fair Isle and Dunrossness. Hence the boats from these districts were called the Fair Isle yoal, and the Ness yoal (Figs. 3, 4). Within the Ness yoal

Fig. 1. *Burra to Quarff to ferry passengers. Photo: J. H. Smith, circa 1900. Courtesy of Shetland Museum & Archives.*

Fig. 2. *Sixareen* Industry *racing under dipping lug sail at Walls. Photographer: unknown. Courtesy of Shetland Museum & Archives.*

category there was a smaller type of four- or six-oared boat called a halv yoal. These halv yoals are considered a separate type to that of the Fair Isle and Ness yoal (Fig. 5) (PI, Moncrieff and Wishart, B. 2015).

The Shetland terms fourareen and sixareen are broad classifications of a general boat type, and within these broad categories there were also other distinct types of boat. For example, the smallest sized fourareen was called a quillie or whillie, and the fishing this type of boat engaged in was known as the eela (a term used to describe the inshore fishery) and, occasionally, these whillies were simply referred to as eela boats (Nicolson 1981: 8). Within the six-oared boat category there were a variety of other sub-categories defined by the type of fishing these boats primarily engaged in (or in some instances the time of year that the fishing took place). These sub-categories were the haddock boat, and the cod boat – sometimes called the summer boat (Figs. 6, 7) (Nicolson 1981: 6). As well as these vernacular craft there were two other rarely mentioned types, the flattie (it had a transom stern and, as its name suggests, a flat bottom) and the pramm dinghy, which also had a transom stern (Figs. 8, 9). These boats were used on lochs, in harbours, and on the sheltered waters of voes. Both were in common use until recent years, and it is important that they are mentioned, even though they do not fall within the conventional realm of the Shetland vernacular boat (Tait, 2014: 20).

Fig. 3. *The Taft yoal* Dolphin *(built as a joint effort by the crew) in North Haven, Fair Isle, circa 1900. Photographer: unknown. Courtesy of Shetland Museum & Archives.*

Fig. 4. *Ness Yoal* Kate *LK152, owned by Brian Wishart and Leslie Moncrieff. Photographer: unknown. Courtesy of Shetland Museum & Archives.*

Fig. 5. *The six-oared halv yoal* Phar-Lapp *(blue and cream). Shetland Museum & Archives boat collection. Photo: M. Chivers.*

Fig. 6. Christina *LK2, a haddock boat.*
Photo: J. Peterson, circa 1930. Courtesy of
Shetland Museum & Archives.

Fig. 7. *Summer/cod boat* Ann *LK126, Shetland*
Museum & Archives boat collection.
Photo: M. Chivers.

Fig. 8. *Tommy Mainland of Bressay rowing a flattie. Photo: C. Stout, circa 1930. Courtesy of Shetland*
Museum & Archives.

Fig. 9. *Group in pramm, Eela Water, Northmavine. Photo: W. Brown, circa 1900. Courtesy of Shetland Museum & Archives.*

Early boat use

Until relatively recently small open boats were essential modes of transport for people in Shetland and the sea was the road upon which all Shetlanders travelled. The majority of families owned a small four-oared boat just as the majority of families own a car today. These boats were built to be lightweight and all the internal furniture was designed so that it could be easily removed, thus making the boat even lighter which enabled it to be hauled up and down a beach with relative ease.

Shetland is an archipelago of more than 100 islands straddling the 60th parallel, 400 miles south of the Arctic Circle. John o' Groats, which is the most northerly tip of the Scottish mainland, lies 104 miles to the southwest. Bergen lies 220 miles east of Shetland's capital town Lerwick, and Tórshavn in Faroe lies approximately the same distance to the northwest (Fig. 10).

The first inhabitants arrived in Shetland 6,000 years ago. This was a gradual northerly European migration, with people travelling from France to the south of England and then on through mainland Scotland, then to Orkney, Fair Isle and eventually the rest of Shetland (Ballin 2011:32). We can only speculate about the design and construction of the craft in which these early settlers travelled (which is beyond the scope of this book). The earliest tangible evidence of boats in Shetland dates from the Norse period which began around 800 CE. The date for Norse settlement has been determined by

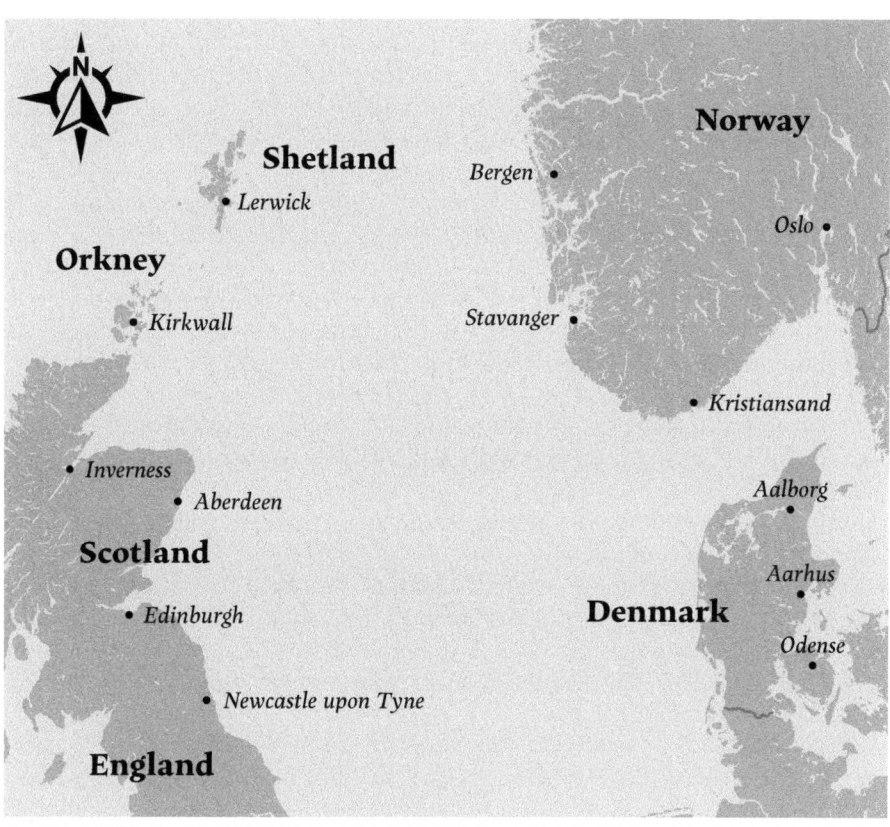

Fig. 10. *Map illustrating Shetland's geographic location.*

the dating of artefacts such as the firebox inserted into the floor of a Pictish dwelling radiocarbon dated to 850-960 CE and material found in middens at Jarlshof and Underhoull (Turner, Bond and Larsen 2013: 4; Barrett 2008: 674; Hamilton 1957: 197-222).

These Norse colonisers came from western Norway and they adopted similar settlement patterns to those found in Faroe (MacGregor 1987: 32). In the Norse world the landscape dictated the pattern of settlement. A Norse settlement required easy access to the sea, a good place to haul up a boat, agriculture potential, grazing, and access to fresh water (Small 1968: 149, Lamb 2010: 85). Settlement therefore occurred around sounds, bays and voes. The colonisation of Shetland was enabled by the development of clinker boatbuilding technology which permitted the Norse to fully exploit fishing, trade and piracy (Hall 2007:50). Norse boatbuilding technology therefore also played a role in determining dwelling site preference, as these vessels were light for their size and so could easily be landed on any suitable beach and then hauled ashore (Lamb 2010: 85). Perhaps the best tangible evidence of the types of small boats used by the Norse during this period was found in a boat burial at Wick of Aith on the east coast island of Fetlar. This site was first formally identified in 1878, and locally is known as the Giants Grave which, according to local folklore, is associated with a seafaring Norseman who died in the vicinity (Batey 2016: 39-40).

The site had previously been disturbed during the 1930s revealing some boat rivets, these were donated to the National Museum in Edinburgh (Batey 2016: 40). The site was excavated in August 2002 by a team of archaeologists from Channel 4s *Time Team* led by Magnar Dalland who had previously excavated the boat burial at Scar on the island of Sanday in Orkney. The excavation revealed a Norse boat burial which is thought to commemorate a woman. The outline shape of the boat was defined by the ferrous fastenings. Almost no wood was preserved, apart from a small section of keel that had the remains of the garboard strakes attached. The excavation revealed that the boat had a maximum beam of 2.6m and was no longer than 8m (Batey 2016: 40-41). Batey described this boat find as a færing, and she drew parallels with other small boat burials. These dimensions, however, are actually too large for a færing, and it is more likely that this boat was a seksæring. To illustrate this point, the færing that formed part of the burial furniture of the Gokstad ship, which was discovered in a mound on a farm in west Norway in 1880, was only 6.5m long and 1.38m beam. (Christensen 1968: 30-32; Greenhill 1976: 212; Williams 2014: 52).

The Gokstad ship has been dated to around 890 CE which is the same period as the boat discovered in Fetlar. The dating of the Fetlar burial was

Fig. 11. *Seksæring boat from the Gokstad ship burial on display Viking Ship Museum, Oslo. Photo: M. Chivers.*

made possible by the discovery of a woman's oval brooch. There were no other finds, and it is now believed that the sole occupant of this grave was possibly a high-status woman who was buried at some point during the mid-ninth century or perhaps later (Batey 2016: 40-41).

What the sagas say

Twelfth century saga evidence, because of its late date, needs to be interpreted with caution. However, the sagas can provide clues about facets of life incidental to the narrative of the saga itself, especially when analysed against historical and archaeological sources (Power 1990: 13; Barrett 1995: 30-41).

In the *Orkneyinga Saga* ships are frequently mentioned and boats occasionally. In the context of this book the most pertinent accounts are of the small boats used for fishing. These, along with the photographs of the small Gokstad seksæring in Fig. 11, provide us with an idea of what these boats were like. For example, there is an account of one Uni rowing from Shetland to Fair Isle with three young Shetlanders in a seksæring (Pålsson and Edwards 1978: 132). Another example is about an occasion when Earl Rognvald, disguised by cloak and cowl, offered his services to a poor farmer whose fishing companion had not turned up. The farmer accepted the earl's help, and they rowed out in a færing in front of Sumburgh Head and inside the islet called Hundholm. There, the roost, a great stream of tide, was running; they had to lie in the eddy but fish outside the roost. The Earl sat in the forward part of the boat andooin (using the oars to keep the boat in position) but he paid too little attention and the boat slipped into the strong tide of the Sumburgh roost. The farmer rebuked the Earl: "Just my miserable luck to take you rowing with me today. Now I am going to die here, and no one to help my family, left penniless if I die." ... "Cheer up, farmer", said the cowled man, dry your eyes. He who let us drift into the current will bring us out of it as well" (Pålsson and Edwards 1978: 159). These two accounts illustrate that small four- and six-oared boats were being used for fishing in Shetland and, as Shetland archivist Brian Smith points out, this text is full of life, enabling us to imagine these events happening in places we still know today (Smith 1988: 37).

Small four- and six-oared boats were perfectly suited to the fishing requirements of the time. The boats were handled by people with a tradition of seafaring; they were efficient for operation in tideways and long swells, they were fast and seaworthy. The high flared prow deflected spray away from the boat which helped keep the water out and the crew dry, whilst its long narrow hull ensured good directional stability in long seas. The low freeboard made for good rowing qualities, and its lightness enabled ease of handling ashore. That these boats had poor load-carrying capabilities suggest that fish were plentiful and could be caught at any time by going just a short distance from the shore (Goodlad 1971: 58).

Shetland's need for timber

Although there is material, and some literary, evidence for boat use in Shetland during the Norse period, there is no evidence for boat repair or boatbuilding. Wooden boats by their nature will have required repairs. Shetland, like the rest of the North Atlantic islands, lacked exploitable woodland and forests and was reliant on driftwood, wreck-wood, timber re-use, and timber imports. Driftwood has long been an important natural resource, with timber drifting across the sea from Canada and Norway to Shetland's coasts, where it was collected from the shore, and by imports from overseas (Tait 2012: 105; Thór 2009: 326, 336).

In Shetland there is a driftwood gathering tradition where material left above the high-water mark is regarded as the property of the gatherer and must not be taken by anyone else. Indeed, the importance of driftwood to the Norse is demonstrated by the number of bays in Shetland that are named Treawick (Old Norse meaning tree bay). Further proof of the importance of driftwood was provided by Shetland museum curator Ian Tait, who identified the conversion of a disused boat noost into a sawpit at Underhoull in Unst (Fig. 12) (Tait 2012: 113). Noosts are boat shelters that were generally, but not always, unroofed. This is one of a pair of remaining noosts which have recently been dated by a team of archaeologists from the University of

Fig. 12. *Thirteenth century noost in Underhoull, Unst. Note the addition of an internal wall structure that transformed the noost into a sawpit during the sixteenth century. Photo: M. Chivers.*

Glasgow to the late Norse period. The dating used a technique called optically stimulating luminescence whereby mineral sediments are tested to determine when they were last exposed to daylight. The results indicate that the noosts were constructed in the early part of the thirteenth century and that the conversion of one of the noosts into a sawpit occurred during the middle part of the sixteenth century (Kinnaird, Sanderson, Preston, Dugmore and Newton 2017: 43-44). The dating is important as it provides us with tangible evidence of a continued boat and timber use tradition.

Conjecturally, timber imports from Norway to Shetland began when Shetland was first colonised by the Norse. This opinion is supported by sources that indicate that timber was being exported from Norway to Iceland during the Norse period (Thowsen 1969: 147; Fenton 1978: 552; Osler 1983: 15; Davis 2011: 34). Indeed, if timber was being imported from Norway then, speculatively, boat components such as stems, keels and pre-cut strakes were also coming to Shetland via this route and these pre-fashioned items would have saved valuable cargo space (Osler 1983: 18).

Historian Chris Smout pointed out that "... Scotland and Norway have had an immemorial history of political and commercial contact, reaching back to the distant days of Viking rule, and to the alliances between Scottish and Danish/Norwegian kings" (Smout 1963: 153). The first documented evidence for Shetland's trading relationship with Norway was provided in the form of a speech made in Bergen by King Sverre in 1186. King Sverre denounced

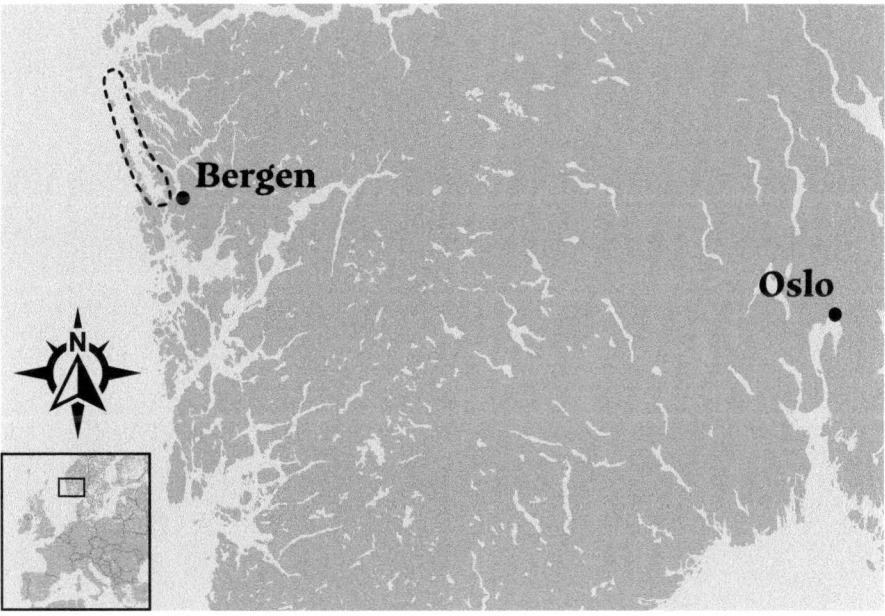

Fig. 13. *Map illustrating the location of Hjeltefjorden.*

German wine traders from Rhineland in favour of merchants from England, Orkney, Shetland, Faroe and Iceland: "We thank all Englishmen because they came here, those who brought wheat, honey, flour and cloth. And we further thank all those who have brought linen and flax, wax and kettles, and we also mention amicably those who have come from the Orkney or Shetland or Faroe Islands or Iceland ..." (Storm and Bugge 1914: 113).

The evidence supporting this long-standing trading relationship is further strengthened by the fjord in Norway that leads to the entrance of Bergen harbour, called Hjeltefjorden (Old Norse meaning Shetland fjord) (Fig. 13). This is a main shipping route into Bergen, and Shetlanders must have frequently sailed along it for it to be named after them.

Chapter 2
Shetland fishing boats 1500-1740

Everyday life of "common" people in Shetland was seldom documented so the sixteenth and seventeenth century evidence for boat use in relation to fishing is limited. However, there must have been plenty of boats, by dint that settlement in Shetland was predominantly coastal and, as there were no roads, all travel was by sea (Donaldson 1958: 44). The population survived through subsistence farming and fishing and both required the use of a boat (Tait 2012: 45).

Shetland Documents 1580-1611 has references to boats that are listed amongst the items of people's moveable property (Ballantyne and Smith 1994: 189, 203, 219). Whilst there is very little detail about the actual boats, and scant information about their use, the available information does provide us with an idea of the types of boats that were commonly being used during this period. The first mention of these boats appears in the schound bill of Peter of Kirkabister, in North Yell, dated October 1605. A schound bill in Orkney and Shetland was the legal division of a dead person's property, and listed amongst Peter's possessions was "... ane auld sixarin boit ..." The use of the term "auld ... boit" is frequently used in documents, but this does not mean the boat was actually old. As historian Gordon Donaldson explained, the use of this term lowered the boat's value and thereby the total value of the estate which meant that less tax (quot) would be payable (Donaldson 1958: 46).

The next mention of a boat was found in the schound bill of James Spence of Midbrak, dated March 1607, in which a "sex haring bot" was listed amongst the "inventarie of the movabill guddis and gaeir." As previously described the nomenclature for these types of craft had, as the main descriptor, the number of oars the boat used, and this followed the naming convention used in western Norway. The term "sixairn boit" (Old Scots) is the same in form as the nineteenth century Shetland term "sixern boat"; "sex haring" is a slightly different variant of the word, but it has precisely the same meaning. The people so far described as owning boats were wealthy but boat ownership during the sixteenth and seventeenth centuries was not the sole preserve of the rich, as even a poor man such as Donald Johnson at Vollister in Yell, whose estate was worth just £26 13s. 4d., had his own boat (Donaldson 1958: 46).

More documented evidence of boats appeared in the testament of Margaret Stewart, spouse of William Bruce of Symbister. This testament, written in September 1608, listed amongst the moveable goods "2 yollis, price of both £16" (Ballantyne and Smith 1994: 219).

The term yoll

During the seventeenth century the word yoll was used to describe a small double-ended type of boat (Online Scots dictionary 2016). There was a similar timber and boat trade between the coastal communities in Northern Ireland and Trondheim in Norway. The boats imported to Ireland were known locally as drontheims (Madill 2008: 51-52). Donal MacPolin wrote about the vernacular boats of Ireland, and claimed that the term yawl, in the Irish Donegal drontheim context, was derived from the Old Norse word yol (MacPolin 2008: 62).

MacPolin's claim is curious, because Jakobsen, in his dictionary of the Norn language, did not list any of the word variants of the term yol. This is perplexing, considering that this boat-term was commonly used in south Shetland and in Fair Isle during the 1890s, which was when Jakobsen visited Shetland (Osler 1983: 81). Jakobsen therefore must have been familiar with the yoal as a type of boat but, as Tait percipiently observed, "... he obviously chose to ignore it, which suggests that the word yoal is not of Scandinavian origin, but is instead of Scots origin with English and Dutch variants" (PC, Tait 2016; Online Scots dictionary 2016).

Robert Monteith mentioned a yole in his 1633 manuscript account of the shipwreck of the Duke of Medina, Admiral of the Spanish Armada, in 1588. Medina and his crew were shipwrecked and stranded in Fair Isle for the winter which put unsustainable pressure on the islanders' food stores which resulted in a famine. Monteith wrote: "... they sent a small Boat or Yole to Zetland desiring a ship to carrie them out, lest all the inhabitants at the Isle should be famished" (Sibbald 1845: 53-54). This yole must have been similar to the yalls described by London merchant Captain John Smith who sailed from Gravesend to Shetland in February 1633 and wrote: "... With their small fishing-boats, called yalls, they will row into the main about two or three leagues [6-9 nautical miles], more or less, ... in one of the boats rowing with two men, and sometimes four according to the largeness of the boat ..." (Smith 1673: 256). Smith provided a vague description of the size of these boats stating that "... the Inhabitants do for the most part trade withal is ling and cod, which they take with hooks and lines in small boats, called yalls, about the bigness of Gravesend Oars ..." (Smith 1673: 253-254). The Gravesend oars Smith refers to were probably used by the long ferry barges and maybe the smaller passenger-ferrying tilt boats (tilt refers to the awning used to cover passengers). These ferries provided an important service transporting people and goods along the river Thames to and from London. Comparing the size of boats with the size of "Gravesend oars" is unhelpful due to an absence of evidence concerning the length of these oars. Smith's use of the term yall illustrates the amorphous use of the generic term yoal in the seventeenth century. For example, he uses the word yall when stating that the small boats were rowed by two men and the larger boats by four. The use of the term as a catch-all word for a small double-ended boat means that Smith could arguably be describing four different types of boats as illustrated in Fig. 14: (1) the smallest boat being rowed by two men is a four-oared boat, with each rower pulling one pair of oars; (2) the larger boat rowed by four men could be a four-oared boat; (3) or it could be a six-oared boat, with two rowers sat next to each other amidships pulling one oar each, with one rower sat forward of the midships pair, and one rower sat aft of the midships pair, each pulling one pair of oars; (4) it could be an eight-oared boat with each rower pulling one pair of oars. This means that the word yall, or any of its variant forms in documents, actually tells us nothing about the boat type other than it was small, open, clinker constructed, and double-ended.

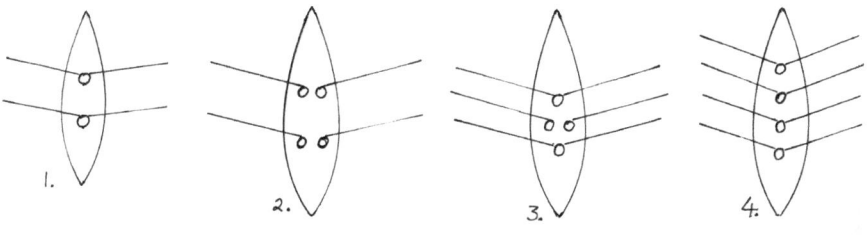

Fig. 14. *Two and four man rowing combinations.*

Boats for fishing

The use of boats for domestic transport, ferrying and trade were of great importance but there was one role upon which Shetland's economy was becoming increasingly dependent, and that was fishing (Donaldson 1958: 45). The development of Shetland's vernacular boats was intrinsically linked to the growth and expansion of the white fish trade. Soon after the mortgaging of Shetland from Norway and Denmark to Scotland in 1469 there began an influx of north German merchants travelling each summer to trade in Shetland (Smith B.1990: 31). These merchants traded directly with the farming and fishing tenants. The tenant was in control of the fishing and the German merchant organised the fish-curing and the trading of the cured product (Smith R.1986: 58). This system worked simply because there were already plentiful boats in Shetland and these were already being used for subsistence and commercial fishing (Goodlad 1971: 76). Subsistence fishing was as important as commercial fishing and, there is no doubt, the boats being used commercially were moulded by their subsistence use, as the distances being sailed or rowed to the fishing grounds, and the methods of fishing employed during this period, in either case, were the same (Smith 1673: 253-256; Donaldson 1958: 49).

In this era Shetland became economically dependent on the annual summer trade. The fishermen traded or sold their catches directly to the German merchants who rented stony beaches that they used for air-drying the fish. Some merchants also had stone booths erected – for which they also paid rent to the proprietor – in which the apparatus for curing fish, the goods for trading, and traded goods were stored (Gifford 1786: 28). The trading role of these German merchants was described by the wealthiest and most powerful of Shetland landowners, Thomas Gifford, in 1733, who stated that 10 or 12 small ships came annually to Shetland from Hamburg and Bremen. Although completed in 1733 Gifford's book was not published until many years later in 1786.

These German merchants imported yearly "... hemp, lines, hooks, tar, linen-cloth, tobacco, Spirits, and beer, for the fishers, and foreign money wherewith they purchased their cargoes" (Gifford 1786: 28). The German trade was a carefully regulated affair in Shetland, and the merchants were told where they could trade and the prices they could charge for goods. But there was more to this trading relationship than straightforward buying and selling (Smith B. 2003: 3). The German merchants fostered dependency on Shetlanders, by placing them in debt through the use of credit in the supply of goods they could otherwise not afford, the credit being settled the following year. This credit scheme had mutual benefits to both tenant and merchant but it also had an unforeseen impact in restraining local enterprise (Smith B. 2003: 3). It has been estimated that Shetland's fishing industry contributed over 10 per cent by value of air-dried fish, called stockfish, entering international trade in the sixteenth and seventeenth centuries. White fish exports at this time were in the region of 500 tons; ling accounted for most of this, with a small percentage of cod and skate making up the remainder of this export trade (Smith H. 1984: 20).

During the sixteenth and seventeenth centuries trading relationships remained constant and dependable. The greatest innovation in the fishing industry at this time was the introduction of the longline, which was introduced by English fishermen to Iceland about 1482 (Thór 2009: 337). In Shetland the longline was first mentioned about 1570 and is thought to have been introduced to Shetlanders by the English and Dutch who by this time had established fishing operations in Shetland (Goodlad 1971: 76). A picture of the types of fishing that was taking place in Shetland is further provided by the 1576 complaint of the people of Fetlar against Laurence Bruce of Cultmalindie, in which three types of fishing tackle were mentioned: the small line, the great line, and the hand line (Donaldson 1958: 49).

As well as the German, English, Dutch and Scottish merchants there were also some other very wealthy seventeenth century entrepreneurial men who organised a commercial fishery and owned several boats. One of these magnates was Robert Sinclair of Brough who had lands in Nesting, Delting, Sandsting, Aithsting, Walls, Whiteness, Weisdale, Northmavine, Bressay, Burra, Dunrossness, Unst and Fetlar. Sinclair's merchant status is irrefutable "... as he owned a ship called the Swanne ... ane great boit for passage ... four greit fisching boitis ... five sixareens ... and four fourareens" (Donaldson, 1958: 81). Of note is the mention of a "great boat" for passage, and this boat type is discussed in chapter three. Unfortunately, there is no evidence that describes the "great fishing boat" so it is impossible to determine what this type of boat looked like. Four of Sinclair's sixareens were kept at Skerries which gave them easy access to the rich fishing grounds to be found off that shore (Donaldson, 1958: 81). Other less wealthy local merchants were Robert Swinton, who was minister of Walls who had three boats, Nicol Gutteromson in Cullivoe, Yell, and Nicol Thomasson at Brek in Walls who had two boats each. Out of all these magnates, James Spence of Midbreck in Yell was the wealthiest but he only had "ane auld boit with her lynis", and the reason for Spence only owning one boat was that his business interest was in farming not fishing (Donaldson, 1958: 45-46).

In addition to fishing for ling and cod Shetlanders were also fishing for saithe and Captain Smith wrote:

> There is also other small fish which the inhabitants do catch with angles sitting on the rocks, and in their small boats with hooks and lines in the sounds, and between the islands; and these small fish are very considerable, for although they cannot spend them by reason of the multitude they take, and have not industry to make use of them for transportation, yet the livers they preserve, and with the livers of the ling and cod, make train-oyle; ... (Smith, 1673: 254).

These small fish were sillocks (immature saithe). The sillocks were caught during the winter when they were close to shore and their livers boiled to release the oil which was collected in barrels (Goodlad, 1971: 71). This trade in saithe-liver oil is known to have begun during the seventeenth century. The livers, once drained of oil, could be rolled in oatmeal and eaten, or they could be made into pies and cooked. Sillock and saithe formed an important part of Shetlanders' everyday diet and this, unlike crops such as grain and kale, was always plentiful, filling nutritional gaps when other food sources failed (Fenton 1978: 527-529). Another important fish caught by Shetlanders with nets from their boats were herrings, which were driven shoreward as the shoals were split by the Dutch herring busses: "... Herrings flee near the Shore, and through the Sounds, where these small Boats, with those Nets they have, take them ..." (Smith 1673: 257).

Further fishing boat evidence was provided during a dispute between Andrew Gifford and Jacob Tait in 1602, in which Gifford bought from Tait "ane new sax earing boit" but Tait refused to make delivery of the boat, "with hir airis and furnitouris," until Gifford had taken him to court (Donaldson,1958: 48). A new detailed descriptive account of a fishing boat was found by Ballantyne (2016) in a disposition made by James Magnusson to Thomas Chesser in March 1626:

... of ane new and sufficient four airing fisheing boit, with hir hail graith, ger and [torn]
[illegible], sick as her bandis, toftis, tilferis, airis and unteris necessaries belonging to hir
quatsumevir, quilk boit perteines to me and in my possessioun [torn] presentlie standing
upon the ground of Quytisnes at the shoir thairof [torn] that place of the same callit
Stanetoo; ... Witnesses: Gilbert Hendrie, merchant, brother german to Thomas Hendrie,
minister at Wals, and Arthur Sinclair, eldest lawful son of William Sinclair of Reawick.
John Neven, notary public (OA, SC11/5/1628/1).

This not only tells us about the boat and where it was lying when it was
sold, but also tells us about the witnesses, two of whom were brothers, one a
merchant, and the other a minister.

The changing pattern of fishing

The pattern of close-to-shore fishing changed from about 1660 onwards
according to the minister John Brand, who visited Shetland in 1701. Brand
commented that the number of fish taken had much decayed during the
last 30 to 40 years, and that the fishermen had to go further out to sea in
their boats: "... until they almost sink the land or else they cannot catch any
fishing worth their expense and pains which cannot but be very toilsome
and dangerous, in case storm should arise and blow off the Land, and so
put them to sea, with their little boats or yoals, ..." (Brand 1701: 194). Brand's
comment that the fishermen "... almost sink the land ..." must be viewed
cautiously, as it contradicts Captain Smith who perhaps should be more
readily believed as he (unlike Brand) was actively engaged in the fishing
industry (Smith 1673: 256). Indeed, Brand later contradicts himself, by
stating that the fishermen caught fish between the islands of Bressay
and Whalsay (the total distance from island to island is 10 miles, which
is the same distance previously stated by Smith) (Brand 1701: 198). Brand,
however, did provide other evidence of Shetlanders' ability in boat handling:
"... and can with some dexteritie and skill attained by experience manage
their boats not only because of their frequent passing from Isle to Isle, and
going over the voes or lochs which lie in upon and cut the mainland, it by
reason of their great fishing ..." (Brand 1701: 198). This perhaps is a more
credible account because Brand will have witnessed this himself first-hand
as he was transported about Shetland by boat.
  Although we now know what types of boats were being used during
this period we do not know what they looked like, nor the detail of how
they were constructed. For this we need to look to Norway, which is where
Shetland's timber and boats came from during this period as confirmed by
Smith who observed in 1633 that "... the inhabitants of the island of Ounst
usually have a Bark that they trade with to Norway, where they may buy ...
deal-boards, tar, ships, barks (a small ship) and boats of all sorts ..." (Smith
1673: 256).

The Norwegian boat export trade

The supply of boats and timber to Shetland from Norway has, I believe, become shrouded in a romantic Norse mist that has clouded the reality of this trade, which was based on the simple economic reality of convenience and affordability. Shetland's neighbour, Norway, had a plentiful supply of timber. It also had the water sawmill and boatbuilders who constructed boats that Shetlanders, because of the longevity of the trade, were accustomed to using. By the sixteenth century Scotland had a powerful presence in Shetland but still boats and timber continued to be imported from Norway. So, with Scotland's increasing dominance in Shetland, why was this timber and boat trade still centred in Norway? The answer is straightforward. Scotland had used up all its easily accessible resources and was itself importing Norwegian timber on a much larger scale than Shetland and Orkney (Smout 1963: 153).

Scotland's large timber import trade was called Skottehandelen by the Norwegians. It was founded on the Scottish parliament's declaration in 1503 that, as a result of building a navy, Scotland's woods were utterly destroyed (Newland 2010: 46). During this period Scotland had an enviable reputation for shipbuilding which, the Scottish historian Christopher Smout informs us, had been eroded to such an extent by the time of the Act of Union in 1707 that the Scots were buying their ships from overseas, from places such as Norway and Holland (Smout 1963: 47). The Scots during the sixteenth century saw the timber trade with Norway and the Baltic as essential to the development of Scotland's economy and Norway was referred to as the "Store Keeper of her [Scotland's] Naval Supplies" (Newland 2010: 46). In 1562 the Danish and Norwegian government, which was keen to protect its own timber resources for its own navy, placed restrictions on timber exports. And so, in the following year, a Scottish ambassador was sent to Denmark to negotiate the restoration of the right of Scottish merchants to purchase timber from that country (Thomson 1991: 1). The importance of this timber trade is shown by the fact that in 1573 a statute banning the export of Scottish salt was waived for those who were trading with Norway for timber; and then, in 1663 a ban on the export of bullion was introduced, but trading in timber was also exempted from this ban (Newland 2010: 46).

Easily accessible timber

Western Norway benefitted from an extensive forest-fringed network of fjords that stretched many miles inland. As well as easily accessible timber it had, as previously mentioned, water driven sawmills which made the conversion of trees into boards and deals very quick and efficient (Newland 2010: 50). The annual trading cycle began around March or April and continued, depending upon weather, until September each year. The merchants would trade direct with the suppliers of timber and timber goods, and the trade extended from Trondheim in the north down the coast to Sognefjord, Kristiansund, Bömlo, Haugesund, Stavanger, Egresund, Mandal, Kristiansand, Larvik and Drammen (Lillehammer 1990: 101, Smout 1963:153).

The earliest documented evidence for this trade was found in the Norwegian customs and excise accounts analysed by Norwegian maritime historian Atle Thowsen who stated that in 1519, out of 88 ships that visited Bergen, one of these was from Shetland (Thowsen 1969: 148). In 1521 out of the 108 ships that visited Bergen two were from Shetland. Then, during 1566-7 a total of 45 Scottish ships paid customs, and a total of 35 boats were exported from the region of Sunnhordland (17 went to Shetland, 12 to Orkney, four to Kirkcaldy and two to Leith) (Sunde 2010: 19). The 17 boats that came to Shetland were transported in seven ships, equating roughly to five boats per shipment (Sunde 2010: 19; Thowsen 1969: 148). Throughout this period Sunnhordland was the most important supplier of boats and timber to Shetland, and the main boat exporting municipalities were Os, Tysnes, Fusa, Strandvik, and Samnanger (Fig. 15) (Thowsen 1969: 150).

It is important not to adopt an isolationist view of Shetland's boat trade relationship with Norway during the sixteenth century, and it is vital to recognise that Shetland and Orkney played a small role in the much larger Scottish timber import trade. But it has to be borne in mind that Shetland, at this time, was not yet fully assimilated into Scotland and so its trade with Norway might be regarded as an ongoing trading tradition. Although Shetland's role in this trade was small by comparison, the analysed evidence which is discussed later in this chapter demonstrates that the proportion of boats coming to Shetland and Orkney from Norway was far greater than the number going to mainland Scotland.

As identified earlier, mainland Scotland, as well as importing timber, was also importing small open boats which were the same boat types that were being imported to Orkney and Shetland. It has become apparent that Norway had developed a niche market in selling boats to places which had no timber resources of their own, such as Ireland, Faroe, Shetland, Orkney and, to a lesser extent, mainland Scotland. In Shetland's unique case, this convenient boat trade continued until the mid-nineteenth century when the timber trading pattern changed and it became cheaper and easier to build boats at home (Chivers 2016: 67).

Smout ascertained that in the seventeenth century unassembled boats were being imported to mainland Scotland from Norway and Gothenberg in Sweden (Smout 1963: 49). These small "unsetup yoalls" purchased by the Scots were imported mainly to the Forth and to the extreme north for use in "quick communication across the straits, and for fishing" (Smout 1963: 155). The destinations were specific; they were bound for Shetland and for the Firth of Forth, which lies on Scotland's east coast, and it appears that these imported Norwegian boats were used for the same purposes in Shetland and on the east coast of Scotland. This fact suggests that the Norwegian boat imports were

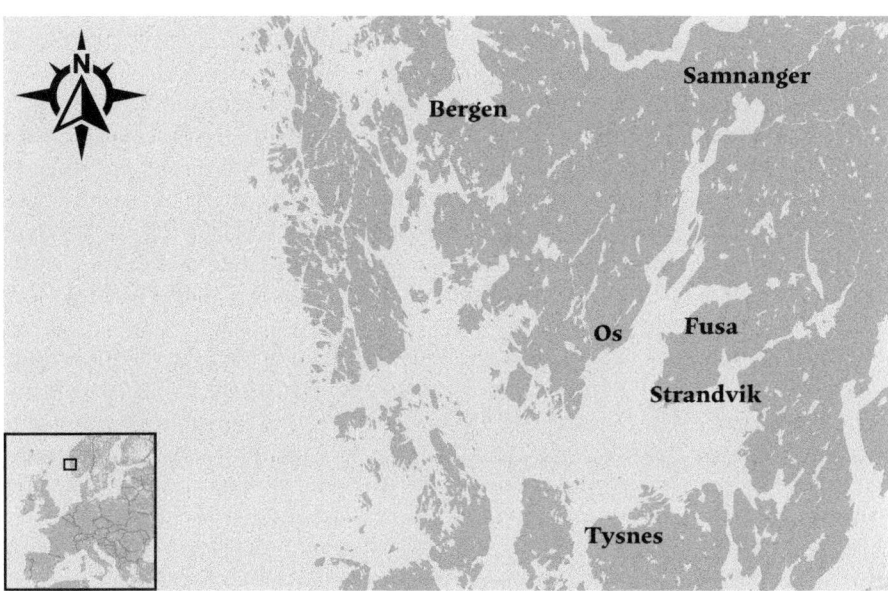

Fig. 15. *Map illustrating the main boatbuilding municipalities which supplied boats to Shetland.*

of a general-purpose type, which I believe, illustrates the off-the-shelf nature of the boat buying enterprise at that time. This reference to "unsetup yoalls" coming to mainland Scotland in the seventeenth and eighteenth centuries assists in highlighting that these Norwegian prefabricated boats were not intended solely for use in the Northern Isles, but were in fact manufactured in Norway as a general export item. Smout also mentioned that during the seventeenth century boats were being imported from Gothenberg which illustrates that Norway was not alone in this small-boat export market. Arne Emil Christensen has indicated that the boats from Gothenberg were probably built in the Bohuslän district, which was formerly part of Norway until the treaty of Brømsebro in the 1660s. "Those boats would in all probability be very different from those from Bjørnefjorden, as the marked difference between east and west Norwegian boatbuilding seems to go back to c.1600" (PC, Christensen 2016).

Smout concluded that some Norwegian ships came to trade, on spec, on the Scottish side of the North Sea. But there are no records of this speculative Norwegian commerce taking place in Shetland during this period, which suggests that it was just mainland Scotland where these Norwegian timber merchants plied their trade. The bypassing of Shetland by these Norwegian speculators again highlights that Shetland played a minor role in this largely mainland-Scottish dominated timber trade. Downplaying Shetland's role in the Scottish timber import trade does not detract from the fact that Shetland's connection with Norway during this period remained close. This is illustrated by the fact that Christian Johnson Forsell, the Burgess of Bergen was a native

of Yell, where he had inherited property from his mother, Merette Williams-
dochter around 1594.

Another important connection between Norway and Shetland was described
by legal historian Jørn Øyrehagen Sunde who provided an account of the
landowner Andrew Mouat. Mouat moved to Shetland from mainland Scotland
at some point in the sixteenth century and, after the death of his first wife
Ursula Tulloch around 1587, obtained from the Scottish king a licence to "joyne
him self in marriage with any parties quilk he sall finde aggreable to him
within the town of Birrhem in Norraway or ellis quhair within the bounds of
said cuntrey" (Sunde 2010: 65).

Mouat at this time was a regular visitor to Norway and it is believed that
he was heavily involved in the profitable Scottish-Norwegian timber trade.
The peak years of this trade were 1550-1650. During this period mainland
Scotland exported grain, flour, bread, cloth, fish, spirit and tobacco to Norway
in exchange for timber and a few boats. Andrew Mouat moved to Norway
around 1590, whereupon he married Else Tronsdochter, a noblewoman. They
settled in Tysnes and it was their son, Axel, who later became the largest land
and property owner in western Norway (Sunde 2010: 65). Axel Mouat played
a key role in the Scottish-Norwegian timber trade, and it is probable that this
Shetland timber and boat trading link explains why Tysnes in the seventeenth
century became the specialist exporting district of boats to Shetland.

During the sixteenth century the import of Norwegian boats was a free-trade
enterprise in which Scottish tax duty was not paid (Sunde 2010: 19). In order
to remedy this situation Lord Robert Stewart, via his foud (governor) Laurence
Bruce of Cultmalindie, attempted to control the import of boats from Norway.
Around 1575 Lord Robert ordained that no-one was to bring boats to Shetland,
nor sell them, without his consent. Furthermore, he sought to specify prices
at which boats could be sold. This attempt to control the boat trade backfired,
as up until this time, Shetland and Orkney had retained a tax-free status with
Norway (even though Orkney and Shetland had been under Scottish control
since 1472). This tax-exemption privilege was revoked in 1580, probably as a
consequence of Lord Robert's attempts to control the trade in boats (Sunde
2010: 19).

Even though Orkney and Shetland now had to pay duty on their imports
from Norway the evidence suggests that this did not affect trade between the
two countries (Thowsen 1969: 149). Shetland historian Brian Smith identified
that this import business was organised by a small band of landowners, some
with Shetland surnames and some with mainland Scots, who began to fit
out their own barks and go to Bergen and the surrounding area for timber,
stock-stove houses and boats (Smith, B.1980: 23). Brian Smith contested the
view of Shetland historian Hance Smith who suggested that trade between
Shetland and Norway during this period was organised solely by the owners
of large Shetland estates. Instead, Brian Smith argued: "My strong impression
is that there is a distinctly plebeian flavour about the trade, organised as it

was by people like John of Windhouse, the Nisbets of Kirkabister and David Sanderson Scot of Reafirth, all in Yell" (Smith, B. 1990: 32). Shetland during this period became an entrepreneurial society organised on a small scale and everyone became a merchant in their own way. The evidence for this entrepreneurial society is provided in the form of "merchant usit marks" (Smith, B. 1990:32). These were authenticating marks that were occasionally incorporated into paper seals. The people using these marks were native small landowners and tenants. Brian Smith argued that Shetland was a flourishing society with a vigorous government and a trilingual population being positively influenced by Scotland, Norway and Germany (Smith, B. 1990: 32).

However, Shetland's trade with Norway was not reciprocal as ships sailed to Norway in ballast (Smith, H. 1984: 34-35). Shetland had nothing to trade in return for the boats and timber that were imported. This timber and boat trade was, therefore, either funded using credit agreed in advance with a broker in Norway (someone like Axel Mouat), or cash was taken by the ship's master with which to purchase the cargo. This casts doubt on Brian Smith's view that this was a plebeian trade, especially as Shetland during this period was largely a cashless society (Smith, H. 1984: 20). This implies that it was only the landowning class who were able to take part in this trade, as they gained a cash rental income from the German merchants, and rental income from their tenants in the form of butter and fish oil that could then be converted into cash.

The scale of the boat import trade

The number of ships sailing from Shetland and Orkney to buy boats and timber in Norway during this period was collated by Atle Thowsen and is reproduced in Table 1 (Thowsen 1969: 150). One way to interpret this data is to divide the total number of ships by the total number of boats to give an approximate average number of boats per ship's cargo. This shows a peak in 1610, when 17 Shetland and Orkney ships purchased a total of 112 boats (a cargo of approximately seven boats per ship), and another peak in boat trade activity in 1621, when a total of 21 Shetland and Orcadian ships brought back a total of 107 boats (approximately five boats per ship), and then a third, more curious peak between 1624-25 when 19 ships imported a total of 83 boats. This last entry is peculiar, as there were more ships buying fewer boats (approximately four boats per ship) which lends credence to Brian Smith's view that this was a predominantly "plebeian" trade, organised on a small scale with minor landowners going to buy boats as and when they needed them. By contrast, in 1620, only seven ships sailed from Shetland and Orkney to Norway but with an average of 10 boats per ship.

Hance Smith in his examination of the Norwegian customs accounts included the number of ships that sailed from Scotland to Norway, given here in Table 2 (Smith, H. 1984: 33). Comparing data from Shetland and Orkney

Year	Orkney and Shetland Ships	Total Boat Exports
1597	11	080
1610	17	112
1611	11	077
1612	12	076
1614	07	073
1620	07	071
1621	21	107
1624-25	19	083
1626-27	10	081

Table 1. *(Thowsen, 1969: 150).*

Year	Orkney and Shetland Ships	Scottish Ships	Boat Exports
1597	12	41	082
1610	18	57	114
1611	12	39	076
1612	12	44	076
1614	11	43	073
1620	06	39	067
1621	19	66	107
1624	19	47	086
1627	14	62	090

Table 2. *(Smith, H. 1984: 33).*

with that of mainland Scotland makes the large-scale Scottish involvement in the seventeenth century timber trade very clear. It can be seen that mainland Scotland's interest in the boat trade was minor, with the around 98 per cent of boat imports going to Shetland and Orkney. Hance Smith also noted that there were more four-oared boats than six-oared boats imported to Shetland during this period which supports the view that the fishery operated inshore. The majority of the boats imported during this period were in a complete, or "set-up" form and it was only at the beginning of the eighteenth century that "unset-up" or "boats-in-boards" became the normal means of shipment (Smith H. 1984: 35). Smuggling was rife during this period and a customs inspection in 1665 revealed that for every legitimately imported boat there was at least one that was smuggled (Sunde 2010: 20). This suggests that the import of boats during this period was perhaps double that of the official statistics.

Analysis of the complete Customs & Excise Accounts of Orkney, Caithness and Shetland from 1668 until 1673 serve to illustrate that trade between Shetland and Norway during this period had stopped completely (NRO E72/17/1, E72/17/2, E72/17/3). However, this was not so in Caithness and Orkney, where the import of boat related items continued. In the Caithness accounts for May

1669 Robert Barber imported "40 fir toafts" (thwarts) and then in July Johne Sinclair imported "half and hundred boat oars", and John Brigg imported "30 toafts of fir" (NRO E72/17/1). That September, in the Orkney accounts, Harrie Moncrieff imported "5 duzen oars, 24 pairs off boats timbers and 4 pairs of oars" (NRO E72/17/1). These boat items were just a minor part of large quantities of timber cargo. By contrast there were no timber imports recorded in the Shetland accounts during this five-year period. Indeed, the only customs and excise entries in these Shetland accounts were 10 German merchant ships (NRO E72/17/2, E72/17/3). These German merchants, amongst their cargoes, imported boat sem (boat nails) to Shetland, which shows that boat repair and possibly construction was taking place. The fact that there are no records of Shetlanders importing Norwegian boats and timber at this point in the seventeenth century is puzzling. Unfortunately, the available customs and excise account evidence is limited and the implication is that the trade with Norway was economically dependent on income from the fishing industry which, by 1660, was experiencing difficulties (Brand 1701: 194; Robinson 2009: 136). The records therefore imply that by the late seventeenth century Shetland's trade with Norway had ceased which contradicts Hance Smith's view that during times of uncertainty Shetland's trade links with Germany, Norway, Scotland and Orkney remained stable (Smith, H. 1984: 36-37). However, Sunde's observation that for every boat imported one was smuggled suggests that the trade continued – it was just not declared (Sunde 2010: 20).

The early 1700s was a period of turmoil, which Hance Smith described as "cataclysmic", with war, famine and the first of many smallpox epidemics gripping Shetland (Smith, H. 1984: 35). To compound these problems, Shetland was strategically placed on the trade routes of Europe, which meant that it became a victim of direct attack which caused disruption to local trade. One such attack took place in 1673 when the Dutch burned the fort in Lerwick along with the few houses that then constituted the town. This was followed in the 1690s by the French, who came to plunder in Shetland (Smith, H. 1984: 38). Trade was continually interrupted by war during this period and, in 1703, the French destroyed the Dutch herring buss fleet in Bressay Sound, from which the enterprise never completely recovered (Simpson 2011: 37).

From the available evidence, or lack of it, Brian Smith suggests "... this indicated that Shetland was in economic depression, and that the Norwegian relationship ceased to exist for quite a few decades." Smith pointed out "that is what happened to the Shetlanders' cloth trade with the Norwegians – it stopped circa 1643, and never recommenced." Further evidence for the gap in Norwegian trade was noted in the parish reports around 1683 where there is no mention of any Norwegian trade (PC, Smith 2015).

The customs accounts strengthen the argument that Shetland's relationship with Norway was not a reciprocal one. Shetland needed timber and wood products but after 1643 had nothing to trade in return. The only Shetland produce the Norwegians would have been willing to import was grain but

Shetland was not self-sufficient. This is illustrated by the fact that the north German merchants exported grain to Shetland (NRO E72/17/2, E72/17/3). So clearly there was no surplus grain for Shetland to trade with Norway. Trade with Norway at this time, if it took place, must have been paid for in cash, or by credit. The only other possible explanation why Shetland ships importing goods from Norway are absent in the customs records is that these goods were smuggled. However, the evidence points fairly clearly to Brian Smith's view being correct – that regular trade with Norway at this time did not take place.

The union between Scotland and England gave rise to the imposition of a series of newly created Acts of Parliament, called the Trade and Navigation Acts. The enforcement of the navigation acts accompanied by the War of Spanish Succession made, as the social economic historian Frances Shaw suggested, trade with the German merchants in Shetland unviable (Shaw 1980). Maritime historian Kathrin Zickermann highlighted another problem, which was the increased difficulty for the German merchants to obtain Swedish sea passes after 1708. The prelude to this was the Nine Years' War (1688-1697) which made it increasingly perilous to send commodities from Shetland to Hamburg as French privateers sank several German ships during this period (Zickermann 2011: 47-49). Sweden and Denmark remained neutral so Hamburg skippers obtained Danish flags of convenience from Altona and Glückstadt. Unfortunately, these still did not prevent attack from the French so the merchants sought protection elsewhere. They found it under the Swedish flag and moved their operations to the southern banks of the Elbe which was governed by the Swedish Stade. From 1703 the majority of Hamburg and Bremen skippers managed to obtain Swedish sea passes by becoming token citizens of the Stade. The destination for the Shetland-caught fish purchased by the German merchants was Portugal, and without a Swedish sea pass it was not possible to safely travel and trade in Lisbon. So for five brief years the problem of reducing the threat of attack and being able to trade with Portugal was resolved. Then, in 1708, the Portuguese government complained that the Swedish sea passes were being issued to German skippers of German vessels, so the Swedish government tightened-up the regulations. This in effect denied German access to the Portuguese market which, when combined with the prohibitive nature of the navigation acts, made trade with Shetland unviable (Zickerman 2011: 47-49).

When the German trade ended Shetland tenants no longer had the means to trade on their own account for goods they needed, and the loss of the rental income from the German merchants left landowners with no cash and dwindling capital. This was a disastrous time for everyone, and for many of the landowners it meant that for the first time they had to become entrepreneurs. The landowners were unaccustomed to merchant life and this was a difficult task which, for some, led to financial loss and, for others, ruin. An easing of this crisis came when a bounty on all Scottish cured fish was introduced in 1727 (Goodlad 1971: 92). This bounty, it seems, created the impetus to further develop the deep-water (haaf) white fishing industry. As Hance Smith pointed out, this bounty was entwined in the rules on salt duty which were many and complex. Shetland was reliant on foreign salt imports for fish curing and things became easier from 1718 when the duty on foreign salt was offset by the payment of a bounty – paid out of the duty itself – provided the cured fish was for export (Smith 1984: 77). Hance Smith's observation is supported by the recent discovery of a list of 27 boats imported by Thomas Gifford in 1719. Titled "The Norway Cargo" this details the names of the tenants who had ordered boats, the type of boat they had requested and the manner in which it was imported. This was either "boarded", meaning set-up, or "unboarded", meaning unset-up (SMA, D17/6/10). One piece of boat import evidence precedes this 1719 date. This consists of a simple note written by Andrew Sinclair in September 1708 to an unknown person ordering two boats, one of which was for Andrew's brother and the other for Laurence Strong (SMA, GD144/34/17).

The development of the haaf fishery was further spurred on in 1728 with the opening of the Spanish market which became, until the end of the nineteenth century, the biggest consumer of Shetland's salt-cured white fish (Goodlad 1971: 93). The gradual growth of the fishing industry gave impetus for the advancement of Shetland's vernacular fishing boats. This era of entrepreneurship was when the fishing industry began to grow and the pattern of fishing changed, which meant that more boats of bigger size were needed.

The need for bigger boats

The first substantive evidence for the renewed trade with Norway is found in correspondence between Thomas Gifford and James Wallace in 1728: "... I did not recive Your favour of 24th August last till the 2d Inst:1 which covered Your Acct for the Cargoe shipd at Noraway in the Godsend, [Godøysund] ..." (Johnston and Johnston 1913: 6). Also in that year was a statement of an account current between Thomas Gifford and James Harrower, who imported for Gifford amongst many other items: "3 Dozen 6 oarin oars at 4/6 ster per dozen. ... 1 Dozen 4 oarin oars ditto" (SMA, GD144/40/32). Then, three years later in 1731, Thomas Gifford wrote to Robert Barclay in Bergen requesting amongst other cargo: "Six 'pises hemp linin for boats sails' £18. One 'long hundred' planks, a full inch thick and 16ft long, cost £25, and half a hundred 'sawen in two' £12 10s for the boatbuilders, much being supplied already cut to shape" (March, 1970: 36-37).

This proves that boatbuilding was taking place in Shetland. Of significance is that some of the boatbuilding timber being imported was pre-shaped and this is discussed further in chapter six. Two years later, in 1733, Thomas Gifford wrote to James Wallace in Bergen, informing him that he had "given orders to John Harrowar to proceed with his sloup, [the Mary of Yorry] from Hamburg to Norraway, and there to load boats for my acct" (SMA, Norski boat. doc: 5). Harrower was a novice in the business of procuring boats, and Gifford was concerned about Harrower being duped by the "Bouers" [builders] and he asked Wallace: "youll give your good advice and recomend him to some friend at the woods to see that the bours doe not Impose upon." It is worth pointing out that the term "at the woods" was a colloquial name for a region of western Norway where much of the timber trade took place. This trade was centred around Bjørnefjord, and specifically the district of Tysnes.

Harrower was instructed to purchase and load "... only 30 four oared yoals and all their apartinant less or more of them as your sloup can contain, but no six oared boats." Gifford aired his concern to Harrower of him being sold poor quality boats by stating: "... take non but Good large four oard Boats and tell the Bouers youll tak non but Such as ar Good and Sufficient, for if you take not Care they will impose upon and Give you Insufficient yoals, which will be useless to me ..." (SMA Norski boat.doc: 6). It is important to note that Gifford's instruction equates to five times more boats per single cargo than the average cargo of six boats imported in 1627. This indicates a major step-up in the scale of the boat trade, and therefore in commercial fishing. As previously discussed, Harrower's voyage was the typical triangular Shetland to Hamburg, Norway, and then home to Shetland route. After discharging his cargo of fish in Hamburg, Harrower was instructed to load five to six lasts (10 to 12 tons) of salt to take as ballast, and then sail to Norway. This reaffirms the fact that Shetland had nothing to trade with Norway, and that the purchase of these boats and the other timber products had to be paid in cash which Harrower was instructed by Gifford to obtain from James Wallace (SMA: Norski boat. doc: 6).

Gifford also stipulated that: "I allow you also to tak one Anker [A cask or keg that held 8 and 1/3 imperial gallons] of watters [spirit alcohol] with you from Hamburgh Give the Noraway Bowers [builders] in Drams, which they most have when they Bring the boats which they Take down and let them be all Right marked" (SMA Norski boat.doc: 6). This reaffirms Hance Smith's view that boats during the eighteenth century were imported more frequently "unset-up" in board form. This would partly explain the ability of ships to carry larger cargoes of boats and, although the ships at this time were becoming larger, these fore and aft rigged sloups, as they were called, were still comparatively small, which local historian and author Charlie Simpson suggests allowed them to be drawn-up and beached for safe winter storage (Simpson 2011: 39). It is noteworthy that Gifford only wanted large four-oared boats, which suggests that fishing continued to take place within 10 miles of the shore. Gifford made no other specification so we can assume that these boats were the standard færing type from Sunnhordland.

The standard færing was typically 10 ells long between the stems (18ft or 5.5m) with a beam of about 5ft (1.5m). The ell was the standard Norwegian boat measurement in the sixteenth century. Originally this was the measurement from the tip of the elbow to the tip of the middle finger which became standardised to 24 Norwegian inches (55cm) (Christensen 2014; Økland 2016: 65).

Of course there was variation in boat sizes, as illustrated by the nineteenth century færing from Austevoll which was 19.7ft (6m) long (approximately 10.9 ells). Gifford's boats will have been somewhere in the range of 18ft-20ft (5.5-6m) and during this period would have been rigged with the square sail as illustrated in Fig. 16.

An itemised account between James Wallace of Bergen and Thomas Gifford of Busta, dated September 1733, confirms the successful completion of Gifford's order: "Cash to Mr John Harrower for purchasing a cargo of boats etc. at the woods for our account as per your order of the 20th July last" (SMA, GD144/10/11). James Wallace, resident in Bergen, was part of a wave of Scottish migrants who moved to Norway. This immigration wave occurred in the early eighteenth century, and was the result of an accord between George II, and his son-in-law, Frederick of Denmark and Norway. This agreement incentivised Scottish Episcopalians to settle and trade in Norway, tax-free (Thomson 1991: 14). Scottish merchants living in Norway were therefore able to act as timber export agents for those living on the Scottish mainland, Orkney and Shetland, and this made the import of boats and timber from Norway much easier.

An unaddressed and unsigned document titled "Instructions for Steness"

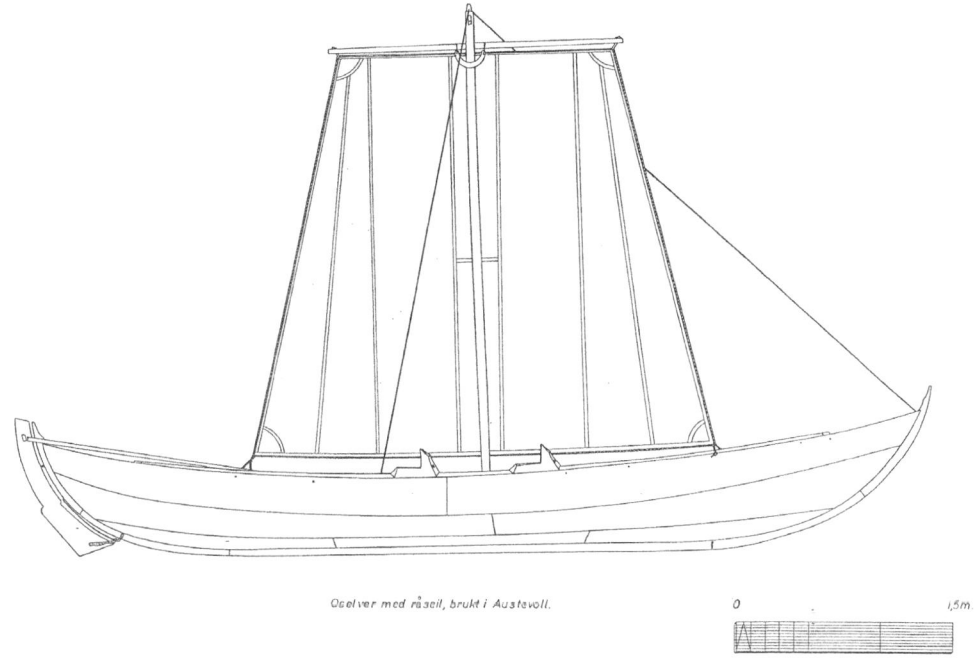

Fig. 16. *Færing from Austevoll rigged with square sail. Drawing: Arne Emil Christensen. Courtesy of the Norwegian Maritime Museum, Oslo.*

dated 3rd July, 1736, provides an insight into how this trading triangle between Shetland, north Germany, and Norway functioned. Analysis of these detailed instructions revealed seven key steps:

> 1. Sail to Hamburg deliver my letters and cargo to Mr. Hendrick Scholle. 2. Spend no more than one week trying to get freight for Bergen. 3. If you can get no freight take four to five lasts of salt for ballast and proceed to Godasund [Godøysund] in Norway. 4. Put on my account anker waters, or two 8 or 10 pound of tobacco from Mr Scholle, for the Norway bowers [builders] and upon your own lads. Also 100 yards of good sail linen for my great boat. 5. Go to Bergen and obtain from Mr Wallace credit to buy cargo. 6. Goods to be shipped at Noraway are as follows: 24 good quality four oared boats with their furniture; Six or eight six oar boats ditto;10 doz ploughs, 300 voys of bark, 10 doz deals; 2 ankers juniper berries; . doz young fir trees with earth about their roots. If you have space left on your ship buy more good and sufficient boats. 7. Sail back here as fast as possible as I might have another trip for you (SMA, GD144/97/2).

This document illustrates the pivotal role that the merchant contacts in Hamburg and Norway played in this triangular trade. As in the aforementioned correspondence between Gifford and Harrower, concerns were raised about the quality of the boats, as the author of the instructions stipulated "... stand not to take none but such as are good and sufficient." This suggests that Norwegian boatbuilders may have been using inferior timber and possibly the quality of their workmanship also varied.

Other evidence for the increase in the number and the size of boats was found in the Statistical Account of Scotland 1791-1799. Two of Shetland's ministers, the Reverend Patrick Barclay, and the Reverend William Jack reported a change to the size and type of boats used for fishing around 1740 (Withrington, Grant and Sinclair 1978: 386; 465-466). This change was so important that 59 years later it was still significant enough to merit mention and illustrates that little else had changed during the intervening era. This suggests that the period was one of relative stability and economic growth in Shetland (although some might argue that it was only the landowning class who benefitted at the expense of their tenants).

The Reverend Barclay, in the parish of Sandsting, described the change from the four-oared to the six-oared fishing boat: "... Many persons now alive remember when there was not one six oared boat in the ministry; and the first master of a boat to the Ha-af, or ling fishing, from Sandsting is still alive." Barclay also stated that prior to the haaf fishing people found as much profit staying at home farming as they did when they "... went to Northmavine fishing for fees and they paid their rents to their landlords and nothing more was asked." This situation changed, and as previously discussed, the landlords then took control of the fishing enterprise, and they provided tenancies "... on this express provision, that they [tenants] should fit out a sixth share of a boat to the ling fishing; ..." (Withrington, Grant and Sinclair 1978: 386).

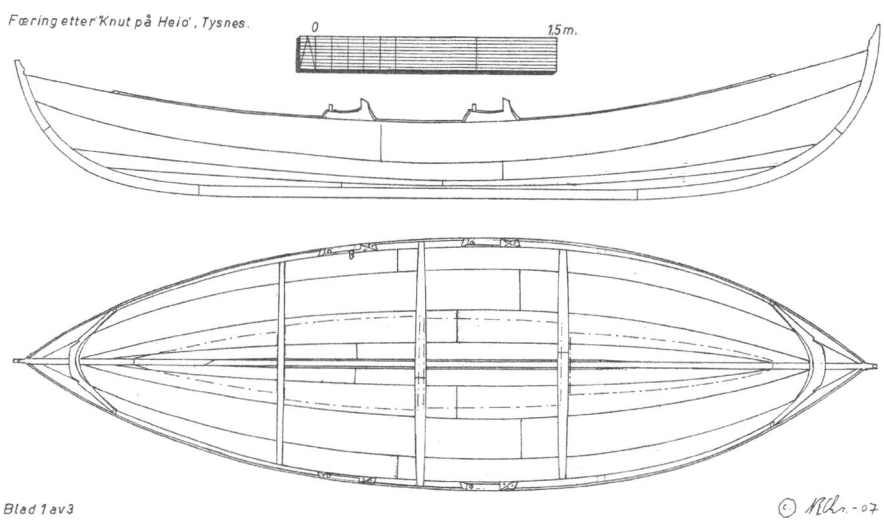

Fig. 17. *Færing from Tysnes. Drawing: Arne Emil Christensen. Courtesy of the Norwegian Maritime Museum, Oslo.*

The Reverend Jack, in his parish of Northmavine, described a similar situation and stated that between 1712 to 1740 the fishing was not more than eight to 10 miles offshore, and this was conducted from four-oared boats. However, around 1740 this changed, and the boats grew in number, "... which induced them to seek out further to sea, to avoid their lines entangling, when crowded along shore. Finding a new bank, they enlarged their boats, and increased their number of lines, till they gradually arrived at the present state" (Withrington, Grant and Sinclair 1978: 465-466). So again, Jack reported that it was 1740 when the fishing pattern changed to the one that was still in use in 1791. And prior to 1740 fishing was conducted from four-oared boats that fished relatively close to shore. It seems that 1740 was the turning point when the number and the size of boats increased. This was when the landlords made a concerted effort to expand the industry, exploiting the discovery of a new fishing bank. This is when the haaf fishery began, and which continued until the end of the nineteenth century.

So, while during this period four-oared boats continued to be dominant, the six-oared type gradually began to become more commonly used as the haaf fishery developed. As well as these common Norwegian boats there were also some less well-known types of larger craft and these are now examined.

Chapter 3

The 'great boats'

hat there were less well-known larger boats in use during the sixteenth and seventeenth centuries is suggested by the previously mentioned "great fishing boat" and "great boat" (Donaldson 1958: 80; SMA, GD144/97/2). At present there is no further evidence for the "great fishing boat", therefore this cannot be discussed further, but there is a growing body of evidence for the "great boat". Before we examine the "great boat" there are some other types of larger craft worth looking at. The largest of these is really a type of small ship called a skuda. This type of vessel has been completely overlooked by researchers but evidence suggests that this was the type commonly called a bark. Barks were used up until the latter part of the seventeenth century to transport boats, timber, and other wooden goods from Norway to Shetland. There is one other type of boat I am going to discuss called the eight-oaring. The eight-oaring is the smallest of these larger craft and so let us begin by examining this first.

The eight-oaring

According to Shetland antiquarian Robert Stuart Bruce eight-oared boats were commonly used in Shetland during the early modern period to transport goods to and from the fishing stations. He described the eight-oaring as being an enlarged sixareen (Bruce 1934: 316-317). These boats had a dual purpose and when not being used to transport goods were used by the lairds for travelling, when according to Bruce, they were referred to as barges (Bruce 1934: 316-317). The earliest documented Shetland evidence of the eight-oaring was found by Bruce in correspondence between James Omand (factor) to Laurence Sinclair of Brough, Nesting (landowner) in 1640. Omand wrote to Sinclair informing him that the aucht oaring [eight-oared boat] had been loaded with butter, and that this had been transferred on to the ship of Buillister which was to sail to Norway. During this period there was still some Norwegian owned land in Shetland and this butter export was a rental payment "to the lordis of Norroway" (Donaldson 1958: 71). Brian Smith recently found another mention of an eight-oared boat in the testament of Ursula Edmondston who was the wife of Ninian Neven. Ursula and Ninian were very wealthy and had huge establishments at Windhouse and Sandwick in Yell, and Gremista in Lerwick. Ursula Edmonston died in December 1646 and listed amongst her extensive possessions was an eight-oaring boat, two sixareens and three fourareens (SMA 30 September, 1648 Shetland Commissariat Register).

An eight-oaring was mentioned in a letter of instruction written by Lady Margaret Bruce of Symbister, Whalsay in July 1742. This was addressed to William John Neven of Windhouse in Yell: "... You'll receive from on board Lunas sloop twenty six short hundred ling, and in the eight oaring six hundred and forty ditto hundreds; ..." (SMA GD144/15/14). This is particularly interesting as it also provides us with a glimpse into merchant life at the time which previously was assumed to be a solely male activity; this proves that this was not the case. During this period these landowning merchants were sending their fish to the Lisbon market. However, we know that in 1744 Neven also tried to infiltrate the Irish market; this venture was a commercial failure because his ship reached its destination after the period of Lent, and thus he obtained a very poor price for his fish (Hance Smith 1984: 86). Lady Margaret's letter of instruction further supports the claim made by Bruce that the eight-oared boat was primarily used to carry cargo. Unfortunately, no further documentary evidence for the use of eight-oared boats in Shetland has so far been found.

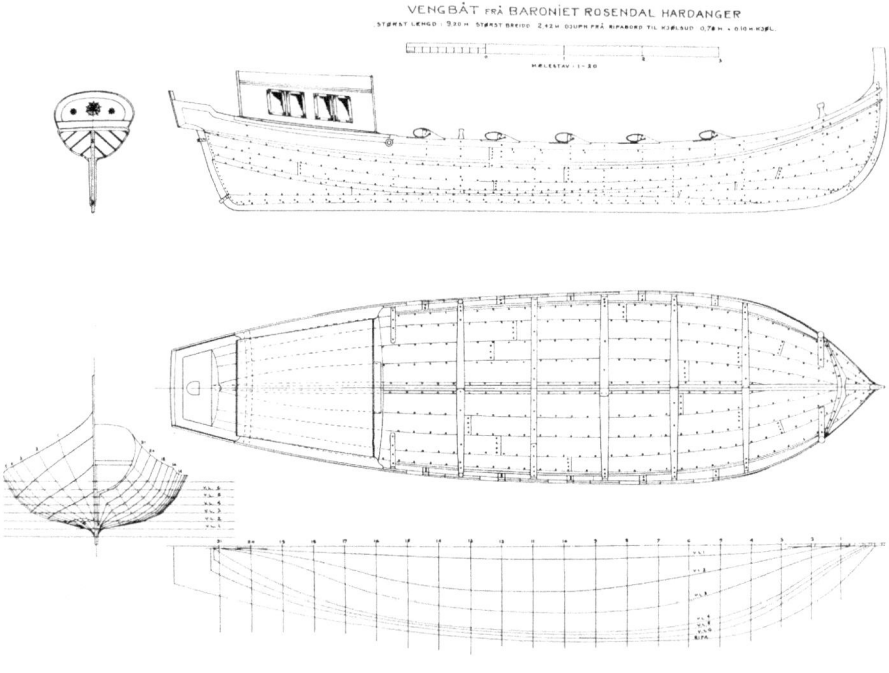

Fig. 18. *Vengbåt from Rosendal, Hardanger. Drawing: Bernhard Faærøyvik. Courtesy of the Norwegian Maritime Museum, Oslo.*

Maritime historian Adrian Osler in his book *The Shetland Boat South Mainland and Fair Isle* discussed the eight-oared boat's use for travelling (Osler 1983: 26). Osler cites the Reverend George Low who, in 1774, was taken on a tour of inspection by Thomas Gifford, the laird of Busta, who "... was so obliging as to accompany me in his barge thro' the islands of Yell Sound ..." (Low 1879: 131). Osler suggested that, because Low used the southern English term "barge", this was a special, grander type, with perhaps proper seating, and maybe even a canopy or cabin. This type of traveling boat with a cabin is in Norway called a vengbåt and Osler suggested that it may have been one of these that the laird of Busta owned, and which Low referred to as being a "barge" (Fig. 18)(Christensen 1979: 33, Osler 1983: 26). However, the term barge in a Scottish context simply meant a small vessel (The online dictionary of the older Scottish tongue 2016). Low was Scottish, not English, and it is unlikely that he would have used the term "barge" in a southern English context but rather in the Scottish meaning of a small vessel.

Perhaps the key argument against the use of the vengbåt in Shetland was that when the "barge" was not being used as a travelling boat it was used to carry cargo, which suggests that there was nothing particularly grand about the eight-oaring. An examination of the nomenclature strengthens this assertion. The naming convention of eight-oared boats in Shetland referring to them as "aucht oaring" and "eight oaring" uses the same nomenclature as western Norway (Thowsen 1969: 166-167). The vengbåt had a transom stern, and the veng part of the word simply means a cabin (Christensen 1979: 33).

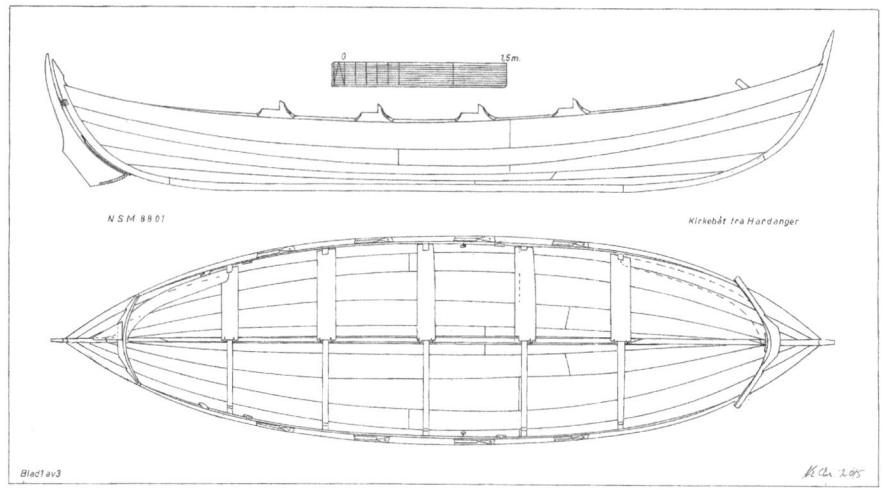

Fig. 19. *Church boat from Hardanger: Arne Emil Christensen. Courtesy of the Norwegian Maritime Museum, Oslo.*

The clincher to this argument is that the vengbåt was a status symbol, and only used by the Norwegian elite for travelling. The eight-oaring's primary function on the other hand was a cargo boat and it seems unlikely that a status symbol would be used for freighting cargo (Bruce 1934: 316-317). In Norway there is eighteenth and nineteenth century evidence for other types of commonly used eight-oared boats and I believe that these were similar to the eight-oarings used in Shetland.

An eight-oared boat in Norwegian is called an åttring. In eighteenth and nineteenth century western Norway eight-oared boats (åttring båter) were often referred to as church boats (kirkebåter) and it was common for a small group of farms to collectively own a church boat, such as the Hardanger åttring illustrated in Fig. 19. These eight-oared boats conveyed farming families to church each Sunday. They were also used for weddings, funerals and for carrying large cargo, and it is this type of boat that I believe was used in Shetland.

Church boats varied in size along with the number of oars they used; the largest were 10, 12, or 14-oared (Christensen 1979: 39, 45, 70, 72). The first impression of these documented Shetland eight-oared boats is that they were not particularly big, being around 21.8ft (6.64m) to 26.4ft (8.04m) long. This challenges the claim made by Bruce (1934: 316) that they were larger than a nineteenth century sixareen which was approximately 30ft (9.1m) long. In the eighteenth century the sixareens described by Low in 1774 were 24-25ft (7.32-7.62m) long, and so even these were larger than most åttring båter.

The Hardanger church boat was 23.5ft (7.16m) long over the stems with a beam of 6ft (1.83m) which is close in size to the sixareens described by Lowe. On close examination of Fig. 19 it can be seen that the forward rong (stameron in Shetland) projects up above the sheer line of this craft. These rong horn projections served as handles and were used to aid hauling the boat up and down the beach. A larger eight-oared church boat from Gloppen in Nordfjord was documented by the Norwegian boat ethnographer Bernhard Færøyvik (Fig. 20). This church boat was 26.4ft (8.04m) over the stems with a beam of 5.9ft (1.80m). As well as being used to travel to and from church it was also used in the summer as a fishing boat. It was versatile – fishing inshore with nets to catch saithe and off-shore using long-lines for ling (Christensen 1979: 70). However, Gloppen is some 140 miles north of the known boat export sites to Shetland, therefore it is less likely, and there is no evidence, that these boats were exported to Shetland.

Of importance is that the eight-oared church boat was a multipurpose craft, used on the one hand for important social occasions, whilst on the other being used for common activities such as freighting and fishing. I believe it was this multipurpose function that made it suitable for Shetland use. Åttring boats of the western Norway type are most likely to have been the same, or very similar, to those used in Shetland.

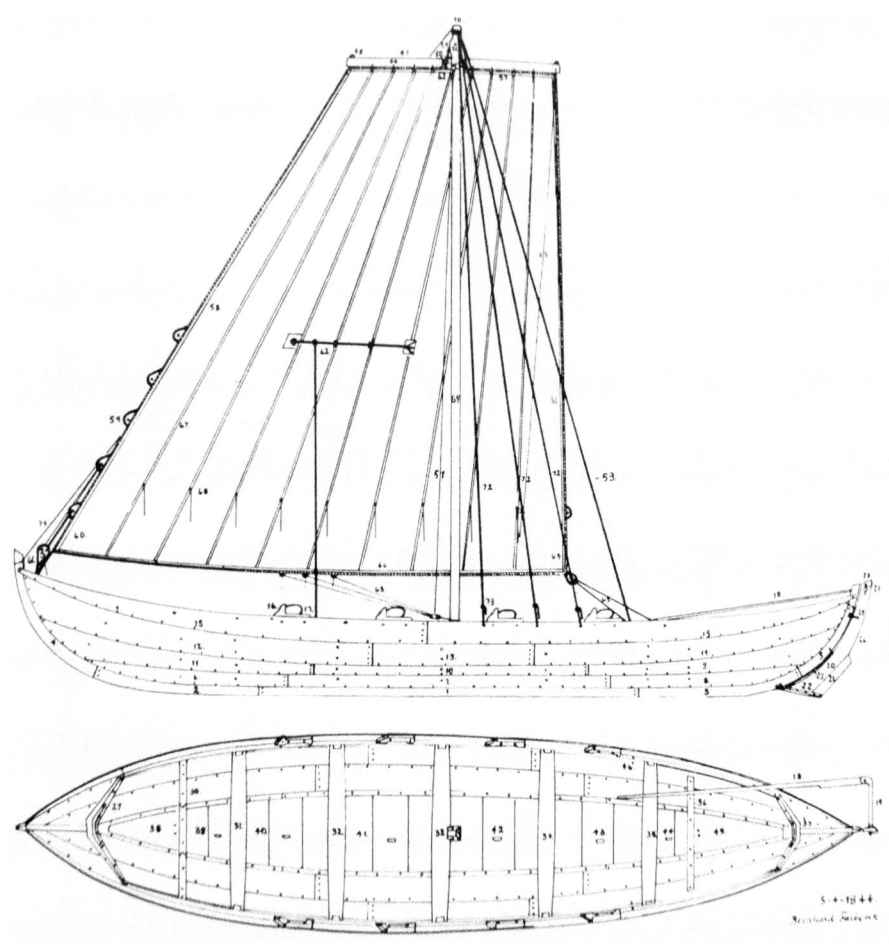

Fig. 20. *Kirkebåt from Gloppen, Nordfjord. Drawing: Bernhard Færøyvik. Courtesy of the Norwegian Maritime Museum, Oslo.*

Large noost evidence

At Burra Ness, in the island of Yell, there is an oral history tradition about a noost – a Shetland term for a boat shelter – that purports to be where the laird kept his eight-oared boat (PC Tait, 2016). The source of this was former Shetland Museum curator Andrew Williamson, who was born in the 1920s. The current curator, Ian Tait, obtained this information from Williamson during the 1980s when he visited the noost which he described as "dug into the bank, with revetted sides. Inside width eight feet at lower end, five feet wide at upper end. The upper end is rounded, almost flat. Sides are revetted, with a slight free-standing wall extending above ground level. Walling is overall around four feet high inside. The nust is unusually long, at 32 feet, with a further 'steed' of approximately 30 feet below this. Andrew Williamson reports this structure had a roof, and that the boat was eight-oared and belonged to the landowner, perhaps in eighteenth century" (PC Tait 2016).

During the summer of 2016 I visited the noost with my son, Matt, and we re-measured and photographically documented the remains of the structure. The mouth of the noost faces northwest and the width of the noost, at the mid-length point, was 5.9ft (1.80m) and at the closed end was 4.1ft (1.25m). The noost's entrance was badly eroded, and so it was not possible to determine its width, as there was nowhere to establish a datum point from which a measurement could be taken. The noost's width determined the maximum beam of the boat, which of course would have been slightly narrower in order for it to fit. Having determined the beam permitted the boat's length to be estimated. The length of the boat was determined by comparing the noost's width with the beam measurements of the previously described kirkebåter. We can conclude that the Burra Ness noost housed a craft approximately 26.4ft (8.04m) long, which was about the size of an eighteenth century sixareen (Figs. 21-24).

This analysis contradicts Bruce's claim that the eight-oared boat was an enlarged nineteenth century sixareen. Of course, there is the possibility that the Norwegian eight-oared boat was adapted to a Shetland specification but there is currently no evidence to support this idea. The fact that there is so little documented evidence for the use of eight-oared boats in Shetland (unlike four- and six-oared boats) disposes of Bruce's claim that these types of boats were in common use. The lack of documentary evidence suggests that they were used in a more limited and restricted way and that they were used less frequently than the four- and six-oared varieties.

The Great Boat

Hance Smith suggested that great boats were originally a variant of the Norse longship, and that these vessels were slightly bigger than the largest late nineteenth century sixareens, which were approximately 30ft (9.1m) long (Hance Smith 1984: 225-226). The idea that great boats were larger than the largest sixareen follows the line of thinking adopted by Bruce, who described the eight-oaring also as an enlarged sixareen. This suggests that these boat types have become conflated with each other. Hance Smith's comparison of the great boat with the Norse longship is a romantic idea but what evidence is there to support this claim? The great boat, Hance Smith believed, was the last vestige of a medieval shipping system, where open boats were used in all external trade, and that these vessels remained in use at least until the middle of the eighteenth century.

Seventeenth century evidence for the use of great boats has recently been discovered by Brian Smith in "the rental of Shetland crops 1611 and 1612 with

Fig. 21. *Noost in Burra Ness, Yell. Photo: M. Chivers.*

Fig. 22. *Note the squared end which suggests the noost had a roof. Photo: M. Chivers.*

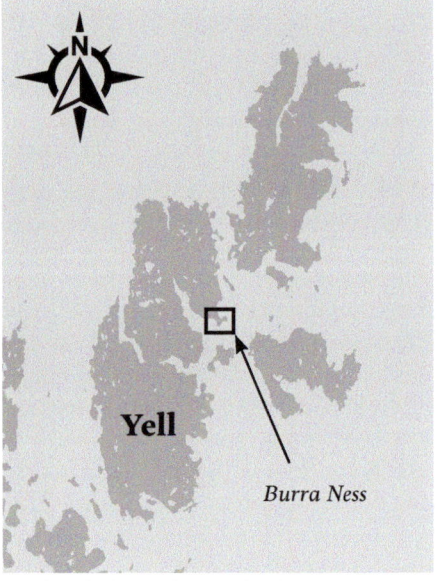

Fig. 23. *The eroded entrance to the noost. Photo: M. Chivers.*

Fig. 24. *Map illustrating location of Burra Ness, Yell.*

account of denunciations of land, 1613" (NRO, E41/3). The denunciation of the lands in Shetland followed the change of administration after the arrest of Earl Patrick Stewart in 1610. In 1612 Bishop James Law was placed in administrative charge of Shetland. So the denunciation of the lands was a symbolic act of removing these lands from the rule of the Stewart's, and handing them back to King James VI of Scotland. In this document is an account of expenditure incurred in the denunciation of the lands which itemises the cost of passage by both ship and great boat.

> [folio 192v]
> Item, for the comptar and his witnessis thair fraucht fra Orknay to Yetland quhen he yeid to denunce the lands thair, quha frauchit ane bark bound to Norroway to putt thame in Yetland, £15." (National Records of Scotland, E41/3).
> [folio 193v]
> Item, for ane gritt boitt to the comptar and his witnessis fra Walles to the ile of Thoulay, to denunce that ile, £6 13s. 4d."
> Item, for ane gritt boitt fra the port of Laxfurd to the iles of the Skerryis to him and his witnessis, the space of fortie myles or thairby in dangerous seyis, to denunce, etc., £10."
> [folio 194r]
> Item, for ane grit boitt to the comptar and his witnessis, fra Dunrossnes to the Fair Ile, and for victuellis and drink to him, his witnessis and men that rowit them, for feir of evill wether and tarrying lange thair, £20.
> (NRO, E41/3)

This account proves that the great boat was a seagoing vessel, capable of travelling to the furthest of Shetland's islands, in this instance from Fair Isle to Shetland, a distance of 24 nautical miles (48km). The account is further supported by other evidence from 1653, discovered by historian John Ballantyne, which supports the seagoing capabilities of the great boat and provides an important clue about its size. On the 29th March, 1653, James Keith of Benholm sailed from Laxfirth to Cullivoe in Yell, in William Bruce of Sumburgh's great boat, with a retinue of 14 named men, plus a number more, who were all "provydit with bellicall [military] furnitour" to confront the republican Ninian Neven (NRO, JC26/23). Clearly if an armed, and armour-clad, retinue of 20 or more men were in this great boat then it had to be larger than the biggest nineteenth century sixareen.

In eighteenth century correspondence great boats are sometimes referred to as large or big boats (SMA, GD144/97/2; Norski boat.doc:7; GD144/104/19; GHA, L33: 61). The earliest piece of new eighteenth century great boat evidence was found in a set of instructions for the purchase from Hamburg of "... 100 yards good sail linen for such to my great boat ..." (SMA, GD144/97/2). The instruction to buy 100 yards (91m) of sail linen hints that the great boat was a sailing vessel.

In 1774 Gideon Gifford wrote to Alexander Wallace in Bergen: "... As I have occasion for a large boat, I beg the favour you would purchase an East Sea boat for me if to be got at Bergen about 9 Tons, Wholly of Oak & well rigged ..." (SMA, Norski boat.doc: 7). It is interesting to note that Gifford requests the boat to be built wholly of oak which suggests that it was a different boat type to the ones available in western Norway which were constructed from Norwegian pine. Indeed, Gifford was unable to obtain this type of boat as Wallace wrote: "The East Sea boat was not to be got here it seldom happens that any are brought here for sale" (SMA, GD144/104/19). The familiar way in which both Gifford and Wallace use the name East Sea boat suggests that this was a well-known and common type of craft, that probably originated somewhere along the Baltic coast, as Østersø (East Sea) is the Norwegian name for the Baltic.

Further documentary evidence is found in a letter written by Wallace and addressed to Gifford that illustrates that nine years later, in 1783, Gifford was again in need of a large boat: "We have ordered the [torn] boat to be built, have received answer that it will take more time before she can be ready being uncommonly large ..." (SMA, GD144/57/25). This brief mention provides no indication about the type nor size of this boat, it just simply states that it was uncommonly large.

Within a letter written by Robert Robertson, to an unknown person in September 1772, further evidence for the use of great boats was found. This large boat was being used to freight slate from Bressay to Fethaland, a passage of approximately 33 nautical miles (63km) and the skipper wrote: "... I am sorry for this disappointment as it will not be convenient this season of the year to return the boat especially as there are no men to be got to sail her ..." (SMA, GD144/54/19). The phrase "sail her" suggests that these types of boats were principally sailed.

It is apparent that these sailing boats were used mainly to freight goods as this description, found in Thomas Mouat's ledger dated June 1788, illustrates: "... Mr Gilbert Henderson of Liverpool partner of Sellar & Henderson ... To goods per my big boat consignd to his disposal Vizt 23 barrels of whale oil filled up 390 large ling fish cured & dried wt 20 cwt £59. 19.. 24 calf skins only 22 delivered ..."(GHA, L33: 61).

Finding out the load carrying capacity of the big boat can help us determine the size of the vessel. The weight of this particular cargo was calculated as being approximately 3.1 tons (3,154kg). Obviously, it is not possible to determine if this was a full cargo, although knowing the weight provides us with a baseline from which the minimum size of this vessel might be estimated. To determine the vessel's size we can compare it with the load carrying capacity of a sixareen in 1881. These boats were 28ft (8.5m) long and were reported to be in good sailing trim with 1.3 tons (1,321kg) of fish (Sandison 1954: 17). Hance Smith previously stated that the sparse evidence suggests that the great boat was larger than the biggest nineteenth century sixareen (Smith 1984: 223). This has now been proven by the seventeenth century account of the armed retinue that went to confront Ninian Neven by great boat in 1653 and is further supported by a description of one of the largest nineteenth century sixareens, the *Ark*, which was about 33ft (10m) long and which regularly carried 40 cran of herring (6.7 tons, 6,807.5kg) (PI, Moncrieff and Wishart, 2015). Working on the premise that the great boat was larger than the average nineteenth century sixareen it is safe to assume that Mouat's big boat was not fully burdened, and was approximately the same size as the *Ark*.

The only known surviving picture of a great boat was identified during the analysis of Thomas Woore's 1828 painting of St. Magnus Bay (Figs. 25, 26). In the foreground is a large boat, with a gangplank and a canopy that covers its well-dressed occupants. The viewer of this painting is provided with an overall impression of a, somewhat naively painted, large two-masted boat. The proportions of the mast in relation to the length of the boat are exaggerated, and this over lengthening of ships' masts along with other proportional discrepancies are a common feature in Woore's paintings. There is a man standing on the beach, holding onto one end of a pole, the other end of which is being held by a man standing in the bow of the boat. It seems that the pole's primary purpose was to serve as a handrail, steadying the gentleman who is seen walking up the gangplank to board the boat.

Fig. 25. *St. Magnus Bay painted by Thomas Woore (1828). Courtesy of Derek and Tim Heath.*

Fig. 26. *This close-up note the sprit sail rigged jigger, canopy and the gang plank. Courtesy of Derek and Tim Heath.*

Fig. 27. Sif Ege *(1990) – a full-scale replica from Frederikssund of the coastal carrier* Skuldelev 3, *largely identical with* Roar Ege *of the Viking Ship Museum. Roskilde Fjord, August 2009. Courtesy of Ole Kastholm.*

Shetland boat aficionado Leslie Moncrieff described the boat in this painting as being "... a huge sixern-looking boat, with a canopy, which I imagine would be the laird's boat. Now to me that looks bigger than a sixern" (PI, Moncrieff and Wishart 2015). The analysis of Woore's painting illustrates that some of these boats may have had a main mast with an accompanying spritsail-rigged jigger, and it seems that the boat in Woore's painting was potentially an eight-oared boat. As previously discussed, the nomenclature of the great boat was its size, not the number of oars it may have used. The boat in the painting, although it has room for eight oars, in fact falls within the category known as the great boat. Hance Smith believed that the great boat remained in use until at least the middle of the eighteenth century, and it is now proven that these boats were still in use during the first half of the nineteenth century. The provenance of the great boat, unlike the now discussed Norse skuda, cannot be determined.

The skuda

Jakob Jakobsen in his etymological dictionary identified the Norn word skuti, which he stated in Old Norse means skúta (Jakobsen 1928: 822). The Norn word skuda means the same as the Norse word skúta (a general-purpose ship) (Heide 2014: 97). Jerzy Litwin, the former director of the Polish National Maritime Museum, divided medieval Scandinavian trading vessels into two categories that he defined as either large or small. In the large category were the knars (in Shetland called knorrins) and in the smaller class were vessels such as the skúta. These vessels, Litwin stated, were primarily sailing vessels which could also be rowed (Litwin 2016: 149). Associate professor Elda Heide defined the skúta as a small and light general-purpose ship and suggested that the verb skúta means "to jut" and the masculine form skúti means a "jutting rock" which he argued implied that the skúta had a jutting stem rather like Skudelev 3 (Fig. 27) (Heide 2012: 97, 134).

During the medieval period a regional variant of the skúta was also used to fish for herring around the waters of the Isle of Man where it was called a scowte, or scoute (Fig. 28) (Megaw and Megaw 1941: 92). During this period the word skúta reached England, where the variant used was skoute which came via the Dutch form schuite, and this term was recorded as early as 1326. The term schuite also had Irish and Scottish variants known as sgoth or scoth which have been defined as a skiff or Norway skiff. In the Isle of Man a regulation was passed in 1662 that stated that these craft must be able to carry a burden of four tons (Mcgaw and Mcgaw 1941: 93).

The skuda was documented in the seventeenth century serving as a trading vessel to Norway, and to Scotland via Orkney (Hibbert 1822: 414). The Reverend James Gordon, minister of North Yell and Fetlar, reported in the *Statistical Account for Scotland 1791-1799* an oral history tradition: "After the Danes took possession of Shetland, which, as above observed, they did between the eighth and ninth century. The settlers here were supplied with all their necessaries from the Kings of Norway, and there were ships fitted out for the purpose, of a particular construction, called Scudas, who carried from Norway wood houses ... this trade continued till the time of Patrick Earl of Orkney, who among the rest of his enormous crimes, robbed the Nisbets of Kirkabister, heritors in this parish, of the last vessels used in the trade ..." (Withrington, Grant and Sinclair 1978: 558).

According to Gordon this trade was halted by Earl Patrick in the seventeenth century. This claim by Gordon is incongruous, as it was in fact Patrick's father, Lord Robert, who attempted to control the import of boats from Norway in 1575. Evidence provided by Ballantyne and Smith indicates that the merchants in Yell were in fact persecuted by Bruce of Cultmalindie

Fig. 28. *Manx scowte. Detail by J. Goldar, an engraving of a painting by Richard Wright, 1760.*

(Ballantyne and Smith 1999: 213). The fact that Cultmalindie was prosecuting and fining the merchants for trading with Norway without his permission suggests that it was he who confiscated their skuda. The timing of Cultmalindie's prosecution falls within the same period as Earl Robert's previously discussed attempt to control the boat import trade, so it is certain that Gordon's oral tradition is incorrect and has been altered over time in order to further vilify Earl Patrick's reputation.

These Yell merchants were not wealthy and powerful and the skudas in which they traded to Norway would have been much smaller vessels than, say, the previously described ship the Swanne which was owned by the rich and powerful Robert Sinclair of Brough (Donaldson 1958: 81). The notion that the skuda was a small vessel fits with Brian Smith's previously discussed view that the merchants in Yell orchestrated the Norway timber and boat trade, which was "plebeian" in nature (Smith, B. 1990: 32). Testimony provided by Captain John Smith in 1633 further discredits Gordon's oral history and shows that the trade continued after Earl Patrick's execution for treason in 1615. As previously discussed, the bark Captain Smith referred to was more than likely a skuda which suggests that it was not confiscated. Alternatively, the merchants had acquired a new vessel, which may have been a skuda, or perhaps another type of small ship (Smith, J. 1673:256). This statement by Captain Smith further supports the plebeian trade theory, because of the way he phrased the beginning of his sentence, stating that it was the "inhabitants of the island" who were engaged in this trade. Brian Smith believed that Captain Smith would have written his journal entry differently, if for example, a big and powerful Unst landowner such as Bruce of Muness had orchestrated this trade (Smith, B. 1990: 34).

As well as trading in their barks to Norway it seems that Shetlanders in the first half of the seventeenth century were also trading fish and fish-liver oil in their barks to Scotland where they also bought commodities they wanted (Smith, J. 1673: 256). This is important because Shetland was a cashless society and the merchants needed to convert their goods into cash before sailing to Norway to buy boats and timber. Other skuda evidence was provided by Hibbert, who stated: "Planks were cut in Norway of such a shape, as that they might form, when joined, proper habitations. These were said to be constantly imported from the mother country in large, twelve oared boats, named 'Scudas'" (Hibbert 1822: 414). Hibbert's skuda evidence is further strengthened by his description of the Papa Stour sword dance which he stated was controlled by a "director, named a Scudler*, who is ornamented by ribbons ... *An ancient Shetland name given to the pilot of a scuda or twelve-oared boat" (Hibbert 1822: 560). And, finally, there is cartographic evidence of twelve-oared boat use found in the place name Skuda Sound in Unst (Fig. 29). There is no further evidence of Shetland's twelve-oared skuda but it is likely that the Shetland skuda was the same type of vessel as the Scandinavian all-purpose small ship called the skúta.

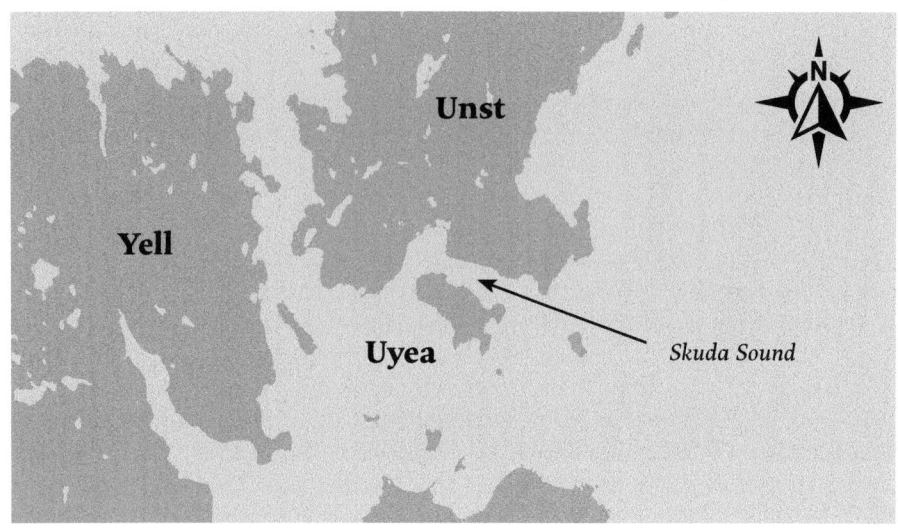

Fig. 29. *Location of Skuda Sound, between Uyea and Unst.*

Chapter 4

To flit and fure 1550-1850

Organised road building in Shetland did not begin until the 1840s so most travel around Shetland, up until the latter part of nineteenth century, was by boat (Donaldson 1958: 44). This chapter looks at the common ferry routes and the types of boats used. This analysis is bolstered by contemporary accounts of people's experiences of ferry boat journeys. These, together with the analysis of ferrying, give an insight into the importance of waterborne travel that fundamentally did not change during this three-hundred-year period. When discussing ferrying the Shetland terms to flit and fure are used. The term flit means to convey goods and passengers a short distance by sea, whilst fure means to ferry passengers and goods by sea.

Ferrying during the sixteenth and seventeenth centuries

An oral tradition, recalled by the nineteenth century English geologist and antiquarian Samuel Hibbert, illustrates that an organised ferry system was established by the late 1500s. Lord Robert Stewart, the first Earl of Orkney and Lord of Shetland, employed an armed retinue who were scattered throughout Shetland guarding the common ferries for the purpose of preventing complaints of his deeds reaching the government of Scotland (Hibbert 1822: 236).

The people of Shetland at this time were placed under a duty to ferry the administrators of Shetland day or night, and these exactions were so onerous that a complaint was raised by the parishioners against Lord Robert Stewart's foude (a Norn word which means sheriff) Laurence Bruce of Cultmalindie on 24th April 1577 (Ballantyne and Smith, 1999: 209). Ferrying was just one component of the complaint made against Bruce by parishioners who lived between Tingwall and Scalloway. It seems these parishioners were exceptionally burdened by the day and night duty placed upon them to ferry the foud, his servants, and his goods and gear. In their complaint they stated that they were accustomed to providing a ferrying service for Shetland's administrators but in times past this was not so onerous "… and quhair as thai war bot thryss in the yeir wount with flitting and furing, and gat allowance and payment thairfoir, now he compellis thame continualie to flit and fure him and his geir as he hes ado, but ony payment or allowance, quhairthrow thair boitis ar broken and thame selffis put to utter wrak" (Ballantyne and Smith 1999: 209). The translation reads "… and whereas there were but three times in the year would with flitting and furing, and get allowance and payment therefore, now he compels them continually to flit and fur him and his gear as he orders, but without payment or allowance, through which their boats are broken and themselves put to utter wrack."

Obligations were also placed on the residents of Burra to make their boats available by keeping them on the east side of the isle for Lord Robert's son, Earl Patrick, and his deputies to use when Patrick was resident in Shetland (Donaldson 1958: 45; Fenton 1978: 553). As well as demanding the use of boats whenever he needed them the Earl, it seems, also wished to control the movement of goods, speculatively to prevent smuggling and theft. Burra residents were therefore forbidden from transporting goods by boat at night and there were also other obligations placed upon them "... for the flitting of strangers and passengers from their island to Scalloway or to Maywick, and were commanded to subscribe among themselves for the purchase of a ferry boat for this purpose" (Donaldson 1958: 45).

So, not only were the people of Burra to ferry whenever required they also had to provide their own boat at their own expense for the purpose. The rates for this service to strangers were "ilk four earing boit to Maywick or Skalloway for one flitting one half mark and ilk sax earing ten shillingis" (Fenton 1978: 553). All this ferrying and hauling of goods had an adverse impact on the residents of Burra, Trondra, Quarff and Gulberwick whose fishing was consequently much neglected (Ballantyne and Smith 1990: 209). The Burra ferry was one example of many small open boat ferries that existed (and in Burra's case continued to be operated between the islands right up until the 1970s, when the bridges were constructed linking Burra and Trondra with the mainland). It must be pointed out that Lord Robert (and later Earl Partick) and Bruce of Cultmalindie were not the only ones to abuse their position of power. In 1604 Hugh Tarrell was accused of abusing the King's authority by demanding the inhabitants of Whalsay to ferry him to Reafirth (Donaldson 1958: 45).

In August 1615 the Shetland court assumed a legislative function and passed or adopted a code of some 25 Country Acts. One of these acts appertained to the hire of boats and provides an insight into how the ferry system operated. It was a requirement that all men should be sufficiently provided with boats for the purpose of ferrying the administrators in the course of their work. Those being ferried were expected to pay a reasonable fare, and if they failed to do so they could be fined £10 Scots. This act also provides us with evidence that the ferry service in Shetland had been established a long time before, and that its operation should "... conforme to the lovable custome observeit in tymes bygane." (Donaldson 1991: 163-164). Maps of Shetland's seventeenth century ferry routes, taken from Donaldson's transcript of the Country Acts, are found in Figs. 30-31.

These maps provide a picture of how the system operated. A boat would be hired from any available local person, and the rate of charge would have been

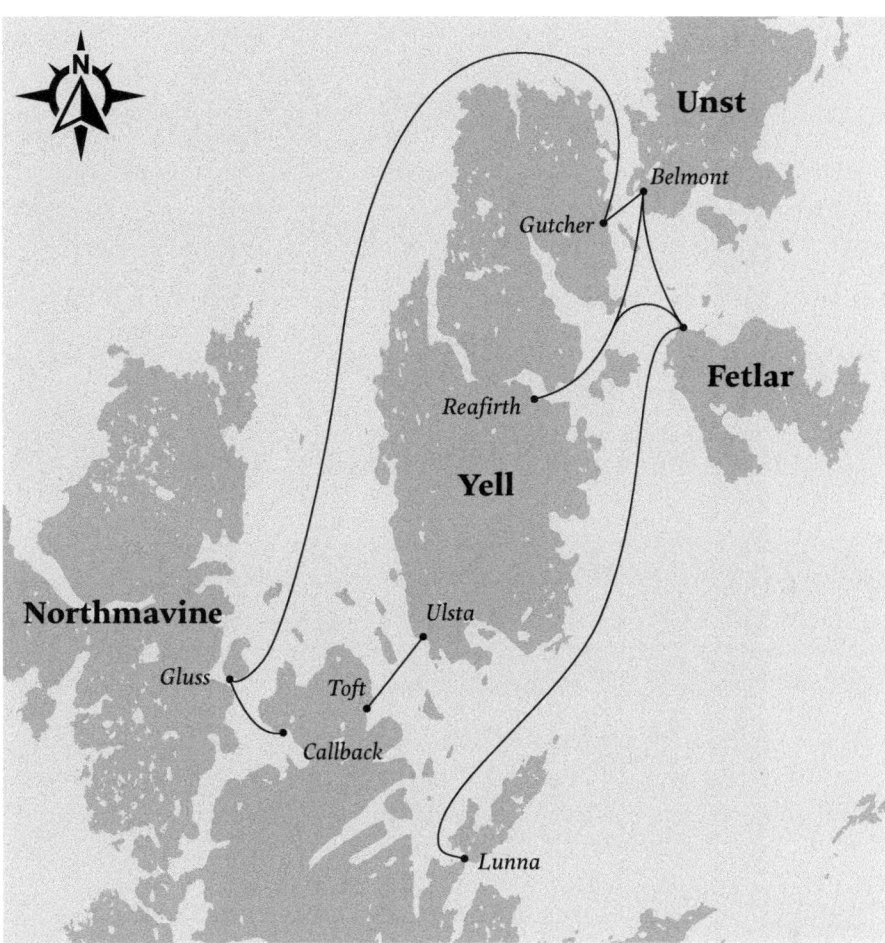

Fig. 30. *Seventeenth century ferry routes between Unst, Fetlar, Yell and Mainland.*

no less than the regulated ferry rate. This did not preclude the negotiation of higher ferry charges, which were locally negotiated, and paid according to local circumstances (Hibbert 1822: 16). It appears that this was an ad-hoc system, which serves to highlight that practically every family had access to a boat and also that during this period there was a lot of movement of goods and people throughout Shetland.

The Country Acts forbade the use of boats on the sabbath for secular matters, and in some districts of Shetland there was considerable church-going by boat. An example of this was the laborious regular Sunday journey of the minister for Bressay, Burra and Quarff who travelled from Bressay by small boat to Easter Quarff, he then walked two miles to Wester Quarff, whence he and his Quarff congregation travelled by boats to the kirk of Burra

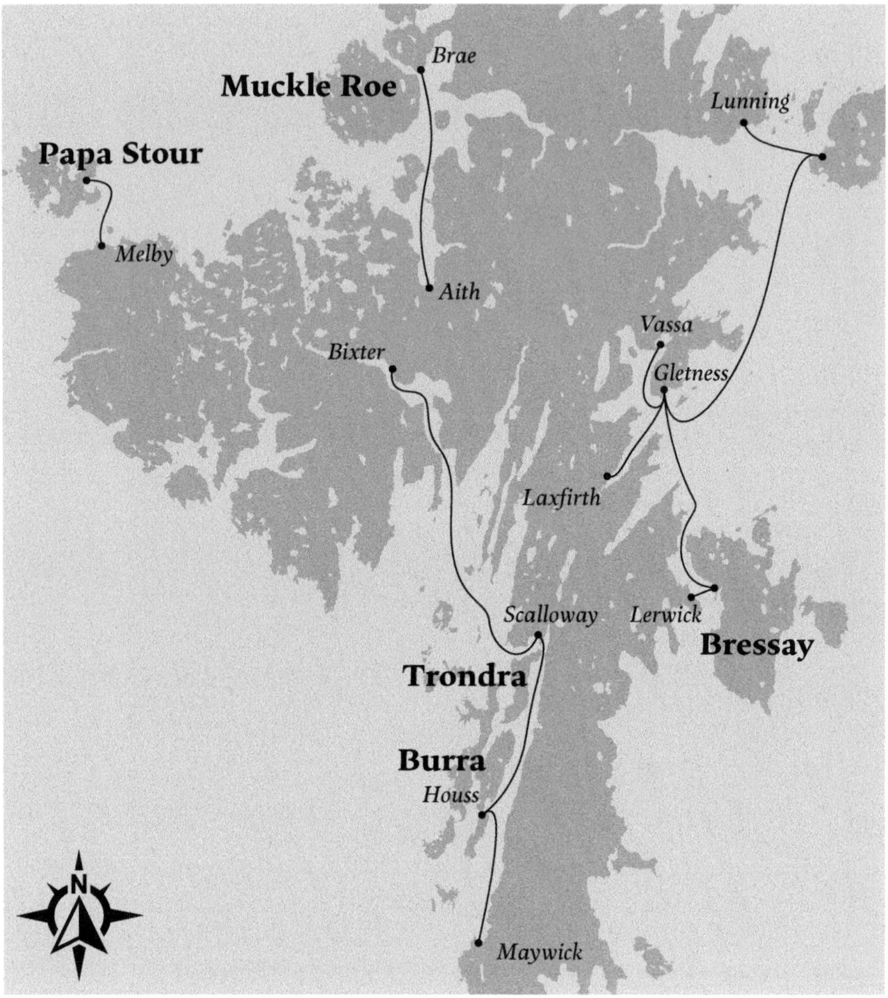

Fig. 31. *Ferry routes in seventeenth century Shetland.*

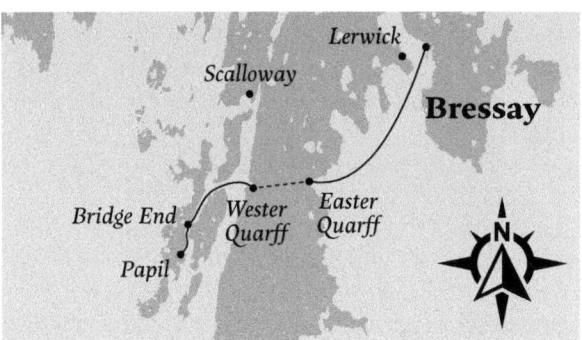

Fig. 32. *The minister of the united parish of Bressay, Burra and Quarff's Sunday journey.*

(a round trip of 32 miles, 51.5km). This ministerial duty took a minimum of eight hours (Fig. 32) (Osler 1983: 27). As well as travelling by boat to church, the residents of Quarff also went to Burra for marriages, christenings, and funerals. Burra resident Laurina Herculson recalled an oral tradition about someone who died in Quarff: "... and the weather was bad for days, they could not travel by boat to Burra, so they buried him somewhere on the banks ..." (PI, Herculson, 2016).

The amended ferry freights

More detailed evidence for the hiring of boats for ferrying people and flitting goods was found within the Mouat papers, in a copy document of the amended ferry freights, dated 1733. This Gardie House document was previously discussed by Hance Smith who described it as the most complete account of statutory links as it lists the ferry routes and the wages that were paid to those who "serve on board of great boats within the said Country" (Hance Smith1984: 223, GHA.292.1733). It says that these ferry services should "conform to the ancient practise of the country." This reinforces the previous seventeenth century ferry rates document, further illustrating that ferry services in Shetland had been in existence for a very long time.

Comparison of the ferry routes described in 1615 with those of 1733 shows that the number of prescribed routes had more than doubled in just over 100 years. It seems unlikely that travel in Shetland had changed much during this period, especially when considering that small boat transport had remained constant throughout Shetland's Norse, medieval, and modern history period; and the evidence seems to suggest that most people had access to a boat. The reason for this ferry route anomaly must be that only the most important ferry crossing points were described in the 1615 Country Act, whereas, in the 1733 ferry freights document, all the known common routes were described. I believe the reason for this more detailed description of ferry routes in 1733 was simply an attempt to centrally control and standardise all the ferry rates charged to passengers (Table 3) (Figs. 33-34). This attempt to control ferry rates was discussed by Hibbert who called this document a "dead letter" when he complained about the lack, and exorbitant cost, of ferry hire during his Shetland travels in 1817 (Hibbert 1822: 455).

The ferry freights document uses the curious phrase quoted above: "to such as serve on board of great boats within the said Country". This is misleading, as it implies that great boats were used to provide all the described ferry services. This of course will not have been the case as great boats, as we have seen, were the preserve of the wealthy and four- and six-oared boats will have been adequate for many of these shorter passages. It is also surprising to note that the offshore islands of Out Skerries, Fair Isle, and Foula were not listed as part of this organised ferry system. As previously discussed, travel to these outer island groups by the denunciator and his retinue in 1613

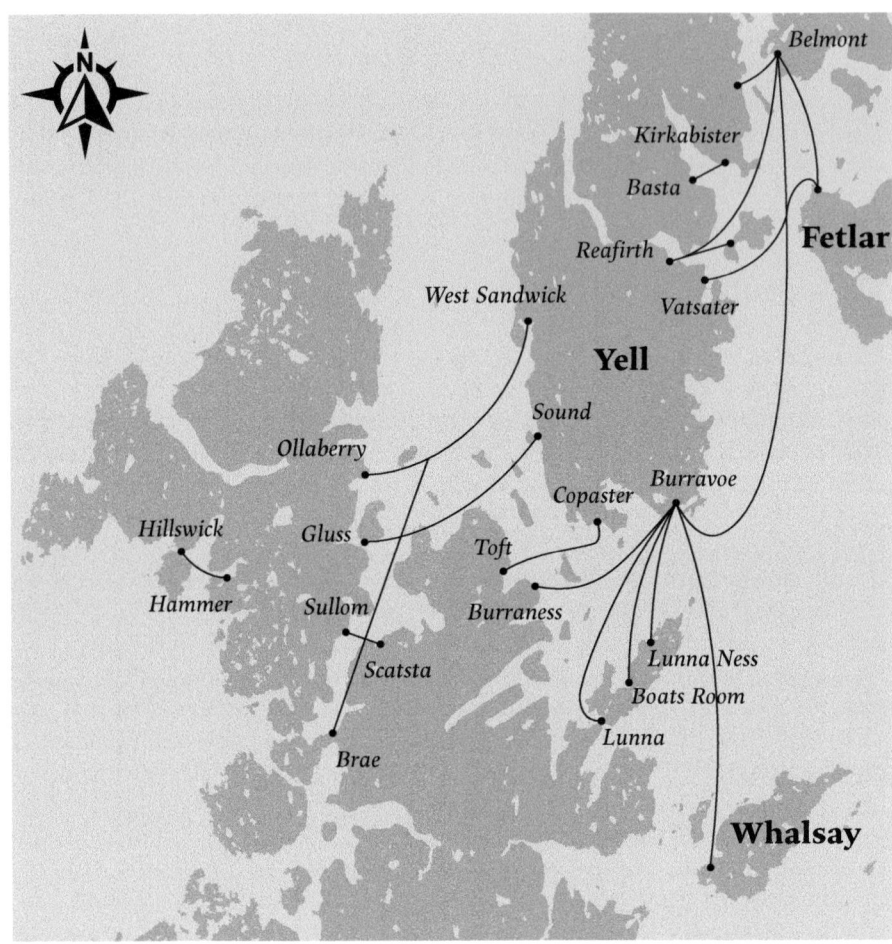

Fig. 33. *Ferry routes connecting North Mainland, Whalsay and the North Isles in 1733. Data for map construction obtained from the Gardie House Archive: GHA.292.1733.*

was undertaken in a great boat and, as will shortly be argued, there is late eighteenth and early nineteenth century evidence that demonstrates that these islands were indeed connected. These services were organised at a local level on an ad-hoc basis and the rate of hire was locally agreed upon. It is noteworthy that between the seventeenth and eighteenth centuries the cost of hiring a ferry did not significantly increase. As explained by Brian Smith, "Shetland was a very conservative society, and in many ways the rents and taxes were in 1733 very similar to those several hundred years earlier ..." (PC, Smith B. 2016). The evidence clearly points to the reality that some of the longer journeys were undertaken by great boat, when these were available, whilst the shorter journeys were undertaken in a four- or six-oared boat, as described below.

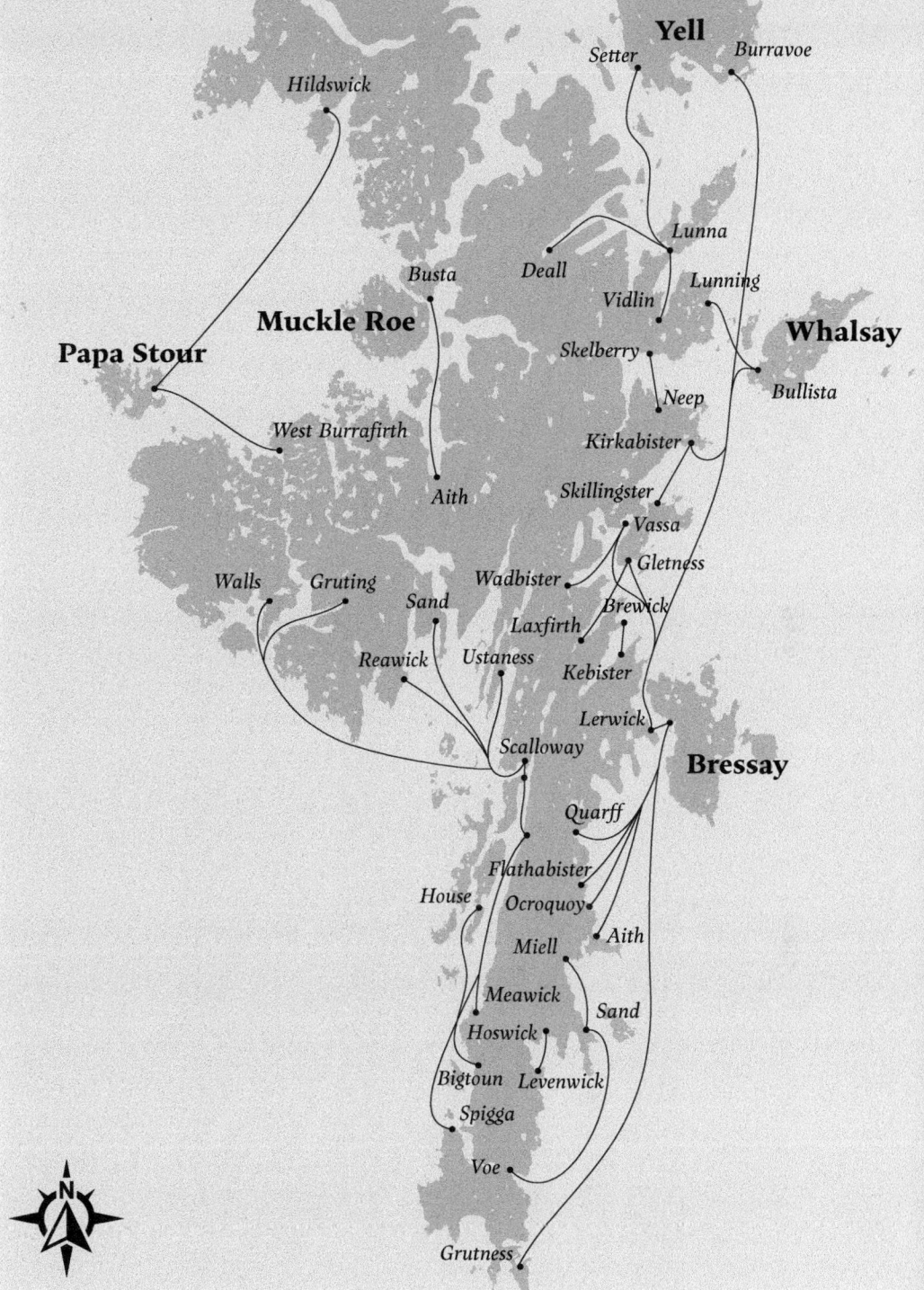

Fig. 34. *Ferry routes connecting Shetland in 1733. Data for map construction obtained from the Gardie House Archive: GHA.292.1733.*

5th July 1733

Extract - *Regulation off ferrie fraights 1733 -* transcribed by John Gifford

Regulation anent the rates of the Ferry's Frieghts & passages within the Country of Zetland & wages to be payed to such as serve on board of great boats within the said Country conform to ancient practise of the country with some alterations made thereupon by the Gentlemen Heritors att their meeting the 5th of July 1733, together with the Stewart Depute of Orkney & Zetland his acct and authority interponed thereto follows vizt:

From -

• Scallaway to Meawick sixteen shillings Scots	• Burravoe, Yell to Whalsey one pound four shillings
• Scallaway to House eight shillings	• Burravoe, Yell to Lerwick three pound Scots money foresaid
• Burra to Bigtoun Banks twelve shillings	• Whalsey to Staverness or Neep six shilling
• Burra to Spigga one pound four shilling	• Lunna to Vidlin four shilling
• Scallaway to Spigga one pound ten shilling	• Lunna to Whalsey twelve shilling
• Scallaway to Walshisare four shilling	• Whalsey to Lunning six shilling
• Scallaway to Trondra one shilling	• Skelberry to Bulista or Durie four shilling
• Scallaway to Ustaness six shilling	• Kirkabister to Burgh or Skillingester four shilling
• Scallaway to Reawick, Sand or Sandsound twelve shilling	• Vassa or Fraister to Burntshamersland two shilling
• Scallaway to Walls one pound 10 shilling	• Vassa or Fraister or Wadabister four shilling
• Selivoe to Whiteness in Walls four shilling	• Vassa, Fraister, Gletness or Realsburgh to Laxfirth six shilling
• Selivoe or Gruting to Burrostow in Walls six shilling	• Gletness to Lerwick ten shilling
• Sandness to Papa Stour six shilling	• Vassa or Fraister to Lerwick fourteen shilling
• Papa Stour to West Burrafirth twelve shilling	• Brewick to Kebister one shilling
• Brindista or Aith to Busta twelve shilling	• Lerwick to Bressay two shilling
• Papa Stour to Hildswick one pound ten shilling	• Lerwick to Laxfirth twelve shilling
• Hildswick to Hammer four shilling	• Lerwick to Whalsay one pound ten shilling
• Sullem to Garth or Scatsta four shilling	• Lerwick to Quarf eight shilling
• Glus to Sound in Yell twelve shilling	• Lerwick to Flatabister ten shilling
• Toft to Copaster six shilling	• Lerwick to Ocroquey twelve shilling
• Burraness in Delting to Burravoe, Yell twelve shilling	• Lerwick to Aith in cunningsburgh eighteen shilling
• Burravoe, Yell to Reafirth twelve shilling	• Lerwick to Virkie or Grutness two pounds money foresaid
• Reafirth to Unst twelve shilling	• Miell in Cunningsburgh to Sands Are four shilling
• Reafirth, Gardie, Cam Besouth the firth to Hascosay two shilling	• Hosewick to Levenwick two shilling
• Vatsater to Fetlor six shilling	• Sandwick to Voe eight shillilng
• The ferry of Bloomasound two shilling	• Quarf to Scallaway four shilling
• Basta to Kirkabister two shilling	• The West Banks of Lunna to Deall in Delting eight shilling
• Fetlor to Unst six shilling	• Setter or Sound in Yell to Lunna or Sweening one pound said money
• Fetlor to Burravoe, Yell twelve shilling	• West Sandwick to Ollaberrie or Northroe sixteen shilling
• Unst to Burravoe, Yell one pound four shilling	• Westsandwick to Brae or Elwick one pound ten shilling Scots money foresaid
• Burravoe to Boats room of Lunna eighteen shilling	
• Burravoe to Lunna Ness six shilling	

Table 3. *The ferry freights, 1773. (Gardie House Archive GHA.292.1733).*

Accounts of ferry journeys

The Reverend Patrick Barclay, minister for Aithsting and Sandsting, in his statistical account report of 1791 described the entrance to his parish, which was from the ocean: "... the parish is everywhere intersected by long voes, the traveller has often occasion to cross ferries. There are, however, no stated ferry boats; but the people are very ready to assist and forward their neighbours, often for nothing, and at best for a very small hire" (Withrington, Grant, and Sinclair 1978: 381-383). This contradicts the 1733 ferry rates document and illustrates the earlier point that ferry crossings were organised at a local level and that the ferry toll was negotiable.

As visiting naturalist Patrick Neill found, some of these ferry journeys that were at times exasperating as his account of a flit between Bressay and Noss comically demonstrates:

> ... yet the only ferry we could procure was a miserable skiff, which could not without difficulty convey two passengers at a time. We observed that one of the boatman was not tugging at his oar half so busily as the other, and consequently that the boat was turning to one side: upon remonstrating with the sluggish ferryman, - he instead of quickening his motions, made a full pause, and hung on his oar gaping with surprise: the other, meanwhile, continued tugging away as hard as ever, nor did he observe what he was doing till he was alarmed by the boat wheeling about, and almost completely in a circle; and all this in the midst of a boiling current, and about equally distant from the shore ... (Neill 1806: 81-82).

Happily, not all ferry journeys were quite so miserable for Neill, as this extract from his August trip from Lerwick to Unst demonstrates: "... On the 28th August we left Bressay Sound in a large open boat, for Unst. ... While we scudded along with a favourable breeze our boat's crew amused themselves with catching mackerel, which swim faster than any other small fish, and may therefore be caught while a vessel is running at the rate of seven or eight knots ..." (Neill 1806: 72-73). This vivid account suggests that the boat described by Neill may have been either a sixareen or a great boat as, when under sail, this craft was achieving speeds of seven to eight knots which suggests a waterline length of approximately 30ft (9.1m). Neill's journey was broken by a midday lunch stop at Gossabrough in Yell, where they ate the mackerel caught earlier that morning. After lunch Neill's journey continued, and he reached Uyea Sound by early evening. This journey from Lerwick to Uyea Sound is a distance of 32 nautical miles (60km) and, assuming that they began at 09:00, stopped at midday for an hour and reached Uyea Sound at 17:00, means that the average speed of the boat was 4.6 knots.

Unlike Neill, Hibbert during his visit to Shetland in 1817 had disappointing, and sometimes miserable ferry trips, as he explained: "There are few gentlemen who, in the trips that they make, are not rowed by their own tenants, and they take such an opportunity of ingratiating themselves in the favour of their dependents, by paying them above their due; it is, therefore, unfortunate that the sum thus given is the least that is demanded from the stranger" (Hibbert 1822: 455). Hibbert's annoyance with the generosity of the lairds for the payment of boat hire runs counter to the commonly held view that the lairds racked-up prices in their own favour (PC, Smith B. 2016). This extra income, which Hibbert bemoaned, was in fact of importance to the boatmen who were very poor. It was common practise during this period to have, as a condition of tenancy, an obligation to fish for the laird or landmaster, selling the catch exclusively to him for a fixed price (Goodlad 1971: 96). The extra income obtained from ferrying would have been extremely important to the boatman and so Hibbert's annoyance was rather ill-placed.

Hibbert continued to vent his frustration over the expense and the quality of boat hire, moaning that it was not possible to pin the ferryman down to an agreed price and that the journey was itself unpleasant because of the attitude of the boatman, who spent his time trying to increase the fare. Indeed, Hibbert expressed incredulity when he recounted an experience of hiring a fishing boat's crew in Walls who "... were under the influence of an old boatman, whose unaccommodating and surly disposition, was in perfect correspondence with the hideous appearance of his figure..." Hibbert then penned a scathing verse:

> An uncouth, savage and uncivile wight,
> Of grisly hew and foule ill-favour'd sight;
> His face with smoke was tand, and eies were blear'd,
> His head and beard with sout were ill bedight,
> His cole-black hands did seeme to have been sear'd
> In smythes fire-spitting forge, and nayles like clawes appear'd.
> (Hibbert 1822: 455).

The Shetlander, Hibbert continued, "... is too often in the habits of considering the extortion to which he makes the stranger submit, as of the same nature as the right that he assumes to plunder a wreck; for he enumerates under the blasphemous title of 'God-sends,' a wreck, a drove of whales, and a boat-fare" (Hibbert 1822: 455).

Like the earlier visitor Patrick Neill, the Danish administrator of Faroe Christian Pløyen, who visited Shetland in 1839, had a better experience of using ferries during his travels through the archipelago. Pløyen briefly described a journey from Scalloway to Burra in an ordinary six-oared Shetland boat. "The boats in Shetland are very like our own ... the ordinary fishing boats are of the size of eight-manned boats with us, but considerably broader, and rowed by six men. These circumstances evidence that the Shetlanders use the sail more than oars ..." (Pløyen, 1896: 23). Pløyen's happy ferry experience was shared by Edward Charlton who first visited Shetland

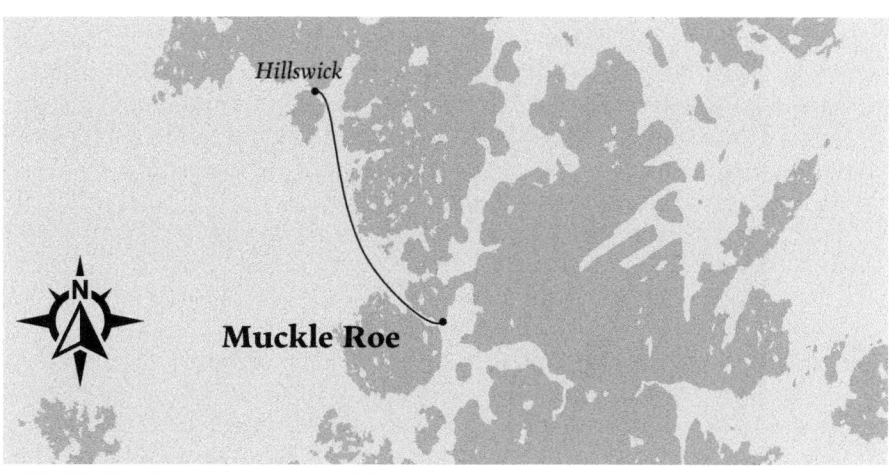

Fig. 35. *Map of Charlton's 1852 boat trip (Charlton 2007: 120).*

as a 17-year-old medical student in 1832, and again in 1852. In his journal
Charlton recalls a trip from Lerwick to Bressay in 1852. "A boatman was soon
found, a ragged poverty-stricken Shetlander, who had been ill for weeks and
could hardly crawl on land, but once seated in his boat the poor fellow gained
new life, and pulled us with great ease across the Sound ..." (Charlton 2007:
95). Charlton also provided a wonderful account of a trip from Hillswick to
Muckle Roe:

> "... the wind blew stiffly from the south west, the sky in that quarter was dark and lowering,
> and our boatmen foretold a gale. They felt no apprehension, however, at the prospect; we
> should reach smooth water, they said, before the gale could rise. Our boat was small and
> old, I should have preferred certainly a six-oared deep sea fishing boat and a younger crew,
> but we found that though three of our men were in advanced years, they had lost none of
> that daring spirit for which the Northmavine men are so famous. Having placed our luggage,
> including two cassies full of minerals, beneath the thwarts of the boat, we embarqued,
> and along with us Mr Hendrie, an active Queen's Messenger of Lerwick. At length when
> we had through the seething green water directly south of the Drongs, we laid in the oars,
> hoisted our sail, and steered for the opening of Muckle Roe Sound. Old Andrew took the
> helm, and Magnus, the youngest of the crew, stood by the sail, holding the halyards, while
> the sheet was in the hands of the helmsman. The wonderful powers of sailing exhibited by
> the Shetland build of boats is well known. When steering the helmsman sits so low, upon
> a smaller semicircular piece of wood inserted in the sharp stern of the boat, that he steers
> with the tiller over his shoulder, and in rapidly shifting the tiller to meet the advancing
> wave, he merely lowers his head and shifts the tiller over to the other side without moving
> from his seat. The advantages of this position are obvious, there is little or no danger of
> the helmsman being struck from his seat by the heaviest wave, and with the sheet in his
> left hand he commands the sail in any sudden squall ..." (Charlton 2007: 120).

It is evident from Charlton's description that he enjoyed this trip and admired the qualities of both the crew and their boat. The boat was a fourareen and this illustrates that even in 1852 smaller types of boats were being used for these types of journeys, and it is evident from Charlton's description that this was a locally organised hire; this route was not listed in the 1733 regulation of ferry freights.

Some 22 years later there is a description of a journey from Watsness in Walls to Foula by Shetland-born Robert Cowie:

> The point of Wattsness marks the termination of this line of coast, on the south. As it is the nearest point on the mainland to Foula, it may be well to proceed thence ... The distance is eighteen miles, and the course south-west. Unless it be the traveller's good fortune to obtain a steamer – and they are by no means numerous in these latitudes – the best conveyance to Foula is a good six-oared fishing boat. A sailing vessel is not so agreeable, for the passage is beset with tideways; and calms and fogs are by no means uncommon in the summer time – and no one who could help it would visit Foula at any other season. About three miles from this island, in an easterly direction, are the Hivda-grind rocks, a dangerous reef of considerable extent (Cowie 1874: 287-288).

This mention for the preference of rowing to Foula provides insight into the hazards faced in making such a journey; although in my opinion, I think Cowie is incorrect, as the choice of whether to row or sail would of course be dependent on the weather. As Charlton previously described, on a fine day with a favourable wind the choice would have been to sail. Generally, Cowie only briefly made statements about the ferryboats he took and gives no details of the boats or what these journeys were like. By contrast John T. Reid provides an account of a perilous ferry journey across Yell Sound in the summer of 1867.

> At West Yell I succeeded with some difficulty in collecting a crew of three, consisting of two lame men, who were sailmakers, and an old man too frail to go to the far haaf-fishing. Down to the boat-noust the two hirpled. They rowed well, and made excellent speed; but when half-way over Yell Sound we got into a string of tide, which on either side rose alarmingly high, and tossed us about like a very air-bell, pitching me repeatedly right off my seat" (Reid 1869: 41).

This description was the type of journey that regularly took place before the steamship *Earl of Zetland* came into service in 1877. The *Earl* provided a twice-weekly service from Lerwick to Unst and the other east-side isles which continued with her replacement, the second *Earl of Zetland*, until 1975. Historian Gordon Donaldson, however, argued that the old system of ferries was more rational. Donaldson complained that there were few, if any, ferries except on the long routes that led to and from Lerwick, with the result that a person travelling from Yell to Northmavine, which is approximately five nautical miles (9.7km) by sea, might have to make an eighty-mile (128.7km) journey via Lerwick (Donaldson 1958: 44). The construction of roads in Shetland, which began in the mid-nineteenth century, gradually reduced the need for travel by boat. This had a profound effect and slowly eroded Shetland's inherited boat culture. An example of this was provided by Shetland Museum curator Ian Tait, who stated: "People stopped taking the ferry boat across Weisdale Voe from Sound to Kalliness once the road came in the 1850s" (PC, Tait 2016). The transition from travel by sea to travel by road was a slow one which only really gained momentum with the development of the bicycle, the motorbike and the car in the late nineteenth and early twentieth centuries.

This analysis on ferrying demonstrates the versatility of these small four- and six-oared boats which, as well as being used to flit and fure, were also used for fishing, moving livestock, and for family travel (see section on subsistence boat use in chapter 10). As already identified, these boats were imported from Norway in one of two ways: set-up or in-boards. This trade continued during the late eighteenth and early nineteenth century. However, at some point during this period Shetlanders began to adapt these imported boats to better suit their own needs, and this gradual adaptation resulted in the development of the Shetland boat types that we are familiar with today. The evidence for this continuing boat import trade and the development of Shetland's own vernacular boats is now examined.

Chapter 5
Boats from Norway 1750-1818

A s already discussed, the boats used to ferry goods and people were imported from Norway. This boat and timber import trade was based on convenience and bolstered by long-shared Norwegian and Shetland cultural ties. The trade is fascinating and archive sources provide a rich narrative that, once woven together, affords us a more complete and accurate picture of the boat import trade during this period. This gives us a glimpse into how the development of offshore commercial fishing drove the development of Shetland's own vernacular boats.

Eighteenth century boat imports

Shetland's quarterly customs accounts are unfortunately incomplete, only beginning in 1742. Within these accounts it would be expected that imported boats, and boat related items, which are sometimes referred to as boat furniture – such as remeks (oars), tafts (thwarts), tilfers (sole boards), stongs (masts) and austkerries (bailers) would have been listed, but this was not the case. The first entry into the accounts of Norwegian timber imports was made on 25th June 1744, with the ship *Providence of Bressay*, whose master, James Calder, imported from Bergen: "Four dozen of small spars, Two dozen Norraway Dealls, A Parcell of timber Ramble [an assortment of timber] valued upon oath £4„3„4, and One hundred & forty Bushells foreign salt in bulk to cure fish" (SMA, SA.1/7/1). In this cargo were 48 "small spars". This might be construed as meaning boats' masts and yards but this was not the case. The term "spar" continually appears in the customs accounts and the term just meant the trunk of a tree, or a pole, which, once in Shetland, may have been fashioned into a boat's mast, or a yard, but equally, may have been made into a roof truss, or a gate post (Tait 2012: 125). Although the evidence for boat imports is lacking at this point in the customs accounts, there clearly was a demand for boat related items as this letter extract, written by Henry Sinclair and addressed to his cousin, dated May 1743, illustrates: "... P.S. Speedy send our sailing linen, ... seam & roves, Oars for yoals" (SMA, GD144/105/13).

In 1745 only one ship was recorded in the customs accounts as importing goods from Norway. The *Sibella* belonged to Thomas Gifford and sailed into Lerwick on 10th September, having travelled from Godøysund. Again, no boats or boat related items were listed in the cargo of spars, barrel hoops, birch bark, and timber ramble. This entry in the customs accounts is noteworthy when it is compared with an "Acct of Cash Disbursed in purchasing our Cargoe at Norway." This document was addressed to Thomas Gifford and written one month earlier, in August, by William Farquhar, from onboard *Sibella*, see Table 4 (SMA, GD144/100/3). It is possible that the 10th of September entry in the customs accounts relates to Farquhar's August voyage. But, surprisingly, the cargoes appear to be quite different. In Farquhar's invoice to Gifford boats and oars are listed but there is no mention of the 2,000 barrel hoops entered in the customs accounts. This suggests that Farquhar's August account of the

Aug 1745	£	S	D
To Expenses Going to Bergin and staying there 8 days	1		
To the lads lodging		10	
To the yaghts Fraieght that Carried Down the Tarr and Deals		8	10
To 9 Barrels Tarr at 15 merk Da per Barrel	4	10	
To 20 4 Oard Boats at 12s	12		
To 6:6 Oard Boats	4	16	
To 250 Voghs Bark at 6s per	6	5	
To 8 Duz 12 Ells at 3s per }	1	4	
To 9 Duz 9 Ells at 1s, 6D per } 13 trees per Duzen		13	6
To 5 Duz 7 Ells at 1s 2D per }		5	10
To 5 Duz & ½ Harpools		2	
To 90 Ploughs		15	
To 6 Duz Oars		6	
To 10 Duz Souples			10
To 1 Duz shovels		2	4
To 1 Duz Ouscari		1	6
To 20 Handstaves			4
To Expenses Going to Hermand Irlands and the woods	1		
To Daily of the Loading and Custom House fees at Hermand ilands	5		
To Act of Tobaco to the Boat Biggers		2	
To the former for preparing the cargoe		8	
To Bier to the Boat Bigers		4	4
To anker Watters to Ditto		1	4
To Two Voaghs Stock fish		3	8
To Two Barrels Lam Bleck		1	4
£H	40	7	2

Table 4. *Acct of Cash Disbursed in purchasing our Cargoe at Norway (Shetland Museum and Archives, GD144/100/3).*

cash disbursed relates to a different voyage, which may have been possible
– provided the weather was favourable, he did not sail via Hamburg, and
that the Norwegian cargo could be got ready and loaded quickly. Even if two
crossings did take place, and the September cargo related to a second trip,
this then begs the question of why the first voyage's cargo was not entered
into the customs accounts? Whichever way this is viewed it is clear that the
correct payment of duty on this cargo was successfully avoided, either by
fraudulently entering the cargo in the customs accounts on 10th September,
or alternatively, if this invoice related to an earlier voyage, the first cargo
managed to avoid HM Customs altogether. The simple fact of the matter is
that the cargo was smuggled.

The number of boats purchased by Farquhar followed the pattern of
buying more four-oared than six-oared boats. Also of note was the continued
procurement of extra oars, along with one dozen austkerries. Farquhar's
account also states that it was the Norwegian boatbuilders who prepared
and stowed the cargo of boats. Although there is an absence of detail about
how the cargo was stowed, Farquhar tells us that the boatbuilders were paid
in tobacco, bier (a type of barley), waters (spirits), stockfish, and lam bleck (a
type of black beer).

An increase in trade with Norway occurred during 1746 when there were
seven ships listed in the customs accounts that imported timber. Again, there
were no boats nor boat items listed as being imported. The cargoes declared
to customs comprised items such as wooden barrel hoops, salt, pipe staves,
barrels of tar, untarred cordage, and one shipment of fifteen hundred Norway
deals. In 1747 and 1748 there was little trade with Norway, and only three
ships imported timber. However, an extremely large consignment of barrel
hoops, pipe staves, untarred cordage, empty barrels, and salt was imported
from Altona aboard the *St. Peter of Altona*, which must have been an extremely
large ship. This vessel was chartered by James Craigie for himself and four
other Shetland merchants; John Robertson, William Spence, James Spence
and Andrew Scott. As well as the *St. Peter of Altona* there were nine other
ships importing cargo from Altona during this period, and their cargoes were
almost identical to that shipped by James Craigie.

There follows a 17-year break in the customs records. Thankfully, there are
other archive sources that demonstrate the continuance of the boat import
trade during this period.

This documentary evidence illustrates that the boat trade was flourishing,
as a letter written by John Davidson (a Lerwick merchant) to Thomas Gifford
of Busta on 26th January 1748, demonstrates. In this Davidson set out his
terms and conditions for delivering a cargo from Lerwick to "... Mavisgrind
upon your risk, for nintain four oard boats and nine six oard ditto, including
those sold by me to your tenants in North Mavine ..." This letter reiterates
that demand for four-oared boats was greater than for the six-oared type. It
also challenges the commonly held view that boats were solely provided to

tenants by their landlord, as Davidson sold these boats directly to Gifford's tenants. Davidson also explained how the cost for delivering the boats was computed: "... tho no man cane judge of my profits, fraight insurance tolls & other charges at Norway & have included beter than your self ... shall accept of Norway faring viz doble of the prime cost to the boat bewlders and twelve and half per cent of said prim cost as reward for transporting them from hence ... " (SMA, GD144/12/12). So, Davidson paid the export duty on the boats and, in order to cover these costs and make a profit, he charged Gifford double what he paid for the boats in Norway. As well as this, Davidson also charged for their delivery to Mavis Grind, at 12.5 per cent of the original Norwegian boat price.

This reveals that the popular belief that the boat import trade was solely controlled by landowners is incorrect. It is likely that Davidson was not the only merchant to be taking part in this trade, and illustrates that the dynamics between landowner, merchant and tenant were more complex than we have previously thought. It is noteworthy that there is no mention of customs duties paid in Shetland, which suggests that these boats were smuggled.

This correspondence between Davidson and Gifford was followed-up by another letter, dated 6th February 1748, in which the delivery of 21 four-oared and four six-oared boats to Mavis Grind by Patrick Torrie was confirmed (SMA, GD144/41/18). It is noteworthy that in the first letter 19 four-oared and nine six-oared boats were to have been delivered. In fact, five times more four-oared than six-oared boats were delivered to Gifford and his tenants. This is somewhat surprising, as this was the time when the haaf fishery was expanding, and six-oared boats were becoming more commonly used. (Withrington, Grant, Sinclair 1978: 465-466).

Other documentary proof of the boat trade was found in an invoice of a cargo purchased at Godøysund by Captain George Richan for Thomas Gifford. Richan's ship *Douglas* does not appear in the customs accounts, and again this suggests that this was a smuggled cargo (Table 5). This invoice itemised the purchase of 10 six-oared, and 24 four-oared boats, yet again illustrating that four-oared boats were in far greater demand than the six-oared type. It is also curious to note that, even though there were fewer six-oared boats, they had far more spare oars bought for them. This suggests that these oars were being lost or broken more frequently than those used in the four-oared boats. It is also evident that Captain Richan paid customs and toll charges when he was in Norway, but no reference is made to duty payments in Shetland.

On 2nd April 1753 Thomas Gifford wrote to William Irvine:

> ... That is upon your delivery to me at Mavisgrind sometime in the Moneth of May next of such a number of Tries (spars) such as 12 Ells, 9 Ells, & 8 Ells, and so many voys of Bark so many dozen of Deals, So may Yols wt. their furniture & So many Barrels of tar conform

to particular Commission yr. Signed by me & upon delivery therof to me atthe said Port of Mavisgrind I am ... to pay you the Common Prime Cost or Value really ... for these Goods in Norway, and 100 p. cent more in full of freight, dutys, port charges and all other Risque & Expenses thereupon. This is the ordinary way I have purchased Many Norway Cargoes And the only Safe way of Making such purchase & Preventingall dispute & grudge and often does in that way of trade ...

The order for the cargo is as follows:

Impro. 6 Six oarings and all their apurtainats of the best kind.

2do. 10 four oarings All yr. furniture Sufficient & of the best kind.

2 or 3 hundr. Voys of bark if to be got or what less can be had.

20 Doz. of their best dealls.

12 Doz. 12 Ell tries of the bigest kind. (For boats' masts).

10 Doz. 9 Ells & 6 Doz. 7 Ells.

6 Doz. Spare Oars larger than ordinary and all the oars of the Yolls most be Sufficiently large which most be noticed as also the tries (which) if not Sufficient will be Cast.

Eight or 10 Barrells of Tar and any quantity of Rumble Such as ploughs shys hazel Cutts & barell hoops is convenient for you or what ever quantity of deals tries or bark You can take Which Shall be Accepted upon the above Writen Conditions ...

(SMA, Norskiboat.doc: 7)

Gifford's business proposal followed a similar arrangement to the one previously presented to him by John Davidson in 1748. As earlier argued, Gifford referred to these boats as "yols" and this reinforces my claim that the term yoal was simply a generic name for a small boat, and that it was not at that time a distinct boat type. After Gifford's letter, there is a six-year break in boat trade documentary evidence. In August, 1754, an invoice addressed to Thomas Gifford detailed the cargo loaded in *Sibella*: timber deals, trees (or spars) of various lengths, and oars – large and small (SMA, GD144/100/3). Then, in April 1756, Thomas Sanderson wrote to an unknown person and described the purchase of one six-oared, and two four-oared boats, plus 30 yards of sail linen (SMA, GD144/240/31).

In January 1762 William Mouat wrote to Alexander Wallace in Bergen requesting that he freight a neutral Danish vessel for the Hamburg and Bergen trade. The vessel was to come to Uyeasound by the middle of June when there would be a cargo for Hamburg ready. Mouat specified that the ship should be between 40-60 tons burden, and that he and his associates were willing to pay up to, but not exceeding, 50 shillings per last. Mouat noted that the highest previous Danish freight was 48 shillings per last (SMA, D.24).

This letter is particularly important. Mouat stipulated that only the best boatbuilders should be employed to build the boats, and it is clear that Mouat knew exactly the type of boats he wanted to buy. He specified the

		R	D	m	s
Invoyse Cap Geo Richan					
Norway cargo					
1748					
two six oard boats @	3,, 4m pr bt	07	2	0	
one Ditto, @	3,, 4m ,, 2s	03	4	2	
one Ditto, @	3,, 3m,,	03	3		
foure Ditto, @	3,, 3m,, 4 pr bt	14	2	0	
two foure oard boats @	2,, 3m,, 4s pr bt	05	1	0	
two ditto @ Ditto		05	1	0	
twenty Ditto, @	2,, 3m,, 6s pr Bt	52	3	0	
three voas of Barke @	4s pr V	00	1	4	
one Ditto @	4 ½ s	00	0	4 ½	
36 Ditto @	5s pr V	03	4	4	
149 Ditto,	6s pr V	18	3	6	
20 ½ Dozen of 12 ells @	4m,, 4s pr Dn	15	2	2	
20 Dozen & 3 nine ells @	2,, 2 pr Dn	07	3	4 ½	
8 Dozen 7 ells @	1m,, 6s pr Dn	02	2	0	
3 Dozen of spare oars for six oard boats @	2m,, 2s pr Dn	1	0	6	
2 Dozen Ditto for four oard boats @	1m,, 4s pr Dn	00	3	0	
54 Dozen of Hazell cuts @	1 ½ s pr Dn	01	4	1	
one mast of 36 foot long @	1	01	0	0	
4 voas of stockfish @	2m,,4s pr V	01	4	0	
Toall & Customhouse fees		31	1	4	
	Errors excepted	176	5	2	

Table 5. *Account of our cargo taken on at Goysound aboard of the Douglas for accompt of Mr Thomas Gifford of Busta with the species numbers and prices (Shetland Museum and Archives, GD144/4/1).*

keel lengths required and ordered that these boats be "in boards." Mouat also ordered 480 oars. These were surplus to the ones that came with the boats, and it is apparent from Mouat's request that these oars were to be the normal type used within the area of Godøysund and Tysnes. This tells us that the type of oars used in Shetland during this period were the same as those used in western Norway and reinforces the earlier point that the boats being purchased were the same types used in that part of Norway. Mouat also requested boatman's boards (boards for use in boatbuilding), and this provides us with evidence that boat repair and boatbuilding were being undertaken in Shetland. This supports my argument that it was economically more efficient to import boats from Norway than it was to build them from scratch at home. Mouat's request for "backs of deals", with which to make tafts that were more robust, provides new insight into adaptations that were made to ensure these "off-the-shelf" purchased boats were better equipped for the Shetland environment in which they operated.

> ... There must be a fitt person employed at our expense to take particular notice that every species be the best of its kind, especially that the best boat builders of Goyasound be employed to make the boats, which otherways will be a loseing bargain. ... all hasards, but that of the sea yours ...
>
> List of goods above referred to
>
> 36 four oard boats in boards, 14 foot of keel, large & well proportioned
>
> 20 six oard boats 16 foot of keel, a few thereof at 17 foot
>
> 40 doz good oars, from Goyasound or thereabouts, besides there for the boats
>
> Some dozens of boatsmens deals good & not exceeding 5 or 6 sh. p. doz.
>
> Please to take care the ship be full hould & decks and according to her siz (which we disire may exceed as litle as possible 60 tons) diminish or add to the bulky articles except the boats which mist not be more. 200 backs of deals which we would have of the best for boats tofts, as the tofts that come with the boats are generally too shore and too thin. A.N. Willm. Mowat ... (SMA, Arthur Nicolson letter book Feb 1761 - June 1764 D.24)

In 1765, after a 17-year break in the Shetland customs records, two ships were listed in the accounts importing cargo from Bergen. The first was *Catherine of Limekilns*, whose master, William Hutchinson imported for John Bruce Stewart, amongst other timber cargo, 72 boat oars. This was followed by another consignment of 100 small boat oars shipped by William Farquhar, master of *Adventure of London*. As well as these oars, and other items of timber, there were quantities of 8.5ft (2.6m) long deals listed in each of these ship's cargoes. Also listed were small pieces of crooked oak, birch and fir wood, used in boatbuilding to make stems, bands, or stamerons (SMA, SA.1/7/1). The use of birch wood seemed strange, as "birch wood is not considered a durable boatbuilding material in western Norway, although it was used for boatbuilding in northern Norway" (PC, Christensen 2016).

It is not known why boat oars, crooked oak, birch and fir began to be listed in the customs accounts. Maybe this was the consequence of an amendment made to the rules on duty, applicable to certain types of timber, which made it impossible to disguise items such as oars, and crooked wood. Alternatively, the duty payable on certain items may have been reduced, thus making it cheaper to declare these correctly to the customs officer. Four years later, in 1769, Henry Forattal shipped aboard *Dolphin* a cargo of boats and timber (SMA, GD144/112/22). This document has been edited and includes boat related items and timber (Table 6). This cargo was not entered into the Shetland customs accounts so either the original entry has been lost or this was another smuggled cargo. For the first time boats were listed as being shipped "set-up" which means ready built. There were just three set-up boats shipped aboard

@ Bergen the 12 aprl 1769 acctt of Goods Shipped on the *Dolphin* for Mr John Henry of Forattal			
TO 7 doz twelve Ells @ 5/4d per	1	17	4
To doz fourteen Ells @ 10 sh per	1	10	
To 200 Hazel Couts @ 1/6 per		3	6
To 248 duble deals @ 4/6 per	5	8	
To 400 Single deals @ 2 sh pr	4		
To 20 Ransom Shiped Ryan & Smith 28 voes 33			
To 1 doz oars 14 feet long @ 1 sh per Pear		6	
To 2 doz Boats scups up @ 8d pr		1	4
To 1 doz [unclear] ditt @1 sh		1	
To 1 doz [unclear] @ 2/6 pr		5	
To 2 [unclear] [unclear] [unclear] @ 14 sh pr	1	8	5
To 5 doz single deals @ 2 pr		10	
To 10 doz Duble ditt @ 4/6 pr	2	5	
To 5 doz 10 feet long @ 4/6 pr	1	2	6
To 1 doz and 4 duble deals @ 4/6 pr		6	
To 1 set up Boat at 1£ 4 sh	1	4	
To 1 ditt @ 12 sh		12	
To 3 doz deals one Deck @ 4/6		13	6
To 1 set up Boat on the Dek @ 12		12	

Table 6. *Cargo shipped onboard the* Dolphin *(Shetland Museum and Archives, GD144/112/22).*

Dolphin in this manner and these had their fastibands (in Norwegian "bete") and stamerons (in Norwegian "rong") removed enabling them to be stacked one inside the other, stowed lashed down on the ship's deck.

Another document, written by Alexander Wallace in July 1769, lists the goods shipped onboard Dilligence by Captain Thomas Brown for William Mouat. Amongst the cargo of timber were a total of 56 boats, and 240 oars (Table 7). Significantly, as with the previously analysed William Mouat document, the keel sizes of the boats were specified. The keel lengths for the six-oared boats were 16.5ft (5m) and 17.5ft (5.3m), and the four-oared type were 14ft (4.3m). This consignment consisted of 40 six-oared and 16 four-oared boats. This is the first time that a consignment of six-oared boats exceeded the four-oared type and, significantly, the document mentions "taking the boats to pieces Ale and Brandy to the Dowers". This again tells us how the "doers" were rewarded, although we don't know if this was their only payment or if it was a perk, and it is not clear if they were the boatbuilders or the ship's crew. Unfortunately, there were no customs account entries for 1769 so no comparison between this invoice and customs entries could be made.

6 Boats 17 ½ foot keel	33.3	
18 do 16 @ 16 ½ foot do	78.4	
16 do ....@ 14 foot do	50.3	
20 Dozen oars	9.3	
Taking the Boats to pieces Ale & Brandy to the Dowers	3.3.12	
Frieght of a yaught	6	
To be speaking the Boats	2.4.4	
Three Expresses	6	
150 Wogs Bark ....@ 1s	25	
4 Dozen 12 Ells ....@ 9s	6	
4 Dozen 9 Ells ....@ 4 ½s	3	
200 Hazel Cutts ....@ do	.4.8	
2 Dozen 8 foot Wrack Deals under the Salt @ 3 ½ s....	1.1	244.3.8
	RD	497 damaged

Bergen 14 July 1769
Alex Wallace & Sons 1769

Table 7. *Invoice of Sundries ship'd onboard the Diligence Capt Thos Brown by order & for accott & Risk of Mr William Mouat of Letland viz ... (Shetland Museum and Archives GD144.59.12.2).*

In June 1771 *May of Queensferry* was entered in the customs accounts as having sailed from Kristiansand in Norway. This illustrates that although Bergen was the preferred port from which to buy boats and timber there were other Norwegian ports that also supplied these items. Of course, without supplementary documents the extent of this trade cannot be determined. Apart from the import of four small boat masts under 20ft (6.1m) long, the cargo was similar to all the other timber cargos listed in the customs accounts. Therefore, it is reasonable to assume that if boat masts were being imported from Kristiansand then it is probable that other boat items, and even boats, were being purchased from that area. This was the first time that masts were entered into the customs accounts. As well as masts, "small spars" were also itemised and this confirms, as previously discussed, that spars in this context were simply the trunks of trees (poles) that came in various lengths and thicknesses.

Another letter, written by Patrick Torrie to an unknown recipient in June 1771, detailed a trip he made to collect a cargo of boats from Bergen. When Torrie's ship reached the fjords it was delayed by unfavourable winds and, when she eventually reached Bergen, he found that the boats from Godøysund had not been delivered. Torrie procured a "yoacht" (by yoacht he probably meant a type of cargo vessel called a "jekt" which may have been of a similar type to the one in Fig. 36). The "yoacht" freighted the boats to Bergen where they were then loaded on board Torrie's ship.

> ... the second day of June gott within the fiords of Norway, the wind proving easterly could not gett to Bergen butt dispatched your letter immediately to Mr Wallace as a small yoal & a few days thereafter got up to town. when to my great mortification the boats from Goisound had not come here, immediately went to the woods in a small boat myself procured the yoacht for carriing them here & seed them load afterwards, the wind proved so contrary that I have been six days impatiently waiting them they are now alongside & your certain no time shall be loosed / ... (SMA, GD144/11/25).

Fig. 36. *A very small jeckt moored in Bergen Harbour. This is basically a small version of the type of vessel used to transport boats in 1771. Photo: M. Chivers.*

Two years later, in May 1773, John Mouat registered a probative writ between himself and Andrew Heddell, which was recorded in the Sheriff Court Book of Shetland (SMA, SC12/53/5). The purpose of this probative writ was to ensure that a transactional obligation between them was legally enforceable (Reid and Zimmermann 2000: 27-28). The writ was actioned, written and signed, by Alexander Wallace in Bergen.

> Invoice of sundry shipt abroad the Isabell Cap. Edward Maxwell by order & for accot. & wish
> of Mr Andrew Heddell of Lerwick.
> 6 sixring boats 17. foot keill.
> 6 do. do. 16. foot do.
> 9 fourring do. 14 do. oars
> Taking the boats in pieces & marking them ale & brandy to the bowers the man for bespeaking
> them & freight
> Landing & delivering in Bergen
> 4 doz 8 foot do. picked
> 6 doz 9 foot oars
> 8 doz 12 foot do.
> 5 doz boats scoups
> 2 boats masts
> 4 boats on deck
> (SMA, SC 12/53/5: 179)

The writ contains some very important details concerning the boats. As with the previously discussed invoice sent by Alexander Wallace to William Mouat – John's father – six-oared boats exceeded the four-oared type in number, and their specified keel lengths were the same as those listed in Wallace's July 1769 invoice. The terms "sixring" and "fourring" were used; these are clearly variants of the terms seksæring and færing and are very similar to the later commonly used Shetland terms sixareen and fourareen. This confirms that during the latter part of the eighteenth century the boats being imported continued to be the west Norwegian type. Of significance is the section about "Taking the boats in pieces & marking them" ... and organising them to be freighted to Bergen.

Comparing this document with the one written by Torrie in 1771 confirms that during this later period boats were in fact prepared for transportation at Godøysund and then freighted by jekt to Bergen, where they were then loaded onto the ship bound for Shetland. This points to a tightening-up of Norwegian/Danish customs control, as confirmed by the closing of the customs house in Eldøy and the opening of the customs house in Bergen in 1753. This seems to have had an immediate effect as twice as many boat exports were recorded the following year (Økland 2016: 25).

Other important information in the writ is the specified length of the extra oars which, using the general rule that oars are twice the length of the boat's beam, means that the sixring was 6ft (1.8m) and the fourring was 4ft 6inches (1.4m) beam.

Off-the-shelf boats

Gideon Gifford, in April 1774, wrote to Alexander Wallace & Son, merchants in Bergen, to place an order for six- and four-oared boats.

> ... As I intend sending a vessel to your place the first of June or thereabout to your consignment, I will have a demand for a Number of boats. In case of her being obliged to wait for them if not bespoke, desire the favour that you will order the following Number to be ready, viz: 6 six oared boats, with Oak keels & Stivers [probably stems] 18 feet long, 8 hassins, 12 of do dementions with fir keels, 6 Six Oared boats 17. feet keel, 4 hassins, 12 four oared boats 15 feet keel, 8 Do. 14 feet, please order likewise 500 voes Bark to be in readyness. The other things I suppose, can be procured upon the vessells arrival.
> (SMA, Norski boat.doc: 7)

The quantity and size of the boats ordered is of great interest as Gifford, like Mouat, was ordering more six-oared than four-oared boats. The specified sizes were very similar to those requested by Mouat, with the exception of the largest six-oared boats, which were 18ft (5.5m) instead of 17.5ft (5.3m) of keel. The mention of oak keels and stems is also significant, as this would make these boats more robust although they would be heavier for hauling up and down a beach. Gifford also requested that these larger boats have eight "hassins" (the forward and aft strake sections). The Shetland variant of the Norwegian word halsane was halsin – Gifford uses the Scots hassin (Jakobsen 1928: 291). These halsin strakes were curved across the face of the board and were specialist items. The curve on the halsin was hewn using an axe and getting the correct curve on these boards was extremely important, as it directly affected the performance of the boat (Figs. 37-38) (Økland 2016: 68-73).

Gifford's instruction that the largest boats have eight halsins indicates that he wanted them to be deeper in the keel in effect creating a double garboard – which became even deeper in the later twentieth century Shetland vernacular racing boats. The creation of the deeper Y-shaped keel section would have improved the windward sailing performance of these boats which indicates that sailing performance was important and, together with the slightly larger size, suggests that these boats were venturing further offshore.

It might seem peculiar that in western Norway boats with five strakes were still classed as four-strake boats. This is because the first narrow strake up from the keel (called the kjølrenne) on these larger six-oared boats was regarded as being part of the keel (Fig. 39) (Thowsen 1969: 187; Økland 2016: 65-66, 449). So it was only large boats, such as the six-oared brugdebåt (basking shark boat), illustrated in Fig. 40 that had a kjølrenne. This brugdebåt from Fjell was built around 1800 and was 26.9ft (8.19m) long, with a 7.9ft (2.4m) beam. These dimensions – apart from the beam which may be slightly bigger – are similar to the six-oared boats ordered by

Fig. 37. *Note the twisting curve of this halsin which was made by Oselvar boatbuilder Hallgier Frostrønen Bjørnevik. Photo: M. Chivers.*

Fig. 38. *Halsin being made by Hallgeir Frostrønen Bjørnevik. Photo: M. Chivers.*

Fig. 39. *Kjell Magnus Økland points to the narrow kjølrenne on this circa 1800 brugdebåt from Fjell, Hordamuseet.*

Gifford. The brugdebåt had eight halsins, comprising one pair forward, and one pair aft, on either side of the boat. The relevance of the shark boat is immediately apparent when examined against Thomas Woore's 1828 painting of Scalloway Castle (Fig. 41). Norwegian maritime historian Kjell Magnus Økland identified the boat on the beach in this painting as being very similar to the one on display in the boat hall of Hordaland Museum (PC, Økland, 2015). This strongly suggests that this type of boat was used in Shetland around 1800 and, I believe, demonstrates that these were an off-the-shelf type imported because they had a suitable hull-form and were available in the appropriate sizes.

Boat varieties

Another source of information about the types of boats being used during this period is found in *The Statistical Accounts of Scotland 1791-1799*, where some of the ministers list the number of boats in their parishes. For example, in the parishes of Aithsting and Sandsting there were 36 six-oared boats, Bressay had 26 large fishing boats (six-oared presumably), Burra, Havera and Papa had 28 boats of lesser size (four- and maybe six-oared), Dunrossness had 200 boats and Northmavine 40-50 (which also included boats from neighbouring parishes), Hamnavoe (Northmavine) fishing station had 12-15 boats, Ronas Voe fishing station 4-5, Uyea 14 boats, and Fethaland – the most northerly mainland fishing station – 60 boats. Unst had 78 boats, Foula 16 (11 of which were from Walls), and the parishes of Walls and Sandness had a total of 42 six-oared and 16 four-oared boats, whilst Fair Isle had 14 boats (Withrington, Grant, Sinclair 1978).

Dunrossness clearly had the largest number of boats, followed by Unst. As well as having the largest number of boats these were the only parishes to mention having two types of six-oared boats, as the Reverend John Mill stated: "... there are three sorts of boats used in the fishing trade, a larger and a smaller size of six oared boats, and 4 oared boats." (Withrington, Grant, Sinclair 1978: 432). Unfortunately, Mill did not provide any more detail about the differences and the origins of these two types of six-oared boat. However, a description of the four- and six-oared boats used on Fair Isle was more precise.

> Their boats, which are 14 in number, lie on the S.W. shore, under the little town of Gelah, from which they go with only two or three men in them, who sit in the middle of the boat, and, with an oar in each hand, row over immense billows, in a short time, to a great distance. These pitiful skiffs, in which a landsmen would scarcely trust his life across a river, they fly to the fishing ground, almost out of sight of the island, where they catch plenty of fine cod, ling, tusk, skate, halibut, mackerel, cyth, and other fish of inferior quality. (Withrington, Grant, Sinclair 1978: 437).

Fig. 40. *Note the unusual rowing positions in this brugdebåt from Fjell built circa 1800. Compare this boat with the boat on the beach in Thomas Woore's painting of Scalloway Castle in Fig. 41.*

Fig. 41. *Scalloway Castle, painted by Thomas Woore (1828). Photograph courtesy of Derek and Tim Heath. Note the rowing positions of the boat in the foreground. Compare this boat with the one in Fig. 40.*

The phrase "... with an oar in each hand" is very important and differs from other accounts of six-oared boat use where boats were crewed by six men (each man pulling an oar) as stated by the Reverend Thomson in his account for the parishes of Walls and Sandness: "Ling is the principal fish caught here. They are fished on a bank from 30 to 60 miles distant from shore. This bank is called the Haaff. ... The large, or six-oared boats, carry each 6 men; ..." (Withrington, Grant, Sinclair 1978: 523).

The number of men crewing six-oared boats was described by Thomas Mouat of Garth and the Reverend James Barclay in their account of fishing in Unst where: "... Five or six row in each boat" (Withrington, Grant, Sinclair 1978: 504). To elaborate, when five men rowed, four men pulled one oar each and the fifth man pulled two oars. So the number of men rowing a six-oared boat was dependent on the boat's keel size which in Unst was either 15.5ft (4.7m) or 18.5ft (5.6m). This brings us back to Dunrossness and its two types of six-oared boat. The smaller six-oared boats being used in Unst may have been similar, or the same, as the six-oared boats being used in Dunrossness. The Fair Isle six-oared boat was described as a "skiff" and the description of them being rowed by two or three men with two oars each is indicative of the Norwegian færing and seksæring which were also rowed by two or three men respectively. Osler suggested that the eighteenth-century Fair Isle "yoal" was in all probability a Norwegian four-oared boat import, and as the boats became more specialised they increased in size and became six-oared (Osler 1983: 68).

Fair Isle born Jerry Eunson cited his grandfather (Stewart Eunson of Leogh) who stated that originally these boats were imported from Norway and put together with wooden pins; the boats were constructed from three spruce boards that were 15 inches (38cm) wide (Eunson 1976: 5). An example of a Dunrossness four-oared "yoal", which was used in Sandwick, was discussed by Charles Sandison who stated that it had a keel length of 14ft (4.3m) and was 20ft (6.1m) long overall, with a beam of 5ft 2ins (1.6m) (Sandison 1954: 14). This boat may have been similar to the four-oared yoals used in Fair Isle, and this two-man Sandwick "yoal" was possibly reminiscent of the Norwegian færing.

Nineteenth century boat imports

Evidence from the first statistical account supports that from the customs accounts and other archive sources and it is clear that the boat trade continued unabated throughout the eighteenth century. Then, in May 1790, the first listing in the Shetland customs accounts of the import of whole, or "set-up" boats was made, when the *Ranger of Lerwick*, master Charles Leask, imported for James Linklater six boats valued at £6.15 shillings (SMA, SA.1/7/2). This was then followed two years later in 1792 by Alexander Wiseman who imported, for Thomas Bolt, four boats valued at £4.10 shillings. Later that year James Linklater imported 17 boats valued at £14 and five boats valued at £4. Timber shaped and unshaped for boat use was also being imported, along with large amounts of other timber and wooden items. Also noted was an increase in the amount of timber being imported from Kristiansand, in southeast Norway, although no boat items were listed amongst these cargoes.

In 1806 12 set-up boats worth £12 were imported in the ship *Eliza of Lerwick*, and then later that year in August four set-up boats were shipped in the *Industry of Lerwick*. Cargoes of between four and 13 set-up boats continued to be regularly imported until the blockade of Norwegian ports by the British navy began in 1807. Just prior to the imposition of the blockade boat and timber imports from Norway continued to be entered in the customs accounts. There were six vessels recorded as importing timber of various descriptions which included quantities listed for boats' use. Along with this timber, there were a total of 41 set-up boats entered into the customs accounts between 20th May and 21st August. The largest single cargo comprised 13 set-up boats imported onboard the *Favourite of Lerwick*. It is not clear why set-up boats suddenly began to appear in the customs accounts, all that can be said is that the tariff on timber imports changed in 1790 and this coincided with the appearance of set-up boats in the accounts (Smith, H. 1984: 144).

A letter written by landowner Thomas Mouat in October 1807 illustrates the point that the duties on boat imports were burdensome: "... The highland society of Scotland gave me reason to think they would interest themselves in procuring an exemption to us from the duty on fishing boats from Norway, and a petition was made out to the Lords of the Treasury at their desire for that end. When you are in London it will be very patriotic and highly obliging to your countrymen if you please to interest yourself therein ..." (SMA, GD144/217/12). Mouat's letter supports Hance Smith's observation that high import duties began around 1790 and that these continued until about 1840. Indeed, up until the blockade a great deal of timber was smuggled. Although high duties on timber began around 1790 the evidence clearly illustrates that smuggling had been continuous and it certainly preceded the period when records began. Smith stated that between 1820 and 1830 there were constant complaints made about the high duty on boats and timber, which was 50 per cent of their value (*ad valorem*). This Mouat letter indicates that a parliamentary lobby against excessive duties was taking place 13 years earlier than previously thought.

The blockade of Norwegian ports was the result of a series of conflicts between Britain and the Napoleonic neutral countries of Sweden, Denmark and Norway. The conflict began in 1807 and lasted until 1814 which is when the blockade by the British navy was lifted and the boat and timber import trade restarted. The Shetland customs accounts suggest that the recommencement of the trade was slow as there were only two ships listed as importing boats and timber in 1814 (SMA, SA.1/7/2). The first was the *Don Cossak*, a prize made free, which arrived in Lerwick on 30th May. In her

Ship: Don Cossak	Length of keel (ft)	Ship: Venus	Length of keel (ft)
12 Boats in Boards	18	19 Boats in Boards	18
3 ditto	16	7 ditto	16
8 ditto	15	17 ditto	13
12 ditto	14	7 built boats	-
13 ditto	12		
5 small built boats	-		

Table 8. *Boats in board shipments, 1814. Shetland Museum and Archives, SA/1/7/2.*

cargo of timber were listed 48 "boats-in-boards" plus five set-up boats. This is important, as this is the first time that boats-in-boards were listed in the accounts. The next shipment was made in December when the *Venus*, master Thomas Leask, imported for George Linklater a total of 43 boats-in-boards (Table 8).

At last boats-in-boards appear in the customs accounts and it is evident that six-oared boats of 18ft (5.5m) of keel were the most popular. This is intriguing and naturally leads to the question of why boats-in-boards were listed in the customs accounts after the lifting of the blockade. The answer is found in a petition letter to the Commissioners of His Majesty's Customs in Scotland which was written by James Hay in August, 1818.

> ... they were in the habit of importing Boats from Norway these at a cheap price as being the best adapted for the purpose – & whereof they had many cargos previous to the last Danish war – That about that time or when there was again a prospect of getting Boats from thence the Petitioners at the desire of other fish curers stated to your Honubl Board the heavy burden it was on the fisheries to pay the same rate of Duties on the thin boards of a fishing boat as on a 3 inch Deal of 19 feet long, wh was then the mode of entering them, at that time when your Honours ^ seeing the impropriety of charging so much Duty on so small a quantity of wood were pleased to direct by letter of 17 April 1813 that boats in boards or set up were to pay duty ad valorem as other manufactured articles. (NLS, Acc. 3250, Folder 4 Box 85)

The answer then, was simply that unset-up and set-up boats were finally recognised as manufactured articles, and so the duty payable on them was now proportionally based upon their value. It is important to note that previously the boats-in-boards were entered as timber deals three inches (7.6cm) thick and under 20ft (6.1m) long which is why they were absent in the customs accounts. The numbers of imported Norwegian boats increased rapidly, from 53 in 1814, to 204 in 1815. The total number of boats entered in the accounts has been calculated, and are presented, grouped according to keel size in Table 9. Evident is that 18ft (5.5m) of keel boats were by far the most popular, with boats of 17ft (5.2m) of keel and 14ft (4.3m) of keel being the next most popular sizes. The 18ft and 17ft of keel boats were six-oared, whilst the 14ft of keel were four-oared boats. In 1815 a total of 118 six-oared boats were imported, contrasting with 73 four-oared boats.

The steep increase in boat imports suggests that the haaf fishery was undergoing a period of expansion, and further evidence for this growth in the fishing industry was provided in a document titled "Instructions," that was unsigned and undated. Shetland archivist Brian Smith analysed the writing in this document and attributes it to James Hay (1750-1831). In Hay's set of instructions is a section regarding changes to currency in Norway. This was used by Yngve Nedrebø, archivist at the state archives in Bergen, to date this document, which he suggests was around 1815. This important letter of instructions is very long, so only the sections pertinent to boats are presented here:

> The cargo should chiefly consist of the following
> Boats in boards, 14, 15, 16, 17, 18, & 19 feet of keel as many as ar ready or can be procured.
> They are subject to a heavy duty
> Enterd as deal, & its not expected the costoume here will admittt them as manufactured wood subject to 50 p. cent ad valorum
> If they must be entered as boats should be carefull few or none of them exceeded 10 feet in length but as broad as possible when they come under the denomination of deal, not exceeding 10 in length & 1. inch in thickness that pay £6.10 — each 120 — The keels & Gunwalls are enterd as spars under 22 feet in length & 4 inch in diam at the middle exclusive of the bark that pay p. 120 — £2.7 —
> The hausens & timbers ar enterd by the number ar crooked timbers for boats use & pay ad valorem.
> Spars Over & above the number that comprehend the boats keels & gunwalls may ship 10 dozen 14 ell trees that run from 21 to 22 feet as many of them may be or indeed should all exceed 4 inch diameter may ship 5 dozen or two quarters spars (not exceeding 6 in diam. at the middle exclusive of bark as long as possible that ar subject to p. 120 £8.18.
> Setup Boats or Whillies — There used be brought from 2 to 3 dollars each & were entered here as above ad valorem. As many of them as the vessel could possibly stow cased within one another upon dek & outside the quarters lashd w. straw ropes should be taken & as many oars along w. them as they coud stow (SMA, D40/243/3/1)

This letter confirms that boats were being entered as other timber articles in order to reduce their taxable value, and as will be discussed in the remainder of this chapter, this implied that Hay was still engaged in smuggling activity.

Of note is that Hay was ordering 19ft (5.8m) of keel boats (this is the earliest known date for this size of boat). Indeed, this size of boat did not appear in the customs accounts until July 1817, when Arthur Cheyne, master of *Eliza of Lerwick*, imported four boats-in-boards of 19ft (5.8m) of keel, each valued at 55 shillings for John Scott. As well as these 19ft of keel boats-in-boards, Cheyne

Total number of boats entered into the customs accounts in 1815

72 Boats in Boards 18 feet of keel valued @	55/ per
27 Boats in Boards 17 feet keel valued @	50/ per
19 Boats in Boards 16 feet keel valued @	45/ per
13 Boats in Boards 15 feet keel valued @	40/ per
25 Boats in Boards 14 feet keel valued @	35/ - 40/ per
8 Boats in Boards 13 feet keel valued @	35/ per
16 Boats in Boards 12 feet keel valued @	30/ per
24 built boats valued @	25/ - 30/ per

Table 9. *Boats entered in 1815 customs accounts. Shetland Museum and Archives, SA/1/7/2.*

declared in the customs records, for the first time, the import of "boat builders boards of nine feet and not exceeding 10 feet in length and not exceeding 1 foot 2 inches in width & one inch thickness partly manufactured valued at 9d. per." This is extremely important and will be discussed in the following chapter (SMA, SA.1/7/2).

It is apparent from Hay's instructions that there was a great demand for boats in Shetland, which was confirmed by Hay using the phrase, "as many are as ready or can be procured." The next section of the letter provides absolute proof that these boats were being entered as deals, and the keels and gunwales were being entered as spars, and the halsins and bands (and probably the stems) were entered as crooked timbers for boats' use. This resolves the mystery of the missing boats in the customs accounts – they were there all the time, hidden amongst the timber cargo, being entered as cheaper forms of timber imports to avoid excessive duty payments.

An intriguing point is that there was no mention of a cargo for the Hays in the customs accounts for 1815, and those for 1816 are lost, so there is no way of determining how this cargo was actually entered into the accounts. Indeed, there was no mention of James Hay & Son in the customs accounts until 30th March, 1818, and in that cargo there was no mention of boats-in-boards, just four "upset" boats were listed, along with 26 oak knees and 56 handscoops.

Letter evidence, dated August 1818, reveals that James and William Hay were in conflict with His Majesty's Lerwick customs officer over the valuation of a cargo of boats. These had been imported in the *Mary* from Bergen which the Hays had valued at £79.5 shillings (NLS, Acc. 3250, Folder 4, Box 85). The customs officer had told them that they had undervalued the boats and gave them with the opportunity to pay an additional sum, or the boats were to be impounded. The Hays refused to pay this and on 19th August James Hay wrote to the collector of customs in Lerwick:

> ... Having for many years been deeply interested in the fisheries of this country we were under the necessity of procuring from different places every material for its prosecution & particularly fishing boats from Norway as untill within late years it was deemed impracticable to manufacture a fishing boat in Shetland, where necessity the mother of invention (during) the late war to 1814 wh rendered it almost impossible to procure them from Norway) stimulated the Shetland carpenters to attempt making boats at home, wherein they have so well succeeded & materials by wrecks & otherwise have become so plenty as rendered importation almost unnecessary but previous thereto our orders had lain with our Agents in Bergen to provide us a cargo, that from time to time they advised was very difficult in consequence of the makers attention having been diverted therefrom by war & the fluctuation in their exchange &c_ rendered the price so precarious However this late winter they advised us having provided the Mary take cargo, that we behoved sent for, a very advanced price least say the Boats formerly cost under £2– now twixt 5 & £6 – there that in honour we were [unclear] [unclear] [unclear] altho' were aware of a manifest loss, had they been exempted from Duty altogether – yet willing to give as little trouble as possible we entered them at the same rate as has been done by all preceeding importers since the boa ... Duty was for the encouragement of the Fisheries commented by the Honl Commissioners for our ad valarum duty & particularly are the same rates as the very late cargo by the Eliza in July 1817 ... (NLS, Acc. 3250, Folder 4 Box 85).

Hay clearly stated that until the blockade in 1807 it was impractical to "manufacture a fishing boat in Shetland". This indicates that the import of boats from Norway was primarily based on economic cost – it being more practical and cost efficient to buy boats in Norway and ship them to Shetland. Hay made his point, stating that this commercial Shetland boatbuilding venture was assisted by the abundance of wreck wood caused by the Danish war. After the lifting of the blockade and, probably because of Norway's independence from Denmark, there were fluctuations in the exchange rate and the cost of boats more than doubled (NLS, Acc. 3250, Folder 4 Box 85). Following an appeal to His Majesty's Board of Customs for Scotland a resolution to the value of the boats was made and Hay was forced to make an additional duty payment.

The fact that the price of boats doubled indicates why smuggling was continuing. In his PhD thesis Jonathan Wills points out that during this period smuggling was endemic amongst the lairds and merchants (Wills 1975: 93). Smuggling timber and gin, Hance Smith states, was the most profitable part of the shipping business in which the merchants were engaged prior to

1801, and that this pattern of smuggling continued (Smith H. 1984: 97-100). Although there were periods of compliance, the decade between 1814 and 1823 was a "golden age" for smugglers and smuggling of timber continued as it had done previously (Hance Smith 1984: 98). Brian Smith points out that the lairds were heavily involved in this, as were some of the revenue employees, and the most prodigious smuggler of all was James Hay (Smith B. 1986:149).

Timber imports from Hamburg

It seems that Norway was not the only exporter of timber during this period as timber and boat's oars were also being imported to Shetland from Hamburg. It was previously known that barrel and pipe staves and wooden barrel hoops were imported from Hamburg but it has not been fully appreciated how much other timber was also coming via this route. The first evidence for this trade is found in a bill of loading of goods, dated October 1741, in which "two planks" and "thirty slitt Dealls" are listed as part of the cargo shipped by James Stephen in the *Sibella* bound for Shetland (SMA, GD144/111/3). Then there was an invoice of the goods imported in the *Clara Margaretta* in May, 1745, which listed "120 deal boards 12 @ 14 feet long" amongst the cargo (SMA, GD144/174/22)

Twenty-five years later, in October 1770, a copy letter and commission from Gideon Gifford to Richard and Octavius Thornton listed wood items to be purchased from Hamburg, and these were: "200ft 1. inch oak plank; 150ft of oak fit for small boats timbers; 20ft ditto plank 1.5 ft broad X 2.5 inch; Oak for a stem & sternpost; and 50 yards of light cloth for sailing" (SMA, GD144/94/15). This shipment was followed a year later by 120 oars, 13ft long, that were listed in an invoice of sundry goods shipped for Shetland from Hamburg by Mr. Thornton for Gideon Gifford (SMA, GD144/104/3). These imports were discussed with Emeritus Professor Arne Emil Christensen, and it was concluded that these were probably re-export items that originated from either Norway or the Baltic (PC, Christensen, 2014). This gives us a new perspective on the timber trade and reinforces the view that these imports from Norway were based solely on economic convenience – that if wooden goods were available in Hamburg this negated the need for a passage to Norway.

The evidence discussed in this chapter highlights that the boat import trade was more complex than previously acknowledged. The import of "boats-in-boards" is frequently described as "kit-boats" and authors, notably Thowsen (1969: 155) and Fenton (1978: 557), have suggested that this was an incipient way for Shetlanders to learn the skills of boatbuilding. As we will see in the next chapter the evidence suggests otherwise.

Chapter 6

Boat-kits and deal boats

B oats-in-boards have often been referred to as "boat-kits" and this term is commonly used to describe boats built in Norway and shipped to Shetland. Prior to shipment the boats had their pieces numbered and marked. They were then disassembled and re-built when they arrived in Shetland (Bruce 1914: 296; Johnston 1932: 11; Thowsen 1969: 151; Goodlad 1971: 107; Morrison 1973: 71; Fenton 1978: 554; Nicolson 1981: 1; Osler 1983: 18-19; Smith 1984: 35; Christensen 1994:93; Munro 2012: 22). This concept of importing boats in "kit-form" has been accepted at face-value by these authors. This accepted opinion can be tested by an analysis of documentary evidence and also by reviewing practical aspects of boat building at the time. This will perhaps give us a clearer understanding of the development of Shetland's vernacular boatbuilding tradition, which has as its background the gradual decline in the Norwegian boat import trade.

Transporting boats from Norway

The earliest evidence for the dismantling of boats prior to their shipment was provided by Norwegian historian Atle Thowsen who cited a Danish report about the diocese of Bergen written on 12th June, 1714, in which it was stated that all boats being exported from Godøysund in Tysnes were "... only clinked together with a few nails and before taken onboard the ship they are numbered and marked and then taken apart again and when the ships arrive at their place of destination, they are discharged and put together again in accordance with the before mentioned numbers and marks – thus a small ship's hold can carry 70, 80, 100 even 120 boats" (Thowsen 1969: 151). Shetland antiquarian Robert Bruce also suggested that this was how boats were imported from Norway. "All Shetland boats are to the present day, clincher built, and it used formerly to be the practice to import from Norway six-oared and four-oared boats 'unset-up' i.e., in bundles all ready to be put together, each piece being properly numbered" (Bruce 1914: 296).

  As previously discussed, it was the boatbuilders who prepared and stowed the cargoes of boats during the mid-eighteenth century. The available documentary evidence indicates that their payment for this service was often ale, brandy, and tobacco (SMA, GD144/100/3; GD144/59/12/2). The idea of building a boat, and to then number and mark, disassemble, ship, and then reassemble it in Shetland, may appear straightforward to those unaccustomed to boatbuilding during this period. However, it has to be remembered that these boats were built by different builders, and all parts of these boats were hand-fashioned (as illustrated in Fig. 42) using simple hand tools such as axes, knives, adzes, augers and planes (Christensen 1972: 249-252). Each boat therefore was bespoke. It would have been imperative that all the pieces of the same boat remained together otherwise reassembly would not be possible, as the bespoke parts would not fit another boat of the same size – even one by the same builder. Thowsen's source states that the boats were "only clinked together with a few nails." At first glance this sounds feasible but how were these clinked nails removed without damaging or destroying the strakes? Clinked means riveted. First an iron nail was hammered from the outside of the boat through a pre-bored hole of the exact size. An iron diamond-shaped flat washer (rove) was then forced onto the end of the nail. The nail was then trimmed to project about 1/16-1/8 of an inch (1.5-3mm) above the rove. The rivet was then formed by the boatbuilder who using two hammers, one to rest against the nail head on the outside of the boat, and the other to hit the trimmed nail end, and this formed a very tight rivet. This process is called clinking.

In order to take a boat apart each riveted (roved) end would have to be filed off and the nail carefully punched back through the pre-bored hole. This would be a laborious process, requiring a lot of care in order to avoid

Fig. 42. *A selection of boat builder tools. These tools belonged to Oselvar boat builder Hallgeir Forstrønen Bjørnevik. Photo: M. Chivers.*

damaging the hand-crafted strakes. These iron fastenings were individually hand-made and removing brand new, perfectly good, fastenings would have been time-consuming, expensive and wasteful.

Thowsen's Danish source also says that, when dismantled, even a small ship could carry "70, 80, 100, even 120 boats". However, Norwegian Oselvar boat historian Kjell Magnus Økland presented a paper at the St. Magnus Conference (held in Lerwick in April 2014) in which he contested the number of boats allegedly loaded in ships during the early eighteenth century. These vessels were small, about 40-60ft (12-18m) long, so it is highly improbable that 120 boats-in-boards could have been freighted in a single shipment (Økland 2014).

Økland further challenged Thowsen's source by stating that the largest annual export of boats to Shetland, Orkney, and Scotland occurred in 1624, when 87 boats were exported. The evidence of both Thowsen (1969: 150) and Hance Smith (1984: 33) shows that during the seventeenth century ship's cargoes consisted, on average, of between four and 10 boats. Further, it has been determined that the boat trade was generally a small-scale enterprise conducted in small ships capable of only freighting small quantities of boats (Smith B. 1990: 32). Thowsen himself stated that between 1755 and 1757 a total of 75 boats were exported annually from Bergen to Scotland, Orkney, and Shetland (Thowsen 1969: 155). Even in 1815, the year after the lifting of the blockade of Norwegian ports, the largest known single consignment of boats-in-boards recorded in the HM Customs Accounts was 72 (SMA SA1.7.2). This throws doubt on the credibility of Thowsen's Danish source, who it seems, had exaggerated the number of boats that could have been shipped in a single cargo to Shetland in 1714.

Økland further challenged Thowsen's 1714 source, arguing against the idea of unset-up boats. Instead, he suggested that boats during this period were imported ready-built, which in archive sources are called set-up (Økland 2014; 2016: 28). According to Hance Smith importing boats set-up was the preferred method until the early eighteenth century (Smith H. 1984: 35). Generally, it was only the smaller types of boat that were imported set-up and these boats were stacked on deck one inside the other. To enable the boats to be stacked they had to have their "betar" (fastibands) and the fore and aft "regene" (stamerons) removed, and it was these items that were numbered and marked. Marking these items enabled the identification of which betar and rengar belonged to which boat, and in what position within that boat they fitted (Økland 2014). This method of shipping was common practice in Norway, and required almost no re-construction, except to refasten the fastibands and stamerons (Økland 2014). These were easy to remove as they were fastened with trenels. As illustrated in Fig. 45, trenel fastenings are held in place by means of a wooden wedge that is inserted into the inboard end of the fastening. This method of fastening was in common use until around 1860. Simply omitting the insertion of the wedge meant that these fastenings could be loosely fitted which will have made removal a very simple process.

The construction of the west Norwegian færing and seksæring bete was different to that of Shetland vernacular boats, as illustrated in Figs. 43-44. The Norwegian bete had a knee at either end, as can be seen in Fig. 44, and this crossbeam was constructed from two pieces of timber, both formed from the grown bends of a tree's branch. The shorter knee was joined to the second piece by means of a feather scarph and fastened by trenels. The bete sat on top of the underband, and the knees at either end of the bete that were fastened through the hull, again by trenels. By contrast, in vernacular Shetland craft the ends of the fastibands were fastened to the band itself and the bands were, up until the 1880s, fastened to the boat's strakes by means of trenels. Unlike ferrous fastenings trenels, being made from wood, were cheap, easy to make, and straightforward to remove. As previously discussed, Eunson stated that the original imported Fair Isle yoal was put together with wooden pins (Eunson 1976: 5). His description implies that these boats were completely fastened with trenels but this is unlikely as boats in western Norway were ferrous fastened, apart from the trenels used to fasten the bete and underband to the strakes that formed the shell of the hull (Fig. 46).

Further evidence for the nineteenth century import of set-up boats is found in James Nicolson's book about the Lerwick merchants Hay & Company. A letter written in 1847, from Hay & Company to Alexander Grieg in Bergen, discussed the import of boats. It states that Captain James Ollason was sent to Bergen for a cargo of boats-in-boards from 19-20ft (5.8-6.1m) of keel. Ollason's instructions were to fill the hold with crooked timbers of fir and oak for building boats from the size of whillies to herring boats. Even more boats were required, and Ollason was told to take a cargo of "upset" boats 10-12ft (3-3.7m) of keel and "Carpenter James Arcus was sent as supercargo and he was told to remove the timbers [bands and stamerons] from the 'upset'

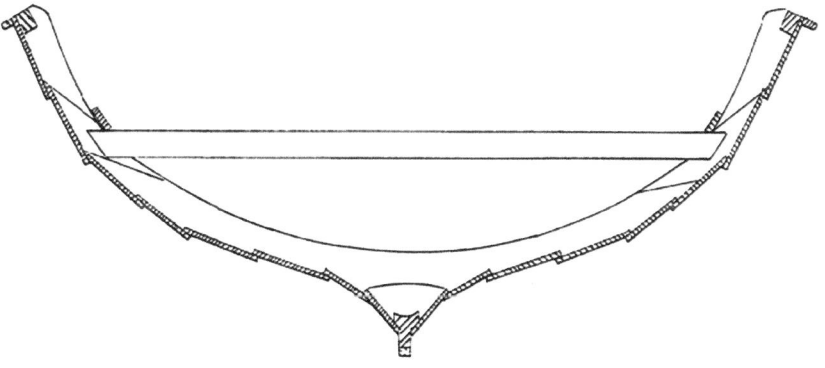

Fig. 43. *Midship cross section from the haddock boat* Brothers LK 96. *Note the construction of the band (frame) and arrangment of the fastiband (cross beam). Drawing: Marc Chivers.*

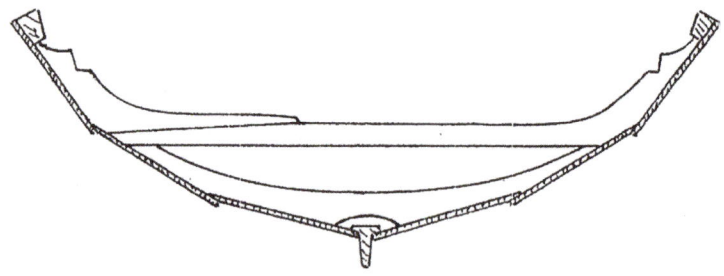

Fig. 44. *Mid cross section of an Oslevar havbåt. Note the arrangment of the bete (crossbeam). Drawing: Arne Emil Christensen. Courtesy of the Norwegian Maritime Museum, Oslo.*

Fig. 45. *An original trenel that fastened the band to the strakes (subsequently the strakes have been replaced).* Ann LK 126, *built by Malcolm Laurenson in Scalloway, c.1860. Photo: M. Chivers.*

boats after first numbering them carefully so that the boats could stand one within another as compact as possible" (Nicolson 1982: 33).

Økland reasoned that building a boat, taking it apart, transporting it, and then rebuilding it, made no economic sense (unless there were tax incentives to dismantle the boats for transportation). However, it was determined in chapter five that boats-in-boards were smuggled in their component parts from at least 1742 until 1814. This demonstrates that there was an incentive to dismantle boats due to the high import duty payable on timber. Indeed, the smuggling of boats only decreased when the import duty payable on boats-in-boards was reduced, and they became recognised by the customs authorities as manufactured timber in 1813.

Import of component boat parts

The precise definition of what constituted a boat-in-boards is ambiguous. This is exemplified by the letter written by Thomas Gifford in 1731 addressed to Robert Barclay in Bergen. In this letter the items listed to be purchased conflict with Thowsen's 1714 report of boats-in-boards (Thowsen 1969: 151). "One 'long hundred' planks, a full inch thick and 16 ft long, cost £25, and a half a hundred 'sawen in two' £12 10s for the boat builders, much being supplied already cut to shape" (March 1971: 34-37). It is clear that Gifford specified the 60 planks (boards) for the boatbuilders to be eight feet (2.4m) long and cut to shape; there was no mention of the boats being built in Norway, then numbered or marked, and dismantled prior to shipping. Gifford simply ordered boards. The specified length and thickness of these boards is important in order to determine if they were of a standard board or deal size.

Katharyne Newland's PhD thesis, about the use of Norwegian timber in Scotland during the seventeenth century, cites the English architect Joseph Gwilt who stated that deals were purchased "... by the hundred which contains 120 deals, be their thickness of one inch and a half and to a length of twelve feet. Whole deal is that which is one inch and a quarter thick, and slit deal is half of that" (Gwilt 1867: 186 in Newland 2010: 22). The *Oxford English Dictionary* defines a timber board as: "Board, bords, sagbord (Norwegian): sawn boards, 'a piece of timber of undefined length, more than four inches in breadth, and not more than two inches and a half thickness ...' A board is technically distinguished from a plank by its thinness, '... it ought to be more than 4 inches in width, and not more than 2 in thickness, but is generally much thinner'."

Newland produced a table of sizes of boards and deals used in the seventeenth century, and this illustrates that these were far from standardised (Table 10). The fact that Gifford requested the boards to be a "full inch thick" and that they were to be cut to shape will have made the best use of valuable cargo space, and also saved the boatbuilders time in preparing the boards for fitting and fastening.

Boards/deals	Length	Breadth	Thickness
Board	?	4 inches	2 ½ inches
Deal (Kristiana, Danzig)	12 feet	9 inches	1 ½ - 3 inches
Ryfylke	8 feet	8 inches	1 inch
Drammen board	10 – 12 feet	9 inches	1 ½ inches
Danish deals	?	?	5 inches
Dutch deals	?	?	2 ½ inches
Sailors' Walk, Kirkcaldy	?	7, 7 ½, 8, 9 inches	1 inch

Table 10. *Summary of the recorded dimensions of boards and deals (Newland 2010: 23).*

Each board (or strake) of a boat varies in its degree of curvature along its length (Fig. 46), and it would save the Shetland boatbuilders even more time if the boards were numbered when they were rough-cut, so their position in the boat could be readily identified. However, there is an anomaly in that the normal thickness of boards on a Shetland boat will have been approximately 3/8 inch (10mm) to 9/16 inch (14mm) thick. Which means that the thickness of the boards would have to be reduced. This was achieved by using an adze to remove the majority of the waste wood, then a hand plane may have been used to dress (finish) the strake. This is hugely wasteful of timber and is a time-consuming process. As previously discussed, the boats-in-boards were being hidden in the customs records – entered as deals – so the fact that the timber was of a recognised deal thickness suggests that these boards were concealed amongst the other timber cargo. In the customs accounts during the 1740s timber boards were entered as Norway deals (SMA, SA/1/7/1). So Gifford's instructions infer that the "kit-boats" may have been no more than timber rough-cut to size and shape, created by the use of templates. This would have saved valuable cargo space and reduced construction time.

The evidence suggesting the probable use of templates is strengthened by the discovery of a letter written in February 1978 by Øyvind Dössland, a teacher in Tysnes, to Shetland scholar and author T.M.Y. Manson. The term "Hjalta-skantar" – Shetland template – is used in connection with the Hjeltebåt (Shetland boat). This is in a nineteenth-century context but may have also applied earlier. The letter suggests that boats-in-boards were

Fig. 46. *Dismantled boards of fourareen, Spindrift. Note the boards are curved. Photo: M. Chivers.*

rough-cut from templates and each strake was numbered to identify its position in the boat (SMA, T.M.Y. Manson collection, uncatalogued letter: Dössland 26/09/1978).

The discussion so far illustrates that Shetland's boat import trade during this period was more nuanced and sophisticated than previously appreciated. An entry in the customs accounts on 9th August, 1774, listed amongst the cargo 360 small pieces of birch and fir wood. These were itemised as "haussins" (halsins). As discussed in the previous chapter, these were specialist boat parts and this shows that they were pre-made in Norway ready for final fitting and fastening in Shetland. This evidence for the import of boat components, boats-in-boards – which were patterned using Hjalta-skantar and rough-cut to shape – and boatbuilder boards, is further supported by remarkable evidence of an account of boatbuilding found in Thomas Mouat's ledgers (GHA, Ledger 49). In the ledger dated 1794 is an account to John Johnson of Oganess, whose occupation was listed as carpenter (Table 11).

It is evident from Table 11 that there were two types of boat construction taking place. First is "By Building a 4erring of Deals ...", second "By setting up Geo Henderson's boat ..." and "By setting up a Sixerring ...". Building from deals – unshaped boards – strongly suggests building the boat from scratch as clearly this was different to "setting up" a boat. Setting-up a boat involved using component parts and deal boards that had been rough-cut to shape using "Hjalta-skantar" in Norway (SMA, T.M.Y. Manson collection, uncatalogued letter: Dössland 26/09/1978). In contrast, the deal boat was built in Shetland from unshaped timber boards imported from Norway. This evidence for an early type of Shetland vernacular boat was described by Thowsen, who stated that this boat type was developed during the period of the blockade with Norway (1807-1814) and that fishermen contemptuously called these craft "deal boats" (Thowsen 1969: 156). However, Thomas Mouat's 1794 letter proves Thowsen's hypothesis to be incorrect. Shetland's vernacular boats were being developed earlier, during the

1794	John Johnson, Carpenter, Oganess	Dr			Crd		
May 6	By Building a 4erring of Deals £10.16 By repairing Jas Jameson Boat £12	-	-	-	22	16	-
	By Setting up Geo Henderson's Boat £7.4 By discot on half an. wrs 12/-	-	-	-	7	16	-
1795 Feb	By Setting up a Sixerring £15 By Setting up a passage boat to J.M £12.12	-	-	-	27	12	-
	By 5¾ days mending Boats pr work book 16/- By mending Ja Scots Boat £1.16 -		-	-	6	8	-
	By mending D Suthds Boat £6 Making 8 oars 31/- Making Door 16/-	-	-	-	8	7	-
1796 Feb	By making a mast 4/-	-	-	-	-	4	-

Table 11. *Extract from Thomas Mouat's Ledger 1794-1796. (Gardie House Archive, Ledger 49).*

eighteenth century. Indeed, the approximate 1794 date for Shetland vernacular boat development fits with the earlier discussion about Gideon Gifford, who specified boats with slightly deeper keels, around 1774 (SMA, Norski boat.doc: 7). Johnson, as well as building and setting-up boats, was also undertaking boat repairs and making oars and masts. This is conclusive proof that small-scale commercial Shetland vernacular boatbuilding was taking place before 1807.

However, the evidence suggests that the 1807-1814 blockade had a major impact on the ability of Shetlanders to obtain boats-in-boards and timber deals. There is no doubt that this was the period when deal boats became the only type of craft readily available and larger scale Shetland commercial boatbuilding began in earnest, although it is not clear where the timber came from. There is evidence from 1818 of Hay & Company selling American timber in Shetland, so perhaps this was the source of timber during the period of the blockade (NLS, Acc. 3250 Box 108). This was probably also when, due to the lack of good quality wide Norwegian fir boards, the strakes on Shetland-built boats became narrower, and increased in number from the Norwegian three or four, to the Shetland six to eight strakes. Building boats with narrow strakes rendered the Norwegian halsane obsolete. The halsane board was replaced with a narrow strake called the garboard (an English term) sometimes called in Shetland the bodam runner (Sandison 1954: 37).

John Johnson of Oganess is mentioned again in 1811, this time in a document called "rents and fishing" written by Thomas Leisk who listed Johnson as setting-up an 18.5ft (5.6m) of keel boat-in-boards (GHA, Thomas Mouat Ledger 49) (Table 12). This document detailed the materials required to set-up a sixareen which, including labour, cost £5.12s.8½d. Another significant document found in the papers of Hay of Hayfield provides evidence for the cost of a boat-in-boards, which was £6, and details the final cost of the boat after it had been built and made ready for sea which was £17.3s.8d. (SMA, D40/181/85/1). The amount of time charged for building this boat was 15 days, which clearly illustrates that setting-up a boat took longer than has been previously acknowledged. Of particular interest in these documents is that the rudder, helm, oars, mast, rooths, kabes, warings, tilfers and fiskavils were not included in the construction price. The boat in Table 12 was heightened by the addition of a reebing strake (sheer strake). The completed sixareen was therefore adapted to become a four strake, rather than a three strake, boat. As well as these items 41 yards (37.5m) of canvas was used to make the sail which suggests that sails were made to a Shetland specification.

Samuel Hibbert provided a contemporaneous description of the boat trade: "... the planks still imported from Norway, so modeled by the carpenter, that, when they arrive in Shetland, little more labour is required than to put them together" (Hibbert 1822: 14). This suggests that the boats were imported in pre-shaped component form, and a letter written by John Mouat of Garth in 1822 to the board of customs in Edinburgh provides slightly more detail about the boat-in-boards: "... am a frequent importer of boats in boards from Norway (proven by

	£	s	d	£	s	d
The Boat in boards				6	~	~
Spirits to the men		1	4			
8½ hundred Seam & ruve @ 1/6		12	9			
Rounds 8/- Claith for Sker Sye 3/4		11	4			
1½ Cans Tar @ 3/-, Nails 5d		4	11			
2 hund'd Seam & Ruve @ 1/6		3	~			
Nails 1/1, Rounds 2/1, Spirits 4d		3	6			
Oak for Rouths 1/4d & for knee heads &c, 3/-		4	4			
Roonds 1/4, Seam -/3d, Rudder work 2/6		4	1			
Seam 3d, a Board for a Rudder 1/6		1	9			
Ribbing wood 6/-, Sailing loft 2/6		8	6			
Deal for Tulfers 6/-; Do for Skuttalds & Wairins		9	4			
Bar wood for Tulfers &c		1	3			
27 feet old boards for fiskafields		2	6			
Nails 1/-; Helm 5d; Rae 1/6		2	11			
6 Cabes /9d; 3 Cans of tar @ 3/-		9	9			
Nails /3d; 1 Cag 4/-; Aft Bank /9d		2	6			
Tar leather		5	~			
6 Oars @ 4/-		1	4	4	10	1
Rigging						
41 yds Canvas No7 for Sail @ 1/10	3	15	2			
Line for Bolt rope		2	3			
Mast & Making		5	~			
Line for draw & Sheet		2	3			
Mast rigging rope		5	~			
Block 10d Twine 2½		1	½	*[4	10	8½]
Men for building				1	2	~

Table 12. *The cost of setting-up a boat of 18½ft of keel. Thomas Leisk, dated 1811 (Gardie House Archive).*

experience to be the fittest for our purposes) ... these boats being light and tender are liable to injury when repeatedly handled and turned over before they are rebuilt" (GA/1822). This supports the idea that boats-in-boards were pre-shaped prior to shipment as he uses the phrase "... before they are rebuilt". Thowsen described the Tysnes county prefect's report of 1836-40, in which "... it is reported that the boat builders in Tysnes construct some larger boats: ... under the name Jæltebaade [Danish form of the Norwegian Hjeltebåtar meaning Shetland boats], in the manner that all the boats materials (keel, frames, planking etc.) are made ready for clinking, the different parts are numbered and transported to Bergen ..." (Thowsen, 1969: 155).

The term Jæltebaade indicates that boatbuilders in Tysnes were building boats to a Shetland specification. This trade was still active in 1860 when the county prefect reported that 30 Jæltebaade were exported to Shetland each year (Thowsen 1969: 156). This suggests that the boats were not pre-manufactured and then taken apart prior to shipment but, like Hibbert's account, were pre-cut and shaped boat components made ready for assembly and fastening. Then, in 1842, James Wilson described being shown around Freefield in Lerwick, by Messrs. Hay & Ogilvy and he mentioned being shown "... a large store full of the component parts of Norway skiffs, brought from abroad, and all numbered in such a way that they could be put into a sea-worthy condition in a very short time." (Wilson 1842: 799).

By 1844 Alexander Grieg & Son of Bergen had become Hay & Company's main supplier of timber and timber products, such as the Hjeltebåt, whose strakes were rough-cut from Hjalta-skantar, numbered and marked, ready for assembly in Shetland (Nicolson 1982: 32, SMA, letter from Dössland to T.M.Y. Manson 26/09/1978). A letter from Hay & Company to Grieg & Son, dated 28th May 1844, indicates that although Alexander Grieg & Son were Hay & Company's main agent in Bergen, Hays were now beginning to look to eastern Norway for timber. However, Hays had no connections in eastern Norway and were reliant on Grieg & Son to act as guarantors to their newly acquainted east Norwegian boatbuilders and timber merchants (SMA, D31/1/2: 846).

Another letter, dated 12th August 1844, from Hay & Company to Alex Grieg & Son, informs us that the trade in Norwegian boats was beginning to go into decline. Part of the reason for this decline, Hay & Company suggested, was because the customs house officers were very much against the importing of boats. We have to assume that this means that import duties at the time were high and this penalised the boat trade (SMA, D31/1/4: 425). This was a gradual but steady decline in the boat import trade. In 1846 there was a drop in demand, and it seems that Shetland was almost self-sufficient in boatbuilding, as this letter from Hay & Company to Alex Grieg & Son illustrates:

> ... we regret that there is no demand here to induce us to send a vessel in ballast for boats but
> we showed the list of those you have on hand to our friends Messrs Garriock and Co. who
> were about to send a vessel – Our people now prefer to build for themselves – and only want

suitable crooks – wh. Hitherto the mode of measurement [unclear] by the Custom house – has prevented our importing – We will be glad you could say at what rate of [unclear] solid foot – you could ship a few loads of such crooked timber as could make boats floors etc (SMA, D31/1/7).

So this was the tipping-point in the boat import trade. Shetland built boats were now more popular than Norwegian boat imports – "our people now prefer to build for themselves". It seems that high customs duties were at least part of the cause of the demise of the boat trade. This fall-off in the trade of both timber and boats must have taken a toll on Alexander Grieg & Son who wrote in 1852 to ask if Hay & Company wished to buy boats, to which Hay & Company responded:

It is now a long time since we had the pleasure of hearing from you -- and during which a great change has taken place in the nature of our trade with Norway, which has chiefly been to the south for timber to build boats instead of to Bergen as formerly for boats -- the price of these built here being less than with you -- and also the mould more liked. -- At present we import East Norway timber laid down here, freight and charges included from 12d to 13d p. cubic foot -- and with us, labour we suppose is not much dearer than with yourselves. -- These circumstances will account for the change which has taken place. -- Still we think a few fishermen used to the Norway boats formerly could not object to them, that some might sell here -- especially if a little fall in price has taken place with you as with us. Please therefore advise us on receipt hereof if you have any boats in hand, the number, sizes, the year they were built, and the prices -- or if you have none -- when a small cargo could be got ready. -- If you should have gone out of the trade, please hand this letter to some respectable party, who will take the trouble to reply to it ... (SMA, D31/1/20).

This letter is very informative. Firstly, boats could be built in Shetland for about the same price as those brought from Norway, and secondly, the shape of the boats built in Shetland had changed and this new form – "the mould more liked" – was favoured by the fishermen. Hay & Company then suggested that the Norway boats might still be preferred by those who were familiar with them, especially if they were offered slightly cheaper. And, it seems, Hays half-expected to find that Alexander Grieg & Son had already gone out of business.

The end of the Norway boat trade

A letter dated 2nd April, 1855, illustrates that Hay & Company were now obtaining timber from outside Norway and this must have been even more disconcerting for Alexander Grieg & Son. To compound the problem there was also an issue with the quality of the imported boats, which was no doubt due in part to Hays continually driving down the price to protect their profit margins. This inevitably took its toll on the boatbuilders who were presented with no choice other than to skimp on the quality of materials and, possibly, also on the quality of the workmanship. So, as can be seen from the letters, this became a vicious circle, and it is sad to see this centuries-old boat trading relationship ending in this manner.

> ... There may not remain in the same demand, as it was in consequence of so many boats having been destroyed by the severe weather we had in winter, and the [unclear] carpenters being so much engaged with these and with stranded vessels, that we saw an opening for a parcel this spring -- When however we found that you could not have them ready, in time, we imported crooked wood from Ireland and other places and will be able to make out [unclear] the needful for this spring and summer fishery. -- We mentioned formerly that the boats we got from you these two years were in some cases very short of the due quality of wood in them -- This it will be well to guard against in future (SMA, D31/1/25).

The trade in boats continued in a much-reduced form but it is evident that it was faltering, as this letter from Hay & Company to Alexander Grieg and Son dated 4th June, 1860, illustrates:

> ... Most of the fishermen find the boats built [unclear] here so much cheaper that they are not willing to go to the expense of the Norway boats -- which you are perhaps aware require a good deal of material and workmanship after we get them to fit them for sea. The latter [unclear] certainly have some advantages and are considered more durable -- and if they could be furnished at anything near the same price would be preferred. Perhaps you will kindly let us know if any and what statement can be made -- and if we see one pay to give an order we shall have pleasure in doing so (SMA, D31/1/36).

This suggests that the Norwegian boats-in-boards required a lot of material and workmanship in order to make them ready for sea. As previously discussed, this equated to 15 days labour, and the end cost of the finished boat was more than double its original purchase price. This validates the assertion that these boats-in-boards were not simple "reconstruction kits" and shows that the builders constructing them were highly skilled. The evidence also points to the fact that defective materials were increasingly being found, which created greater labour and material expense caused by having to cut and shape replacement boards. Despite this it is enlightening to note that, even at this late stage in the boat trade, the Norwegian boat types are being spoken of in a positive way and were still considered to be more durable than the Shetland built boats.

Contrary to these letters, the import of boats from Norway continued for a further twelve years until finally, in 1872, Hay & Company wrote to Alexander Greig & Son:

> Dear Sirs,
> We received your esteemed letter of the 24th ulto. in due course and note the contents, but

we regret to say the trade in boats here has quite changed of late years, and we are therefore unable to take advantage of your kind offer. No boats can be sold here now except those built by our own workmen, and we have to import square timber from the east coast of Norway, for the special purpose of boat-building which is carried on now to a much greater extent than formerly.

We regret that the steamer which has been running the past summer between Bergen and Iceland calling here going and returning has been discontinued otherwise one of our firm would have had the pleasure of paying you a visit and renewing our long acquaintance.

With best wishes

We are Dear sir,

Hay & Co

(SMA, D31/1/58: 261)

This demonstrates that the east coast of Norway became the dominant supplier of timber, lending credence to the hypothesis that Shetland boats have east Norwegian characteristics, as these boats – such as the fourareen and sixareen – have more strakes, which are narrow compared to the wide three- or four-strake boats of western Norway (PC, Christensen 2014). The timber trade with eastern Norway is exemplified by the photograph in Fig. 47 of the Norwegian barque *Walter of Drammen* discharging timber at the Gas Pier in Lerwick, just to the south of where the Malakoff is situated today. It is important to note that by 1885 Norwegian ships were themselves bringing timber cargo to Shetland, rather than Shetland ships going to Norway.

Fig. 47. *North Ness. Photo: G.W. Wilson, (c.1885). Courtesy of Shetland Museum & Archives.*

Chapter 7

Boatbuilding 1770-1890

It has been established that boats-in-boards were not simple self-assembly kits and that the carpenters (builders) who constructed these boats were skilled craftsmen. The earliest mention of a Shetland boat carpenter is found in a letter from John Mitchell on 23rd April 1771 to an unknown landowner. Mitchell requests assistance in building some boats:

> As I am disapoint of a Boat Builder from Walls, his wife being ill prevents his coming, I must therefore apply to you, & beg the favour that you will allow me to send the Bearer to Christopher Tullock at Steness, who I am informed is your tenant, to come here immediately / as I am informed he can easily leave his labourings / in case you are not imploying him, & I must likeways beg the favour that you will inforce my application by a line to him to that purpose; if he cannot come along with the bearer I will be greatly obliged to you if you will send another good Boat Builder that is near you, that can be spared. I want those Boats built immidiately as I intend they should try their fortune betwixt the fair isle & foula before they go to Steness (SMA, GD144/237/64).

It is clear that John Mitchell held Christopher Tullock in high esteem and his letter clearly reinforces the view that the setting-up of boats-in-boards was skilled work. A further letter from Babie and Bruce Scotts, [Grave]land, to William Hay in West Sandwick, Yell, dated 4th June 1781, further illustrates this point: "We have at last got Gilbert Linna to go to Sandwick to sett up the boat which you were so good as promise us on loan. When the boat is sett up, if our men think her a good boat they will perhaps buy it if you are inclined to sell it ... If you want one of our old boats it shall be repared as soon as Gilbert L. returns ..." (Ballantyne 2014: 54).

Clearly, a skilled craftsman was required to set-up a boat-in-boards. Other sources, found in the Gardie House Archive, list the names of eighteenth-century Shetland boatbuilders and sailmakers: "... William Johnson, Carpenter, 1783-87; ... various Deals; a four erring set up for John Smith &c; a pikt deal for heightning said boat, 14/-; ..." (GHA, Thomas Mouat Ledger 49: 20). We learn that boat carpenter William Johnson was paid 14 shillings for setting-up a fouraren, which he adapted by heightening it with an additional strake. This lends further weight to the claim that during the late eighteenth-century Norwegian boats-in-boards were being modified for local Shetland use. John Henderson, a boat carpenter, was paid for setting-up three boats, and repairing three more between 1783 and 1794:

John Henderson of Bothin (1783-94)
March 1786 By Robt Sinclair Accot for his share of Setting up his new
Boat 15/-
By Mags Johnson & James Smith, setting up yr shares of a Boat 1.10/-
April 1787 By mending . of my boat at Hoya 8/-
May 23 1789 By setting up a boat at Hoya . thereof mine, 30/-
January 1790 By mending my . of the boat of Sotland 5/-
July 1791 By mending a boat of Hoya 5/- ...
(GHA, Thomas Mouat Ledger 49: 12)

Then follows evidence of sailmaking, sail repair, rigging and the tarring of boats:

Andrew Sinclair, OGANESS –
Payments to his account for ... ; mending sails, rigging the Shark, tarring;
12/- ... making 2 boat sails £2.8/- ; ... making a sixeren sail to Jo
Wm.son, ... Also work tarring boats ... Belmont, 1795. Leaves in
credit." (GHA, Thomas Mouat Ledger 48: 117).

EDWARD THOMASON, Pund at the Lochend
To his CREDIT: 1801 By his Fee in the Shark agreed for his Land & house
rent; 1804/5 44 days at Sharks repair &c 12/- , , Burrafirth towing 18/-,
various freights, Norw Logs 18/-, shipping kelp 6/- etc. Making a Sail to
James Jamessons Boat 30/-. (GHA, Ledger 47: 103).

These documents give us a fascinating insight into boatbuilding, boat maintenance and sailmaking in Unst at this time. They demonstrate that boatbuilding was not a full-time occupation. People were multi-skilled, and had several jobs such as tailoring, cobbling, house building, and acting as boat-hands in Mouat's boat *Shark* (which was possibly an eight-oaring or a great boat).

Further evidence of Shetland boatbuilding is found in the first Statistical Account (1791–1799). Boatbuilding is a trade mentioned in the parish accounts of Aithsting & Sandsting, Dunrossness, Northmavine and Unst (Withrington, Grant and Sinclair 1978: 387, 432, 464, 505). For example, Robert Thompson, originally from Fair Isle, lived in Dunrossness. He had been a schoolmaster, became a farmer and mariner, and was "... an excellent cooper, a wright, and mason, ... His sloop was built from the keel, and completely rigged and equipped by himself" (Withrington, Grant and Sinclair 1978: 432). Whilst Thompson's adaptability was perhaps regarded as unique by the minister who reported his skills, this nevertheless illustrates that people in Shetland were able to turn their hand to most tasks, and many needed more than one occupation to support themselves and their families.

In October 1812 James Hay & Son wrote to William Anderson of Sound:

Henry Anderson had resolved to give £5 for an old wrecked bottom, with very superficial upper work, of a 13 feet keel boat without an oar or tilfer, which we have dissuaded him from and are to get a new boat built for him. Is it one or two boats we have at West Sandwick – whatever they are will be useless there, and rather wishes you get them sent here at trifling expence. If they can't float, it might be as well take them asunder and send us the haussens, keels or timber that were sound, to build smaller boats on, and what was not fit for that purpose will be needed for ove [roof laths] to your houses ..." (Ballantyne 2014: 263).

The significance of this is that the blockade of Norwegian ports had been in place for four years so timber and boats-in-boards must have been in short supply. Building a new boat was mentioned, along with the recycling of old boats keels, halsins, and other useful pieces which were adapted and re-used to make new, smaller, boats and other artefacts. The remainder of the timber that was not useful for boatbuilding (in this instance) was to be used as roof laths. This demonstrates both ingenuity and boatbuilding skill.

Twelve years later, in January 1824, George Henderson from Baltasound, Unst, wrote to William Hay, stating that he needed a six-oared boat for the summer "... viz of 17½ feet & 18 feet keel ones; if any strong ones of the first size it might do; & as Thoms Smith I believe is always engaged by you, what would your charge be for him Building her, if it suits the men I should like her to be built in Lerwick as all necessaries a could be at hand..." (NLS, Acc.3250, Box 31, Folder 1). Henderson wanted a boat 18ft (5.5m) of keel and was asking for a boat-in-boards to be set-up. He used the term "... Building her ..." which further suggests that these boats were not simple self-assembly kits, particularly as he asked for Thomas Smith to build her in Lerwick, where all the necessary items needed for construction were readily available.

In March that year William Hay instructed the same Thomas Smith to repair and deliver a boat to John Johnson. The repaired boat was returned to Johnson the following day (NLS, Acc.3250, Box 31, Folder 1). A letter from Arthur Nicolson in Fetlar, written in 1825, provides further testament to the continued popularity of boats-in-boards: "... I want a six oared boat for some Papa men, and I should be glad you could desire your man to set up one of your Norway boats, say 18 feet ..." (NLS, Acc.3250, Box 32). At this time the haaf fishing was at its peak and it appears that 18ft (5.5m) of keel sixareens continued to be the most common size of boat.

This all paints a picture of industrious boatbuilding, boat maintenance and sailmaking. It is apparent that the skills to set-up and repair boats and make sails were both in demand and available. The Mouat ledgers show that people were paid for this work, although it is not clear how rates of pay were agreed upon, nor when payment for work was made (GHA, Thomas Mouat Ledger 47: 103, 48: 117, 49: 12, 20).

Payment to the boatbuilder

We do, however, find some evidence of how boatbuilders were paid in the second Truck Commission report, chaired by Sheriff William Guthrie in 1872. It is worth placing Guthrie's 1872 Shetland visit in the wider political context. This was part of a long process that sought to investigate the conditions in which Scotland's crofters – small-holding tenant farmers – worked and lived. As Shetland archivist Brian Smith pointed out "... Shetlanders were the peasant producers of an industrial crop, fish, of course, without enough land for proper subsistence" (Smith, B. 1986: 3). Guthrie's ineffectual report was later followed by the Napier Commission in 1883. Then finally, in 1886, the Crofters Holdings Act (Scotland) was enacted. This at last gave Shetlanders – for the first time – the security of tenure that released them from being bound to their land-master (Smith, B. 1986: 2, 3, 4, 8).

John Anderson, a merchant and fish curer from Hillswick, North-mavine, was examined by Guthrie on 11th January. Anderson testified that boatbuilders were not paid a regular wage but were instead paid a fixed sum, in this instance £3 for building a six-oared boat. Anderson stated that he employed one boatbuilder and that generally he was paid in cash for his work.

By the latter part of the nineteenth century boatbuilders were regarded as specialised tradesmen and worked at nothing else. The boatbuilder Anderson employed travelled about Shetland, building and repairing boats for various people. Boatbuilders, like farmer- fishermen, had accounts with landowners and merchants such as Anderson. Sometimes Anderson paid an advance to the boatbuilder and, whilst building the boats, he and his family would obtain credit from Anderson's shop. When the work was completed this credit was deducted from the money owed to the boatbuilder by Anderson. When questioned by Guthrie as to whether the boatbuilder would be owed any money after the settling-up, Anderson replied "... he has something to get still, because he is building more than one at a time" (Guthrie 1872: 162-163).

This comment gives us a glimpse into how the boatbuilder worked – he built several craft at a time. This was faster than building boats individually. For example, all the keels could be cut and shaped together, then all the stems could be made and then fastened to the keels. The stems and keels once joined and set-up on the building stocks were ready for the strakes to be cut, fitted and fastened; these were made in pairs, one for either side of the boat (Osler 1983: 51-63).

One of Anderson's tenants, John Sandison of Hillswick, was examined by the commission. During his interview, it became apparent that he was employed as a haaf fisherman by Anderson during the summer and then by Laurence Smith during the winter and spring as a boatbuilder. Payment for boatbuilding was not settled after the work was completed but, as Sandison stated, he was paid for this work at the same time as he was paid for his fishing – and this was settled-up in December each year. So Sandison had to wait almost a year before being paid for his boatbuilding work, during which time he will have accrued debt for the goods and money he obtained on credit (Guthrie 1872: 240).

The main fear of Shetlanders at this time, apart from debt, was eviction. This was exacerbated by the fact that during the eighteenth and nineteenth centuries Shetland experienced a steep rise in population which, by the 1850s, was around 30,000. Marriage in Shetland happened early (Smith, B 1986: 4) and families became cramped, living on small farms with no prospect of finding alternative holdings. Eviction was feared, as there was nowhere else to go, and insecurity of tenure was a constant worry (Smith, B. 1986: 4). It is evident that the boatbuilder prior to the crofting acts was in effect tied to his employer – who was the landowner or the merchant. There was an implicit expectation that he would purchase goods – often on credit – from the local shops owned by their employer (Guthrie 1872: 14).

Prominent boatbuilders

During the eighteenth and nineteenth centuries the need for boats gradually increased as the commercial fishing enterprise grew. Shetland began to develop boats which were better suited to this industry which, in-turn, led to more people becoming boat builders, or carpenters as they are generally known in Shetland. The extent of the trade can be gauged by collating all known references from published and archival sources and this is given in Appendix A. An astonishing 61 names appear giving a fascinating overview of boatbuilders of the period. We have their names, when and where they were born, where and for whom they worked, the types and numbers of boats they built, and when they died. And we can pick out some important boatbuilding family lines, foremost amongst which was perhaps the Bruce family from Skaw, Whalsay – Thomas (1811-1894), Laurence "White Lowrie" (1839-1919), and Thomas (1848-1927) (Figs. 48-49) (Shetland Museum and Archives, D62/1/22). The Bruce family boatbuilding line continued into the twentieth century and we return to them in chapter 10.

Another well-known boatbuilding family were the Laurensons, from Sandwick in Dunrossness (Fig. 50). Malcolm "Maikie" became foreman at Hay & Company's yard at Blacksness, Scalloway, where he shared the position with his brother, Adam. Some of their apprentices in turn also became important and highly respected boatbuilders such as Walter Duncan (1869-1944), Thomas Walter Scott (1859-1929), and George Johnson (1859-1941). By 1870 Blacksness had gained a reputation for building high quality small boats, in particular fourareens, cod, and haddock boats (SMA, D62/1/37, D62/1/58).

Fig. 48. *The derelict old Westhouse in Whalsay where Laurence Bruce, "White Lowrie", built his boats. Photo: M. Chivers.*

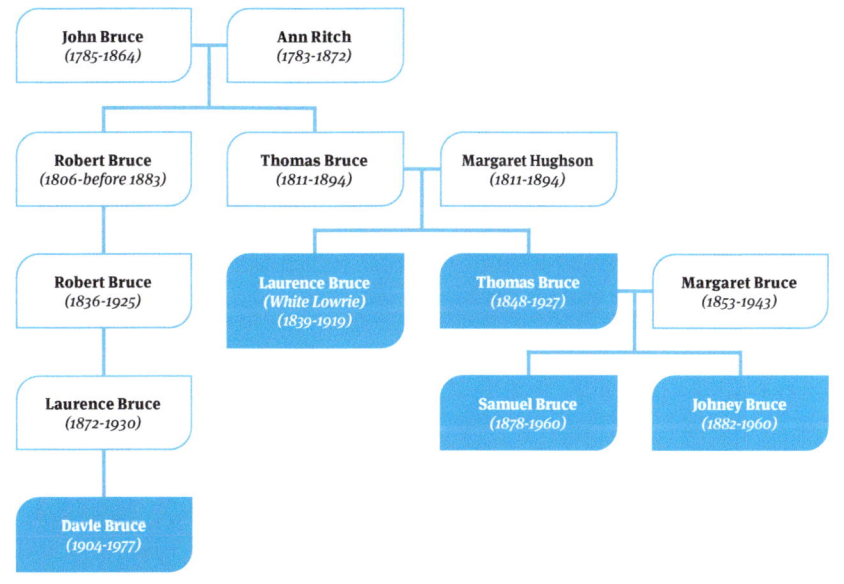

Fig. 49. *Bruce boatbuilding family tree. Boatbuilders in blue. Non boatbuilding siblings not included. (Shetland Museum & Archives D62/1/22; Lythoe 2016, Hutchison 2016).*

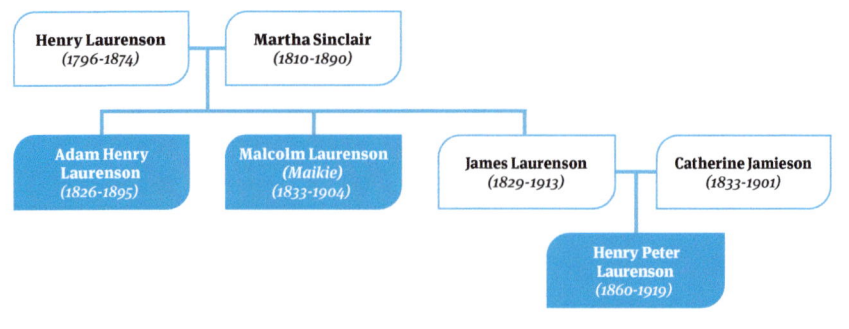

Fig. 50. *Laurenson boatbuilding family tree. Boatbuilders in blue. Non boatbuilding siblings not included (Shetland Museum & Archives D62/1/37; D62/1/58; Lythgoe 2016).*

Laurenson boats

Three of the boats built by Malcolm and Adam are in existence today. The oldest of these is the summer cod fishing boat *Ann*, LK126, which was built for the brothers David and Robert Williamson from South Havera (SMA collection) (Fig. 51). *Ann* was built prior to 1869 – we know this as the boat was listed in the inaugural customs' fishing boat register of that year. The boat was registered as having a keel length of 15ft, six oars and a square sail rig. Used for deep sea fishing with ground lines *Ann* had a crew of three and was jointly owned by David and Robert, with David listed as skipper. *Ann's* registration was cancelled in March 1902, and the reason given was "boat broken up." (SMA, C85/11/5). Clearly this was not the case as it was reported by Adrian Osler that the boat remained in casual use until 1960, which means she was seaworthy for close to 100 years (Osler 1983: 102-104).

The next oldest surviving Laurenson boat is the sixareen *Industry*, LK718, which was built to deliver the mail between Foula and Walls in 1891, and cost £21 ready for sea. The boat was 20ft (6.1m) keel and 30ft (9.1m) over the stems, with a beam of 8.5ft (2.6m) and was originally rigged with a dipping lug sail that was set on a 26ft (7.9m) mast (SMA, catalogue SEA 2007.19, CE85/11, Osler 1983: 106-107). The Foula mail run was instigated by Robert Gear who, after receiving the consent of Queen Victoria, began this service in 1879. Twelve years later, in 1891, the mail contract was awarded to John Jaromson (master), George Hughson, James Twatt, James Coutts and Bruce Fraser from Walls. On obtaining the mail contract Jaromson commissioned the Laurenson brothers to build *Industry*. However, she never actually provided this service. Whilst the sixareen was being built the mail contract was re-tendered, and subsequently awarded to Magnie Manson and Laurie Gray from Foula (SMA, DVD 2010).

Industry, now redundant as a mail boat, was registered for fishing on 1st March 1892. During her 15-year fishing career she took part in at least two of the new annual Walls regattas, in 1895 and 1896, and was reputed to have been a fast boat. Her fishing career came to an end in 1907 and for the subsequent 50 or so years she worked in the summer as a flit boat, transporting peats from Gruting and Olas Voe to Walls. It was at this time that her rig was changed from dipping lug to a standing lug and jib arrangement, the mast being shortened by 4ft (1.2m) in the process. This change was necessary to make the boat more easily handled under sail. Tacking with a dipping lug involves the crew lowering the sail, unhooking it, and moving sail and yard forward around the mast and then hoisting it back up again on the new tack – a process severely hampered with a full cargo. So *Industry*, like all flit boats, was converted to the more easily handled standing lug and jib; her "new" suit of sails being made from the original dipping lug sail (PI, Moncrieff and Wishart 2015).

Constructed in 1897 the three-man haddock boat *Active* LK 950 was built by the Laurensons for William Leask of Scalloway (Fig. 52) (Unst boat Haven Museum collection). With a keel of 13.5ft (4.1m) the boat was 21feet six inches over the stems with a beam of 6.5ft (1.98m). Like *Industry*, *Active* was a six-oared boat rigged with a dipping lug sail. Testament to the seaworthiness of *Active* was the time the boat was caught in a sudden gale when fishing a notoriously dangerous area called the Kist Grounds just southwest of Skeld. William (Tammie) Leask, the owner and skipper,

Fig. 51. Ann *LK126 built by Adam and Malcolm Laurenson prior to 1869. Shetland Museum & Archives collection. Photo: M. Chivers.*

Fig. 52. Active *LK950 Unst Boat Haven Collection. Photo: M. Chivers.*

was fishing with his two sons Tammie Jnr and Adie. When caught by the gale they began to row but made no progress. The skipper's son Tammie suggested that they sail and eventually he persuaded his father that this was the only course of action available to them. They fully reefed the sail and Tammie Jnr helmed the boat, sailing her to windward back the eight miles to Scalloway (Isbister, 1995: 17-18). *Active's* fishing registration was cancelled in 1914, and from then nothing more is known about the boat until 1959 when boatbuilder Jess Goudie fitted a Stuart Turner engine. This was when Tommy Isbister first saw the boat, and a year later she was bought by George Lamont Williamson of Papil, Burra, who used the boat for lobster fishing. He too was caught out in bad weather and commented that "she was a remarkably good sea boat and would run straight before a heavy sea, requiring almost no helm" (PI, Williamson, 2016). In 2008 *Active* was gifted to Duncan Sandison (founder of the Unst Boat Haven).

Following consultation with Tommy Isbister *Active* was restored as close as possible to her original condition by Duncan Sandison, Davy Leask, and Andrew M. Thomson. Following the boat's restoration she was once again sailed under dipping lug, her mast supported by a single strood (shroud) which was moved to the weather side when the boat was tacked. Then, four years later in 2012, *Active* was retired, and is now on permanent display in the Unst Boat Haven museum.

To the uninitiated these three Laurenson boats may look very similar but, as Isbister explains, they were quite different boats:

> Cod boats, sometimes referred to as spring or summer boats, were only used in this area [Scalloway, Trondra, Burra, and South Havera]. The cod used to come right into the voes to spawn, and of course they needed a bigger boat, cos it was bigger fish ... And I mind me saying to an old man in Scalloway, 'why did they not use these boats for the haddock line?' And he said they never wanted to a row a bigger boat than they had to ... I mind seeing one that Jeemsie Williamson had built ... she was lying here in Burwick up til 1953, I think, when a gale blew her away, she was a beautiful boat, and she was a spring boat, and there were a haddock line boat lying alongside her, and so both old boats; there was a tremendous difference in size. One was 17ft of keel, and the other one was say 14ft or 14.5ft of keel. They were a totally different boat altogether, you could put nearly two inside the spring boat, it was just a good piece bigger, ... (PI, Isbister, 2015).

Isbister's description demonstrates a pragmatic approach to boat use whereby a boat would not be used that was bigger than necessary the purpose for which it was needed. This description of the six-oared cod and haddock boat types illustrates the point that they were totally different types of craft. For example, *Active* was 13.5ft (4.1m) of keel, and was a type known as a three-man haddock boat. Haddock boats went up to 15ft (4.6m) of keel and these bigger boats were crewed by four men.

These Laurenson-built boats were described by Isbister as being "... lovely, beautiful boats." When sailing off the wind in a stiff breeze they planed. In Shetland this phenomenon was called "becoming sea loose" which Isbister attributes to the angle of first two strakes up from the keel, which Maikie made as flat as possible in the midship section of the boat: "... the next board had a definite uplift but that's in the boats of 13ft or 14ft of keel, but they planed afore the wind ... I was warned about it, the fellow that sold it to me said 'she'll scare dee but she'll do nothing wrong ...'" (PI, Isbister 2015, Morrison 1978: 16).

Isbister's description of how Laurenson built boats that planed is very important and demonstrates that these boats were principally sailing boats, designed to sail well on all points of the wind. The high-performance sailing ability of these boats further emphasises the skill of the boatbuilder:

> ... the funny thing was that you would of thought she would not be able to sail that well. You might not be able to go to weather so well, and might need a bit more depth [in the keel], but it was the third board coming up again that gied them that, they settled down a bit, and gied them slightly more depth although they still had these two flat bottom boards, and they could sail to weather like the devil ... I had the sail on mine, and she sailed well. So he was a good builder, and funny enough, the ones that was apprenticed to him didn't actually follow the same idea ... they were inclined to make the first two boards slightly steeper ... and then just kinder gradually come out ... (PI, Isbister 2015).

This observation that the Laurensons' apprentices adopted a different approach is intriguing and suggests a change in emphasis towards boat use where sailing performance was either of secondary importance (which is doubtful) or they wished the boats to be less intimidating to use when sailing off the wind (probably more likely). It must be recognised that lives depended on the skill and workmanship of the boatbuilder, and the shape of the boat amidships was a determining factor as to whether a boat would be safe to sail and row. Isbister emphasised that the second board up from the keel, at the midships section, had to be low in angle. To check this angle the boatbuilder would stand a bottle on this board midships, and if it did not topple over the angle was correct (PI, Isbister 2015).

The Laurensons of Quoys, Catfirth, Nesting

Another well-known boatbuilding family, coincidentally also called Laurenson, were from the Quoys, Catfirth, in the parish of Nesting (Fig. 53). The founder of this line of boatbuilders was Magnus (1772-1851) of whom currently nothing is known. His son Dempster (1802-1892) began boatbuilding in 1828 following a period of several seasons at the haaf fishing (Fig. 54). In 1821 Dempster was nearly drowned when the sixareen he was a crew member of was caught in a storm and capsized 10 nautical miles (18.5km) southeast of Bowl Skerry. Dempster's uncle and cousin were also on board and both were lost. The only survivors were Dempster and Robert Robertson of Lunnasting, who were picked up by another sixareen, skippered by Robert Hunter (SMA, D62/1/113).

It has been claimed that Dempster was self-taught but the fact that Dempster's father, Magnus, was also a boatbuilder means that this is unlikely. Proof of the handing down of boatbuilding tradition is found in a John Laurenson fourareen which was built around 1880. This boat is completely original apart from the sheer strakes which Tommy Isbister replaced when he first got the boat in 1959. This fourareen is an extremely important material cultural object, and is unique, being the most complete original boat of its type known to be in existence. This boat has important Norwegian boatbuilding features, which according to Isbister were handed down through the Laurenson boatbuilding line – these features are discussed in chapter 10. Information given to seaman, navigation teacher and maritime enthusiast Tammy Moncrieff, indicates that Dempster built over 400 boats and that all his boats had six strakes (SMA, D62/1/113). The Laurensons built a variety of boats including sixareens. The larger boats were built outside at the Quoys whilst the smaller ones were built in a shed. The boards used to build the boats were hand sawn by the Laurensons at a specially built saw pit which was located on the foreshore banks (Shetland Museum and Archives, D62/1/113).

Other notable builders

John Eunson (1836-1894) was from the Punds, Eastshore in Dunrossness. He mainly built yoals with his sons outside in the yard behind his now demolished house. Boatbuilding outside in Shetland was fairly standard practice

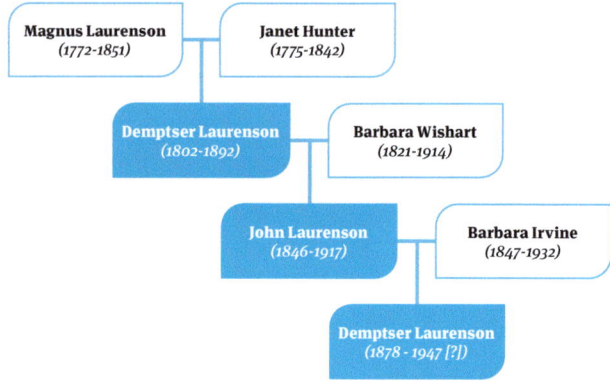

Fig. 53. *Laurenson boatbuilding family tree. Boatbuilders in blue. Non boatbuilding siblings not included (Lythgoe 2016).*

Fig. 54. *Dempster Laurenson. Photographer: unknown (c.1890). Courtesy of Shetland Museum & Archives.*

although the other notable Ness yoal builder of the period, George Johnson (1859-1941), built his boats in a shed at Bodam, Dunrossness. Building boats inside was obviously advantageous, as work could take place even in the poorest of weather. According to George Jacobson, a descendant of John Eunson, this meant that Johnson built many more boats than Eunson, although he was reputed to have built between 200-400 yoals during his career (PI, Jacobson 2020, SMA, D62/1/43). Eunson retired from boatbuilding aged just 55 so during his working life of approximately 35 years he must have built between six to 11 boats per year. By contrast George Johnson, who built his boats in a shed, is reputed to have constructed about 13 boats per year. Not all the boats that Johnson built were yoals, he also built small fourareens and transom-sterned dinghies with steamed timbers (SMA, D62/1/96). One of the yoals built by Johnson is the well-known *Ivy*, LK 237 (Fig. 55) (Osler 1983: 92-94, Osler 2020).

Other boatbuilders of that period such as Walter Duncan built boats outdoors. Duncan left Hay & Company to start his own boatbuilding business around 1887-89, at the herring station, in Hamnavoe, Burra. In 1893 he bought one of the old herring station sheds but then found it difficult to obtain a piece of land on which to erect it. Peerie Walter Duncan explained that eventually his grandfather obtained a site in Hamnavoe but it was not level, so he had to cut into the hillside in order to make a sufficiently large and level earthen floor upon which to erect the shed. This shed was slightly extended in 1910, but otherwise, apart from the usual maintenance and repairs, remains unaltered (Fig. 56-57) (Osler 1978: 77-79, Osler 1983: 49-50; PI, Duncan 2015).

Another less well known, but nevertheless important, boatbuilding family, were the Inksters who lived in East Burra. This line of boatbuilders consisted of Laurence (1785-1866), his brother-in-law Charles (1798-1866), and Charles's son, John "Houllsie" (1828-1912). Laurence built boats at the dock at the North Houlls banks, in a stone walled roofless building. In 1850 Laurence moved to the booth at Houss and left the boatbuilding business to his sister Catherine's son, John Inkster (Houllsie).

John built at least two 19ft (5.8m) of keel sixareens. The first of these was the *Lady*, constructed in 1892, which was built as the replacement Foula mail boat to the previously discussed sixareen *Industry*, LK 718 (Isbister, 2015, Wishart 2015). The Inkster sixareen was named *Lady* after Mrs Louise Traill, who was the factor for Foula at that time and who funded the building of the boat. Mrs Traill hired the boat to Magnie Manson and Laurie Gray and she provided a new sail each year and new oars every second year. Because she was being used during the winter in rough weather, the boat only lasted six years, and was then replaced around 1898, by another sixareen, also built by Inkster, and again called *Lady* (Fig. 58). It was pointed out that the rig of this second Inkster sixareen was unusual for that time, as the boat was rigged with a dipping lug, jib, and a jigger (mizzen) (SMA, DVD 2010; PI, Isbister 2015; PI, Wishart 2015).

Fig. 55. *The Ness yoal* Ivy *LK 237, currently (2021) in storage in Dunrossness.* Ivy *was restored by Jim Harper during the 1980s. Photo: M. Chivers.*

Fig. 56. *The launching of the* Ocean Gift. *Bakkaburn, Hamnavoe. Walter Duncan's shed is in the background. Photo: J.H. Smith, (1912). Courtesy of Shetland Museum & Archives.*

Fig. 57. *Boat shed erected by Walter Duncan senior in 1893, Bakkaburn, Hamnavoe. This photograph was taken in 2015. Shed dimensions 43ft (13.10m) by 26.65ft (8.12m). Photo: M. Chivers.*

Inkster built his last boat, for William Aitken, in the early 1900s. This boat was about 12ft (3.7m) of keel and was later owned by Jeemie "Keelie" Leask, who kept her in the small boat harbour in Lerwick during the 1980s (PI, Wishart 2015). Fig. 59 is a photograph taken about 1900 of William's son, James Aitken, standing in William's boat at Quarff. Note in this photograph the elegant, long, slender, and round-tipped oar blades (PI, Herculson 2016; Lythgoe 2016). Another 12ft (3.7m) of keel Inkster boat was built around 1900 for James Coutts, Malaquilse, Mid Walls. This boat was latterly owned by Martin "Mattie" Williamson (PI, Wishart 2015).

Thomas Walter Scott (1859-1929) served his apprenticeship under Adam and Malcolm Laurenson. He became manager foreman at Hay & Company's Blacksness yard in May 1889. Between then and March 1926 Scott built 215 boats (Fig. 60) (SMA, D62/1/163-168). Scott kept a boatbuilding journal which, remarkably, has survived, and in it is listed every boat he built up until March 1926 (PI, Rendall and Wishart 2016). Each entry in this journal details the boat's length of keel, the name of the person for whom the boat was built, how much the boat cost, plus key dimensions such as band spacings, and board widths. Scott also provided the strake dimensions for boats from 10ft (3m) to 16ft (4.9m) of keel. He also stated the distances between the bands, the depth of the sheer at each band, and the breadth of the boat at each band (Fig. 61).

Scott's journal also tells us where his customers lived, and it is not surprising to find that most of his clients were in the area surrounding Scalloway, from places such as Bixter, Burra, Trondra, Quarff, Oxna, Sand, Whiteness, and Weisdale. However, there were occasionally customers who ordered boats from further afield. For instance, a Mr Inkster from Brae ordered three boats to be built between December 1889 and February 1890. The size and cost of these were: 12ft (3.7m) of keel cost £5.12s., 11ft 8ins (3.6m) keel cost £4.8s., and a boat of 11ft (3.5m) keel cost £4.10s.6d. An interesting entry on 27th January 1896 provides early evidence of building boats for recreational sailing as Scott Christie from Leith is listed as ordering a racing boat, 12ft of keel and copper fastened. According to Scott's journal entry this boat was to be sailed by Laurence Williamson from Papil.

Another notable boatbuilder of this period, who worked for Hay & Company in Lerwick, was David "Davey" Leask, who was born in Burravoe, Mid Yell in 1836. Leask in his early teens built boats in his parents' garden before serving his apprenticeship with Laurence Arcus, who had a boatbuilding business where the Thule Bar in Lerwick stands today. After completing his apprenticeship, Leask worked as a shipwright in Glasgow, and then in 1866 he approached Hay & Company, who immediately employed him as a foreman. One of the boats built by Leask was the three-man haddock boat *Brothers* LK 96, built in 1888 (SMA collection) (Fig. 62). As well as building traditional fishing boats, Leask also gained a reputation for building racing boats as reported in his obituary in *The Shetland Times* on 28th February, 1903: "... Mr

Fig. 58. *Sixareen* Lady *built by John Inkster. Photographer: unknown (c.1900). Courtesy of Shetland Museum & Archives.*

Fig. 59. *James Aitken standing in his father's fourareen built by John Inkster. Photographer: unknown. Courtesy of the late Laurina Herculson.*

Fig. 60. *The haddock boat* Gleaner *LK2878 built by Thomas Walter Scott in 1885. Photo: C. Stobie, (c.1890). Courtesy of Shetland Museum & Archives.*

Leask has shown rare skill as a designer and boatbuilder of pleasure boats some of the 'crack' racers at regattas being the result of his intelligence as a boat builder" (SMA, D62/1/116).

It is evident that all parishes in Shetland had their own carpenters, all of whom probably had their own building styles and preferences. Indeed, local racing sailor and traditional sailing enthusiast Brian Wishart noted that boats built by Malcolm and Adam Laurenson, Thomas Walter Scott, and John Inkster, shared certain proportion similarities to that of the Ness yoal in that they were longer and slenderer, with finer ends and slacker bilges compared with those of the more modern, early-twentieth century boats, influenced for example by Walter Duncan. Wishart pointed out that these nineteenth century vernacular boats belonged to the period when rowing was as important as sailing requiring, above all else, easily driven and sea-kindly hulls (PI, Wishart, 2016).

By the mid-nineteenth century Hay & Company had become the main commercial supplier of vernacular boats. They employed a large workforce of boat carpenters who supplied boats not only to the local area but also to islands such as Foula, Unst, and Whalsay. Vernacular boatbuilding during the mid-nineteenth century was expanding in order to keep pace with the demands of the commercial fishery and, in 1868, The Sea Fisheries Act was

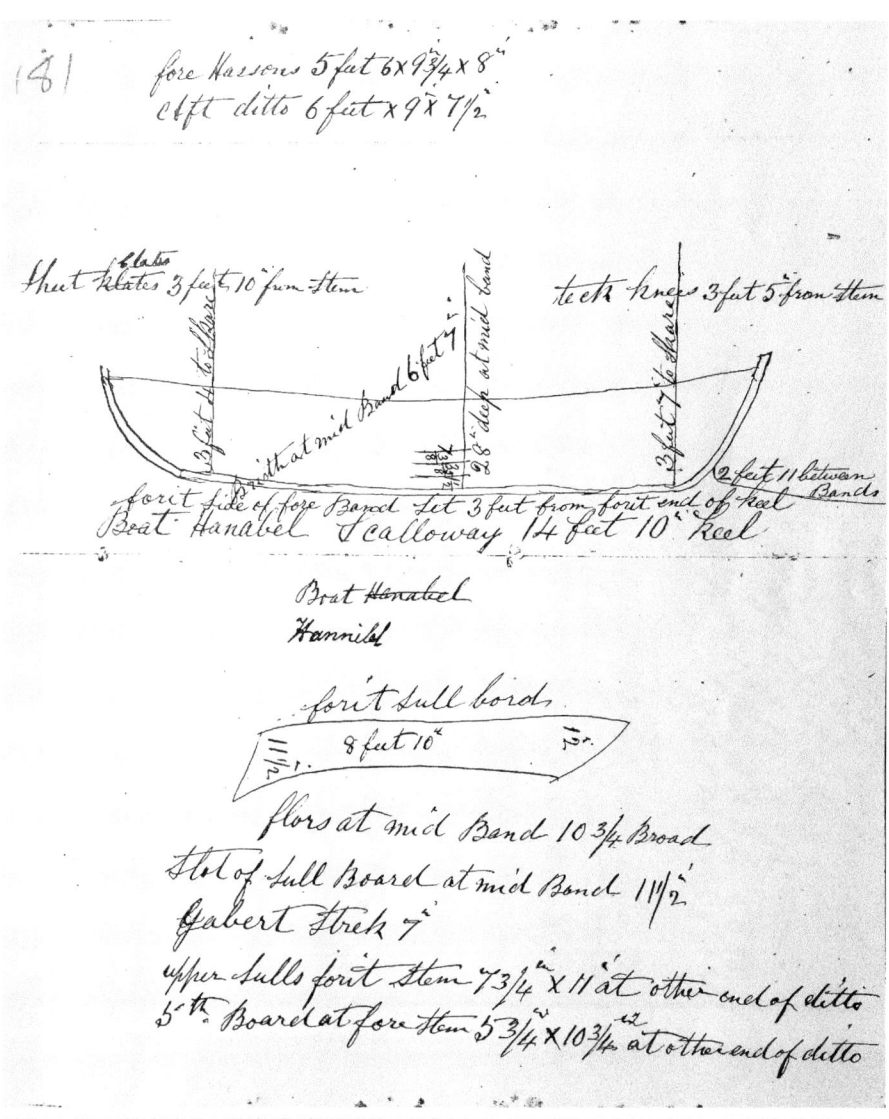

Fig. 61. A copy of Walter Scott's boatbuilding journal in which he provides scantling sizes for boats he built. A. Rendall, 2016. Photo: M. Chivers.

passed and it became mandatory in 1869, under article 22, for all British commercial fishing boats to be registered (Sea Fisheries Act 1868: 327). The penalty to fishermen who failed to comply was a fine not exceeding £20, and the local sea fisheries officer was authorised to seize any unregistered vessel and prevent it from going to sea. This mass registration provides a unique glimpse into the types, sizes, distribution, and ownership patterns of vernacular craft in Shetland.

Fig. 62. Brothers *LK96 built by Davey Leask, foreman of Hay & Co., Lerwick, 1888. Shetland Museum & Archives collection. Photo: M. Chivers.*

Chapter 8

Boat types and their distribution and ownership in 1869

T he inaugural year of the H.M. Customs Fishing Boat Register provides us with a unique snapshot into the number and sizes of commercial fishing boats in Shetland during 1869 (SMA CE85/11/5-6). The register tells us the name of the owner, along with the name of the skipper and where the boat was registered. It also tells us the number of crew, the number of oars, the type of sailing rig and the fishing purpose. In the register the terms square sail and dipping lug sail are used. The square sail, as previously mentioned, was the original sail type. By the mid nineteenth century the square sail was being replaced by the more efficient, higher peaked, asymmetric dipping square sail referred to in the register as "dipping lug".

This information was collated and divided into six-oared and four-oared boats, organised by keel size. The six-oared data was then broken-down into boat types and each boat's location plotted on a map to show the distribution of boat-types and ownership patterns across Shetland. It must be emphasised that this represents only commercial fishing boats; it does not take into account the many other vernacular craft – for example sixareen flitboats and non-commercial fourareens are absent from this record. Therefore, this information represents the minimum number of boats in use in Shetland in 1869. Table 13 lists the boat types that were identified from the register.

There has been a general propensity to assume that the sixareen and the Ness yoal were the dominant commercial fishing boats in use during the mid- to late-nineteenth century. As can be seen in Table 13 this presumption is questionable. The fishing boat register did not list boats by type but categorised them by the number of oars, their keel length, the type of fishing engaged in and whether they grossed less or more than 15 tons. This sometimes makes boat type identification difficult, particularly as there is a crossover between boat types in the keel length range of 14ft (4.3m) to 16ft (4.9m). So, where possible, other sources have also been used in order to help clarify the types of six-oared boats listed in the register. Six-oared and four-oared boats are presented and discussed in this chapter, with geographical data analysed from north to south, beginning in Unst. Following the geographical analysis of boat types, a discussion takes place concerning boat ownership, followed by a brief presentation of the types of sailing rigs listed in the 1869 register. It was remarkable to find that there were only 730

Boat type	Number of oars	Usual number of crew	Approximate Length of keel	Approximate Length over the stems
Cod/spring or summer boat	6	3	15ft (4.9m) - 17ft (5.2m)	23ft (7m) - 24ft (7.3m)
Fair Isle yoal	6	3 or 4	c.16ft (4.9m)	22ft (6.7m)
Four-man haddock boat (smaller sixareen)	6	4	14ft (4.3m) - 15ft (4.6m)	21ft (6.4m) - 23ft (7m)
Fourareen	4	2 or 4	8ft (2.4m) - 15ft (4.6m)	15ft (4.6m) - 23ft (7m)
Ness yoal	6	3 or 4	c.15ft (4.6m)	23ft (7m)
Saithe boat	6	4 or 5	12.5ft (3.8m) - 15ft (4.6m)	21ft (6.7m) - 23ft (7m)
Sixareen	6	6	17.5ft (5.3m) - 22ft (6.7m)	25ft (7.6m) - 32ft (9.8m)
Three-man haddock boat (small sixareen)	6	3	13ft (4m) - 14ft (4.3m)	20ft (6m) - 22ft (6.7m)

Table 13. *Types of boats registered to fish.*

six-oared boats, as opposed to 1,732 four-oared boats registered. This disparity between six- and four-oared boats illustrates the ubiquity of the fourareen against that of the more specialised commercial six-oared fishing boats.

The sixareen

Identifying the larger sized sixareens from the register is straightforward. However, the aforementioned crossover in keel lengths makes categorising the smaller boats more difficult (see Table 13). In 1817 Samuel Hibbert commented that the Northmavine fishing boats had keel lengths of between 18ft (5.5m) and 19ft (5.8m) (Hibbert 1822: 298). Then, in 1845, the Reverends James and John Ingram reported that the boats in Unst were larger than "... former days measuring from 18 to 22 feet in length of keel with six men in each" (*New Statistical Account* 1845: 46). Robert Bruce, in 1914, stated that average keel length of a mid-nineteenth century sixareen was 18ft (5.5m) to 20ft (6.1m) (Bruce 1914: 291). This is supported by the surviving material evidence of the previously discussed 1860s sixareen *Mary*, LK 981, which is listed in the 1869 register as having a keel length of 19ft (5.8m). It therefore seems reasonable to categorise boats with keel sizes from 17.5ft (5.3m) to 22ft (6.7m) as sixareens, that is, a six-oared boat usually rowed by six men.

To further complicate matters some of the boats fall within the keel-length ranges of the four-and three-man haddock boat. However, these boats were engaged in haaf fishing, and it is postulated that these may have been small versions of the sixareen, adapted to suit local conditions.

The analysis of the 1869 register produced some surprising results. Out of a total of 730 six-oared boats, less than half (48 per cent) were conventional sixareens. This illustrates that the types and sizes of boats were more diverse than has been previously appreciated. In the most northerly part of Shetland – Unst – of the 80 six-oared boats registered 54 were sixareens. Conversely, in Dunrossness in the south, with 146 six-oared boats registered, only 21 were sixareens. This demonstrates that the geographical location of the commercial fishery determined boat type distribution. This is further illustrated by 71 per cent of all sixareens being located within the districts of Unst, Yell, Northmavine, Delting, Lunnasting, Whalsay, and Skerries. This is not particularly surprising, as the haaf fishing stations were located in these districts, being physically closest to the fishing grounds, with good stony beaches (ayres) on which to dry cure the fish (Goodlad 1971: 110).

Six-oared boats

Besides the sixareen there were other, smaller, six-oared boats being used for fishing at the haaf. These smaller six-oared boats were also longline fishing inshore for haddock and cod, fished with dorros (handlines) for saithe, and used nets to catch herring and mackerel (SMA, CE85/11/5-6). A good example of this diversity in six-oared boat size is found in Unst, where out of the 80 six-oared boats registered 22 (28 per cent) were saithe boats.

Saithe was an important commodity in Unst – as it was in Dunrossness and Fair Isle – and these were caught in the roost of Skaw around Lamba Ness, and Flugga (Goodlad, 1971: 118). It has not been widely acknowledged that Unst had its own version of the yoal called the saithe boat, a surviving example of which is *Jemima Ann*, LK 1004, built by Robbie Nicolson in Haroldswick around 1892 (Fig. 63) (Munro 2012: 42). Shetland boat aficionado Leslie Moncrieff described the saithe boat: "In the old days, in Unst, the saithe boats, which were very much like yoals, rowed with five men. The aft man had the pair [oars]" (PI, Moncrieff 2015). This information has assisted in the identification of saithe boats in the 1869 customs register.

The keel lengths of saithe boats ranged from 12.5ft (3.8m) to 15ft (4.6m) and out of the 22 boats identified only five used a sail, which suggests that fishing took place reasonably close to shore. As well as the five-man boats there were also three- and four-man six-oared boats listed as dorro fishing inshore. Their keel lengths were in the same range as the five-man boats so it seems reasonable to assume that these were also saithe boats. There were two six-oared boats, both called *Joan*, registered to Skaw. *Joan*, LK 984, owned and skippered by William Clark and *Joan*, LK 1457, owned and skippered by Andrew Clark. All the six boats registered to Norwick, were saithe boats, as were the boats from Burrafirth, Newgord and Westing (Appendix B, Fig. 64).

In Unst the most common sixareen keel lengths were 19.5ft (5.9m) to 20ft (6.1m). Thirty-seven of these boats were registered to Haroldswick, which was

Fig. 63. *Saithe Boat* Jemima Ann *LK1004 built by Robbie Nicolson, Haroldswick, Unst. Unst Boat Haven collection. Photo: M. Chivers.*

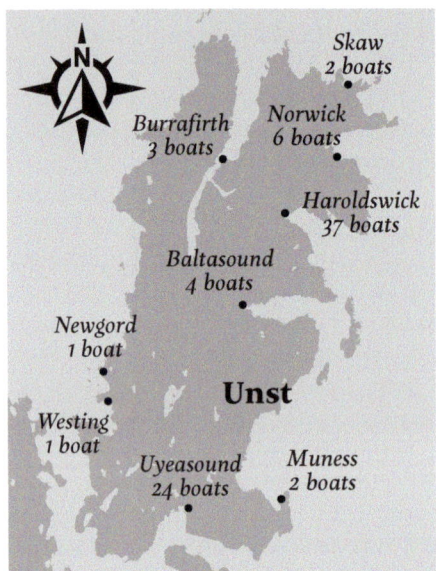

Fig. 64. *Six-oared boat distribution in Unst in 1869.*

an important haaf station, and 24 were registered to the open fishing station in Uyeasound (Goodlad 1971: 117).

Six-oared boats in Yell ranged in keel length from 13.5ft (4.1m) to 22ft (6.7m). Forty-two per cent of sixareens had keel lengths of between 19.5ft (6m) to 20ft (6.1m), and 24 per cent had keel lengths of 22ft (6.7m). The distribution of boats across Yell was fairly even, although there was a high density of 15 very large sixareens registered to Greenbank, Cullivoe, in northeast Yell (Fig. 65). There were two shops in Greenbank and these large sixareens were owned by the merchants who ran these stores. One was owned by Pole, Hoeseason & Co and the other by Alexander Sandison and both hired out large 22ft (6.7m) of keel sixareens (SMA, CE85/11/15:1; Bayanne 2016).

In Northmavine, the most northern part of Shetland's Mainland, there were 62 six-oared boats registered, of which 52 were sixareens. Fifty-four per cent of these boats had keel lengths in the range of 18.5ft (5.6m) to 19ft (8m) (Fig. 66). Anomalies were found in the distribution of these boats, as it was expected that there would be a significant number registered to Fethaland and Stenness which were the two largest fishing stations in Shetland (Kerr 1831: 189-194). Surprisingly, only one sixareen was registered to each of these stations. These anomalies are easily explained, as Fethaland and Stenness were seasonal fishing stations, used between May and August. The boats were registered to where the owner lived, which was not necessarily where they fished. Indeed, both Fethaland and Stenness were remote places, as illustrated by the 1878 Ordnance Survey maps, on which it is possible to identify the small fishermen's böds and the other buildings associated with the haaf fishing industry (Fig. 67-68).

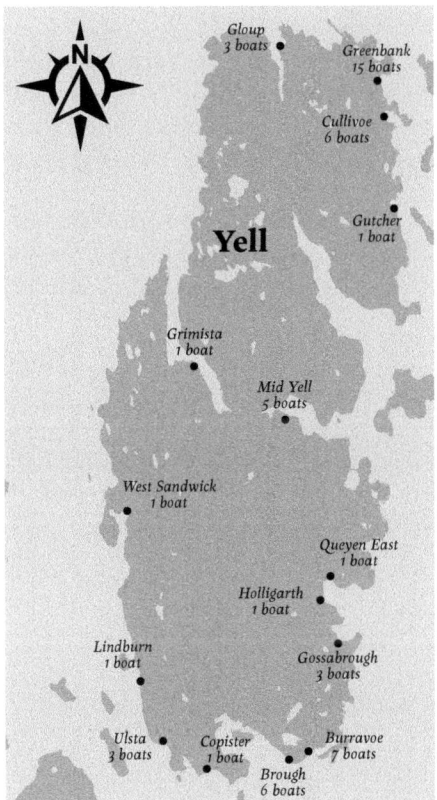

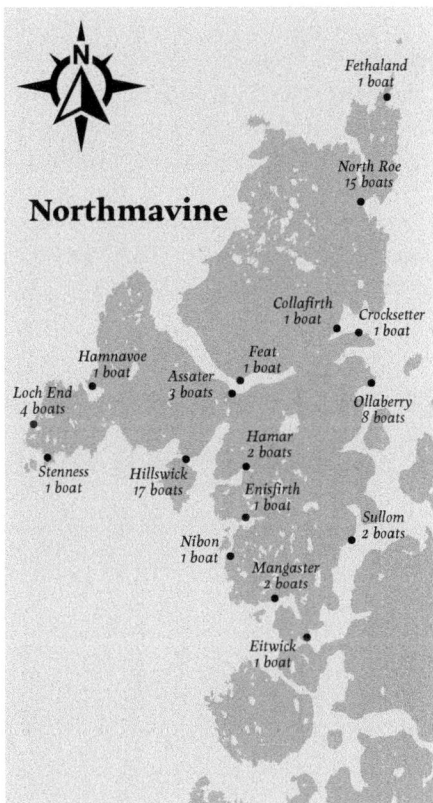

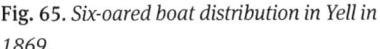

Fig. 65. *Six-oared boat distribution in Yell in 1869.*

Fig. 66. *Six-oared boat distribution in North-mavine in 1869.*

By contrast, on the small east coast islands of Whalsay and Out Skerries the boats fished from the places they were registered (Fig. 69). Like in Northmavine, the keel lengths of sixareens in Whalsay and Skerries ranged from 18.5ft (5.6m) to 20ft (6.1m). All these sixareens were square sail rigged, apart from one Whalsay boat which was dipping lug rigged. It was noted that in Skerries 44 per cent were of a smaller type of six-oared boat, with keel lengths that ranged from 15ft (4.6m) to 16ft (4.9m) (SMA, CE85/11/5). These, like the sixareens, were registered to fish with ground lines at the deep sea. Geographically these stations were close to the fishing grounds and it is probable that these boats were a smaller type of sixareen. This further illustrates the point raised at the beginning of this chapter that boats were built to suit a need determined by local conditions. Of note is that the larger 19ft (5.8m) to 20ft (6.1m) sixareens were also registered to fish with nets, presumably for herring.

Listed amongst the Whalsay sixareens was *Mary*, LK 981, which was registered as being 19ft (5.8m) of keel and square sail rigged. She was built prior to 1869 by Hay & Company in Lerwick at Freefield and is a typical example of a mid-nineteenth century sixareen. *Mary* was registered to Sandwick and was jointly owned by the skipper, William Anderson, and her five crew. This new sixareen was named after Mary Anderson who was born in 1852 and was the daughter of William's brother John, who was one of the boat's shareholders. In 1884, which was towards the end of *Mary's* fishing career, the boat took part in the rescue of the crew and passengers from the stricken Danish barque *Alba*. The *Mary's* skipper at that time was the aforementioned John Anderson who was awarded a silver medal for saving lives by the Danish government (SMA, CUR 8020). *Mary's* registration was cancelled in January

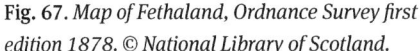
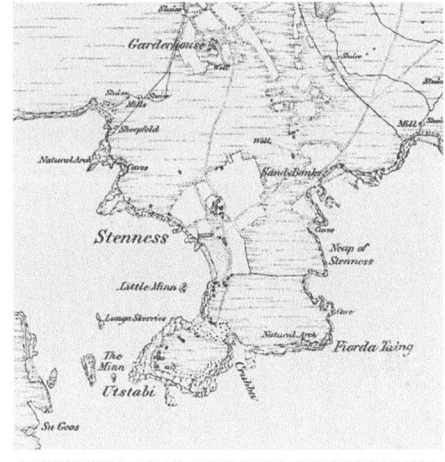

Fig. 67. *Map of Fethaland, Ordnance Survey first edition 1878. © National Library of Scotland.*

Fig. 68. *Map of Stenness, Ordnance Survey first edition 1878. ©National Library of Scotland.*

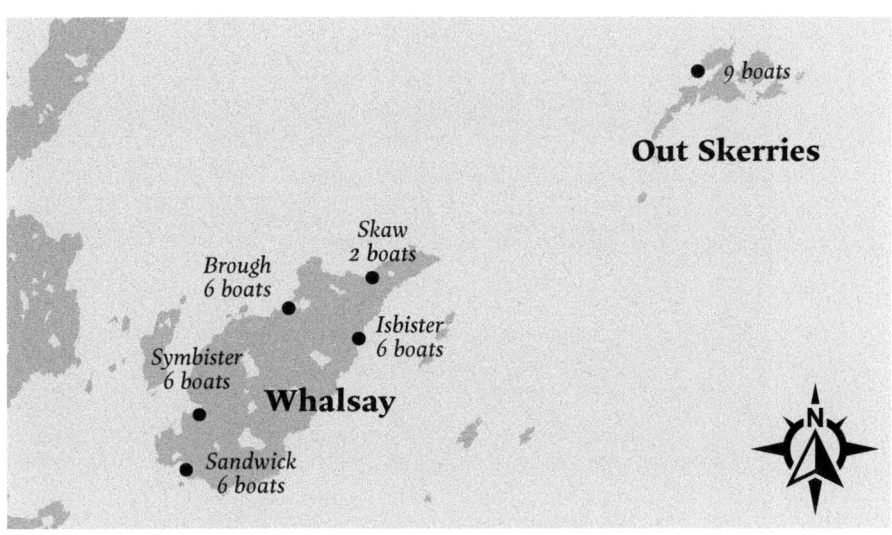

Fig. 69. *Six-oared boats in Whalsay and Out Skerries in 1869.*

1886, recorded as "Boat usless." Although *Mary* was no longer fit for the rigours of the haaf fishery she was still seaworthy, as R.S. Bruce recalled:

> I made a run in Decr. 1891from Sandwick, Whalsay, to Lerwick in the haaf-boat 'Mary' of Sandwick. We had a single reef and a following wind, and I think we got to Hay's Docks in an hour and 30 or 40 minutes. The 'Mary' was thought to be a fine boat on a wind, but not a good runner, but she ran well enough for me! It was like flying when she lifted on a sea, and she scudded on the back of a roller - I enjoyed that run, I can tell you (SMA, D25/95/50).

When no longer fit for sea *Mary* was brought a short distance inland and sawn in half. The two halves were turned upside down to become the roofs for two outhouses. The outhouse comprising the aft section was destroyed during the 1960s leaving only the forward section preserved which is now on display in the Shetland Museum (SMA, FIS 2011.54, Chivers, Stratigos and Tait 2019: 442-446) (Fig. 70).

By 1869 the sixareen as a fishing boat type, in some districts of Shetland, was in decline. An example of this was observed in Fetlar, where in 1845 there had been 17 sixareens (*New Statistical Account* 1845: 27-31). By 1869 there were just five (Table 14). A similar situation was noted in Bressay and Quarff. In 1845 Bressay had 13 sixareens, and in Quarff, there were four (*New Statistical Account* 1834-1845: 15). These Bressay and Quarff sixareens operated from the haaf station in Noss, a small island close to the east of Bressay. However, by 1869 the number had reduced by 41 per cent. Quarff only had two 19.5ft (5.9m) of keel boats and Bressay just five. Although fewer in number, the sizes had increased, and three of these boats had keel lengths in the range of 21ft (6.4m) to 22ft (6.7m) (SMA, CE85/11/5-6: 68, 96, 124, 203, 230).

Number	Boat name	Length of keel	Oars and rig	Type of fishing	Owner's name	skipper	No crew	No boys	Cancelled
1562	Agnes	16.5	Open clinker boat, 6 oars and square sail	Longlines and nets	James Jamieson	James Jamieson	6	0	1878 boat done.
1563	Martha	17	Open clinker boat, 6 oars and square sail	Longlines and nets	Martha Park	Jarm Park	6	0	1871 boat unfit for fishing.
1564	Mary	20	Open clinker boat, 6 oars and square sail	Longlines and nets	Arthur Brown	Arthur Brown	6	0	1873 unfit for fishing sold as flit boat.
1566	Friends	20	Open clinker boat, 6 oars and square sail	Nets	Thomas Murray and others	Thomas Murray	4	0	1872 ceased to be a fishing boat
1658	E.Z.	20	Open clinker boat, 6 oars and square sail	longlines	James Jamieson	James Coutts	4	1	Boat done 1875

Table 14. *Six-oared boats registered to fish in Fetlar in 1869 (Shetland Archives CE85/11/6: 22,23,42).*

Fig. 70. Mary *in Sandwick, Whalsay, in 1993 before being moved to Shetland Museum & Archives, Lerwick. Photo: John Jamieson.*

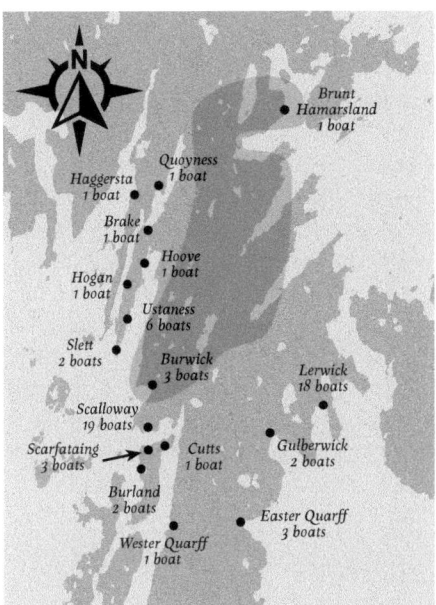

Fig. 71. *Six-oared boats in Tingwall in 1869.*

While some districts had large numbers of sixareens others – being too far from the fishing grounds or with coastline ill-suited to launching boats or drying fish – had none. For instance, in Tingwall there were no conventional sixareens. There were just four six-oared boats registered to this parish, two 15ft (4.6m) keel and two 16ft (4.9m). As the map in Fig. 71 illustrates three of these boats fished from Burwick with a crew of four, whilst the fourth, *Margaret*, LK 1289, skippered and owned by William Irvine, fished from Brunthammarsland with a crew of six. All fished with longlines at the haaf (SMA, CE85/11/5: 12, 217).

By contrast there were 18 six-oared boats registered to the parish of Whiteness but only one, *Hope*, LK 264, was a sixareen. This square sail rigged, 18ft (5.5m) of keel sixareen was owned and skippered by Henry Smith of the Pund who, with a crew of five, fished with longlines. The next largest of the Whiteness boats was the 16.25ft (5m) of keel, square sail rigged *Jane*, LK 352. She was owned and skippered by Robert Laurenson, who lived in Hays, and fished with longlines with a crew of four. Of these Whiteness boats there were just two that were not rigged for sailing: *Swan*, LK 75, 13.5ft (4.1m) keel, owned and skippered by James Sclater from Ustaness that used to fish with groundlines and dorros near to shore with a crew of three; and *Ann*, LK 189, a 13ft (4m) keel boat owned and skippered by James Smith of South Hove, who fished near shore using dorros and rods also with a crew of three (Fig. 72).

In Weisdale there were two small six-oared boats. The largest, *Helen*, LK 1060, was 14ft (4.3m) of keel, dipping lug rigged, crewed by four, and owned and skippered by Robert Leask who lived at Cott. This boat operated inshore and was registered as fishing with longlines and herring nets. The other, *Margaret*, LK 1639, was 13.5ft (4.1m) keel and dipping lug rigged. She was skippered by John Johnson from Heglabister, with a crew of three (SMA, CE85/11/5/6: 38, 171) (Fig. 73).

It was surprising to find no sixareens registered to the west coast island of Papa Stour. The situation here was similar to Stenness, whereby sixareens were only stationed in Papa Stour during the haaf season. There were five 13ft (4m) to 14ft (4.3m) keel six-oared boats registered to Papa Stour. They fished inshore with dorros, were square sail rigged, and crewed by three or four men (Fig. 74). By contrast there were 28 six-oared boats registered to the small islands of Trondra, Hildasay, Papa, Oxna, and South Havera, located to the south and west of Scalloway. Again, none were sixareens – all were either cod or haddock boats (SMA, CE85/11/5) (Fig. 75). One of these "summer boats" – as explained in the previous chapter – was the cod boat *Ann*, LK 126, which had a keel of 15ft (4.6m) and was crewed by three. *Ann* was built at some point in the mid to late 1860s, for David and Robert Williamson from South Havera, and is the second-oldest surviving boat in Shetland and the only remaining example of a cod boat.

In 1869 there were 46 six-oared boats registered to East and West Burra, southeast of Scalloway, and only three of these were sixareens. These sixareens fished at the Burra haaf using longlines and were 18ft (5.5m) keel. Each had a crew of five, and two of these boats were square sail rigged, whilst the third, *Morning Star*, LK 222, which was registered to Hamnavoe and owned by the skipper Matthew Pottinger and others, was dipping lug rigged (Fig. 76).

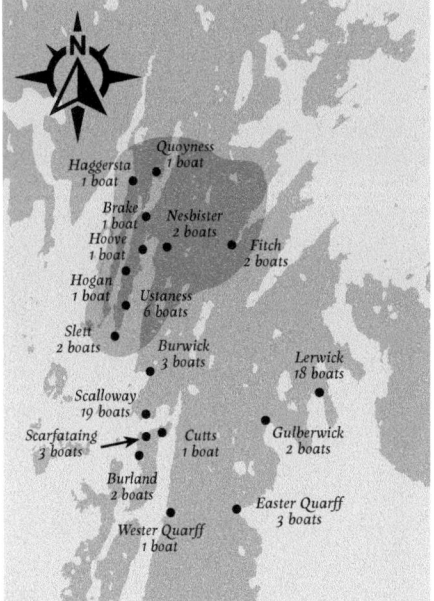

Fig. 72. *Six-oared boats in Whiteness in 1869.*

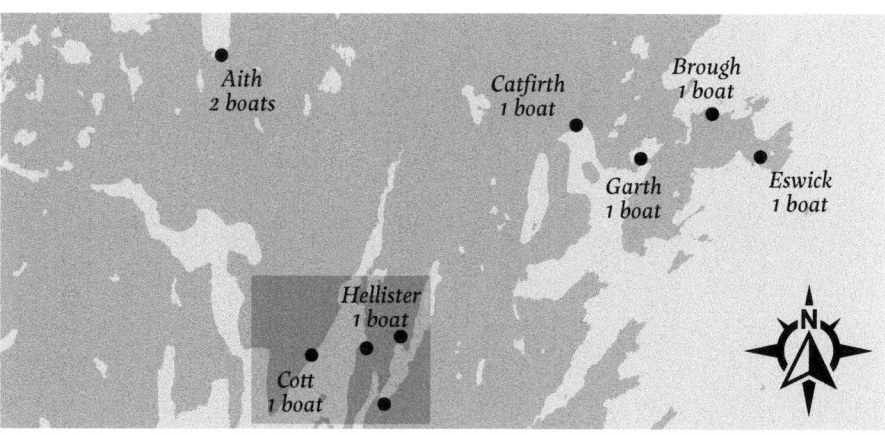

Fig. 73. *Six-oared boats in Weisdale in 1869.*

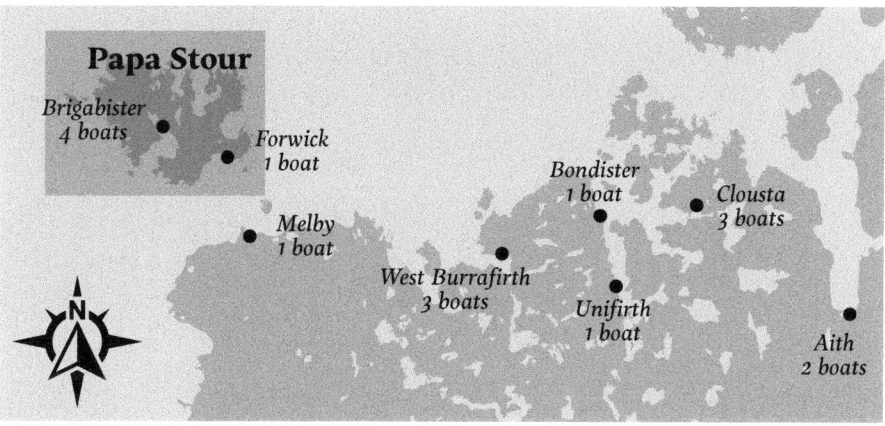

Fig. 74. *Six-oared boats in Papa Stour in 1869.*

Moving down through the southern part of Shetland's Mainland, sixareens begin to become more prevalent again. For instance, in Cunnings-burgh there were 14 six-oared boats, 10 of which were sixareens (Fig. 76). One of these was *Nymph*, LK 1641, which had a keel length of 22ft (6.7m). This boat was square sail rigged and originally hired by Hay & Company to Andrew Smith, who along with his crew, listed as being 4 or 5, fished with ground lines at the haaf and also with nets for herring. *Nymph* was sold in 1871 to John Johnson of Ludd, Dunrossness, who skippered the boat at the haaf with a crew of six until 1879 when the boat's registration was cancelled.

In Sandwick there were 50 six-oared boats listed in the 1869 register, 31 were sixareens, seven of which were 20ft (6.1m) keel (Fig. 77). In the adjoining parish of Dunrossness the number of six-oared boats jumped to

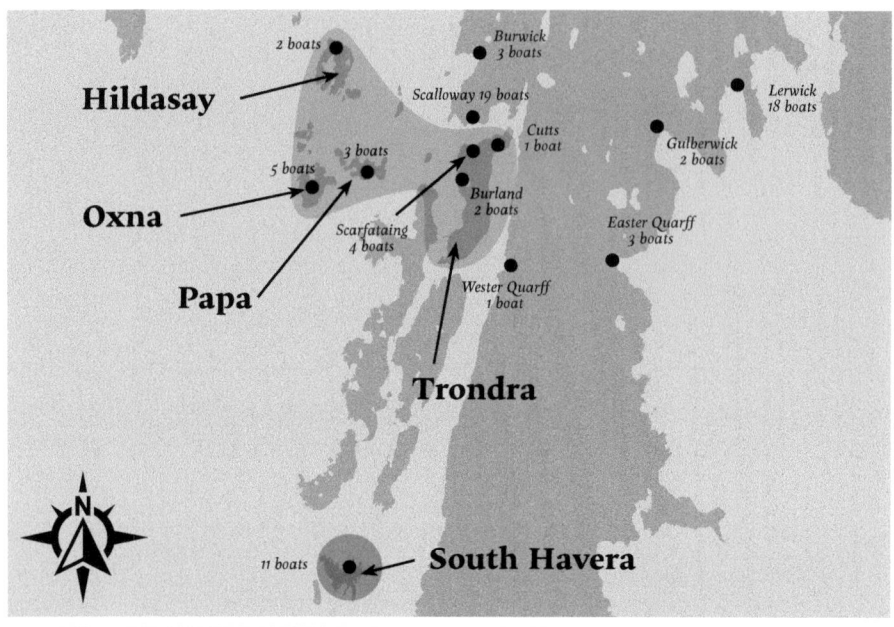

Fig. 75. *Six-oared boat distribution in Trondra, Hildasay, Papa, Oxna and South Havera in 1869.*

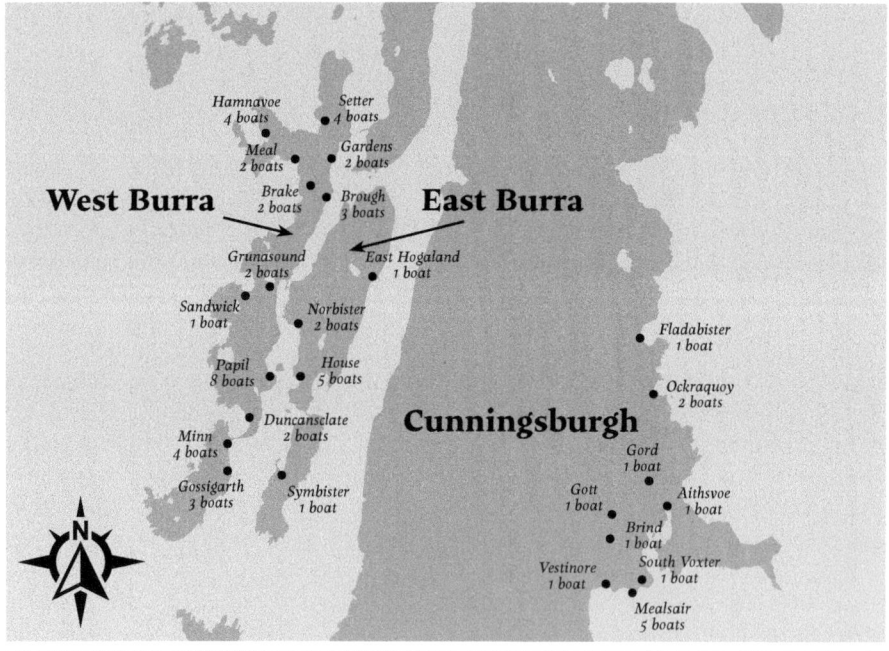

Fig. 76. *Six-oared boat distribution in Burra and Cunningsburgh in 1869.*

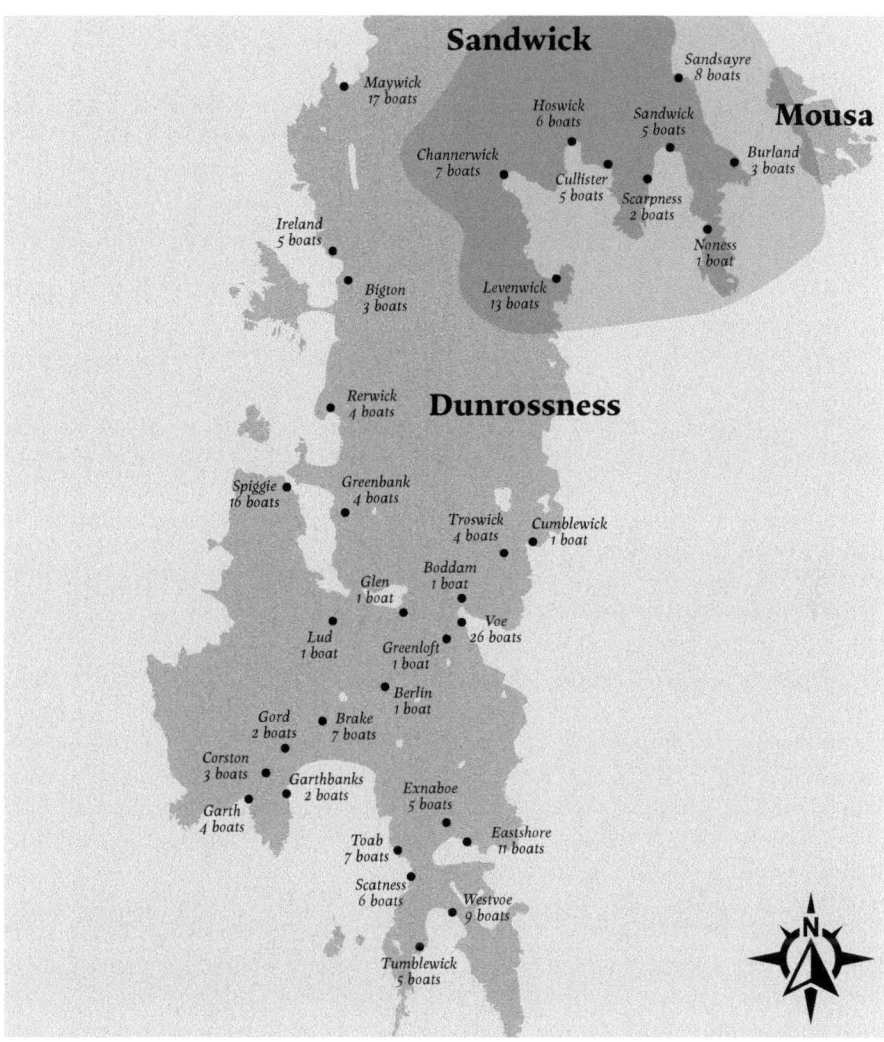

Fig. 77. *Six-oared boat distribution in Sandwick and Dunrossness in 1869.*

146 but only 21 were sixareens. The overwhelming majority of these boats were presumably Ness yoals, as they were 15ft (4.6m) of keel and crewed by three or four men (Henderson 1978: 53; PI, Moncrieff and Wishart 2015). Saithe fishing in Dunrossness, up to the end of the nineteenth century, was always undertaken relatively close to shore using dorros (Osler 1983: 91). It was therefore surprising to discover that, according to the register, only eight per cent of these boats fished inshore with dorros. Twenty seven boats were registered to deep sea fish with longlines, 40 boats were deep-sea longline and handline fishing, 22 were handline fishing near shore and 5

were registered to longline near shore. This suggests that these boats did not just fish for saithe, but also for haddock, ling and cod.

In Fair Isle there were 17 six-oared boats, these were square sail rigged and were 16ft (4.9m) long in the keel. Crewed by three or four men these Fair Isle yoals were used commercially to fish for saithe using dorros. Like the Ness yoals they also commercially fished for other species such as ling, coalfish and cod, and used longlines for haddock and halibut (Fig. 78) (Fenton 1978: 528, Osler 1983: 13, 71). In Foula eight sixareens were registered, four were 18ft (5.5m) and four 19ft (5.8m) keel, dipping lug rigged, and fished with longlines at the haaf with a crew of six.

It has been a prevalent belief that both Ness and Fair Isle yoals were solely used to fish for saithe using dorros but the customs register suggests that they also fished for ling. This suggestion is further supported by the fact that there were approximately 10 ling fishing stations in Dunrossness, and one in Fair Isle (Smith, H. 1984: 115). This, along with the evidence for the use of saithe boats in Unst, indicates that the Norwegian sexæring forerunner to the yoal was probably ubiquitous in Shetland.

The fourareen

Unlike the six-oared varieties, the distribution of four-oared boats was more even across Shetland. Fourareen keel lengths were also fairly uniform and the most popular sized fourareens fell in the whillie category, with keel lengths of 9.5ft (2.9m) to 12ft (3.7m). The 1,316 whillies accounted for 76 per cent of all fourareens in the 1869 register. As previously mentioned, this number only reflects those boats listed for commercial fishing and is therefore the minimum number of fourareens that were in use during that year.

Some anomalies show up. In Fetlar and Fair Isle there were no four-oared commercial fishing boats, and in the large district of Dunrossness there were only 23. The reason, I suspect, is that these districts were specialist fishing areas, with specialist boats. So in these districts the fourareen was not used for commercial fishing – it was simply the family utilitarian boat. Reinforcing this view, within the category of fourareen there was only one variation in nomenclature, the whillie, sometimes referred to as an eela boat, as discussed in chapter one.

In Unst all the fourareens, apart from *Margaret*, LK 1527, were registered as dorro fishing inshore. This indicates that these fourareens were fishing for saithe in the same manner as the specialist saithe boats. *Margaret* was owned and skippered by John Johnson; she was a lug-sail rigged boat of 13ft (4m) keel and fished from Haroldswick with longlines. The most popular keel lengths were 11.5ft (3.5m) to 12ft (3.7m), and there was parity in the number of 9.5ft (2.9m) to 10ft (3m) and 12.5ft (3.8m) to 13ft (4m) keel boats. Nearly all these boats were skipper owned and, as can be seen from the map (Fig. 79), the densest population of fourareens was found at Uyeasound and at Baltasound.

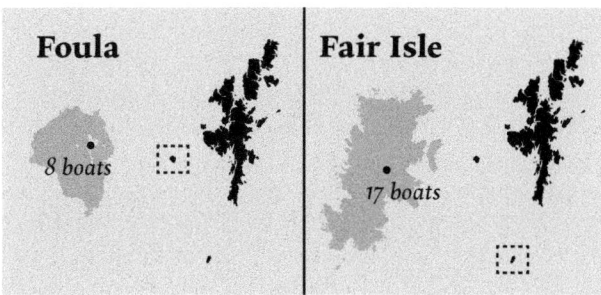

Fig. 78. *Six-oared boats in Foula and Fair Isle in 1869.*

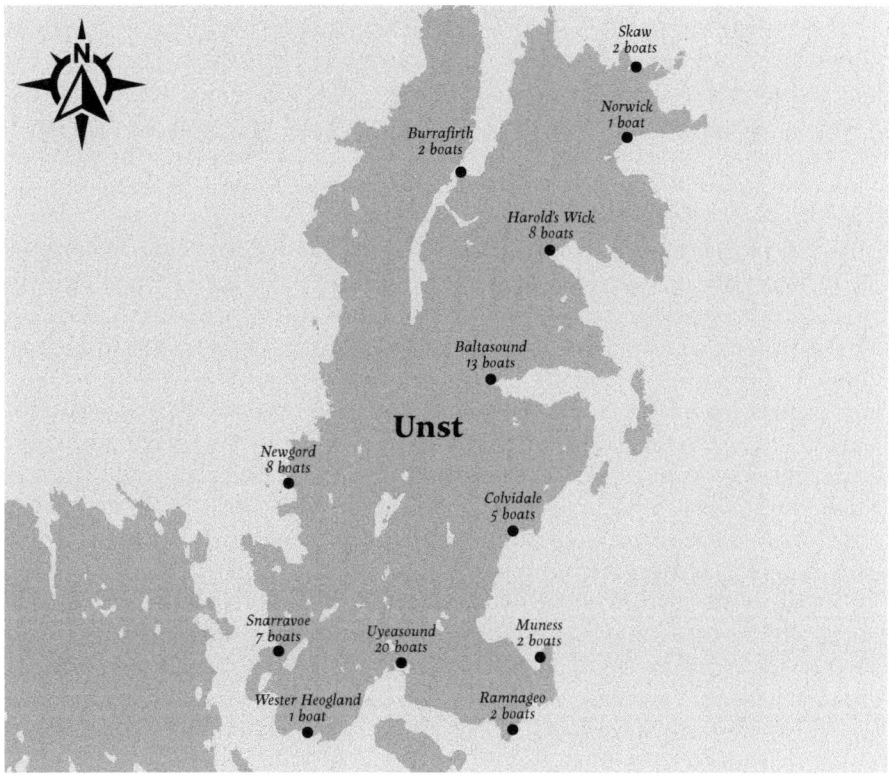

Fig. 79. *Four-oared boats in Unst in 1869.*

In Yell, the most common keel length of a fourareen fell between 10.5ft (3.2m) and 11ft (3.4m), with the next most popular size of boat being 11.5ft (3.5m) to 12ft (3.7m). The majority of Yell's fourareens were longline and dorro fishing and nine of these were only fishing for haddock with longlines (SMA, CE85/11/5-6). The distribution pattern of fourareens in Yell was concentrated around Mid Yell and towards the south of the island. Most notable of all are the total number of fourareens in Yell which was more than double that in Unst (Fig. 80). This is the more striking considering that the population sizes of the islands were very similar (Scotland's People, 2016). From this, and their proximity, it would be expected that the number of boats commercially fishing in these islands would also be comparable. The disparity remains unexplained.

The pattern of fourareen boat use in Mainland Shetland broadly follows that observed in Yell and Unst. On the east coast of Shetland's northern Mainland, within the parishes of Delting, Nesting, and Skerries boats fished with dorros, and also for sillocks using pock-nets (Fig. 81). Sillock-pock – poke-net or pock-net – fishing could be done from the shoreline, or by boat at sea (Fenton 1978: 536). When undertaken from a boat a net was suspended from a hinged iron rim approximately 6ft (1.8m) in diameter. The bait commonly used was offal which was placed into the net, which was then lowered into the water until the netted iron rim lay open on the seabed. It was usual for a shoal of hundreds of sillocks to be attracted to the pock-net. This would then be quickly hauled, and the hinged rim would close trapping the sillocks in the net (March 1970: 44).

In Sandsting, there was an 11ft (3.4m) keel rowing fourareen called *Ann*, LK 5. *Ann* was owned and skippered by James Thomson who, with his crew of four plus a boy, used the boat for dorro fishing and oyster dredging. The Reverend John Menzies described oyster dredging in Burra in 1799: "They have upon their coast a fine oyster scalp, from which they take large rich oysters. Hence they are, in general in easy circumstances" (Withrington, Grant, Sinclair 1978: 398-399). There were some four-oared boats registered to dredge for oysters. Three of these came from Scalloway, and a further three from Burra. The first of the Burra boats was *Star*, LK 39, which was registered to Laurence Inkster at Bridge End. This boat was 12ft (3.7m) of keel, dipping lug rigged, and crewed by Laurence and a boy. Then there was *Lilly*, LK 129, square sail rigged, owned and skippered by Gideon Christie who, along with another man and a boy, dorro fished and oyster dredged inshore. Finally, there was *Swan*, LK 134, owned by Laurence Inkster of Norbister. As well as these oyster dredging fourareens there was also a 13ft (4m) of keel, six-oared rowing boat called *Oak*, LK 302, owned and skippered by William Manson from Norbister in Burra who fished with a dorro and also dredged for oysters.

Fourareen use in the rest of Shetland was fairly consistent with that already described. The boats fished using dorros, longlines, rod and fly, and occasionally nets for catching either herring or mackerel.

Boat ownership

As well as providing us with information about the types of boats, their location, and use the inaugural customs register also provides us with information about their owners and skippers. The register shows that shared

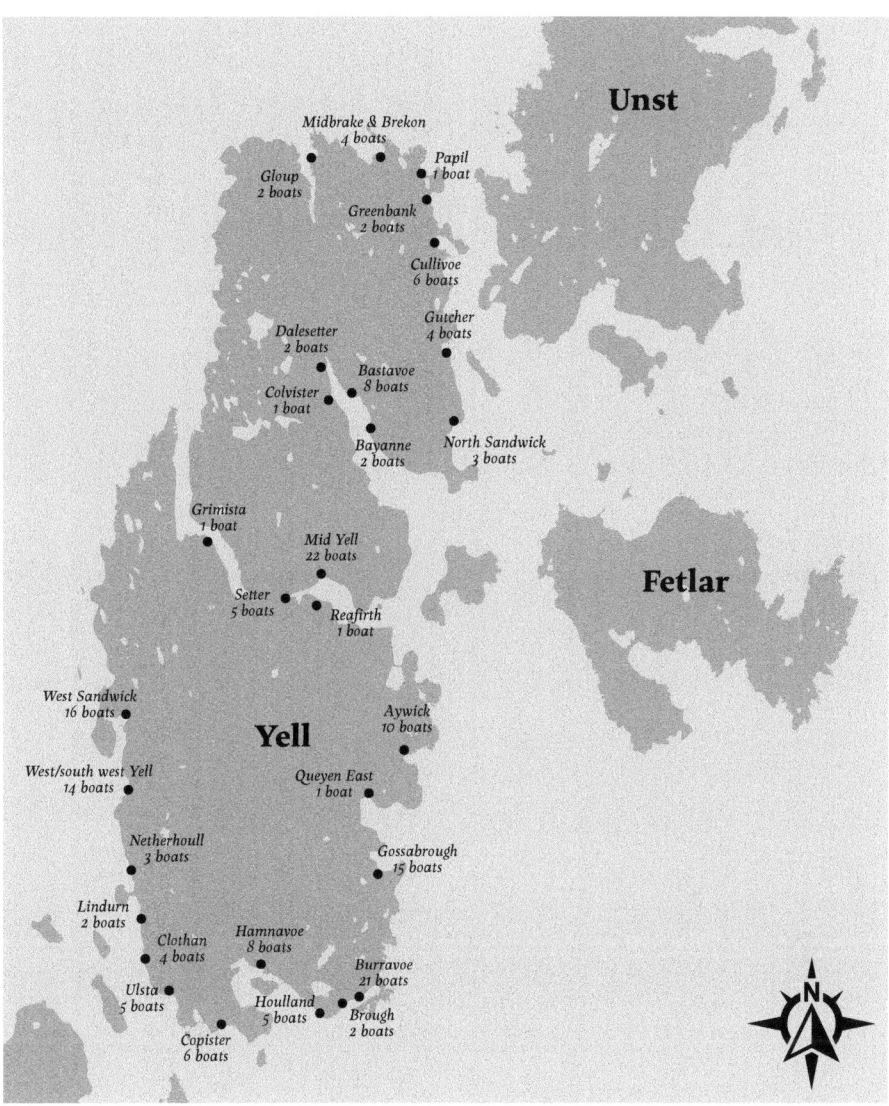

Fig. 80. *Four-oared boats in Yell in 1869.*

ownership was far more common in commercial fishing than previously thought. This, when examined alongside other archive sources, enables us to view Shetland society in a slightly different way, allowing us a glimpse into a world where fishing from small open clinker boats was of the greatest economic importance. Some boats were bought second-hand but the majority were new as they were reasonably cheap to build (March 1970: 56). It is clear that most commercial fishing boats had a hard life, on average only lasting

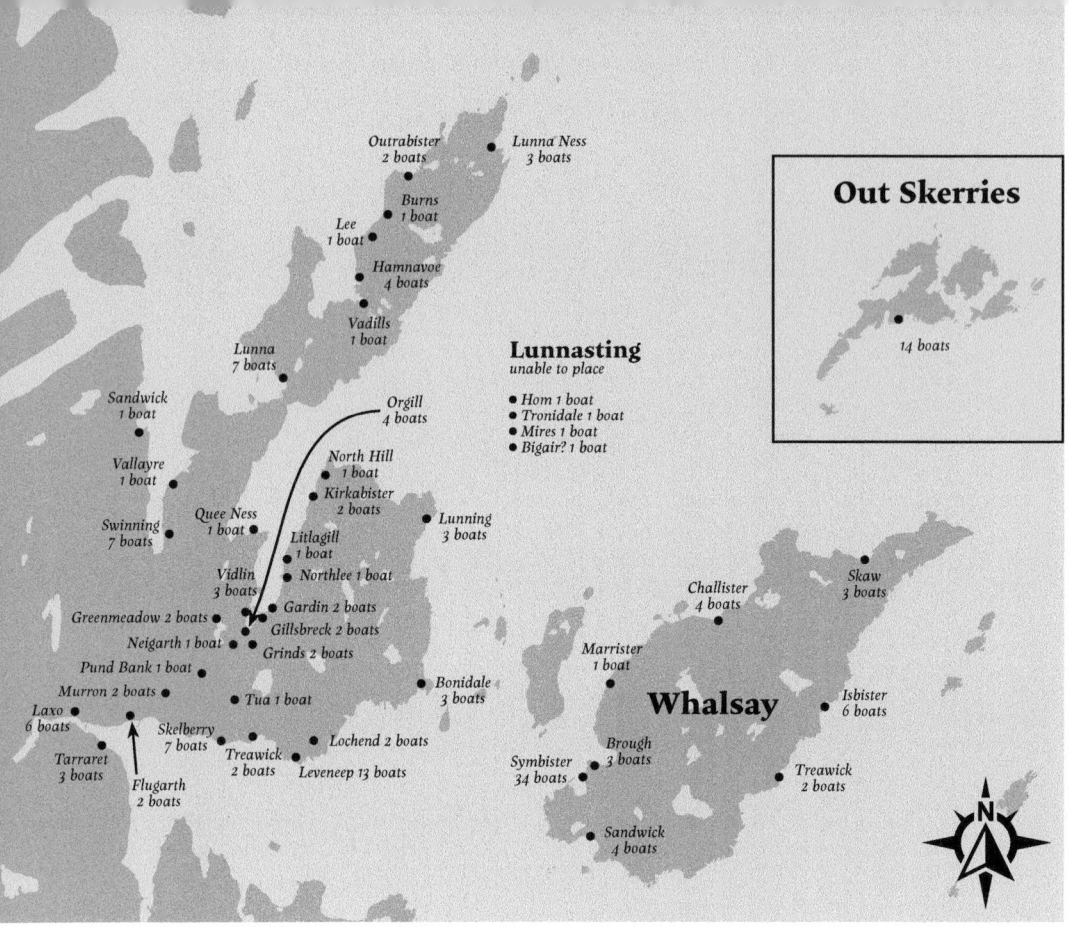

Out Skerries

14 boats

Outrabister
2 boats

Lunna Ness
3 boats

Burns
1 boat

Lee
1 boat

Hamnavoe
4 boats

Vadills
1 boat

Lunnasting
unable to place

● Hom 1 boat
● Tronidale 1 boat
● Mires 1 boat
● Bigair? 1 boat

Lunna
7 boats

Sandwick
1 boat

Orgill
4 boats

Vallayre
1 boat

North Hill
1 boat

Kirkabister
2 boats

Lunning
3 boats

Swinning
7 boats

Quee Ness
1 boat

Litlagill
1 boat

Challister
4 boats

Skaw
3 boats

Vidlin
3 boats

Northlee 1 boat

Greenmeadow 2 boats

Gardin 2 boats

Gillsbreck 2 boats

Marrister
1 boat

Neigarth 1 boat

Grinds 2 boats

Whalsay

Isbister
6 boats

Pund Bank 1 boat

Murron 2 boats

Bonidale
3 boats

Laxo
6 boats

Tua 1 boat

Skelberry
7 boats

Lochend 2 boats

Brough
3 boats

Tarraret
3 boats

Treawick
2 boats

Leveneep 13 boats

Symbister
34 boats

Treawick
2 boats

Flugarth
2 boats

Sandwick
4 boats

N

Fig. 81. *Four-oared boats in Lunnasting, Whalsay and Out Skerries in 1869.*

seven to 10 years. By contrast, large sailing vessels in Shetland, as in other parts of the United Kingdom, often continued in commercial service for 30 years or more and maintained good resale values (Greenhill 1959: 104). This insight into boat ownership raises some important points about the prosperity and well-being of Shetlanders during this period.

Six-oared boat ownership

Forty-four per cent of six-oared boats were owned by their skippers, 31 per cent were in shared ownership, and the remaining 25 per cent were hired. Boat hire was most prevalent in the parishes of Unst, Yell, Northmavine, and Delting, which is where the main haaf fishing stations were located. It is not immediately apparent why boats in these areas were hired instead of share owned. Historian James R. Coull, in his book *Fishing, Fishermen, Fish Merchants and Curers in Shetland*, discusses the use of the term "boat hire" which, he believes, did not necessarily mean that the boats were owned by the firm. Instead, he suggests that this was an accounting convention, whereby men who had a share in the boat would get extra payment for the hire charge. Indeed, Coull suggests this was because in most instances merchants preferred the fishermen to own and be responsible for their own boats (Coull 2007: 15).

However, the customs register is clear that the boats being hired were the property of the merchants or the firms who registered them. Indeed, many of the hired boats were the larger sixareens, and there are several reasons why it made economic sense for crews to hire these. The haaf season itself was short, lasting just three months, and the boats were only used for this purpose, supplemented by some net fishing for herring at the close of the season (Coull 2007: 21-22). Therefore, it made economic sense not to own a boat that was only being used for a quarter of the year as the financial return did not justify the expense of buying a new boat. As already discussed, the largest sixareens only constituted six per cent of the total six-oared boat population. This indicates the specialist nature of these large boats – they were simply not practical for other fishing activities. The only other useful purpose they served was as flitboats after they were downgraded through wear and tear or replaced by better craft.

Fourareen boat ownership

The pattern of fourareen ownership demonstrates the ubiquity of these boats. The vast majority, around 93 per cent, were owned by the skipper, with seven per cent of boats in shared ownership and an insignificant number hired – less than one per cent. The pattern of fourareen ownership was almost universal across Shetland with the exceptions of Foula, Walls, Sandness, Burra, Cunningsburgh, and Dunrossness, where boat share was far more common. Fourareen ownership was within the means of common people, and the 93 per cent of those boats registered to fish – those owned by their skippers – was a subset of a bigger number of boats used in subsistence activities.

Boat ownership as an indicator of well-being

It is accepted that Shetlanders were held in economic bondage through debt and were victims of the system known as a truck (Smith, B. 1986: 3). This system of credit was not unique to Shetland. It was also prevalent in Newfoundland during the same period (Candow 2009: 388). Even though bondage through debt was prevalent a large proportion of the Shetland population were able to afford one boat, sometimes two, and occasionally even more (SMA, CE85/11/5-6). The 1871 census helps elucidate this point, as the total adult population of Shetland between the ages of 18 and 70 was 16,923. When this number was divided into male and female it became more interesting, as there were 11,185 women, and only 5,738 men in that age range (Scotland's People 2016). That roughly equates to three men for every commercial fishing fourareen and sheds a completely new light onto boat ownership and, again, stresses the ubiquity of the fourareen.

Shetland society was economically complex. Money flowed in from men at sea serving in the mercantile marine, taking part in fishing or whaling, or serving in the navy. During the early part of the nineteenth century the presence of positive social change began to be felt. As ethnologist Alexander Fenton pointed out in his book *The Northern Isles: Orkney and Shetland*, even as early as the 1840s there was evidence of social change taking place in Shetland, which was evidenced through the spread of free fishing (Fenton 1978: 584).

This societal change was described by social economic historian Hance Smith who stated: "... in many cases the landowner had become the tenant's confidential agent as far as trade was concerned, standing between him and the merchant, and there often existed an open and tacit agreement that tenants were to fish for certain merchants exclusively when fishing tenures were done away with" (Smith, H. 1984: 127). This change came about as shopkeepers began to take over large proportions of internal trade, which Hance Smith suggested began as early as the 1820s.

It was during this period that business interests focused on the means of production, chiefly the development of the herring and cod fisheries, which in turn increased the opportunity for mercantile businesses to grow. This economic growth continued, and by the 1860s there were over 200 small shops in Shetland's rural communities. The rise of this mercantile trade went hand-in-hand with fish-curing as this was the tenant fisherman's only means of obtaining credit. During the 1840s rents were converted into cash payments and this led to the replacement of fishing tenures by the system of truck. Indeed, these merchants became large landowners by the 1870s as illustrated by such as Adie of Voe, Inkster in Brae, and Anderson in Hillswick (Smith, H. 1984: 128, 129, 130). The Crofters Holdings Act (Scotland) in 1886 assisted this societal change through the provision of security of tenure, and this was later aided by the development and expansion of the herring industry (Smith, B. 1986: 5; Gear 2013: 67). Surprisingly, the system of truck did not disappear with the introduction of the crofters act. This was successfully circumvented by landowner-merchants and factor-merchants who in effect set up localised monopolies by thwarting any potential local business competition, and this persisted until the herring industry gained momentum in the 1890s (Smith, B. 1986: 5).

The flow of cash into Shetland began during the era of the press gang, when it was estimated that around 3,000 Shetland men were serving in the navy in the first decade of the nineteenth century. And the remittances that came home from Shetland sailors serving in the navy amounted to several thousands of pounds annually (Smith, H. 1984: 152). When war ended the Greenland whaling grew and expanded rapidly, and this too brought money into the Shetland economy which Hance Smith estimated to be around £50,000 annually (Smith H. 1984: 152). In fact, the number of Shetlanders making a living at sea in the 1850s was great, and it has been estimated that the 1861 census was short of around 2,000 men, who were serving at sea (Smith, H. 1984: 152). The population of Shetland according to the 1861 census was 31,561 and so perhaps the true figure was between 33,000 to 34,000. If so, approximately six per cent of the male population were employed as seamen, fishermen, whalers, or sailors (Scotland's people 2016).

As previously described by Samuel Hibbert in 1817, the money the seaman brought home was able to be invested in fishing through the purchase of a boat, either by an individual who was the owner as well as skipper, or through the crew share system (Hibbert 1822: 523). As Coull highlighted, income from fishing fluctuated from year to year, in some years fishing was extremely good and fishermen ended up fairly well-off. An example of this was John and Samuel Fullerton from Oxna, who were successful fishermen, and their individual share from fishing in the early 1860s could make them £20 to £30 per annum. Unfortunately, due to the vagaries of fishing, their earnings then slumped in 1867, and Samuel ended-up in marginal debt to Hay & Company, whilst John owed the firm £2.9s.3d. However, their fortunes changed for the better in 1869 when they delivered to Hay & Company in Scalloway over three tons of salt-cured ling, cod and saithe for which they earned £74.1s.6d., plus an extra £10.14s. for their seven crans of early herring and 13 crans of late herring. This left them individually £36.13s. in credit at the end of the year (Coull 2007: 28-29). It is perhaps not surprising to learn that John and Samuel jointly owned two of the smaller types of six-oared boats, *Arthur*, LK 659, which was 14ft (4.3m) keel, square sail rigged and crewed by three (used for fishing with groundlines) and *Ann*, LK 660, 14.5ft (4.4m) of keel, square sail rigged, and also used to fish with groundlines and to dredge for mussels with a crew of four (SMA, CE85/11/15).

The ledgers appertaining to Unst merchant Alexander Sandison's shop at Cullivoe in Yell provides us with more detail about the hire of sixareens (Coull 2007: 33-40). Sandison was a partner in Spence & Company who were heavily involved in the Gloup fishery during 1870-71, and they hired out six sixareens in 1869 and five in 1870 (SMA, CE85/11/5:184; Coull 2007: 33-40). There were 38 boats hired to boat crews in Yell in 1869, and the merchants who hired-out these boats were: Pole, Hoseason & Company, who hired-out 15 boats; William Jack Williamson who hired-out three boats; George Henderson who hired-out 12 boats, and Hay & Company who hired-out two boats. Significantly the skippers listed by Coull as hiring boats from Sandison's in 1870 were the same skippers (apart from A. Williamson who did not hire a boat in 1870) as were listed hiring boats from Spence & Company in 1869. The reason why these fishermen hired boats one year from one merchant, and the following year from another is explained by the fact that both were part of the same company. Spence & Company were recorded as employing these fishermen, and Alexander Sandison (who owned the shop and hired-out the boats) was in fact a partner in Spence & Company (Coull 2007: 33).

Boat hire was not expensive, some of these charges were as low as 5 shillings (25p) and hire charges seldom exceeded £1. Coull suggested the reason for these low charges was because the firm had a share (or shares) in boats, with the fishermen having the bulk of the shares (Coull 2007: 21). To put this into context the estimated cost of a loaf of bread in 1914 was one penny, and £1.11s, would buy £100 worth of goods in 2014 (Denton 2015). Coull identified that there were "... considerable variations in well-being among the fishermen and the communities for whom the haaf was the main commercial activity and the main source of cash income. But fishing was ever a mixture of feast and famines" (Coull 2007: 39-40).

As previously discussed, Yell had thirteen 22ft (6.7m) keel sixareens. These were very big boats, approximately 34ft (10.4m) long, and it must have been heavy work to haul them ashore. It is probable that they were kept moored afloat during the fishing season like the sixareens in Fig. 82. All these big sixareens were dipping lug rigged and belonged to Pole, Hoseason & Company (SMA, CE85/11/5: 1). This company was owned by William Pole and James Hoseason who were merchants and fish curers. Like Alexander Sandison they too owned a shop at Greenbank, Cullivoe, in North Yell, and they also owned a shop at Mossbank in the district of Delting. At these two shops sixareens were hired or sold to the fisherman, and the shops also supplied, on credit to the men and their families, the other fishing necessaries and

Fig. 82. *Sixareen setting off for the haaf at East Wick, Fedaland. Photo: J.D. Rattar, (1890). Courtesy of Shetland Museum & Archives.*

goods that they required. Pole also owned land and was tacksman at Aywick, Sellafirth and North Sandwick. His tenants in these places were obliged to fish for him as a condition of their tenancy. Pole, however, would release tenants from this obligation, one assumes, if all his boats were fully crewed, and they were then permitted to go to the Greenland whaling or the cod fishing in Faroe (Lythgoe 2016).

In Yell there were some smaller sized six-oared boats. The smallest of these boats was *Hope*, LK 1248, which was 13.5ft (4.1m) of keel, owned and skippered by John Williamson. *Hope* was square sail rigged and registered to Burravoe, where she fished using ground lines and dorros with a crew of four (SMA, CE85/11/5). Peep, LK 1459, a 14ft (4.3m) keel boat owned by Pole, Hoseason & Company, Greenbank, was hired to Laurence Manson who used her for long and ground line fishing, with a crew of four (SMA, CE85/11/6: 4). The other 14ft (4.3m) keel, six-oared boat, was *Unity*, LK 1297 owned by George Henderson at Brough, and hired to Peter Grant for ling and herring fishing (SMA, CE85/11/5: 218). *Ann*, LK1454, a 15ft (4.6m) keel, square sail rigged, four-man boat, was owned and skippered by Robert Manson, from West Sandwick, for deep sea fishing using groundlines (SMA, CE85/11/5: 244). Small six-oared boats were also used in Aithsting and these craft were skippered by their owners. The smallest and most interesting of these six-oared boats was *Sarah*, LK 509, a 13.5ft (4.1m) keel boat owned by William Nicolson of Danwall in Brindister. *Sarah* was dipping lug rigged and was registered to fish for haddock near shore. This boat was evidently a three-man haddock boat, a specialised type of fishing boat that has been previously described. This is an important listing as it is the earliest record of a haddock boat found (SMA, CE85/11/5: 79).

The six-oared boats registered to the district of Walls were mainly sixareens, and John Thomson owned five of these 20ft (6.1m) of keel boats, plus two 18ft (5.5m), and one 16ft (4.9m). All these Thomson owned boats were dipping lug rigged and were registered to Houll. Another interesting Walls boat-owning family was also called Thomson. Magnus and his family, originally from Quarff, lived in the island of Vaila (Scotland's People 2016). Magnus owned one sixareen and three smaller six-oared boats, all were dipping lug rigged, and each was skippered by one of his four sons: James, aged 21, skippered the 15.5ft (4.7m) keel *St. Andrew*, LK 872; William, aged 28, skippered the 15.5ft (4.7m) *Success*, LK 869; Thomas, aged 32, skippered the 16ft (4.9m), *Racer*, LK 870; and finally Matthew, aged 34, skippered the 18ft (5.5m) keel sixareen *Dauntless*, LK 871.

Women boat owners

Boat ownership in Shetland was not just the preserve of men. There were four women listed as boat owners in the 1869 register. Entrepreneurial women were uncommon during this period, although in British maritime communities there is clear evidence that they existed, and in many cases flourished (Doe 2009: 41-46). The first of these women boat owners was Martha Sinclair Park, from Fetlar, who owned a boat called *Martha*, LK 1563, a six-oared boat, 17ft (5.2m) of keel, square sail rigged, and skippered by Jarm Park, who fished with longlines and nets with a crew of six. So why did Martha own a boat? The reason is perhaps explained by the fact that her husband, Magnus Sinclair, died in 1858, at the young age of 40. Magnus had been a whaler, merchant seaman and crofter. They had nine children, the last of whom, Mary, was born the day after Magnus died. Following the death of Magnus, I suspect the choices Martha faced were limited. The probability is that she and Magnus had been able to save some of his whaling money, which, we might speculate, Martha then used to purchase a six-oared boat. The skipper, Jarm Park, was in all probability a family member and in that way the control of the boat remained firmly within the family.

Next there was Elizabeth Robertson, who lived in Garden, Lunnasting, who owned *Star*, LK 306, a rowing whillie, 10.5ft (3.2m) of keel, skippered by Alexander Robertson. There is very little information about Elizabeth – it appears she did not marry and it is unclear what her relationship was to Alexander. Then there was Rachel Goodlad of West Hogaland in Burra, who was the registered owner of *Vulcan*, LK 80, a rowing fouareen of 12.4ft (3.9m) keel. *Vulcan* was skippered by James Pottinger, who with a crew of two, fished inshore with dorros. James was in fact Rachel's husband, they were married at Quarff in September 1857 when Rachel was 27 and James just 20. The final female entrepreneur was Christina Anderson from Sullom Voe. Chistina was the owner, and intriguingly she was also listed as the skipper, of an 11ft (3.4m) of keel fourareen called *Ann*, LK 876, which had no sail, and fished using dorro lines with one crew member. The boat's registration was cancelled in 1871, with the reason given that the boat was useless. At present nothing more is known about Christina. I strongly suspect that there were other women boatowners and it would be important to be able to uncover their stories.

Boats rigged for sailing

The prevailing types of sailing rigs used were the square sail and the asymmetric dipping square sail, referred to within the fishing boat register as dipping lug. Both types of rig were common and were often used on the same boat types within the same district. As well as these sail configurations there were other less popular rigs: the fore-and-aft main and jib (possibly standing lug or gunter rig); the smack rig; the spritsail rig; the two lugsail rig; and a three lugsail rig. As well as boats being variously rigged for sailing there were also boats that were only rowed and it was striking how many of these were fourareens. Of course, there was variation between districts. Sandsting, for instance, had the greatest percentage of non-sailing six-oared boats (27 per cent) while Cunningsburgh had the largest percentage of non-sailing fourareens (67 per cent). In part this was due to the distances boats were travelling. For example, if a boat was fishing offshore it would have been rigged for sailing. The selection of the type of sailing rig would be subject to variables such as the availability of sail types, the local sail maker's preference, the owner or skipper's personal preference, affordability, or a combination of these factors. Of importance is that many different rigs were in use in 1869. Shetlanders were being influenced by technological sail rig development from elsewhere, which is not surprising, considering that Shetland men were accustomed to serving in the mercantile marine, navy and at the Greenland whaling (Smith, H. 1984:152).

Chapter 9

The modern Shetland boat: part 1

The modern Shetland boat can trace its ancestry back to the Norse period – or so scholars almost unanimously agree. But we must look at the evidence. Instead of seeking to create or support a pure Scandinavian lineage we can ask when, why and how Shetland's vernacular boat came into being.

The direct linking of the Shetland boat to the Norse era was fuelled by an intellectual nineteenth-century romantic vision of Shetland's Viking past. This, I believe, has blurred reality. The economic and social conditions of the eighteenth and nineteenth centuries and the development of commercial fisheries led to changing fishing patterns and of the boats needed to meet these. While there may be many similarities between the boats built in Shetland and those built-in western Norway, they became a true Shetland product when islanders began to diverge from that tradition around 1780. No longer were they Norwegian boats in Shetland, but true *Shetland* vernacular boats.

Viking romanticism

Charles Rampini, who was sheriff-substitute for Caithness, Orkney and Shetland during the 1880s was one of the keenest exponents of Shetland's Norse myth. This myth was devised in the mid to late nineteenth century by writers and scholars such as Gilbert Goudie, J.M.E. Saxby, and J.J. Haldane Burgess, who gradually created Shetland's modern Scandinavian cultural identity (Brown 1998: 34; Grydehøj 2013: 41). Angela Watt in her PhD thesis identified a cultural male heroic bias that has developed in Shetland, which she termed the "Norseman's Bias." Watt suggests that this is "... a cultural persuasion – or tendency – within Shetland to direct attention towards the Nordic world, by both Shetlanders and non-Shetlanders" (Watt 2012:1). This view is supported by academic Adam Grydehøj who argues that this is a consequence of Shetland developing a cultural distinctiveness complemented by self-identification with Scandinavia (Grydehøj 2013: 41). This is exemplified by Rampini who, during two speeches to the Philosophical Institution, Edinburgh, in February 1884, stated:

> To this day, despite telegraphs and Scotch fishcurers, steam communications and tri-weekly
> mails, despite crowds of summer tourists who yearly invade their shores, and despite,

above all, the four hundred years' connection which binds them to the Crown of Scotland, the islands and their inhabitants are still as essentially Norse as when they formed an integral part of the Scandinavian kingdom of Denmark and Norway ... These 'sixerns,' which like the Fair Isle skiff, the Orkney yawl, and the Faroen fishing-boat, were lineal descendants of the lang-skip of Viking times, were perfect in the eyes of the islanders ..." (Rampini 1884: 14, 80).

The Viking myth grew because of Shetland's status as having been Scandinavian and much of its folk culture has Nordic strands (PC, Tait 2016). The populist Viking imagery therefore subsumed the medieval cultural strands that survived. Shetland became Viking because people beyond Shetland wanted Vikings, not because Shetlanders needed this imagery (PC, Tait 2016).

This chapter seeks to ascertain the influences on the development of Shetland's vernacular boats with a comparative analysis of boats built during the late nineteenth and early twentieth centuries in Shetland, western Norway, and Faroe. We can then see the similarities and differences in hull-form, sailing rig configuration, rowing mechanisms, oar shape, rudder shape, and helm assembly.

The hull: how many strakes?

The number of strakes that comprised the hull of a Shetland boat varied according to its size and depth. In general, the number ranged from five on a wide-strake, low-freeboard yoal, to eight or nine on a deep-freeboard haddock boat or sixareen. In western Norway færings from the district of Sunnhordland were constructed from three strakes and seksærings from four, while the larger seksæring and åttring boats were built with a double garboard called the kjølrenne, so technically these craft had five strakes. However, convention dictated that the kjølrenne was considered part of the keel, so these boats were classed as four-strake boats (Økland 2016: 65-66, 449) (Fig. 83). Faroese boats were constructed in a similar manner to those in Hordaland. Indeed, Faroe had its own version of the kjølrenne called the kjalarborð and, like Norway, this strake was regarded as part of the keel (Mortensen 2000: 321) (Fig. 84). As discussed in chapter five, during the late eighteenth century some of the boats-in-boards imported to Shetland were of the kjølrenne type.

In western Norway, in the districts of Bjørnafjorden and Hardanger, the halsane strake – in Shetland called the halsin – was axe-hewn to the desired shape, and this method of construction was also practised in Faroe (Figs. 85-86). However, in the Shetland boatbuilding tradition there is no evidence that this practice of axe-hewing the garbuird and halsin strakes took place. Instead the desired shape was created by bending and twisting the strake after it had been steeped in water. This was originally done by placing the rough-cut strakes in a stream, weighing them down with stones, and leaving them for several days to soak. A strake would then be gently heated over a fire which softened the wood fibres, allowing it to be twisted and bent into the correct shape (Figs. 87-88). By the early twentieth century steam was commonly used. Some later twentieth century Shetland boatbuilders preferred an alternative method to soften wood fibres; this involved coating the part of the strake to be bent and twisted with linseed oil, which was then carefully heated with a blow torch to soften the wood fibres.

Whether using steam or heating the oil-soaked strake with a blow torch, the method to ensure the strake maintained the required shape was the same. It would be clamped in position and left overnight while the fibres cooled and stiffened taking on the new shape. The following day the strake would be final fitted and then fastened into position (PI, Tommy Isbister 2015).

Strake similarities

The Shetland halsin strake, the Norwegian halsane and the Faroese flaborð were all similar. It was divided into three components: a forward end-piece, a middle section and an aft end- piece. In Shetland these components were the fore-halsin, the middle section was the boddam runner, sometimes called the gabuird stroke or the slot, and the last section was called the aft-halsin (Jakobsen 1928: 291) (Fig. 89). Curiously, during the course of my research I observed that three Shetland boats had a forward facing scarph (sker)

Fig. 83. *Kjølrenne on a brugdebåt from Fjell, West Norway. Note the diamond ferrous roves and the axe-hewn kjølrenne and halsane strakes. Boat collection Hordamuseet. Photo: M. Chivers.*

Fig. 84. *Faroese åttamannafar, note the steep rise of the kjalarborð. Photo: M. Chivers. Unst Boat Haven collection.*

Fig. 85. *Oselvar boat builder Hallgeir Forstrønen Bjørnevik beginning to axe the hals into shape. St. Magnus Conference, Lerwick, May 2014. Photo: M. Chivers.*

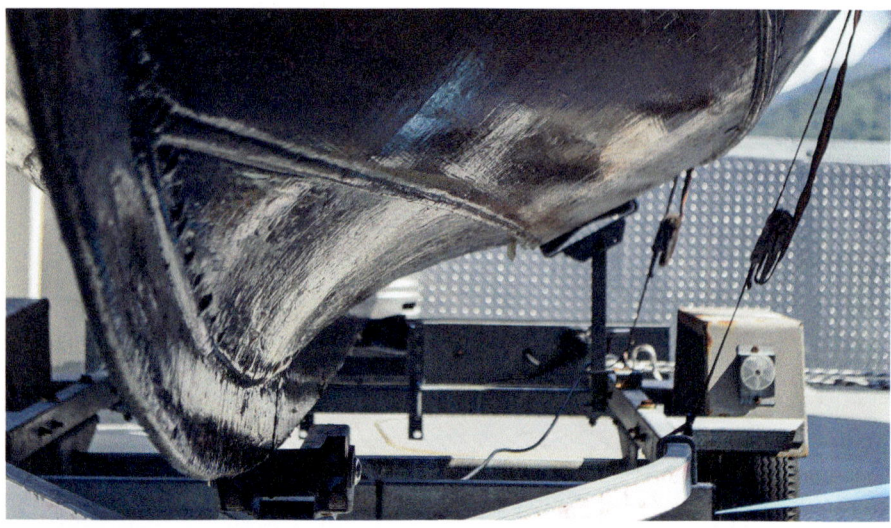

Fig. 86. *Note the wide axe-hewn halsane strake and the entry shape created on this Oselvar. Photo: M. Chivers.*

Fig. 87. *Note the straight garbuird strake with minimum twist on the fourareen* Spindrift. *Photo: M. Chivers.*

Fig. 88. *Note the similar entry shape created on the Gardie boat. This does not have axe-hewn garbuirds or halsin strakes. Unst Boat Haven Collection. Photo: M. Chivers.*

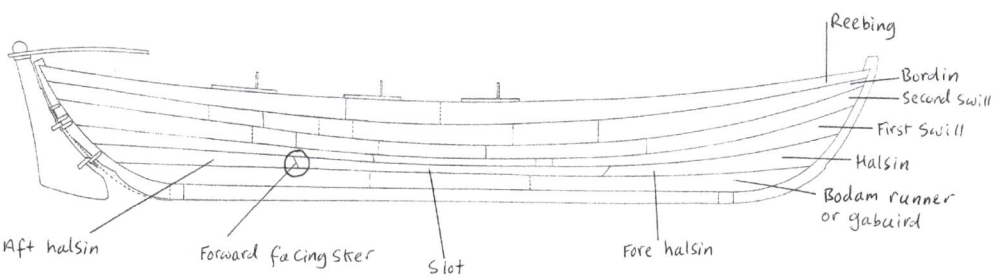

Fig. 89. *Profile plan of the halv yoal* Phar-Lapp *illustrating the names of strakes with the forward facing sker on the aft halsin highlighted. Drawing: M. Chivers.*

Fig. 90. *The John Laurenson fourareen in-situ in Tommy Isbister's barn. The position of the forward facing sker is symmetrically placed on either side of the boat. Photo: M. Chivers.*

joining the slot with the aft halsin, which was symmetrically placed on both sides of the hull. This is unusual, because normal boatbuilding convention dictates that scarph joints should always face aft. Recently I have observed symmetrical port and starboard forward facing skers on several John Eunson and George Johnson built Ness yoals which are currently in private storage (which I hope to document and publish).

This symmetrical port and starboard forward facing sker is easily explained as it originates from western Norway. Until the latter part of the nineteenth century it was traditional boatbuilding practice in the districts of Hardanger and Bjørnafjorden to have a forward facing sker (skaring) on the aft section of the halsin strake, which in Norwegian is called the bakhals. Today this tradition is only practised by builders of Oselvar boats. It was noted by

Shetland boatbuilder Tommy Isbister, who recalled a conversation he had some years ago with the well-known reputable Oselvar boatbuilder, Harald Dalland:

> ... and this board was hewed out. Started with a three-inch plank and he axed it out. And he had a board with the sker going the wrong way [facing forward] so I said, 'Harald, what's the meaning of putting the sker the wrong way?' 'What do you mean? he says ... it's always been done like that.' So I said, 'well what is the reason?' 'Is it easier to repair?' And we both thought about it, and it was nae. And he never knew the reason" (PI, Isbister 2015).

This forward facing sker was also part of the Faroese boatbuilding tradition (PC, Christensen, Bjørnevik and Økland 2014. Mortensen 2000: 321). It seems that this Hordaland tradition was practised in Shetland by some late nineteenth century Shetland boatbuilders, namely: John Laurenson, the Quoys, Catfirth, Nesting; an unknown boatbuilder(s) who worked under the foremanship of Davey Leask for Hay & Company, Lerwick; and John Eunson, Punds, Eastshore, Dunrossness. There is a caveat where Davey Leask is concerned, in that another boat built by him, which is in private ownership on the island of Whalsay, does not have forward facing skers on the halsin strakes. It has to be remembered that Davey Leask was foreman at Hay & Company in Lerwick which had a large boatbuilding concern, and it is traditional practice for the foreman to take credit for each boat built under his foremanship. As there were several boatbuilders working at Hay & Company each might adopt different techniques. The other boatbuilders mentioned were individuals who worked by themselves or with family members.

It seems that Shetland boatbuilders, certainly by the twentieth century, regarded forward facing skers on the halsin strakes as incorrect, and when repairing these strakes corrected this original "error". Indeed, when I mentioned this to contemporary traditional Shetland boatbuilders they all (apart from Tommy Isbister) assumed that the original boatbuilder had made a mistake. The only reason these boats retained this feature is because the strakes in the aft section of these boats are original and have not been replaced.

Figures 90-91 illustrate two of the three Shetland boats that have this forward facing sker. These boats are: the fourareen built by John Laurenson around 1880, which until recently was owned by Tommy Isbister and is now in the Shetland Museum and Archives boat collection; the haddock boat *Brothers*, LK 96, built under the foremanship of Davey Leask about 1888; and the halv yoal LK 203, built by George Eunson around 1910, also in the museum collection. The Laurenson fourareen is in fact a unique material cultural object because it is almost completely original, and provides us with valuable insight into the mind of the late nineteenth century boatbuilder who constructed craft suited for local conditions but continued to follow some Hordaland boatbuilding practices.

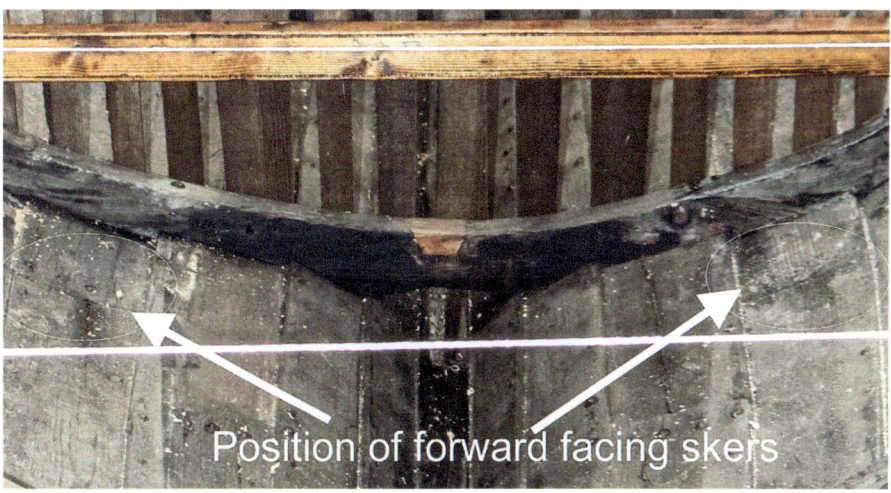

Fig. 91. *The haddock boat* Brothers *LK96. Curiously this sker falls on the fourth strake. Note the fiskvils in the background of this photograph which are attached to the band and bekk-fastiband. Photo: M. Chivers.*

Snikk

Another example of a continued Hordaland tradition was the practice of incorporating a moulded bead on the top inside edge and the bottom outside edge of each strake. In Shetland these mouldings were called the snikk and the tool used was the snikk høvel (translated into English it means snikk plane) (Fig. 92). It is important to note that even Shetland boat luminaries such as Charles Sandison thought the snikk inconsequential, as his letter to T.M.Y. Manson in 1953 illustrates:

> Thank you very much for the P.C. showing one of the small boats from the Gokstad ship. What immediately caught my eye was the shallow bede and line along the inner, upper edge of the planks, in way of the roves. I felt sure I had noticed this in some Shetland boats, but ignored it as meaningless and useless. Today I dashed round and visited 23 Shetland model boats in the north parish - 4 of these have the identical bede and line ... a feature that must have been handed down by tradition! 2 Norwegian skiffs seen at the same time also have it. Another point of interest is that this boat has just 5 planks a side, and it was just this number of planks that the old carpenter was able to give me names for – Boddam Runners, Hassings, First Swille, Second Swille and Reebin (what we would now call the sheer strake) (SMA, D37/1/85/81/1).

Oselvar boatbuilder Hallgeir Forstrønen Bjørnevik says that the snikk, although now considered decorative, actually served a function in that it enabled the boat strakes to flex slightly at the point where they were joined:

Fig. 92. *Snikk høvel that belonged to Jack Shewan. Owned by Robbie Simpson, Vevoe, Whalsay. Photo: M. Chivers.*

> ... the whole boat benefits from this flexing ... because the boat will be more soft to work in when out fishing. In a stiff boat your body will start hurting sooner than in a more flexible boat. This was important for the fishermen, and the first thing they did with a new boat was to shake it to see how flexible it was. Fishermen said it was better to take in some water than have a stiff boat. (PC, Bjørnevik 2015).

This snikk pattern dates from 1,000 CE, and can be found on a few twentieth century Shetland boats, but now is often consigned to the reebin (sheer) strake, an echo of its original purpose (Figs. 93-98).

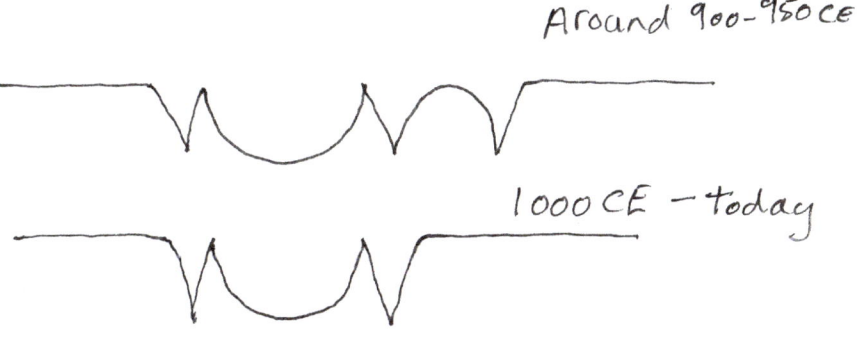

Fig. 93. *Gokstad færing with Norse moulding visible on the stem. Viking Ship Museum, Oslo. Photo: M. Chivers.*

Fig. 94. *The moulding in use from 900-950 CE and from 1000 CE until the present day. Drawing: M. Chivers after Arne Emil Christensen (2015).*

Fig. 95. *Note the same snikk detail on the fourareen built by John Laurenson c.1880. Photo: M. Chivers.*

Fig. 96. *The same snikk on the brugdebåt from Fjell c. 1800. Hordamuseet collection. Photo: M. Chivers.*

Fig. 97. *The same snikk can be seen on this Oselvar built by Stig Henneman, Oselvarverkstaden, Hamnevegen, Os. Photo: M. Chivers.*

Fig. 98. *Again, the same snikk pattern on this fourareen built by Tommy Isbister, Burland, Trondra. Photo: M. Chivers.*

Fastenings

Until the latter-part of the nineteenth century the strakes on Shetland's vernacular boats, as in other parts of Northern Europe, were ferrous fastened, using hand-forged nails (sem) and diamond roves (røv). The roves were made from black iron strips. These strips first had holes punched through, and then the strips were partially cut-through, at an angle, making each rove rhomboid in shape. When needed the rove was simply snapped-off the strip, driven onto the sem by means of a tool called a sem kløv which was also used in the process of forming the rivet (Fig. 99) (PC, Christensen 2014 and PC, Tait 2016). By 1880 manufactured nails and round roves were commonly being used as can be seen in the aforementioned boats, the fourareen built around 1880, by John Laurenson; the haddock boat, *Brothers*, LK 96, built in 1888; the sixareen *Industry*, LK 718, built in 1891 by Malcolm Laurenson; and the fourareen *Ann*, LK 15, built in 1899 by Laurence Goodlad, Lerwick (Fig. 100). It is worth noting that Shetland began using manufactured nails and roves some 20 years prior to western Norway, where mass produced boat fastenings only began to be used around 1900. That Norway did not use these mass produced items earlier was at least in part due to it being economically impoverished during this period (PC, Christensen 2014).

There was a cross-over period when both the new manufactured round roves and the old hand-forged diamond roves were being used. This can be seen in the Shetland Museum and Archives' exhibit, the sixareen *Mary*, LK 981. A detailed constructional analysis of the *Mary* was undertaken in 2016 by marine archaeologist Dr Michael Stratigos, museum curator Dr Ian Tait, and the author. The *Mary* was built prior to 1869 and is constructed from nine strakes fastened with ferrous nails and diamond roves. We initially thought the hull was fastened with hand-forged ferrous fastenings. On closer inspection we were surprised to find evidence of galvanization which suggests that these were in fact early industrially manufactured galvanized items (Fig. 101). The use of galvanized diamond roves had previously been found by Tait

Fig. 99. *Sem kløv at top of photograph, below sem and røv (nails and roves). Photo: M. Chivers. Courtesy of Shetland Museum & Archives.*

on the remains of a boat believed to have been *Hope*, LK 352, which was built in 1899 in Skerries (Chivers, Stratigos, and Tait, 2019: 455). This material evidence is further supported by newspaper advertisements for galvanized boat fastenings found, by Adrian Osler, in the *Newcastle and Tyne Mercury* dated Saturday, 21st February, 1846, and in *The Cumberland Pacquet, and Ware's Whitehaven Advertiser* of Tuesday, 24th February, 1857. This points to the early use of galvanized boat fastenings by provincial boatbuilders (PC, Osler 2020).

During the *Mary's* working life damaged or rotten strakes were replaced. One repair was made with galvanised diamond fastenings and we think this is the earliest repair. Later repairs were made with industrially manufactured round galvanised roves. An example of a repaired strake is illustrated in Fig. 102. As well as replacement galvanized round roves the indentations from

Fig. 100. *Original round iron fastenings on the fourareen* Ann *LK15. Note also the snikk. Shetland Museum & Archives boat collection. Photo: M. Chivers.*

Fig. 101. *Some of the* Mary's *original galvanized diamond fastenings. Shetland Museum & Archives collection. Photo: M. Chivers.*

Fig. 102. *Replacement strake on the* Mary *LK 981. Note the imprint of the original diamond rove fastening with the nail hole plugged. Shetland Museum & Archives collection. Photo: M. Chivers.*

Fig. 103. *The sixareen* Industry *built using manufactured round roves and then later repaired and heightened by the addition of two thin strakes fastened with hand-forged roves, presumably old stock. Photo: M. Chivers.*

the previous diamond roves are clearly visible on the planking, as are the wooden pegs, used to plug the old fastening holes. These fastenings provide us with a provisional transitional period for the gradual development and use in Shetland of industrially manufactured galvanised boat fastenings. The period spans the working life of the *Mary*, which was prior to 1869, until sometime after 1891 (Chivers, Stratigos and Tait, 2019: 446; 449 - 4450; 455). As mentioned previously, the sixareen *Industry* was built using round roves, and it was surprising to find that later repairs had been made using the hand-forged type –presumably these roves were old stock (Fig. 103).

Boats built for local conditions

The evidence thus far has led me to believe that Shetland boatbuilders began to develop their own eclectic tradition from around 1770. Indigenous developments in boatbuilding were no doubt spurred on as a consequence of the development of the haaf fishery, the availability of raw materials, and individual, or district wide, boatbuilding preferences. My opinion falls in line with that of the boat ethnographer Eric McKee who, in *Working Boats of Britain*, published in 1983, described how indigenous boats become locally modified as a consequence of a change to their surroundings, the availability of materials, or the boat's purpose (McKee 1983: 18). In Shetland's case there was a west Norwegian influence on Shetland boat design. An example of this is found in the manufacture of the stameron, which in western Norway was called a rong, and which was always made from a grown crook (Fig. 104). The previously discussed eighteenth and nineteenth century evidence for the importation of crooks from Norway illustrates that these were also used in Shetland. However, when this boat and timber import trade stopped it became difficult to obtain these items, and this is probably when local builders adapted and crafted the stameron from several separate pieces of timber as illustrated in Fig. 105.

Bands

Other variations in hull construction are found in the manufacture of the bands (frames) sometimes spelt baunds. The positioning of these bands in Shetland and west Norwegian boats was very similar, but this was not the case in Faroe where the bands were more numerous, and their scantling sizes were reduced (Figs. 106-108).

As can be seen, there is a variance in the construction of these bands. Each is distinct, with some similarities and some significant differences. The Norwegian and Faroese bands are similar in that the cross beam is constructed from two grown crooks (one either end of the band). In this context these grown crooks are called knees. The Norwegian cross beam (bete) however, ends beneath the inwale, whereas in the majority of Shetland and Faroese boats the frame ends at the inwale's top inside edge. The Fair Isle yoal is an exception as its bands

Fig. 104. *The aft rong is made from a grown crook in this post boat built in 1848 from Fusa, Bjørnefjorden. Hordamuseet collection. Photo: M. Chivers.*

Fig. 105. *Fore stammeron constructed from three pieces of timber which have been joined with half-lap joints and then rivetted together. Fourareen* Girl Chrissie *built by Davie Bruce in 1949 at Skaw, Whalsay. Photo: M. Chivers.*

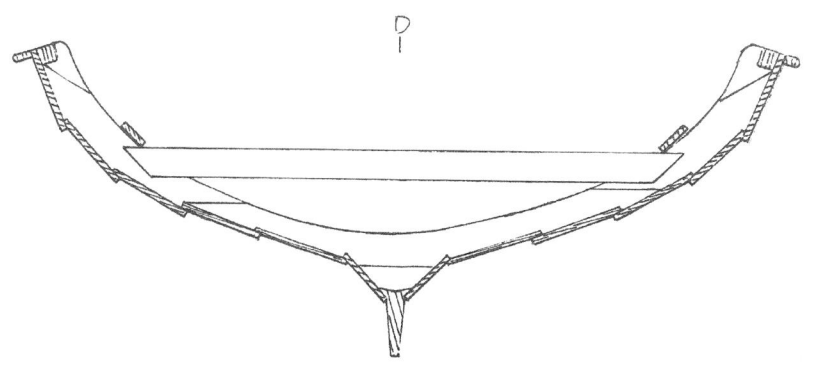

Fig. 106. *Mid cross-section of the fourareen* Ann *LK 15. Built by Laurence Goodlad in Lerwick, 1899. Drawing: M. Chivers.*

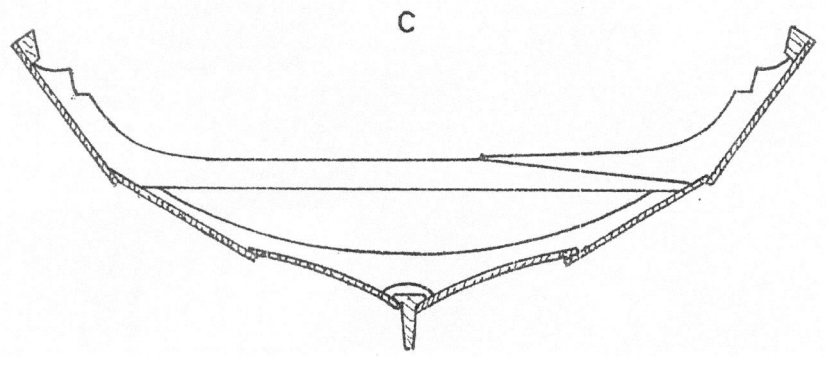

Fig. 107. *Mid cross-section of an Oselvar havbåt. Drawing: Arne Emil Christensen. Courtesy of the Norwegian Maritime Museum, Oslo.*

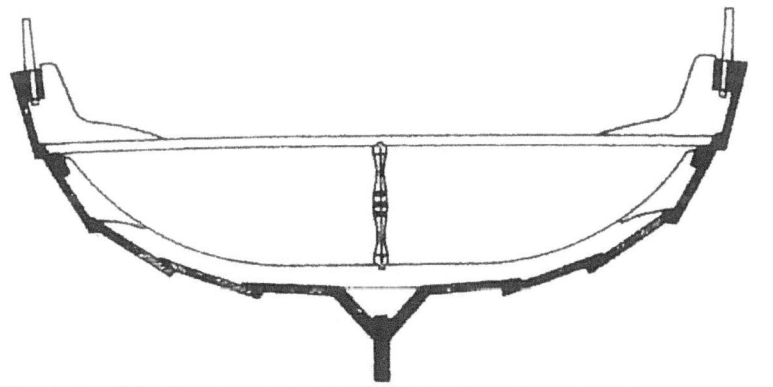

Fig. 108. *Mid cross-section of a Faroese tríbekkir. Drawing: Andras Mortensen. Courtesy Andras Mortensen.*

end below the inwale (Osler 1983: 70-71, 77-78). The two knees that comprise the bete also have a notch cut into them onto which the bench, called a toft in Norwegian, fits. Conversely the Faroese cross beam (bekkur) is not removeable and is fixed in position by the knees. As can be seen in Fig. 108 the bekkur is supported by an upright central member – this feature is absent in both the Oselvar and the fourareen.

Of note is that the Shetland fourareen has a rubbing strake (rimwol) fastened to the outside of the reebin (sheer strake) which is absent on both the Norwegian and Farose boats. The cross beam on the fourareen – which in Shetland is known by various regional names such as bekk, fastiband or haddabaund – was constructed from a separate piece of timber fastened in place by nails or, in more recent construction, screws. On top of the bekk, on either side of the hull, is a stringer running fore and aft called the warin, sometimes called wearing, upon which the taft (thwart) rests. It can be clearly seen that the Shetland and Faroese builders developed their own methods for making bands. Both in Shetland and in Faroe the construction and arrangement of frame, crossbeam, and thwart has departed significantly from that of the boat types from Hordaland, whose frame construction remains remarkably similar to that of the Gokstad færing (Fig. 109). Noteworthy is that the Shetland and Norwegian mid-section hull shape is similar, in contrast to the Faroese boat which has a much fuller shape and a distinct Y shaped keel and garboard arrangement.

An interesting find was made by Alan Moncrieff around 35 years ago when Alan and his brother Jim were erecting a fence in Bigton, near Spiggie Loch. They were digging a hole for a straining post when Alan discovered a Norwegian style bete (Figs. 110-111). This is now in the possession of the Shetland Museum and Archives. This bete is unusual as it has no moulding and is fastened together with manufactured nails and round roves, suggesting that it was made in Hardanger at some point during the early twentieth century (PC, Christensen 2015). However, there are some anomalies in that the scarphs are fastened by means of manufactured galvanized ring nails, something that would not have been done in Hardanger, where the scarph would have been riveted. There is also a trace of toredo worm which suggests that either it was constructed from driftwood, something that would not have been done in Norway, or that the bete itself had spent a period of time in the sea (PC, Tait 2016). The provenance of this bete continues to be speculated.

The hinnispot

The Faroese linguist Jakob Jakobsen, in his dictionary of the Norn language, described the hinnispot (breast hook) as being a triangular piece of timber that tied the two sides of the hull together (Jakobsen 1928: 314). The hinnispot is present on all Shetland vernacular boats and is fastened in place by means of diagonal riveting and nailing through the inwale and reebin strake (Fig. 112). Notably the breast hook is absent in all the west Norwegian and Faroese boats.

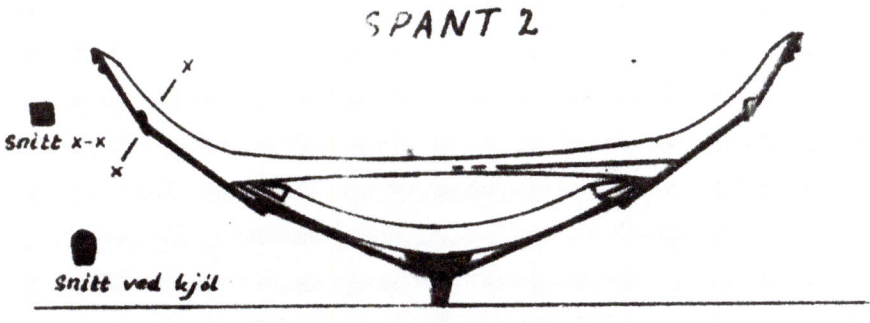

Fig. 109. *Mid cross-section of the Gokstad færing. Drawing by Arne Emil Christensen (1959). Courtesy of the Norwegian Maritime Museum, Oslo.*

Fig. 110. *Bete found by Alan Moncrieff about 35 years ago in Bigton. Photo: M. Chivers.*

Fig. 111. *Note the grown crook knee. Photo: M. Chivers.*

Fig. 112. *The hinnispot on the John Laurenson built fourareen (c.1880) previously owned by Tommy Isbister and now owned by Shetland Museum & Archives. Photo: M. Chivers.*

Hinnispot is a Norn word which suggests that it has been part of Shetland boat construction terminology since the Middle Ages. This is puzzling, as the documentary evidence illustrates that the boats imported from Norway came from the Bjørnefjord and the Hardanger districts and boats from these places during that period did not have breast hooks.

A possibility is that the hinnispot was adopted from another boatbuilding culture, maybe from mainland Scotland, but its Old Norse provenance means that this is unlikely (*Dictionary of the Scots Language* 2016). More likely is that the hinnispot was originally used in the construction of larger vessels, such as the previously discussed skuda, and its use was later transferred to the fourareen and sixareen, when the Norn language was still in common use in Shetland. This must have been prior to the late eighteenth century which is when Norn died-out (Knooihuzen 2008: 110). Speculatively, the hinnispot lends further credence to the adaptation of Norwegian imported boats to suit Shetland sea conditions and its Norn provenance fits with the evidence so far discussed.

A comparison of hull shapes

Faroese and Shetland vernacular boats developed from the west Norwegian boats that were once imported. Comparing the similarities and differences between the hull shape of boats from Shetland, west Norway and Faroe tells us a lot about how they have developed from the original west Norwegian four-oared boat of the Norse period (Figs. 113-126). To assist us we are fortunate to be able to use

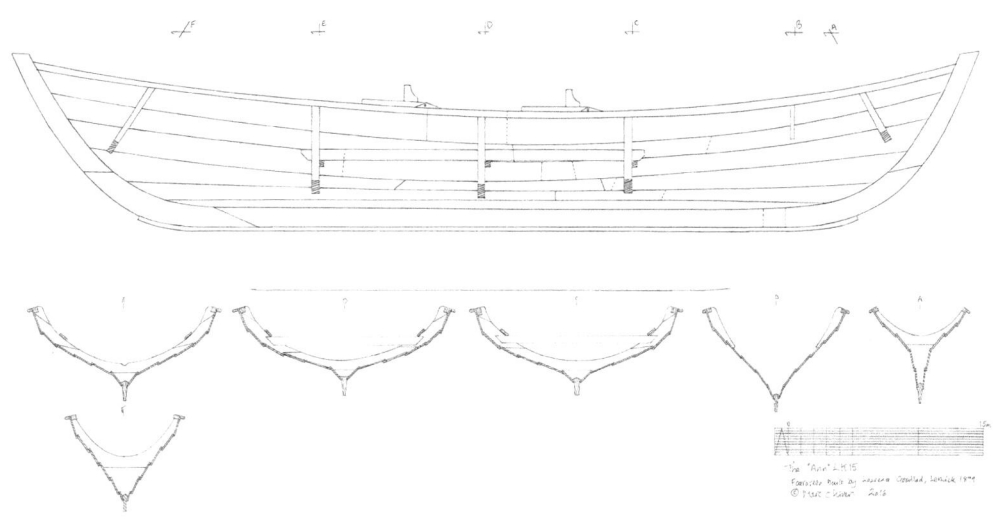

Fig. 113. Ann *LK 15 in cross-section view. Built by Laurence Goodlad in 1899. Length of keel 10.3ft (3.14m), length overall 17.5ft (5.34m), beam 5.5ft (1.68m). Drawing: M. Chivers.*

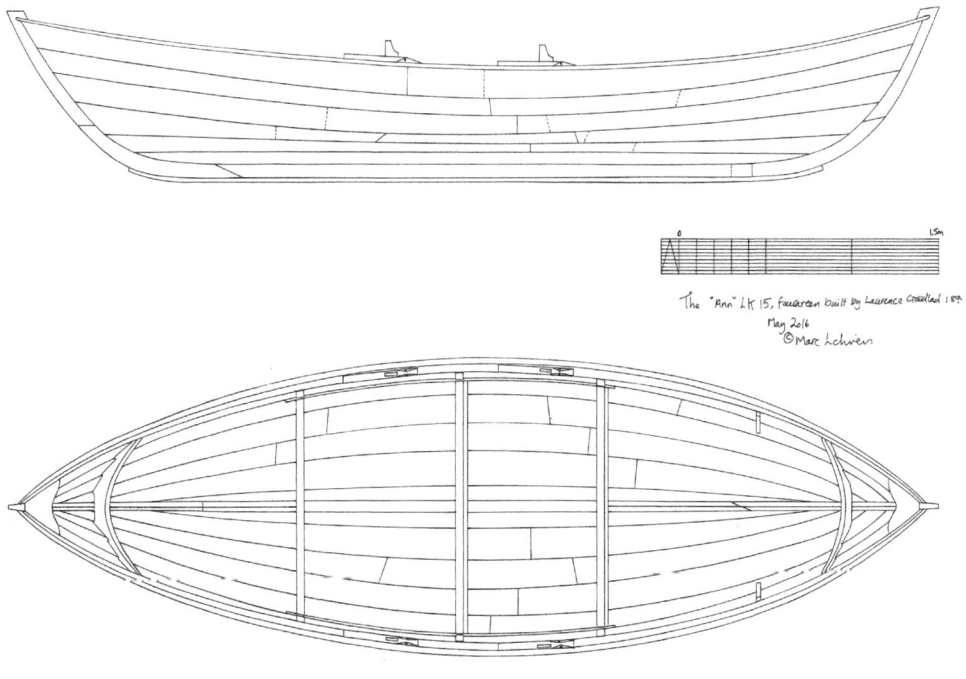

Fig. 114. Ann *LK 15 in profile and plan view. Drawing: M. Chivers.*

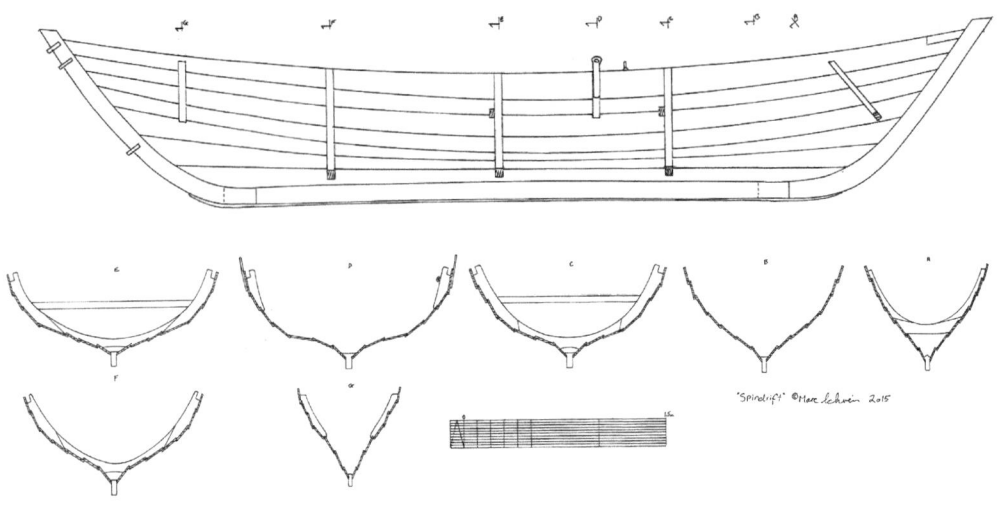

Fig. 115. Spindrift, *a racing fourareen, in cross-section view. Built by Lowrie Smith (c.1937). Length of keel 10ft (3.05m), length overall 16.8ft (5.12m), beam 5.2ft (1.58m). Drawing: M. Chivers.*

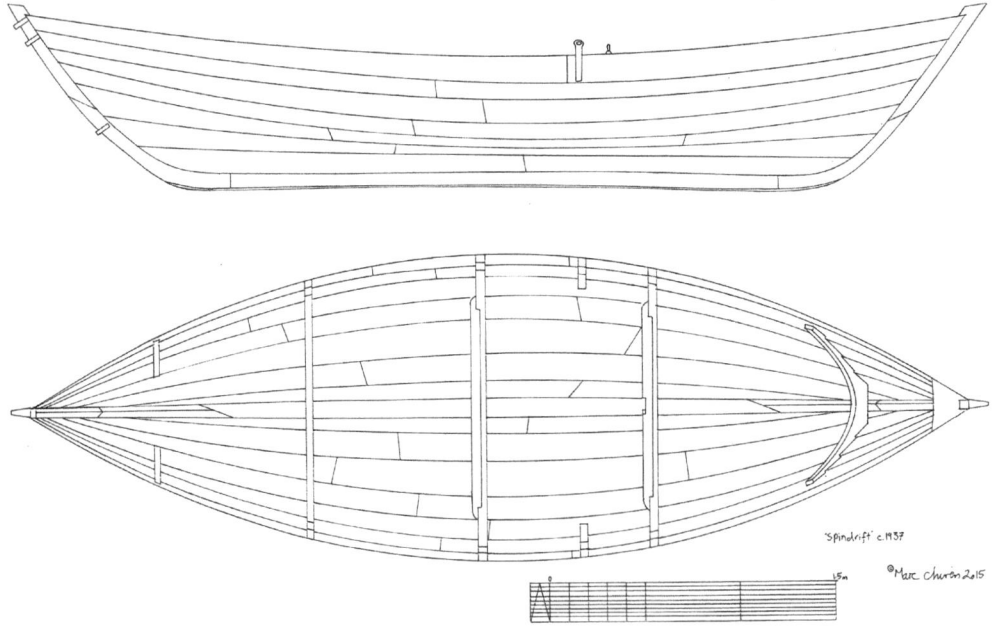

Fig. 116. Spindrift *in profile and plan view. Drawing: M. Chivers.*

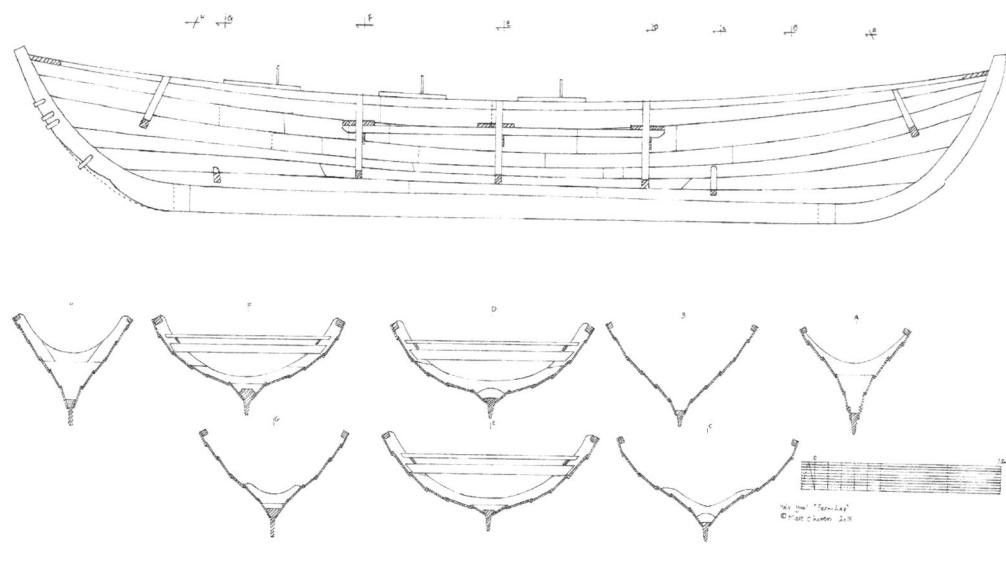

Fig. 117. *Halv yoal, latterly called* Phar-Lap, *in cross-section view. Built by George Eunson (c.1890). Length of keel 13.3ft (4.04m), length overall 19.9ft (6.06m), beam 5.3ft (1.61m). Drawing: M. Chivers.*

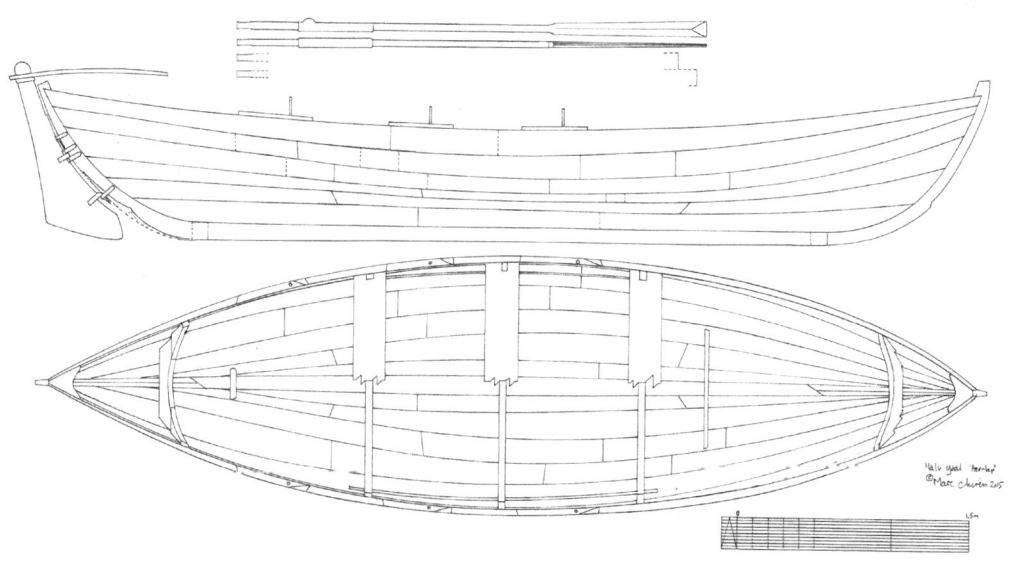

Fig. 118. Phar-Lap *in profile and plan view. Drawing: M. Chivers.*

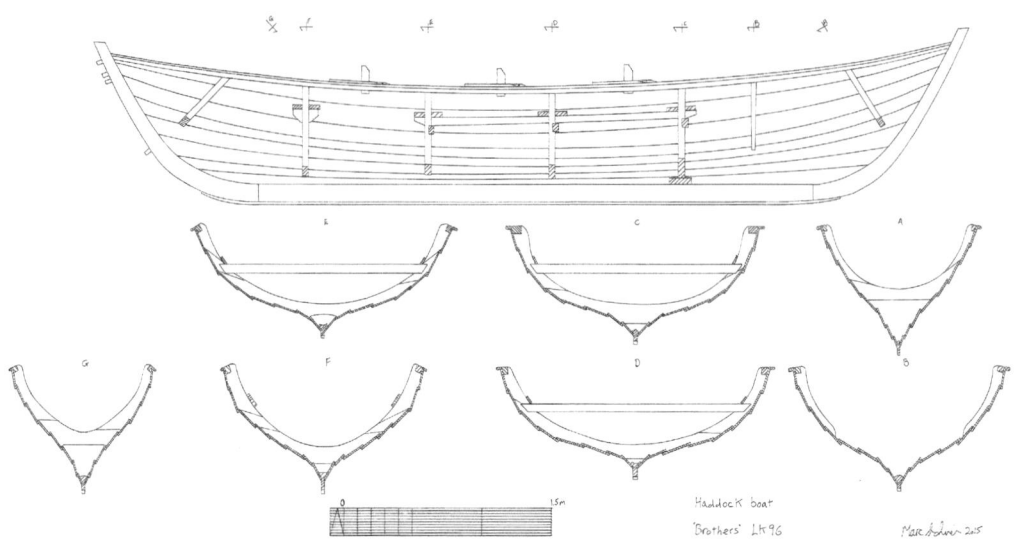

Fig. 119. *Cross-section view of the haddock boat* Brothers *LK 96. Length overall 20.7ft (6.32m), beam 6.6ft (2m). Built by Davie Leask, Lerwick 1888. Drawing: M. Chivers.*

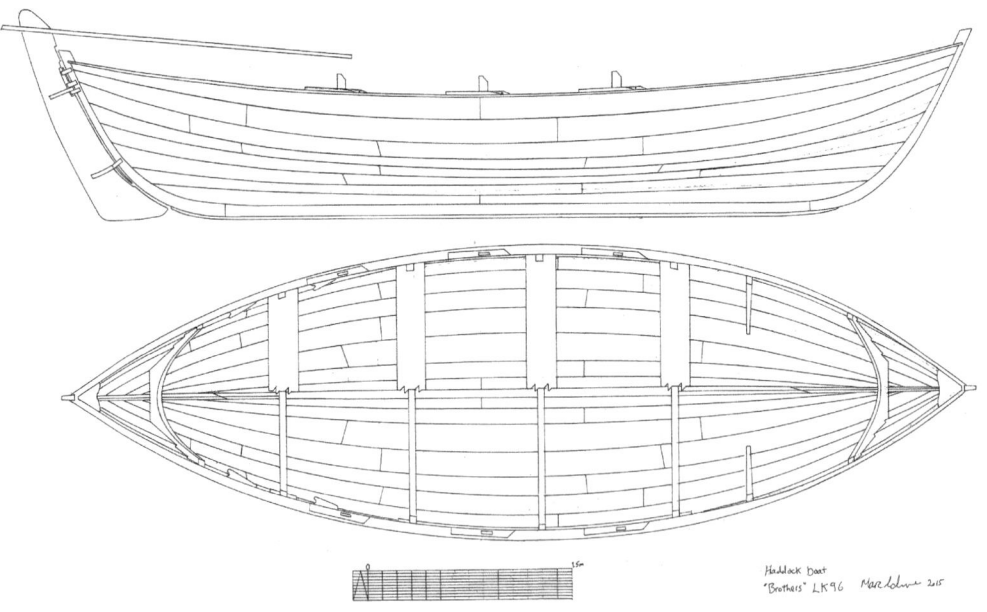

Fig. 120. *Profile and plan view of haddock boat* Brothers *LK 96. Drawing: M. Chivers.*

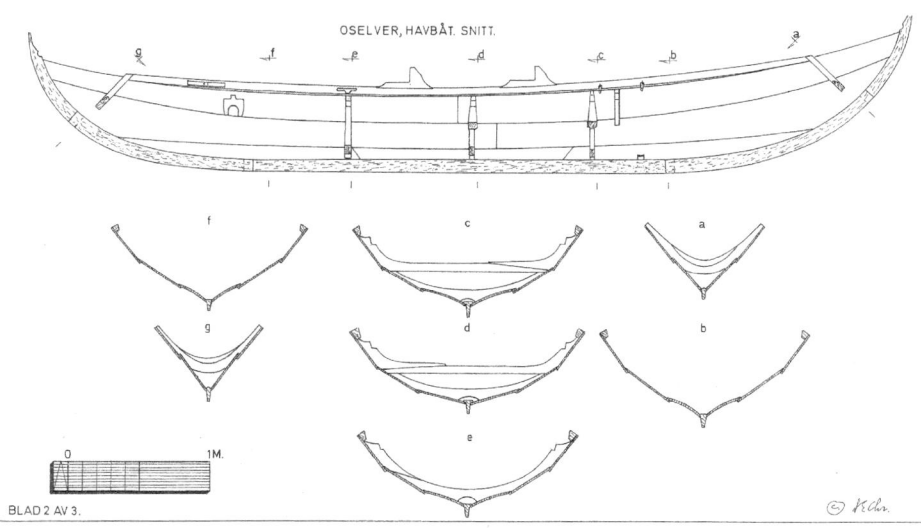

Fig. 121. *Cross-section view of an Oselvar havbåt. Length of keel 9.84 ft (3m), length overall 17.7ft (5.4m), beam 4.8ft (1.4m). Drawing: Arne Emil Christensen. Courtesy of the Norwegian Maritime Museum, Oslo.*

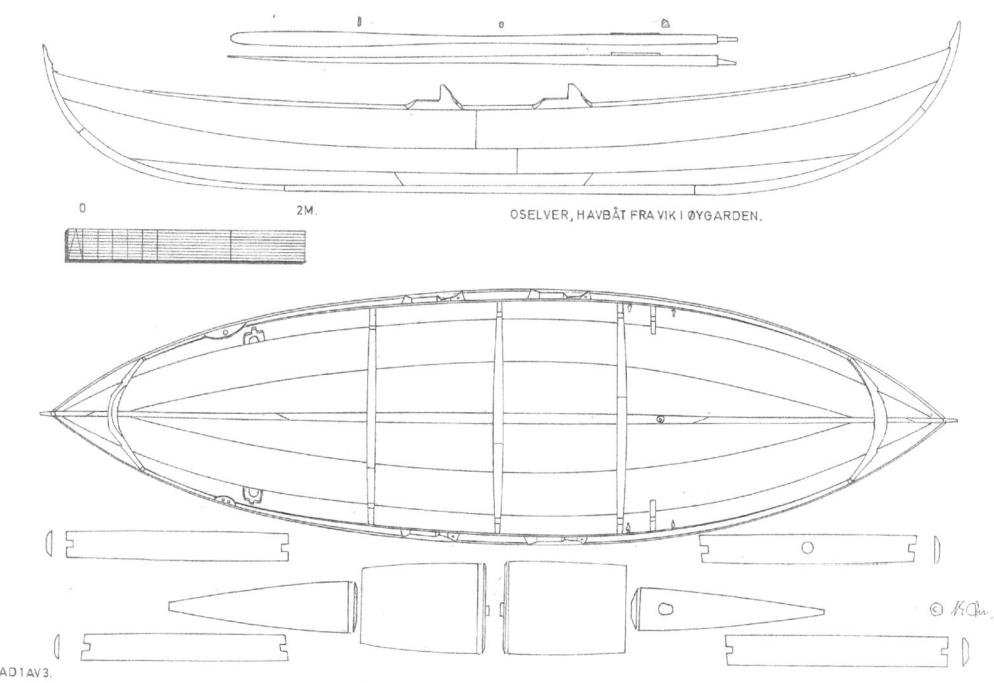

Fig. 122. *Oslevar havbåt in profile and plan view. Drawing: Arne Emil Christensen. Courtesy of the Norwegian Maritime Museum, Oslo.*

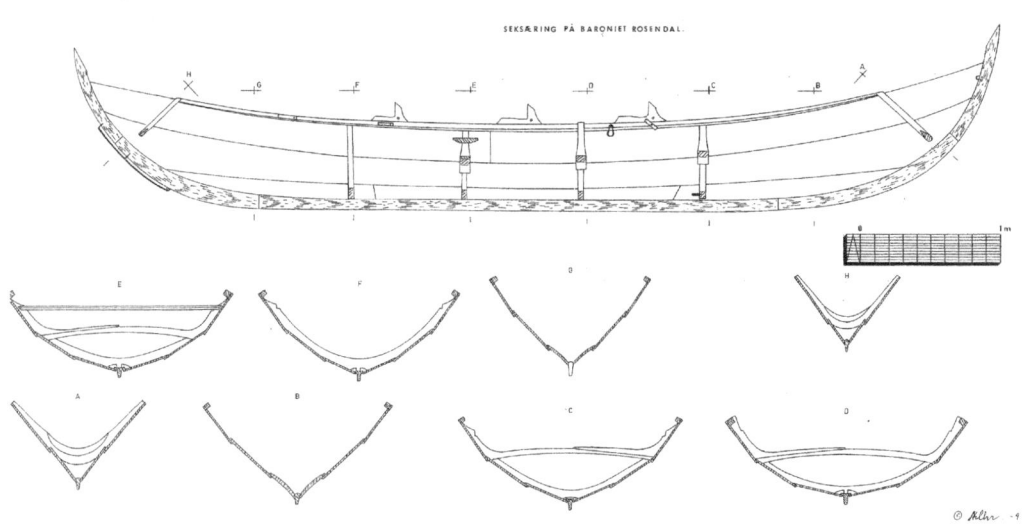

Fig. 123. *Cross-section view of a seksæring from the Barony Rosendal. Length overall 19.7ft (6m), beam 5.2ft (1.6m), depth midships 1.5ft (48cm). Drawing: Arne Emil Christensen. Courtesy of the Norwegian Maritime Museum, Oslo.*

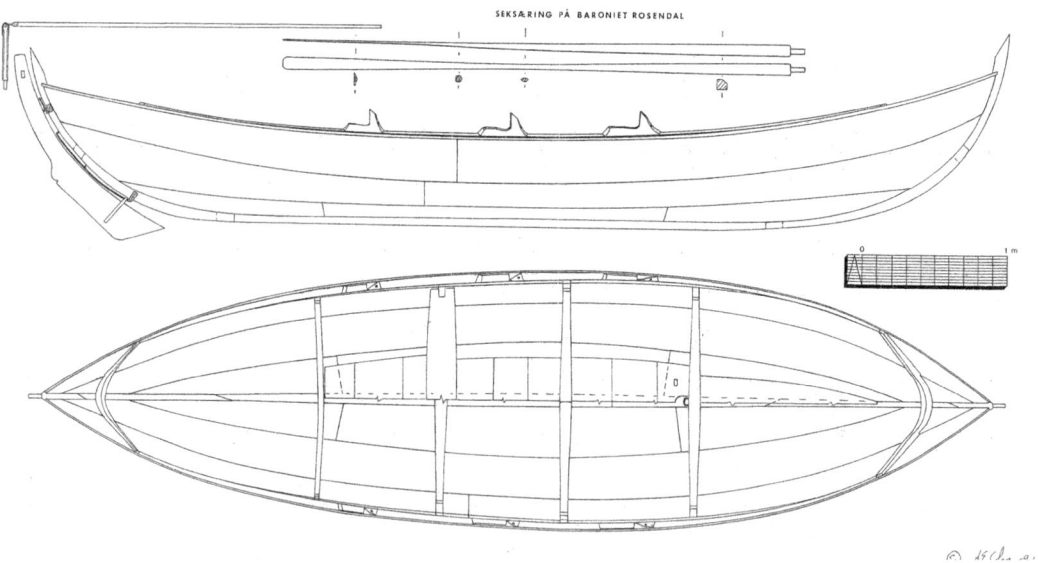

Fig. 124. *Profile and plan view of the seksæring from the Barony Rosendal. Drawing Arne Emil Christensen. Courtesy of the Norwegian Maritime Museum, Oslo.*

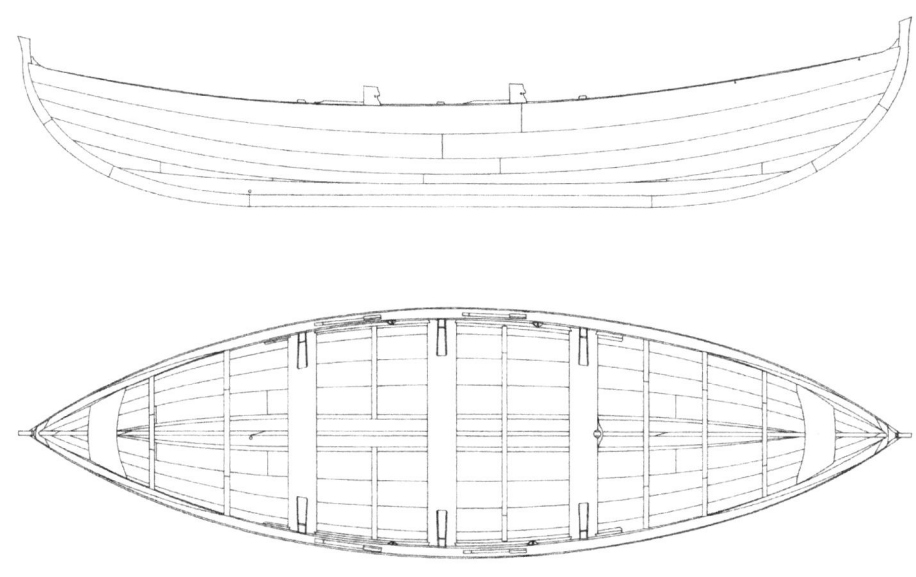

Fig. 125. *Profile and plan view of Faroese tríbekkir. Built by Tummus Jakku c.1922. Overall length 17.3ft (5.3m), beam 4.1ft (1.2m). Drawing: Andras Mortensen. Courtesy of Andras Mortensen.*

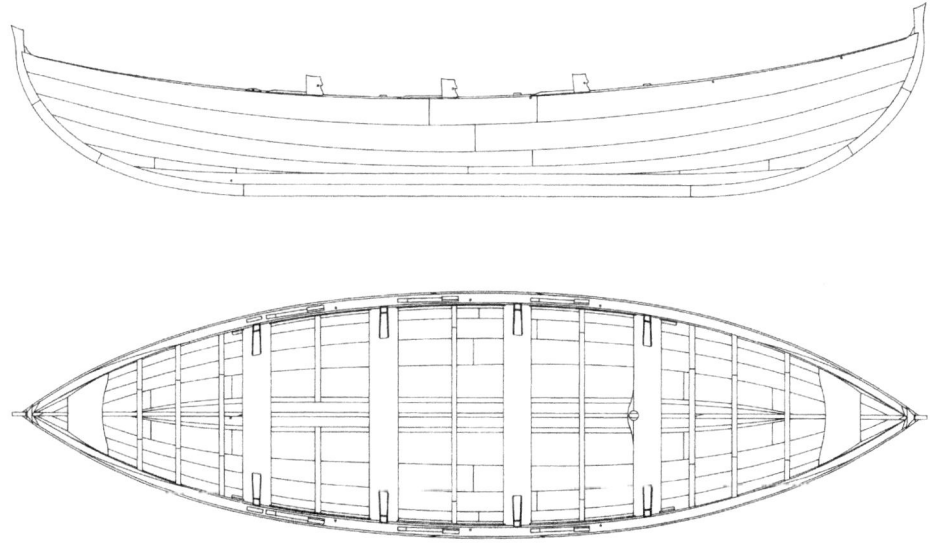

Fig. 126. *Profile and plan view of a Trista. Built by Hans Petur Simonsen c.1911. Length overall 18.1ft (5.5m), beam 3.5ft (1.1m). Drawing: Andras Mortensen. Courtesy of Andras Mortensen.*

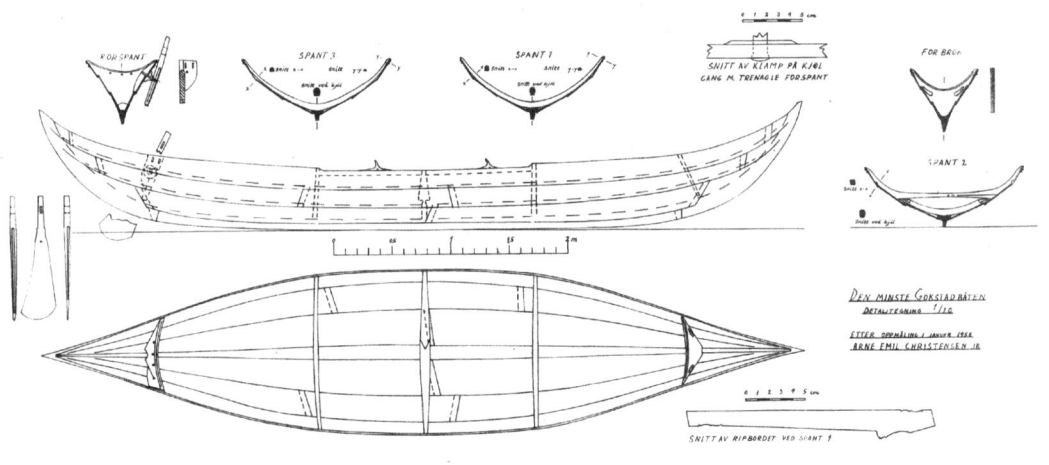

Fig. 127. *Cross-section and plan view of the Gokstad færing. Length overall 21.3ft (6.2m), beam 4.4ft (1.3m). Drawing: Arne Emil Christensen. Courtesy of the National Norwegian Maritime Muesum, Oslo.*

the oldest surviving færing, dated to around 890 CE. As previously described this færing was part of the furniture of a large ship burial found at Gokstad farm in Sandar, Sandefjord, Vestfold, Norway in 1880. The Gokstad færing was documented and drawn by Norwegian maritime archaeologist Emeritus Professor Arne Emil Christensen in 1959 (Fig. 127). This is used for comparison with the hull shape of various Shetland, west Norwegian and Faroese late nineteenth and early twentieth century boats.

One simple method used to compare hull shape is the length to beam ratio. This is obtained by dividing the length of the boat by its beam (maximum width). Boats with a length to beam ratio of 2.6 and under are considered broad whilst those over 3.75 are classed as narrow (Table 15). Another simple ratio tells us if it is deep or shallow. This number is calculated by dividing the beam of the boat by its depth, measured from the height of the sheer line to the top of the keel. Numbers of two and under are considered deep whilst those of three and above are shallow (Mckee, 1983: 81) (Table 16).

As can be seen from Table 15, the length to beam ratio amongst this selection of boats was reasonably close. The halv yoal *Phar-Lap* was of the same proportion as the seksæring and the tríbekkir and these were slightly narrower than the Norwegian havbåt. It is striking how close in proportion the havbåt and the tríbekkir are. It is also interesting to note that the two Shetland fourareens and the haddock boat were similar in respect of their length to beam ratios, all having an average beam for their overall length. The Gokstad færing, on the other hand, had the largest length to beam ratio, making it the narrowest boat for its

Boat type & name	Length overall	Beam	Length to beam ratio
Fourareen Ann	17.5ft (5.3m)	5.5ft (1.7m)	3.1
Fouareen Spindrift	16.8ft (5.1m)	5.2ft (1.6m)	3.2
Halv yoal Phar-Lap	19.9ft (6.1m)	5.3ft (1.6m)	3.8
Haddock boat Brothers	21.0ft (6.3m)	6.5ft (2.0m)	3.2
Havbåt	17.7ft (5.4m)	4.8ft (1.4m)	3.9
Seksæring	19.7ft (6.0m)	5.2ft (1.6m)	3.8
Trîbekkir	17.3ft (5.3m)	4.8ft (1.4m)	3.8
Trista	18.1ft (5.5m)	4.9ft (1.5m)	3.7
Gokstad færing	21.3ft (6.5m)	4.4ft (1.3m)	5

Table 15. *Comparative length to beam ratio of boats.*

Boat type & name	Beam	Depth	Beam to depth ratio
Fourareen Anne	5.5ft (1.7m)	1.7ft (53cm)	3.2
Fouareen Spindrift	5.2ft (1.6m)	1.9ft (57cm)	2.6
Halv yoal Phar-Lap	5.3ft (1.6m)	1.8ft (56cm)	2.8
Haddock boat the Brothers	6.6ft (2m)	2.3ft (70cm)	2.9
Havbåt	4.8ft (1.5m)	1.5ft (48cm)	3.1
Seksæring	5.2ft (1.6m)	1.6ft (50cm)	3.2
Trîbekkir	4.1ft (1.2m)	1.5ft (46cm)	2.6
Trista	3.5ft (1.1m)	1.4ft (44cm)	2.5
Gokstad færing	4.5ft (1.4m)	1.6ft (49cm)	2.9

Table 16. *Comparative beam to depth ratios.*

overall length. The shallowest boats were the fourareen *Ann*, LK 15, the havbåt and the seksæring; all the others fell within the middle range. This, combined with a close examination of the drawings illustrates some striking similarities in hull shape. This representative sample of boats from the late nineteenth and early twentieth centuries illustrates that proportionally they were comparable. Such comparative ratios were previously examined by Sandison (1954) and Osler (1975, 1983) with comparable results. The fourareen *Ann*, the halv yoal, havbåt and the seksæring being the most similar.

The shape of the stem profiles of the west Norwegian and Faroese boats are similar to that of the Gokstad færing, whereas the Shetland boats are markedly different, and this illustrates a departure from the west Norwegian tradition. This suggests that the Norse lineage is present in the wide sense but the final developed Shetland hull-form has moved away from its predecessor, as shown by the shape of the stems. Christensen observed that Shetland boats, having narrower and more numerous strakes, resemble boats from eastern Norway. This is possible because, as we have already seen, Shetland's timber imports became centred there during the nineteenth century (PC Christensen 2014). In his book *Boats of the North: A History of Boatbuilding in Norway* Christensen discussed the Norse boatbuilding legacy which, he stated, still existed on the west coast of Norway and on the Baltic coasts of Finland and Sweden (Christensen 1968: 12). These regions retained much of their boatbuilding traditions, including the hull form that was present in the Norse period. By contrast western Sweden, eastern Norway and Denmark have boat types further removed from those of that period.

The original west Norwegian boats imported to Shetland retained characteristics handed down from the Norse period. Indeed, by comparing the Gokstad færing with the havbåt and the seksæring, it is evident that there is a continuation in boatbuilding tradition that has clear links with western Norway's Norse boatbuilding past. However, it is apparent that in Shetland the remaining echoes of a west Norwegian boatbuilding tradition were disappearing rapidly by the latter part of the nineteenth century. As previously discussed, this falls in line with the ending of the Norwegian boat and timber import trade, by which time Shetland boatbuilders had already been exposed to many other boatbuilding influences – from Scotland, the rest of the United Kingdom and overseas.

The sail

As we have already discovered, the dominant types of sailing rigs used in Shetland during the late nineteenth century were the square sail and the asymmetric dipping square sail, often referred to as a dipping lug. Other, less common, spritsail and smack (fore-and-aft configured) rigs were also being used in Shetland at this time. During this period in the counties of Rogaland and Hordaland in western Norway the square sail gave way to the more popular spritsail rig. To improve the performance of boats with this rig builders in Rogaland constructed boats that were slightly broader in the beam (Christensen 1979: 26). The mast was moved from the centre of the boat to approximately two-thirds of the way forward from the aft end (Fig. 128). It can be surmised that these changes to boat shape and mast position must have also occurred to boats that were similarly rigged in Shetland.

The Danish Governor in Faroe, Christian Pløyen, who visited Shetland in 1839, observed that sail was used more frequently than oars. He also described

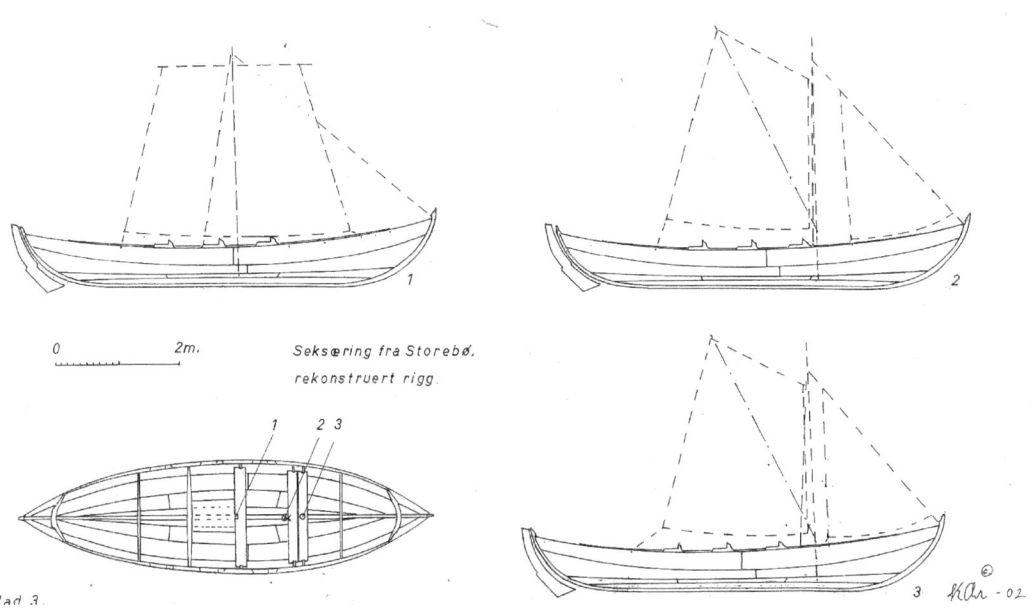

Fig. 128. *Different mast positions for the square sail rig (1) and the spritsail rig (2, 3) on a seksæring from Storebø. Drawing: Arne Emil Christensen. Courtesy of the Norwegian Maritime Museum, Oslo.*

the mast, which in Shetland "is very tall, and the sail, which is a square sail, is likewise high, but narrow in proportion to the yard; it is furnished with two or three rows of reef points, which are commonly used." He thought that this type of sail would not be suited for use in Faroe "on account of the frequency of heavy squalls, which rush down our steep hills …" Pløyen also described the sheeting arrangement:

> … but the sheet which is very long, is fastened from the outside through a hole in the gunwale of the boat, this again is passed through a thimble or a small block, which is in the corner of the sail, and the end of it is held in one of the steersman's hands. He thus holds the rudder in the one hand, and the sheet in the other, and can at pleasure veer and hale at the moment he considers it necessary, and this too he can do without apparent exertion of strength, as the sheet runs through a block, which increases the power (Pløyen 1896: 23-24).

Jessie Saxby wrote, in 1880, that the mast on the sixareen was generally the length of the keel, and was placed in the mid-room taft, a little forward of the centre of the boat (SMA, D1/134/3:226). This mast length rule of thumb was confirmed by the Yell fisherman and boatbuilder John Smith who stated that before 1840 the sixareen's mast was much shorter, and its rigging was made from tarred hemp. There were two shrouds (stroods) per side and the sail was perfectly square (March 1970: 55). The square sail had two rows of reef points, one at the head and one at the foot. The reef points in the head of the sail meant that when the sail was wet the water ran down and off its foot. Conversely, if the sail was double-reefed (at the foot) any water running down the sail would collect in the reefed part and the sail would remain wet and heavy. The rule of thumb for sail making was to allow 1.5 yards (1.4m) of cotton for each foot of keel (March 1970: 61).

Shetland author Arthur Johnston, in the May 1932 edition of the *Model Yachtsman and Marine Model* magazine, described how the sail on a sixareen was rigged. The sail was hoisted by means of a single halyard (draw) which was attached to the yard (rae) which ran through a dumb sheave in the mast (stong) that was held in position by a turn taken around the cleat at the stong's foot (Fig. 129). This end was also attached to the rae making an endless rope, thus forming both the down-haul and the up-haul (Fig. 130). The rae was held in postion against the mast by means of the rakki, a semi-circular collar made from sheep/cow horn or bone (Fig. 131). There was a bowline in the fore luff of the sail and the sheet hooked onto the lee gunwale (Fig. 132) (Johnston 1932: 9).

When tacking a dipping lug the sail had to be dropped. The rakki, mainsheet and tack were undone, the bowline loosened and the yard and sail passed around the fore side of the mast. Once this procedure was complete the rakki and mainsheet were re-attached and the tack loosely fastened on the new leeside – this was fully tensioned and made fast once the sail was almost hoisted. The final job, if the boat was sailing to windward, was to tension and secure the bowline. This remains the common Shetland method for tacking both small and large asymmetric dipping lug rigged boats. However, in a correspondence between T.M.Y. Manson and Charles Sandison another method was discussed, where instead of passing the yard and sail around the fore side of the mast it was instead passed aft (Fig. 133) (SMA, D37/1/85/81/4/1).

Fig. 129. *The slippery hitch used to secure the draw (halyard). This simple hitch pushes the load into the mast not away from it and can be undone and the sail dropped in an instant. Drawing: M. Chivers.*

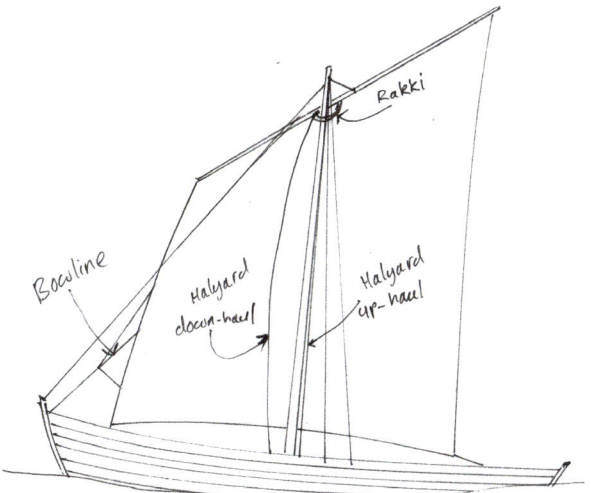

Fig. 130. *Illustration of the halyard up-haul and down-haul on a sixareen. Also observe the rakki and the bowline. Drawing: M. Chivers.*

Fig. 131. *Rakki on model of a sixareen made by David Henry, Foula, c.1870. Courtesy of Ian Tait.*

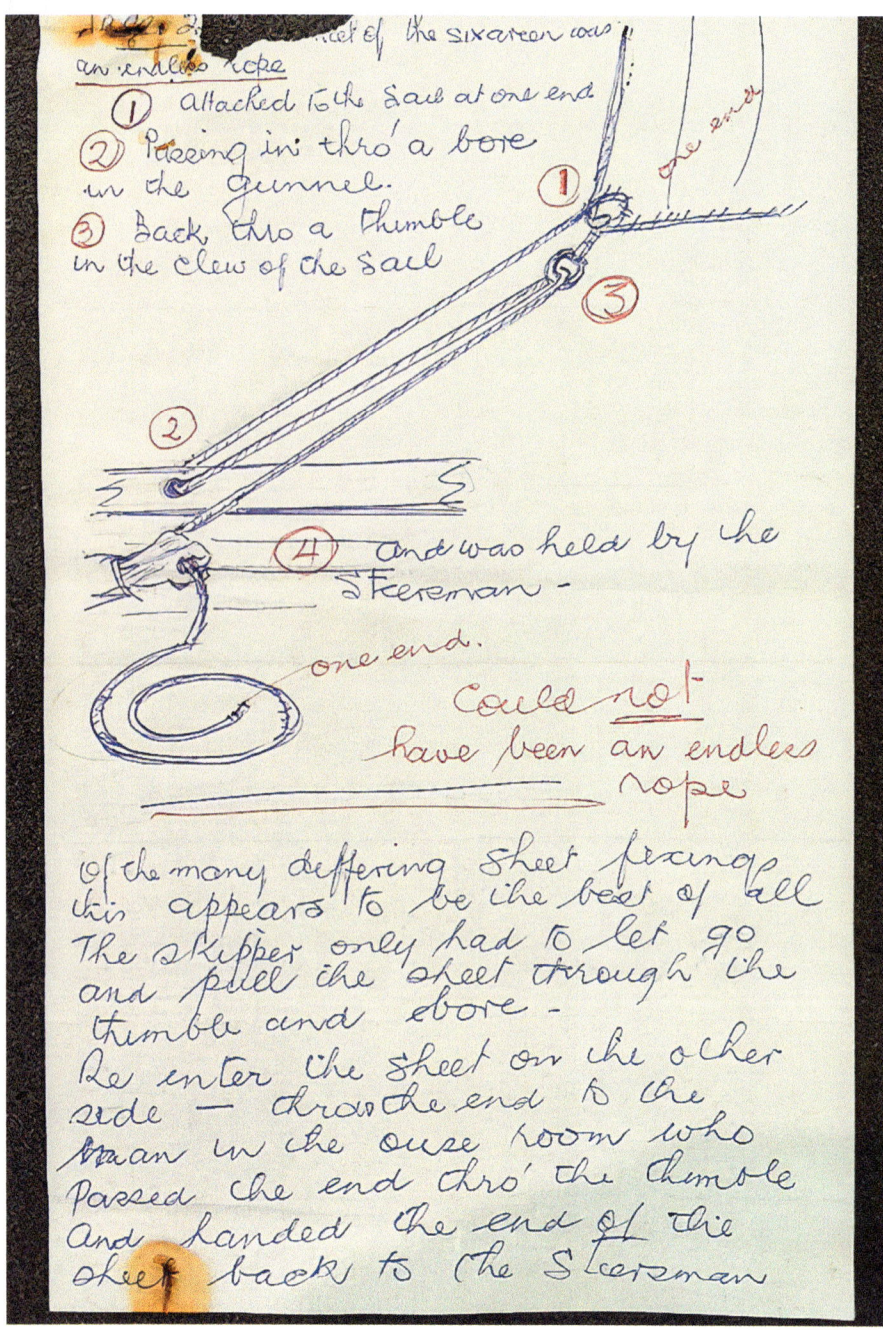

of the many differing sheet fixings
this appears to be the best of all
The skipper only had to let go
and pull the sheet through the
thimble and bore -
Re enter the sheet on the other
side — thro the end to the
man in the ouse room who
passed the end thro' the thimble
and handed the end of the
sheet back to the Steersman

Fig. 132. *Illustration of the sheeting arrangement. Shetland Museum & Archives uncatalogued correspondence between Dr T.M.Y. Manson and Charles Sandison, 9th September 1966. Courtesy of Shetland Museum & Archives.*

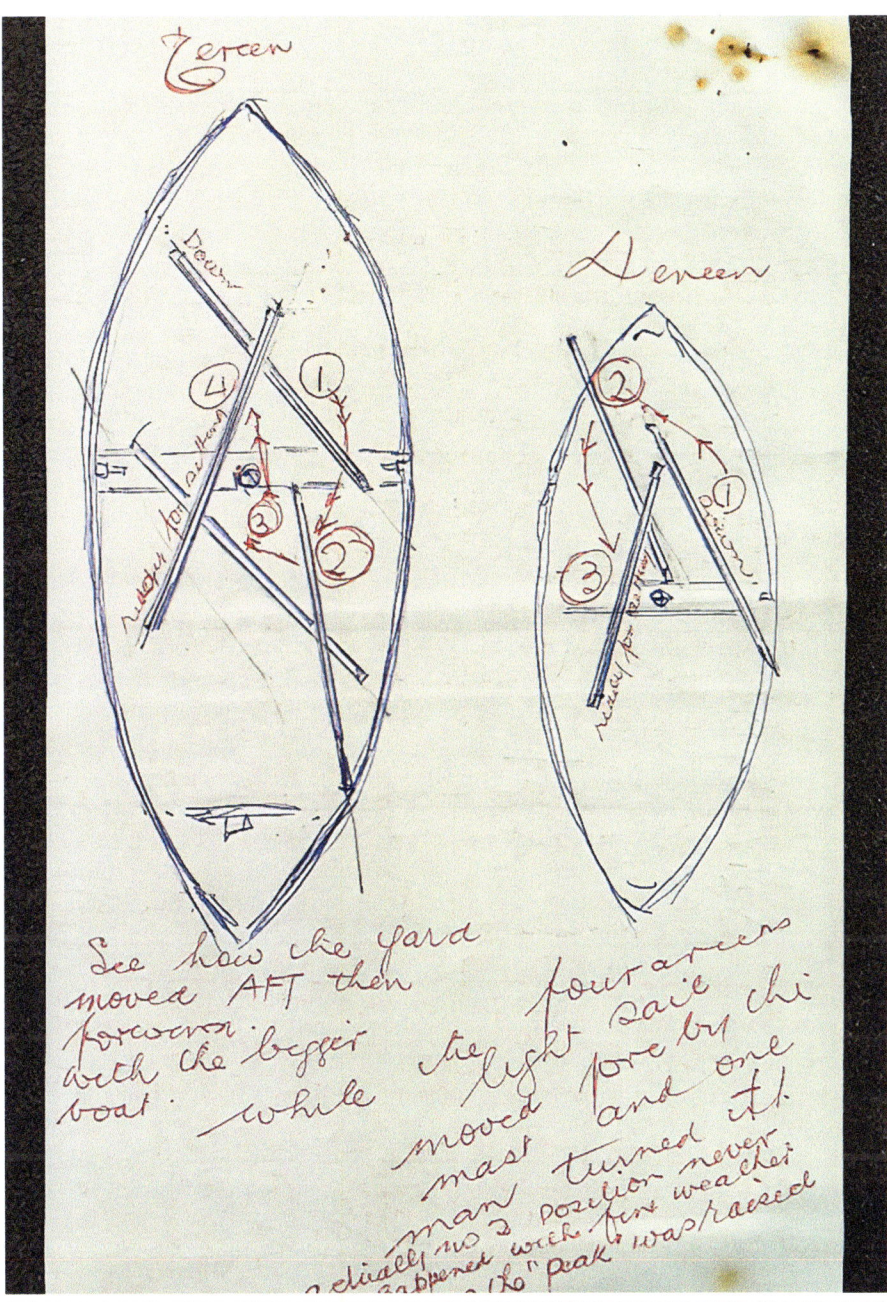

Fig. 133. *Alternative ways of passing the yard around the mast. Correspondence between Dr T.M.Y. Manson and Charles Sandison, 9th September 1966. Courtesy of Shetland Museum & Archives D37/1/85/81/4/1.*

By the early nineteenth century sailing – as opposed to rowing – to windward was becoming the preferred option, as noted by the physician Arthur Edmondston who wrote: "More lately it has been the custom to try and gain the land by tacking, and fewer boats have been lost since the adoption of this practice" (Edmondston 1809: 239). As previously discussed, there is evidence that by about 1770 the Norwegian kjølrenne, which created a slightly deeper keel, had been adopted in Shetland. There is also evidence from this period for the heightening of some boats by the addition of an extra strake. The combination of a slightly deeper keel and an extra strake made boats better suited for sailing to windward.

The improvement in sailing performance, I believe, is due to the development of the haaf fishery when rowing long distances in rough conditions would not have been viable. As has already been discussed, the sixareen only became dominant over the fourareen as a haaf boat around 1770, which suggests that this was when the distant water fishing commenced. This was the period when boats that were able to sail well to windward in all weather became important. John Smith, cited by Edgar March in the first of his two-volume book *Inshore Craft of Britain in the Days of Sail and Oar* emphasised that both the square and dipping lug sailing rigs required judicious handling, especially during squally spells. When sailing before the wind the sailsman, sometimes called the towsman, was responsible for the lowering of the sail when a strong gust struck, then hauling it up quickly once the gust had passed. The lives of the crew depended on his skill in judging when to lower and raise the sail (March 1970: 49).

The skill of the towsman was equally important when beating to windward, especially when tacking. Timing was everything. If the towsman misjudged the lowering of the sail and it was caught aback, pinning it against the shrouds and mast, the leverage exerted by the wind on the pinned sail could capsize the boat (March 1970: 50). The forces generated in the luff of the sail, when the boats were being sailed hard to windward, meant that the reebin, and the strake below it, the bordin, were prone to splitting in the boat's headrum area. To rectify this, from the early part of the nineteenth century, a pair of ribs, one on either side of the boat were fitted. These ribs called "bettin bands", were fitted between the stameron and the fore band (Fig. 134) (March 1970: 60).

The nineteenth century Shetland author Jessie Saxby provided a, perhaps somewhat romanticised, description of sailing a sixareen to windward in storm conditions:

> There must be, at least, two men skilled in managing a boat on board, viz, one to steer, and the other to hold the halyards – called respectively the skipper and the tow-man. The services of the latter are seldom required unless when running before the wind ... When a storm comes off the land, and the boat is close hauled, the helm's-man has the sole management and control. He holds both helm and sheet, and with one, or the other, or

both of them he regulates the movements of his boat. He must be very watchful of breaking seas on the weather bow, and also that the boat does not take in too much lee water. If he sees a threatening "lump" he will not allow the boat to go into it with full speed, no, he will put down the helm a little, and give her an arm length of sheet, thus deadening her way, and bringing her to the wind she will top the breaker like a see-mew. It is extremely useful on such occasions to have an oar out on the weather side, as by its help the boat's head will pay off more quickly, and acquire an onward velocity ... If the wind comes in gusts, the boat will often not be able bear the sail, although reefed down to the average force of the storm. In that case the skipper must ease off the sheet, thus spilling the sail of the wind, and allowing the boat to upright. He must not, unless a sea is to be headed, put down his helm and bring up the boat to the wind, as this occasions considerable leeway before the boat can resume her onward course (SMA, D1/134/3:226).

John Smith also described the use of the sail when running before the wind and he said: "It was essential that the boat did not run too fast, or slide on to the crest of a following sea, lest she be driven under or broach-to" (March 1970: 60). The towsman, Smith said, "sat with the sole of his foot on the garboard strake and could tell by the trembling and vibration of the plank if the sixareen was running too fast" (March 1970: 60). If the boat was running too fast the towsman would ease the halyard and pull down the sail using the downhaul, hoisting it again when the danger had passed. It was essential that he maintained concentration, because when the boat was in the trough of a wave the power in the sail would be reduced and, as the boat

Fig. 134. *Bettin band on the sixareen* Vaila Mae. *Note how the sail tack is secured via two bores in the gunwale. Observe the bowline passing through a bore in the hinnispot. Photo: M. Chivers.*

began to rise onto the wave crest, the full force of the wind would be exerted on the sail, and Smith recalled that "when running, a sixern appeared to fly through the water" (March 1970: 61).

Saxby, in 1882, wrote in depth about handling a sixareen in heavy seas:

> ... the most dangerous position in which a sixern and its crew can be placed is when running before the wind in a stormy sea ... The trim of the boat should be carefully attended to. She must not be trimmed too much by the stern. The tendency of the sail before the wind is to raise up, or make more buoyant the fore part of the boat, and consequently the afterpart will dip ... The towman ... must keep a keen lookout behind the boat, and if a wave is threatening to break at any considerable distance astern he will hoist the sail a little, and the boat with increased speed will run from it. He must not neglect to look ahead as well, because he may happen to overtake a breaking sea, in which case he must lower the sail a bit, and when the wave has spent its furry he will follow up in its rear with increased velocity. The greatest danger arises from a wave overtaking the boat. When such is the case, the boat's stern will of course, first lift on the sea, and she will seem as if running down hill ... Steady the helm! Don't yaw. The sail must now be lowered, and the boat's headlong progress retarded, then as soon as the wave has passed forward the sail must be hoisted again, and so run behind it with all possible speed (SMA, D1/134/3:226).

We have already discussed reports that Shetland boats were able to semi-plane off the wind. Tommy Isbister attributed this to the flat sections amidships on the halsin strake. This phenomenon was, in Shetland, called sea loose, and in Norway "letting go of the sea" (Morrison 1978: 16). Arne Emil Christensen and Ian Morrison noted that the fishermen from Nordmøre said that a good færing should lift one strake out of the sea when sailing and half a strake when being rowed by two people. Also noted were the high speeds –15 knots – achieved by the replica fembørings which sailed to Iceland in 1974 (Christensen and Morrison 1976: 277). Norwegian Anders Gjellstad described this letting go of the sea phenomenon in the Oselvar as being similar to a hydrofoil, and was noticeable when sailing hard downwind, the boat suddenly letting go "and shooting forward like an arrow without any possibility of steering or control" (Gjellstad 1969: 21).

There is pictorial evidence drawn by Samuel Hibbert in the 1820s which is curious, as the mast, in the majority of his boat illustrations, is positioned about one-third of the way along the keel (Figs. 135-136). Yell fisherman and boatbuilder John Smith recalled that "the mast in the boats was amidships; then, when the lugsail was introduced the mast was placed in the fore thwart ..." and it was found that with the mast in this position the boat steered much steadier in a running sea (March 1970: 50). This is an important observation by Smith, and on close inspection of Hibbert's illustrations this is exactly where the mast is positioned. Therefore, what Hibbert's text must mean is a dipping lug (which Shetlanders in recent years often term "square sail"). This suggests an earlier date for when the asymmetric dipping square sail was

Fishing Station of Feideland.

Fig. 135. *The boat in the centre of this print has the mast positioned amidships whereas the boats between it and the shore have their masts positioned two thirds foreward. Print by Samuel Hibbert 1822.*

Drongs in the Bay of St Magnus.

Fig. 136. *It is curious that the mast is positioned two thirds of the way forward in this print by Samuel Hibbert 1822.*

developed in Shetland. It must be stressed however, that during the latter part of the nineteenth century the mast was located as described by Saxby just slightly forward of the centre of the boat (SMA, D1/134/3:226).

John Smith recounted an old tale he was told by a Shetland haaf fisherman who claimed that the fishermen were averse to sailing when a lot of tacking had to be done:

> They hauled their lines but as it was a head wind for home the crew were getting ready to row as usual ... The son expressed the wish to put the sail up and tack for windward. The father replied that if there was any tacking he would refuse to steer, but gave the son a free hand. The sail was hoisted, the son took charge; the old men grumbled that it would

be a waste of time, caring apparently nothing for an easier journey ... But the son had too
much experience of square rigged ships to be annoyed ... he tacked the sixareen home,
close-hauled, tack for tack. They were home hours before the other sixareens that were
rowing and this was really the introduction of tacking the square sail as it became general
after that (March 1970: 57).

Adrian Osler suggested that the critical period in sailing rig development
took place during the 1830s and 1840s, the square sail falling out of common
use in most parts of Shetland by about 1850; although, in some places such
as Fair Isle, the square sail continued in use until the early 1900s (Osler 1983:
44). This innovation in the development of an asymmetric sailing rig may
have come about in various ways: through direct innovation by an individual;
a transference of dipping lug sail practices seen elsewhere to indigenous
boats; or through copying, from an existing asymmetric dipping lug rig, such
as the type used in the Møre region of Norway (Osler 1983: 47).

Samuel Hibbert's drawings, when cross referenced with the oral history
provided by John Smith, leads to the probability that the dipping lug sail
may have been in use in Shetland from around 1820. However, as Osler
pointed out, there is precious little information about the development of the
higher peaked asymmetric dipping square sail in Shetland, and as previously
pointed out, this sail retains many features of the square sail and is therefore
possibly unique to Shetland (PC, Wishart R. 2020).

Osler made an interesting observation about the dipping square sail, that
it had its first reef at the sail's head, which did not run parallel to the yard.
When used this reef transformed the asymmetric sail to a square sail configuration (Fig. 137). Osler speculatively suggested that this reefing system may
have been advantageous to the boats operating on the west side of Shetland,
as the square sail was better suited for running or broad reaching. The wind
frequently blows from the southwest so a returning West Side boat, laden
with fish, often sailed before the wind from west to east (Osler 1979/80: 4).

Sails, like oars, were the motive power of the boat and therefore their
correct design and construction were incredibly important. Making a good
quality sail, with the correct shape, was a complex task; the sailmaker being
the marine engineer of the sail and oar era (PI, Moncrieff and Wishart 2015).
It is thought that the asymmetric square sail first became peaked higher
on the west side of Shetland – a consequence of contact with the Scottish
mainland luggers, whose sails were higher peaked. Shetland sailing rig development was also probably influenced by naval practice, which many Shetland
men will have become familiar with during the French wars of the 1790s
and early 1800s. As Brian Wishart pointed out, the influence of naval sailing
practice was probably the major contributory factor in the development of the
high peaked dipping lug sail in Shetland (PI, Moncrieff and Wishart 2015).

Of importance to the evolution of the sail was the further development
of the bowline. The bowline was important in controlling the shape of the

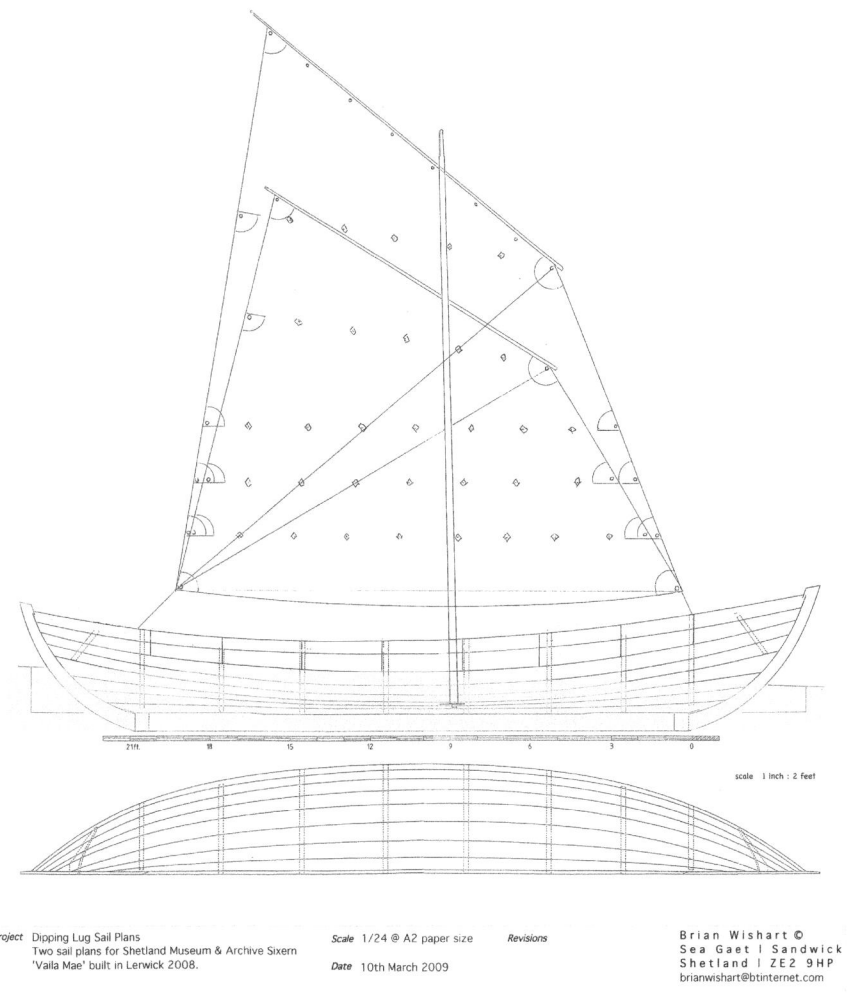

Project Dipping Lug Sail Plans
Two sail plans for Shetland Museum & Archive Sixern
'Vaila Mae' built in Lerwick 2008.

Scale 1/24 @ A2 paper size *Revisions*

Date 10th March 2009

Brian Wishart ©
Sea Gaet I Sandwick
Shetland I ZE2 9HP
brianwishart@btinternet.com

Fig. 137. *Sailplan for the sixareen* Vaila Mae. *Observe how when used the top row of reef points convert the sail into a true square sail. Drawing: Brian Wishart.*

sail when sailing to windward, as when pulled tight it flattened the sail and when loose it allowed more fullness in it. Thus the correct use of the bowline ensured the optimum aerofoil shape was achieved to create maximum lift and drive (Smith and Preece 1994: 17-18). Pløyen was very impressed by the Shetland bowline which he said was far more efficient than the type used in Faroe. The Faroese version consisted of just one line that ran from the middle of the sail's luff and was made fast at the stem. The superior Shetland bowline enormously helped the windward sailing ability of the boat, enabling it to point much higher (Pløyen 1896: 25). Shetland antiquarian Robert Bruce described the bowline and its use in the sixareen which in its later years was configured as illustrated in the upper drawing in Fig. 138 (Bruce 1934: 312; 338). The bowline configuration in the lower drawing in Fig. 139 was the older form and this was the one used in western Norway and Faroe; although it is not clear if the use in Faroe came about as a consequence of Pløyen's visit to Shetland (PI, Moncrieff and Wishart 2015).

Bruce described how the shape of the crowsfoot bowline was obtained by way of a piece of wood with holes bored into it. The bowline went through a hole in the stem head, aft of the forestay hole, and the line led aft usually to the fore taft where it was hauled taught and made fast (Fig. 139) (Bruce 1934: 313). This form of the bowline was very similar to the one used on the Ness yoal and was similar to the Norwegian three-part crowsfoot. There were several patterns for that particular type of bowline and, for simplicity, on the West Side and in the North Isles they just had a single one, which was roughly in line with the second reef, the idea being that it ran in a straight diagonal line from the peak of the sail to the stem, this was close to the pulling point on the luff of the sail's bolt rope (PI, Moncrieff and Wishart 2015).

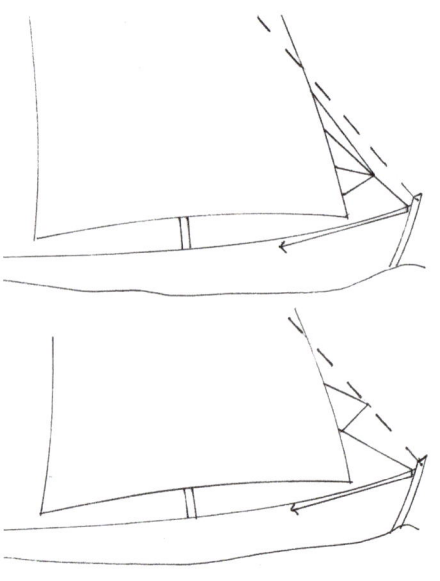

Fig. 139. *Forward hinnispot with hole for the bowline to pass through. Model sixareen by David Henry, Foula c.1870. Courtesy of Dr. Ian Tait.*

Fig. 138. *Two types of bowline. Top – crowsfoot with fixed knot. After Pløyen (1894) and Osler (1983). Bottom – single line via forestay and reef cringle. After Stuart Bruce (1934) and Osler (1983). Drawing: M. Chivers.*

An interesting aside is the observation made by Bruce who noted that until about 1860 fishing lines were shot from the sixareen under oar, until a Whalsay skipper had the idea that the lines could be better shot under sail to save time. This skipper and his crew experimented by taking an old fourareen's mast and sail with them, and before they began to set their lines they took the pump-rod out the sixareen's pump box and stepped the fourareen's mast inside the box, creating a mizzen sail. The sheet was led back to a staple that had been secured to the rudder's head. This development was later followed by some Whalsay fishermen using small jib-headed mizzens. Bruce admitted that he never actually saw this temporary rig, and he did not know if it was used anywhere else in Shetland. He also noted that the sails of the Whalsay boats were always white and were never barked (Bruce 1934: 314). White sails were commonplace in Shetland, as clergyman Alexander Kerr observed whilst on passage from Scotland. As the ship approached Shetland Kerr observed "... and getting close with the coast it was a cheerful and interesting site [sic] to see the ocean spotted, in every direction, with the white sails of the boats, glittering in the sun as they were making for their respective fishing grounds" (Kerr 1830: 190). Indeed, it seems even in the twentieth century white sails remained common as reported by John Smith who noted that sails were generally white and only rarely were they barked (March 1970: 61).

Rowing mechanisms: kabes and humlibands

The mechanical operation of the oar has been documented in detail by Adrian Osler in his book *The Shetland Boat: South Mainland and Fair Isle* (Osler 1983: 41). Osler noted that the system of rowing in Shetland was the same as that employed in western Norway and Faroe: "... all Shetland rowing methods were based on the use of oar pivots consisting of removable wooden kabes (tholes) inserted in the boat's gunwales with humlibands (grommets) to retain the oar in position ..." (Osler 1983: 41) (Figs. 140-142). Humlibands were traditionally made from rawhide which, when wet, created sufficient friction to prevent the oar from slipping out of the humliband when the oar was let go by the rower. This allowed rowers to simply let go their oars when fishing or having a rest and the oars would just swing back to lie dangling in the water alongside the boat, conveniently placed to be easily picked-up when rowing was resumed (PC, Christensen 2014).

Shetland had its own general rowing arrangement, with one regional variation of kabe mounting system found in Whalsay where it was mounted on the inside of the inwale rather than through the inwale itself. This was preferred because the inwale was structural, its purpose was to stiffen the boat, and cutting a slot weakened the inwale thus partially defeating its structural purpose (Fig. 140) (PC, Hutchison 2014).

In Shetland both the kabe and ruth were traditionally made of oak, this prolonged the life of these components, as oak was more resistant to wear from the friction generated by rowing than either pine or spruce. The removable Faroese oak "tollur" was very similar to the removable kabe. The tollur or kabe were removed when the boat was fishing with nets, or when sailing, thus preventing the nets or mainsheet becoming snagged (Fig. 140-141). Unlike the kabe and tollur, the west Norwegian oak "keipe" was permanently fastened on top of the inwale (esing) (Fig. 142). Latterly in Shetland, certainly by the early twentieth century, the kabe was gradually replaced by the more popular fixed steel tholepin, which was found on boats not used for net fishing or sailing, an example being the Bressay Lass, used to flit lambs from Noss to Bressay by John and Wendy Scott during the early 1970s (Fig. 143).

The Shetland oar, its blade shape and flex

Until the mid-nineteenth century oars, as well as boats, were imported from places such as Godøysund in the parish of Tysnes in western Norway (SMA, D.24; NLS: Acc. 3250, Folder 4 Box 85). However, as has been previously noted, there may have been some variation in oar type, as eighteenth-century

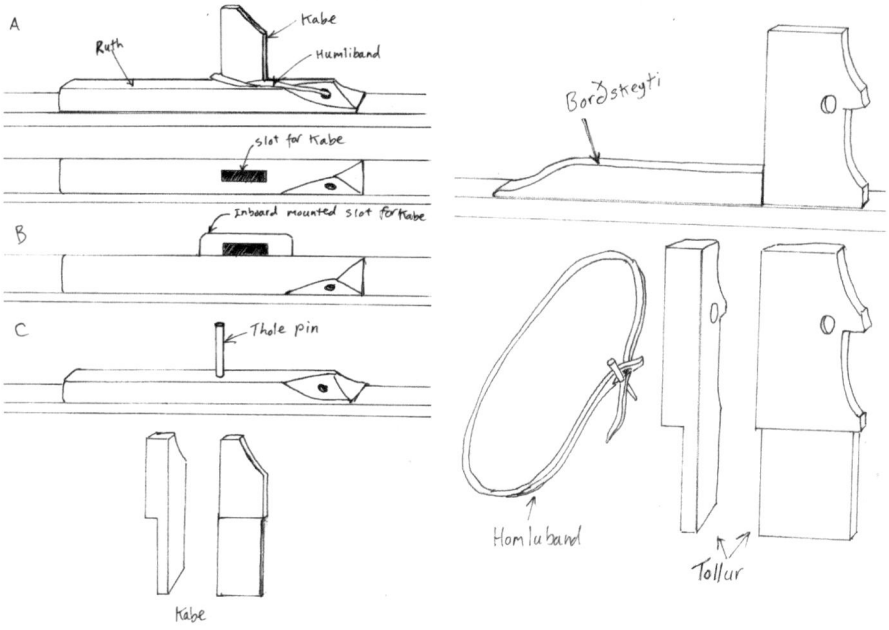

Fig. 140. *Shetland kabe styles. A. Common style of wooden kabe. B. Whalsay inboard mounted kabe. C. Modern style thole pin. Drawing: M. Chivers.*

Fig. 141. *Faorese tollur. Drawing: M. Chivers.*

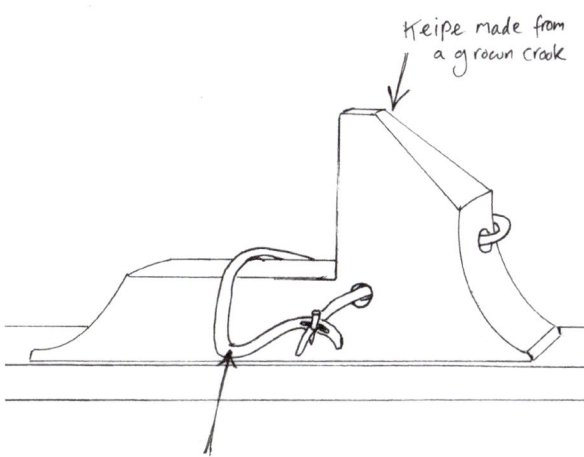

Keipe made from
a grown crook

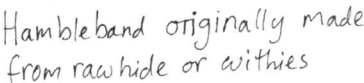

Hambleband originally made
from rawhide or withies

Fig. 142. *Norwegian keipe with hamleband. Drawing: M. Chivers.*

Fig. 143. Bressay Lass *owned by John and Wendy Scott. Photo: M. Chivers.*

documentary evidence illustrates that oars were also imported from Hamburg, although these may have been Norwegian re-export items (SMA, GD144.104.3). Late eighteenth-century evidence for the making of oars in Shetland was shown in chapter six (Table 11). Unfortunately, there is no descriptive, nor material evidence, of these early Shetland oars, and so we have no idea what they were like. It may be assumed that, like the boats, there was a transition period from the west Norwegian to the Shetland oar type.

Oars for west Norwegian boats such as the Oselvar were made from a tree that had been cut into quarters (PC, Isbister 2015, Økland 2016: 87). Indeed, the oars documented by Christensen in Figs. 144-145 clearly illustrate this and also that the shape of the blades are different. Rowing mechanisms and oar shape vary quite considerably in Norway as Christensen explains:

> East Norway to the border between Vest-Agder and Rogaland uses two tholepins, round oar with symmetrical rather wide, blade; oar can be turned 90 degrees. Rogaland is a transition zone. Hordaland to Nordmøre uses keip and oar where the cross-section at keip is a quarter circle, long narrow blade with a slight curve. Trøndelag and North Norway round oar in rounded keip or tholepins, symmetrical blade, narrower than East Norway. Old North Norwegian oars narrow at loom, widest at end, nearly a pointed triangle (PC, Christensen 2016).

The regional Norwegian variance of oar and blade shape combined with rowing methods as identified by Christensen are important. In eastern Norway it seems that the oar was able to be turned through 90 degrees, and so could be feathered at the end of each stroke, whereas in Hordaland, and Nordmøre the rowing system was the same as in Shetland and Faroe, the oar in effect was captured, with the blade always being held at 90 degrees to the water. Northern Norway used tholepins, and the oar was round in section which allowed the oar to be feathered at the end of each stroke. Because of Shetland's boat trade connections with western Norway it would have been surprising if there had been a difference between the mechanism and style of rowing between Hordaland and Shetland.

It is interesting to note the Norwegian pramm being rowed, seen in Fig. 146, captures the oars by means of wooden thole pins and the oars are round in section. As Christensen previously pointed out this means that this boat was probably built somewhere between Vest-Agder to the border of Rogaland. In contrast the oar visible in the foreground of this photograph is quarter round, with a triangular pointed blade tip which is similar to the oar in illustrated in Fig. 145. The oar in the foreground of the photograph pivots against a keipe, and so this boat was probably a færing from the Hordaland or Nordmøre region. This photograph is undated but, judging by the dress of the pramm's occupants, was taken around 1900.

A typical Shetland oar was made from spruce or pine, its handle was rounded, and below this the loom was square in section. Two protective

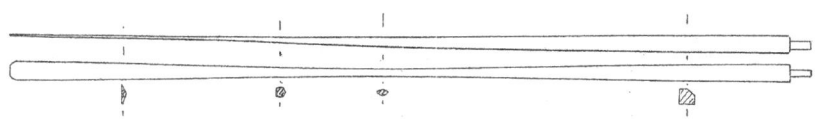

Fig. 144. *Drawing of oars belonging to a seksæring from the Barony Rosendal. Drawing 1:10. Drawing: Arne Emil Christensen. Courtesy of the Norwegian Maritime Museum, Oslo.*

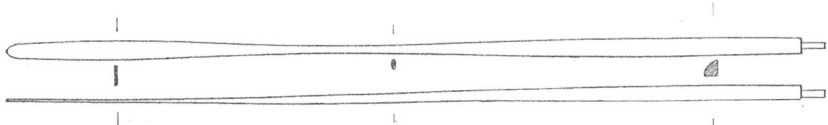

Fig. 145. *Drawing of an oar belonging to a seksæring from Selbjørn, Hordaland. Drawing 1:10. Drawing: Arne Emil Christensen. Courtesy of the Norwegian Maritime Museum, Oslo.*

Fig. 146. *Norwegian pramm and færing, Eela Water, Northmavine. Oselvar bottom right the keipe and oar blade shape and compare to Fig. 149. Photograph c.1900. Courtesy of Shetland Museum & Archives.*

shaped pieces of oak called sklettes were nailed to the oar at the point where it pivoted against the kabe and ruth (Figs. 147-149). As the loom tapered it became round or occasionally oval in section, the round/oval section was narrowest at the neck of the oar's blade (Fig. 149).

The amount that the oar blade flexed was an important factor in rowing as boatbuilder Tommy Isbister explains "... the Norwegian oar is very heavy on the inboard piece, so you dinna have weight in your hand. The oar blades, they have to bend evenly you ken. It's flat on one side and slightly curved on the other" (PI, Isbister 2015). In later years the shape of oar blades in Shetland diverged from the west Norwegian type, culminating in the oars that are prevalent in Shetland today of the type that were made by boatbuilder Jimmy Smith up until the 1970s. These Jimmy Smith oars have thicker blades, with pronounced keels (the ridge running vertically along the centre of the blade).

Tommy Isbister owns a pair of oars that were made by boatbuilder Jack Shewan who built sixareens for Hay & Company in the late nineteenth and early twentieth centuries (Fig. 150). The blades of this pair of oars are tapered, the full width being reached at the tip of the blade. Isbister, described the technique used when rowing with these oars: "... the first stroke is important, as this puts the whip into the blade, and at the end of the stroke the blade flips back with its own flexibility and gives you power" (PI, Isbister 2015).

The oar in Fig. 151, like the Jack Shewan oar, in my opinion is elegant. The oar's blade is thin and very flexible. This Sandwick oar was frequently

Fig. 147. *The handle and top section of an oar's loom with oak sklettes. Oar made by Jack Shewan around 1900 which belongs to Tommy Isbister. Photo: M. Chivers.*

Fig. 148. *Rear face of the loom revealing the oak sklettes. Photo: M. Chivers.*

Fig. 149. *The full length oar which is 11.5ft (3.5m) long. Blade is 3.8ft (1.16m) long. The lower loom is round in section. Photo: M. Chivers.*

used, as the sklette is worn through, and it was obviously very important to someone, as they had gone to a lot of trouble to repair the loom which had split (Figs. 152-153). The blade tip of this oar is rounded whereas all the other oars examined by me during my research were straight ended, which indicates a possible regional variation in oar blade pattern.

Salient points about the possible stylistic development of oar blade shape were made by Brian Wishart: "... Ness yoal oars I have seen, probably by Johnson, being later and most productive, do not have a central ridge, but a generous convex rounding over most of the blade, diminishing towards the tip. These oars looked purposeful and simple, and are very attractive as a result, to my eye at least" (PI, Wishart, 2015).

Oars with a distinctive central ridge and a more complex shape tended to be the product of the bigger boatbuilding establishments found in Scalloway, Burra and maybe Baltasound. This probably led to more rapid and stylish development, resulting in spawned copies by associated craftsmen (PI, Wishart 2015). Brian Wishart, who grew up in Walls, on the west side of Shetland's mainland, moved to Sandwick during his career as a teacher. Through years of observation Wishart concluded that there was a regional variation in oar blade shape, which in part may have been influenced by local boatbuilder preferences. An example of this being the distinct style of the oars commonly used in yoals; these oar shapes were much more homogenous compared to the oars on the west side of Shetland. "The best example of this homogeneity were the oars from a group of boats from Rerwick, south

Fig. 150. *Tommy Isbister demonstrating the flexibility of the Jack Shewan oar. Photo: M. Chivers.*

Fig. 151. *An oar of unknown origin from Sandwick belonging to Davey Johnson. Photo: M. Chivers.*

Fig. 152. *Note the wear on the sacrificial oak sklette. Photo: M. Chivers.*

Fig. 153. *Someone went to a lot of trouble to repair this oar. Photo: M. Chivers.*

of Bigton, now all gone. Thanks to Osler's work we know that the oars were made by the two main builders John Eunson and George Johnson." The crews who used these oars will have discussed their needs with the boatbuilders, in much the same way as they will have discussed alterations and refinements to hull shape to enhance boat performance (Fig. 154-155) (PI, Wishart 2015).

Oar blade shape began to become more homogenous during the twentieth century. This was possibly due to the increased popularity of the small inboard Stuart Turner engine during the 1950s, which meant that people were less dependent upon oar and sail as the main means of propulsion. Also, during this period Hay & Company were manufacturing oars and these were bought by people from all over Shetland. Allister Rendall described how his father (Robbie) took over the responsibility for making oars at Hay & Company from 1959 until he retired in 1973 (Fig. 156). Oar making was not Robbie's main job, he was employed by Hay's as an assistant sawyer, and when

Fig. 154. *Adrian Osler demonstrating the balance point of this Ness yoal oar of unknown date and possibly made by George Johnson. Photograph c.1980. Courtesy Adrian Osler.*

Fig. 155. *Adrian Osler illustrating the slender neck of this yoal oar. Photograph c.1980. Courtesy Adrian Osler.*

he began oar making there were no templates for the shape of the oars, and so he asked around and took advice from people. Allister recalled "… every week he would always have two or three pairs of oars to make … Normally it took a couple of nights to make a pair of oars, but, if they were really pushing with somebody wanting oars he could start at 6 at night and have them finished by 11 o'clock … That would be the sklettes and everything" (PI, Rendall and Wishart 2016).

Customers could also buy blanked oars from Hay & Company to finish shaping at home. Rendall pointed out that it was not just Hay's who made oars, but boatbuilders such as Jimmy Smith in Lerwick, and there were also boatbuilders in the isles who will have made oars for local customers. However, if you needed oars during the 1950s, 60s and 70s it was Hay's where you would naturally go to purchase them. Wishart emphasised: "… everybody's wood came from Hay's. It's important to get that picture across, that was really the source. Maybe a few oars might have been made by a boatbuilder like Jimmy Smith, but it would not tend to be something you

Fig. 156. *Pair of unfinished oars made by Robert Rendall and owned by his son Allister. Photo: M. Chivers.*

would set-off to do" (Fig. 157-158). Hay's owned big frame saws and band saws, which meant that people would also go to them for other boat parts (PI, Rendall and Wishart 2016).

Rudder

There are no Shetland indigenous rudder and helm artefacts that predate the late nineteenth century except those found on scale models of boats, the earliest being a Fair Isle yoal by an unknown maker in the Science Museum collection. This was documented by Adrian Osler during the late 1970s (Fig. 159). He conservatively dated the model to 1850 and featured it in his book *The Shetland Boat: South Mainland and Fair Isle* (Osler 1983: 78).

Fig. 157. *Two different blade patterns. Top oar made by Jack Shewan c.1900. Lower oar made by John Laurenson c.1880. Photo: M. Chivers.*

Fig. 158. *White and blue oars made by Johny Bruce, Whalsay for the fourareen he built called* Eclipse *(c.1940). Yellow oars made by Jimmy Smith. Oars and boats owned by Allister Rendall. Photo: M. Chivers.*

To compound the lack of material evidence no written descriptions of these items has been found, and there is no documentary evidence that these items were imported from Norway. This leads me to surmise that rudders were constructed in Shetland from the mid to late eighteenth century.

In Shetland the rudder was secured to the aft-stem using a captured gudgeon and pintle system. On the aft-stem was an upper pintle and a lower gudgeon. The pintle, on the upper aft-stem, consisted of a sliding bolt that in effect captured the rudder and held it in position preventing it from accidently becoming unshipped. The Science Museum model's rudder uses the Shetland gudgeon and pintle system as does the model of the sixareen built by Foula resident David Henry about 1870 (Fig. 160). The use of this system in these models demonstrates that this method of attaching the rudder was established before 1850, which means that this system was possibly developed during the early 1800s, possibly even earlier. Fig. 161 illustrates the difference between the pintle size of a sixareen and a fourareen. The sixareen's pintle is from a boat that was latterly at Uyeasound, Aithsting, and the fourareen's pintle is from a boat that was from Kurkigarth, Delting (PC, Tait 2016).

A captive pintle system was also used in Hordaland, west Norway. This system was different to that used in Shetland as the lower rudder hanging consisted of a very long upward-pointing curved pintle (Fig. 162). This Hordaland system was particularly useful as the lower pintle began above

Fig. 159. *Model of Fair Isle yoal. Science Museum Collections, London (Osler 1983/78).*

Fig. 160. *Shetland rudder and helm assembly on a model sixareen constructed by David Henry, Foula c. 1870. Photo: Ian Tait.*

Fig. 161. *Comparison between pintles, larger from a sixareen, smaller from a fourareen. Photo: Ian Tait.*

the waterline, enabling the easy location of the lower rudder gudgeon which was simply slid onto the pintle and pushed down, until the upper rudder gudgeon was located and secured by the sliding pintle on the upper aft-stem. In Faroe the system of rudder attachment was similar to that in Hordaland, although the pintle seen in Fig. 163 was shorter, ending below the waterline. So, whilst there are some similarities in the way that the rudder was attached to the aft-stem of boats in Shetland, western Norway, and Faroe there are also some marked differences.

The rudder securing system in Shetland is unique and has certainly not changed in form for at least 167 years. There is no evidence as to why the Hordaland rudder securing method was not adopted. This may have been due to the cost and the availability of iron, or it simply may have been easier for small non-commercial blacksmiths to make the Shetland style of rudder hangings (PC, Tait 2016). Whatever the reason, the Shetland pattern of rudder hanging has proven itself, which is why the pattern of these fittings remained static, even when boats began to be used for organised recreational racing around 1880.

It is noteworthy that the rudders from Shetland, Hordaland and Faroe are similar in shape. Of particular interest is that all three extend below the keel line (Figs. 162-164). Shetland rudders during the twentieth century normally ended in line with the keel, (Fig. 165) however prior to this it may have been common for them to "... extend a good piece below the keel ...". This observation by Wishart is further supported by Osler's blog post on the subject written for Moder Dy CIC. (PI, Rendall and Wishart 2016, Osler 2019). The material evidence from the nineteenth century constructed model boats is unequivocal: rudders in Shetland extended below the keel line. This would have increased the boat's ability to manoeuvre under sail, and will not have impinged upon it when being rowed ashore, as the rudder will have been unshipped prior to rowing; the boat being steered by the person taking the stroke. Indeed, this was how rowing boats were steered in Norway and Faroe, and it is only in very recent times, in Faroe and Shetland, during rowing competitions, that the rudder has been used. Although the rudder in modern times rarely extended below the keel it was wider, thus making-up for the deficit in length, as the overall below waterline surface area was approximately the same (PI, Rendall and Wishart 2016).

Helm

The type of helm used in Hordaland was completely different to the one used in Shetland. Instead of fitting over the rudder's head-stock the Hordaland helm was attached via a mortise located on the head-stock's side, through which a tenon slotted, and this was retained by a peg or pin (Fig. 162 - 166). The Hordaland rudder and helm arrangement are clearly illustrated in Hans Dahl's late nineteenth century romantic painting titled *the Coming Storm* Fig. 167.

The Hordaland helm assembly is similar to that used in Faroe. According to Mortensen the adoption of the rudder came late to Faroe and appears to

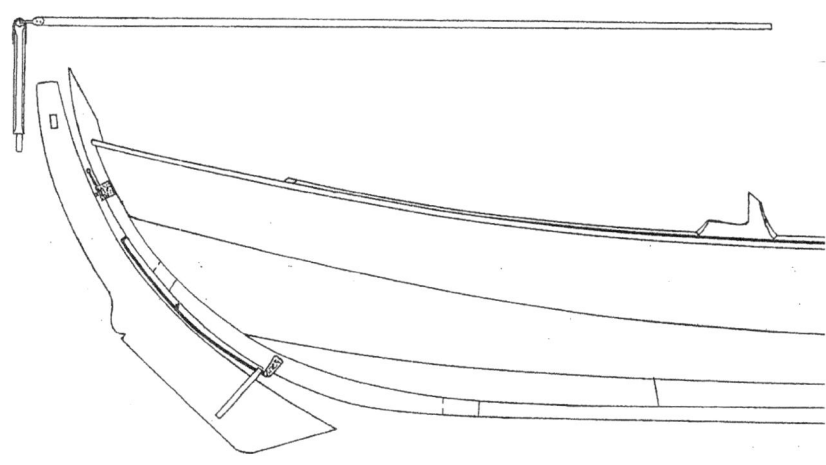

Fig. 162. *Pintle and gudgeon arrangement on a seksæring from the Barony Rosendal. Observe the captive sliding bolt, upper stem, and the lower long pintle. Drawing: Arne Emil Christensen. Courtesy of Norwegian Maritime Museum, Oslo.*

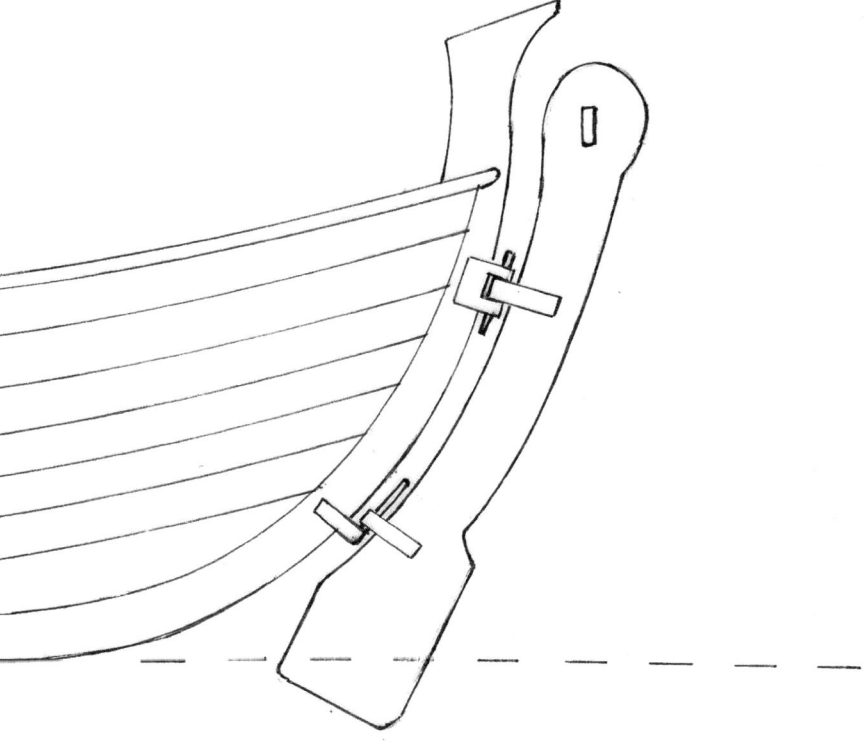

Fig. 163. *Rudder attachment on a Faroese boat. Drawing: M. Chivers.*

coincide with the adoption of the asymmetric dipping square sail, which, as previously described, was probably brought to Faroe by Pløyen following his trip to Shetland in 1839. Prior to this Faroese boats were steered by an oar (Mortensen 2000: 322).

The Shetland helm slotted onto the rudder head-stock, which was curved. This enabled the skipper to unship the helm quickly, simply by lifting and levering it backwards over the curved head-stock (Fig. 168). The rudder head-stock seen on the model of the Fair Isle yoal, if original, is of an unusual form (Osler 1983: 78). The head-stock, upon which the helm slots, is square. To remove the helm would necessitate pulling it vertically upwards (Fig. 159). The head-stock on the model of the yoal when compared to that of the Foula sixareen is similar, in that the head of the rudder is slender, although the Foula sixareen has the usual Shetland curved head-stock form (Fig. 160). This was a far more secure method of securing the helm, and the headstock and helm assembly on the model of the Fair Isle yoal appear flimsy. This therefore leads us to question the provenance of the rudder on this model yoal. Is it original? Or was the original lost or damaged, and a new rudder made? On the other hand this rudder may be original and if so illustrates a transition from a Norwegian style of rudder to a Shetland one (Osler 1983: 78).

Summary

So what have we learned about the origin and development of Shetland's indigenous boats? We have seen that they are Norse in origin but that they have been much adapted over time. Although originally Norse Shetland's indigenous boats are not of an unbroken Norse lineage. This is because boatbuilding in Shetland was far less conservative than in western Norway, as exemplified by the Oselvar which has retained many Norse boatbuilding features, an example of which is the axe-carved hals. The development of Shetland's indigenous boats began during the late eighteenth century and this maritime heritage is more nuanced, and interesting, than previously appreciated.

Shetland's boatbuilding tradition was eclectic, adapting practices to suit local circumstances and individual boatbuilder preferences. More than that, because of the limitations that geography and economy imposed, there was little opportunity, or need, for islanders to radically change their boatbuilding practices. Instead change was incremental and only accelerated as trading boomed from the late nineteenth century. The slow rate of change meant that local names were retained for the constituent parts of boats, which gives a false impression of an unbroken Norse lineage. The nineteenth century was when Shetland boats became a true vernacular product – they were developed to suit local conditions and meet the needs of a changing commercial fishery.

Fig. 164. *Rudder on the model of the Ness Yoal* Venerable *LK 596 built by Jack Shewan (date unknown). Photo: M. Chivers. Collection Shetland Museum & Archives.*

Fig. 165. *Rudder assembly on the Walter Shewan built ballasted racing boat* Miss Gadabout. *Note the rudder ends in line with the keel. Unst Boat Haven collection. Photo: M. Chivers.*

Fig. 166. *The articulation of the Norwegian helm. This system is still used today. Boat Hall in the Hordamuseet. Photo: M. Chivers.*

Fig. 167. *The Coming Storm, West Norway. By Hans Dahl. Oil on canvas 40¾ by 57⅝ inches (103.51 X 146.37 cm). Photo: Jueqian Fang. Courtesy of the Frye Art Museum, Seattle, USA.*

Fig. 168. *Rudder from an old yoal. Note the curved headstock over which the helm was levered on and off. Photo: A. Osler. Courtesy of Shetland Museum & Archives.*

Chapter 10

The modern Shetland boat part 2: boat use

T he development of Shetland's vernacular boats was driven by the needs of the fishing industry. As this industry changed so did the boats; as observed in other North Atlantic fisheries in western and northern Norway, Faroe, and Iceland (Starkey 2009: 16). By contrast the everyday use of boats in Shetland had remained constant. Boats were used for subsistence activities such as fishing, going to the shop, moving livestock and flitting peats. The important role that boats played in the day-to-day life of Shetlanders has previously been understated. Perhaps this is because the everyday use of boats was commonplace, taken for granted, and therefore not documented. In this chapter we will explore how boats were used, and this will provide us with a clear picture of how central the boat was to everyday life.

The fundamentals of the haaf fishery

The haaf fishing season, during the nineteenth century, was short. It began around 20th May and ended about 12th August (Edmondston 1809: 234). Late May to early August is when Shetland experiences the longest period of daylight hours. During these months the nights are very short, and it is never truly dark; locally this is called the simmer dim. This is also the period when Shetland's weather is, for the most part, benign. As a rule, boats went twice a week to the haaf. This was, of course, weather dependent. It is generally accepted that the average distance to the far haaf was 30 to 50 nautical miles (56 to 93km) (Bruce 1914: 296, Sandison 1954: 17, Goodlad 1971: 102, Fenton 1978: 575, Hance Smith 1984: 49-52, Munro 2012: 24-26). In Shetland there has been a popular, and exaggerated, cultural belief that boats on the west coast often fished within sight of the clouds above Faroe, and on the east coast within sight of the mountain peaks of Norway (March 1970: 55, Goodlad 1971: 102). This is a romantic claim, and there is absolutely no evidence to support it.

The available evidence, found in the 1869 fishing boat register, illustrates that a boat's size was dictated by the distance it had to travel to the fishing grounds (SMA, CE85/11). A notable example was Sandness where there were no sixareens registered. Instead fourareens were used for longline fishing. Burra is also an interesting example. In 1869 there were 46 six-oared boats, and out of these only three were classed as typical 18ft (5.5m) of keel haaf sixareens. All the other six-oared boats had a keel length of 15ft (4.6m) which suggests that their fishing grounds were relatively close to shore. This view is supported by the Reverend James Gardner's report of there being 10 six-oared boats of 15ft (4.6m) of keel in Burra in 1845. According to Gardner these boats only had to venture one nautical mile from shore: here the fishermen set their lines in the evening, returned home, and then retrieved their lines the following morning (New Statistical Account 1845: 15). With such close-to-shore fishing grounds it is not surprising to discover that in Burra the number of six-oared boats had quadrupled by 1869.

By contrast the fishermen from Quarff and Bressay (on the east side of the same parish as Burra) operated from the Noss fishing station and were reputed to travel as far as 50 nautical miles (93km) from shore, sometimes spending two nights at sea (New Statistical Account 1845: 15). The precise location of many of the haaf fishing grounds is now forgotten, although their general regional location is known. These common fishing grounds were located off the east coast of Unst, near to what is today called the Pobi Bank. The boats from Fetlar, Whalsay and Out Skerries fished a poorly defined area known locally as the Fetlar haaf, and similarly, the fishermen operating from Noss went to the Bressay haaf, an area which is now called the Forty Mile Ground (Goodlad 1971: 102).

The Havera haaf is also frequently mentioned but it is not possible today to identify its exact location (Goodlad 1971: 102). An oral history of the distance to the Foula haaf was provided by Tommy Isbister, whose ancestors were from Foula:

> ... They went from 12 to 20 miles nor west o' Foula, that's where the normal fishing ground was, and the Papil [Burra] boats would have gone to the same place, west side o' here [Trondra] and Walls and Sandness they would have all gone to that area. And they tell me on Foula that the farthest they went was 30 mile due west from Foula. But it had to be very fine weather; the last time they were there was 1870 when the Franco Prussian war broke out ... This old man, he was a cousin of me father, ... and he said that they crossed deeper water then came to shallower water; so, I get to the chart and I look at it, and it's on the chart as the Otter Bank and it's exactly 30 mile due west fae Foula ... (PI, Isbister 2015).

This oral history contradicts the Statistical Account. However, as Isbister highlighted, the distance the fishermen travelled was weather dependent. Sandy Gorman (a pen name, this person's real identity remains unknown) in the account of his first year at the haaf, when he was 16, recalled that on one occasion he was at sea two nights and that they caught about one ton of fish which was considered a very good haul (Gorman 1885: 5). Charles Johnson, a haaf fisherman from a well-respected fishing family, and a survivor of the 1881 disaster, recalled his experiences at the haaf in *Manson's Shetland Almanac* in 1932. Johnson described the distances travelled to the fishing grounds:

... up to ten miles off shore was reckoned the inshore fishing-ground. About 16 miles was reckoned the mid, or trading ground, off and on according to fish and weather. With suitable weather and few fish on the trading ground, fish were sought further off, up to 20 miles. The furthest offshore ever I was, and the old men said so too, was in the 1881 disaster, when we were four hours under sail to land. Had it been clear weather we would not have been so far off, but as it was we had gone further than intended (Simpson 2017: 47).

Johnson spoke more about the distance travelled to the fishing grounds and stated that he had read that open boats had "gone the land down" and as far as 70 miles. This he said was "bunkom". "They had a rule not to go out of sight of land, and in fact it was seldom ever they lost sight of more than the low lands ... The men in my time were too wise to try nonsense of that kind, and men before my time were wiser still with their open boats" (Simpson 2017: 47).

Haaf fishing preparations

The process of haaf fishing can be divided into the following general categories: the preparation for fishing; the actual process of going to the fishing grounds; setting and hauling the lines; and bringing the catch back to shore. The first chore was the procurement of bait. Haddock or piltock were the preferred bait for the haaf fishery and these were caught using limpets, piltocks or mussels (Shirreff 1814: 86; Gorman 1885: 5; March 1971: 40; Coull 2007: 7, 9). Piltocks were caught with a rod and line from a small whillie close to shore, and lures or limpets were used as bait (Shirreff 1814: 86; Gorman 1885: 5; March 1971: 40; Coull 2007: 7, 9). Limpet bait was obtained at low-tide, when normally submerged rocks on which they were attached were exposed. Clamped tenaciously to rocks, limpets were gathered by levering them off with the aid of a knife (Fenton 1978: 528). If mussels were to be used as bait then these were obtained by dredging, usually from a fourareen (Coull 2007: 9).

Generally, four out of the six crewmen would go and fish for haddocks. This was classed as an inshore fishery that extended up to six nautical miles. The remaining two crew members prepared for the following day's haaf fishing by gathering-up the fishing lines once they had dried, repairing any damaged line as they went. The two crewmen then baked bread to be taken to the haaf, and cooked a meal ready for the crew returning from haddock fishing. Once all preparations been attended to the crew would sleep before rising early the following morning (Shirreff 1814: 86). During the haaf season lack of sleep was a constant problem, with the men having no more than three or four hours sleep in every forty-eight (Shirreff 1814: 86). In benign conditions the lack of sleep would just be irksome, but when the weather deteriorated this would be a serious problem. Concentration, crew co-ordination, and fast reflexes are essential in handling a small open boat in heavy weather. I believe it highly likely that fatigue, combined with the effects of dehydration, hunger and cold-slowed reflexes which caused poor judgement, and this would have been a factor in the tragic loss of many boats and their crews. Unfortunately, there is no documentary evidence to inform a balanced argument; although the fact that sleep deprivation was mentioned by Shirreff suggests that it was a recognised problem.

Hauling boats

Shetland's indigenous boats were launched and recovered from beaches and, when not in use, were kept in simple structures called noosts. Where the shoreline was rocky boat draws were constructed, and good examples of these have been observed at Hamnavoe, Papa Stour, and at Skaw in Whalsay (Figs. 169-170) (Tait 2012: 473-475). Launching and recovering boats from a beach meant that there were limits on boat size and weight. The practice required boats that were lightweight with easily removeable tafts and tilfers to further reduce weight (PI, Wishart 2015).

Boat hauling was relatively easy on the stony beaches found at haaf fishing stations, but on sandy or shingly beaches was much more difficult. In these circumstances runners called linns were placed beneath the boat's keel; these were an essential aid to the hauling process. The preferred material for linns were whale ribs, which had the benefit of not floating. Friction between the boat's keel and the linns was reduced by covering the linns in seaweed before dragging the boat over them (PI, Wishart 2015). Traditionally Norwegian pine (latterly Scottish larch) was used to construct the first three strakes up from the keel and the remaining strakes above these were constructed from white wood (Sitka spruce) (PI, Hutchison, McNeil 2015; PI, Isbister 2015). Sitka spruce is less durable but half the weight of pine or larch boards, and this significantly reduced the weight of the boat, thus making it easier to handle ashore. As previously discussed, due to their size and weight the larger sixareens were kept moored afloat during the haaf season.

Boat handling at the haaf

We have already seen that the preferred motive power was sailing. By 1809 there is evidence that boats usually sailed to and from the haaf and that when caught in bad weather the crews opted to sail for land (Edmondston 1809: 239). Indeed, attempting to row to the land in severe weather sometimes resulted in men dropping dead at their oar from exhaustion and exposure (Kerr 1831: 189 -194). However, the principal problem with sailing an asymmetric dipping square sail rigged boat in big seas was tacking. When tacking, the sail had to be lowered and the yard dipped and moved from one side of the mast to the other in order that the sail could be raised on the new tack. Undertaking this manoeuvre in heavy seas put the boat at risk

Fig. 169. *Examples of boat noosts with boat draws just visible below the tide line. Hamnavoe, Papa Stour. Photo: M. Chivers.*

Fig. 170. *Large boat draw in Skaw, Whalsay. Photo: M. Chivers.*

from broaching and, in extreme situations, this could result in a capsize before the sail could be re-hoisted on the new tack (Kerr 1831: 189 -194). An eye-witness account of the sail being used during the infamous storm of 1832 was provided by 17-year-old medical student Edward Charlton, who had sailed from Leith to Shetland and arrived in Lerwick in time to witness the great storm from the deck of the ship, which was in quarantine as the authorities thought that there was an outbreak of cholera onboard. Charlton recalled: "... It was a really beautiful but withal anxious sight to watch these poor fellows ... one managed the helm, and the other three attended to the sail, as the boat dashed through the heavy surf. As each white squall swept down, dashing spray in sheets into the air, we saw the sail lowered and then cautiously raised again ..." (Charlton 2007: 15). The 1832 storm began on 16th July and raged for five days during which time 31 sixareens and 105 men were lost at sea.

Charlton's vivid description of a boat running for shelter during the summer storm of 1832 illustrates that the survival of the crew depended equally upon the expert handling of the sail and the steering of the boat. Generally, boats went to the haaf in a company of two, the supporting boat was called the ranksman. They endeavoured to keep as near to one another as possible and the crews pledged to help each other in case of distress. In this way many lives were saved (Clark 1837: 450). An eye-witness account from the Gloup fishing disaster of 1881, when 26 sixareens and 36 men were lost, illustrates the role of the ranksman. In this account a boat skippered by William Henry came in with Magnus Scollay. All went well until they approached land and Henry's boat foundered. Scollay at once brought his boat up to the wind and stood to the upturned boat, where four of the crew were seen clinging to the keel. Scollay tried to approach the upturned boat but was driven back by an exceptionally large wave, which also swept away two of the four stranded men. Scollay refused to give-up, and when he could not approach the upturned boat under sail he tried to reach the stricken crew under oar. Unfortunately an oar broke and another was lost: it was only then that Scollay realised that he would not be able to save the two remaining crewmen (SMA, *The Shetland Times,* 23rd July, 1881).

Oral accounts of boat handling in extreme conditions illustrate the importance of the sail in order to make landfall. In the 1832 disaster a boat from Funzie, in Fetlar, was observed pulling under oars with its mast laid down. The boat was appearing to be making headway, but maintaining this for hours was impossible; the wind was so strong that it blew the tarpaulins off of the steeples of fish scattering them about the beaches, and so there was no chance that this boat could have made land (Laurenson 1963: 25-27). Another oral history, this time from John Smith, who was present at the Gloup fishing disaster in 1881, described the important use of the sail in running from a storm. The skipper was experienced in managing boats in extreme conditions, and he insisted that the men, who wanted to cut the fishing lines and run as soon as the storm struck, continued to haul them during the short summer night. There were two reasons for his decision: the first was that they needed the fish to ballast and trim the boat, and second, it was safer to wait for daylight before running. This was an important factor, as Smith stated that many boats were lost because they ran at night, when the conditions, combined with darkness, made it impossible to see where they were going:

> The daylight had well come when we got all our lines, which I think was the means of saving our lives ... we got the mast and sail on our boat, every reef tied in and the balance reef also ... the reef down the after leech of the sail to equalise it on every side of the mast which made the boat easier to steer. We run away, our little boat behaving well in such awful weather ... We were now coming into the 'strings', that is the tide rips running west which was making the sea very steep. A large sea made on our weather quarter when the skipper could not avoid it, he put down the helm and the great sea broke over our stern, taking about five hundredweight of fish overboard. I looked aft and all I could see of our skipper was his head through the white foam ... up went the sail and drew the boat ahead and what water came on board was soon gone out by the pump and bailer (March 1970: 64-65).

This account by Smith adds weight to Osler's previously discussed observation that the first set of reefing points at the head of the sail did not run parallel to the yard. This he surmised was so the lug sail, when reefed, would revert to a true square sail, which would be more balanced when running before the wind. A letter written by James Balfour to T.M.Y. Manson in 1950 confirms Osler's observation: "... the haaf boats sails had a slight peak ... which they used to reef off to make the sail square when running before a breeze ..." (SMA, letter from James Balfour to T.M.Y. Manson 18/02/1950. Box 21/1). In John Smith's account of reefing the sail he mentioned the "balance reef" which ran the entire length of the sail's leech making the sail narrower and more balanced when running before the wind.

Another account of sailing in bad weather, provided by Gorman illustrates how the boat was handled when sailing to windward:

> ... we got ou sail an' med for da land. Da wind wiz be dis time aboot nor'– nor' wast, an' wir coorse wiz a wast, sae it took iz a wir time ta lie it. We took a single reef, in dey wir mony a time 'at we wid needed a dooble een ... We sailed fir seven 'oors an' it took twa haands a' da time bailin' oot lee water as hard as iver dey cood pelt (Gorman 1885: 5).
>
> ... we got out the sail and made for the land. The wind was by this time about north-north west and our course was west, so it took us a long time to lie it. We took in a single reef and there were many times we needed a double one ... We sailed for seven hours and it took two hands at a time to bail out as hard as they could the water that was coming over the lee side.

Here the asymmetric shape of the dipping lug sail was helpful, as this created more lift and enabled the boat to point higher, thus sailing a course closer to the wind (Simpson 2016: 36). This description of managing a sixareen in bad weather illustrates further that sailing was the key to survival. The boat beating to windward, with just a single reef in the sail, was over-pressed, and if the sail had been double-reefed the boat would not have taken as much water over the leeward side. Johnson, writing of his experience of the 1881 disaster, stated that the sail was vital to the survival of the boat; it was not speed they were after, but the ability to manoeuvre to avoid the worst of the seas (Johnson 1932: 189-196).

Setting and hauling lines

Each member of the crew had their own set of fishing lines, called a pakki (Figs. 171-172). Each pakki was made-up of bughts of line, the length and number of which varied from region to region. A boat's total number of pakkis was called a fleet of tows and when the lines were being set each pakki was tied together. It is now apparent that it was not always the case, as suggested by Halcrow (1950: 75) and Goodlad (1971: 107) that the biggest boats used the longest lines (Table 17). The regional variation in the length of longline used was in some instances considerable and it is not known why there was such great variation in the total longline length. For instance, in the parishes of Sandsting and Aithsting each bught of line was 50 fathoms long and there were 16 bughts of line to a pakki. When all the lines were joined and set the longline was 4.7 nautical miles (8.9km)

Fig. 171. *The fishing hooks on this six bught line are rigged at three fathom (18ft or 5.5m) intervals. Photo: M. Chivers.*

Fig. 172. *Six bught of line belonging to Tommy Isbister, Burland, Trondra. Each bught is 40 fathoms. Fishermen in Foula carried two of these six bught lines in the boat which made the fleet of tows 2.8NM (5.3KM) long. Photo: M. Chivers.*

long (*New Statistical Account* 1845: 130-131). Conversely, boats from Bressay and Quarff carried 50 bughts, each 50 fathoms long, which when joined and set made a longline of 2.4 nautical miles (4.5km) (*New Statistical Account* 1845: 15).

The haaf men set their lines in the evening so they would leave for the fishing grounds between six and eight in the morning, not returning before the following evening (Shirreff 1814: 86-87). Once at the haaf they would bait and set their lines, the hooks being spaced between 20ft (6.1m) to 30ft (9.1m) apart. If the weather was moderate this would take about three hours but if rough this process would of course take much longer (Shireff 1814: 86-87; March 1970: 40). The lines, once set, lay along the seabed held in place by four flat stone weights called kappis

Fishing boat data described by Edmondston (1809) & ministers in the New Statistical Account (1845).

Number of boats	Fishing station, island or parish	Length of keel - feet & (metres)	Alleged distance to the haaf -nautical? or statute? miles	Total length of line - nautical miles & (kilometres)
13	Bressay	18 – 20 (5.5 – 6.1)	50	2.5 (4.6)
10	Burra	15 (4.6m)	1	?
?	Fethaland (Northmavine)	?	40 – 50	5.9 (10.9)
17	Fetlar	13 – 19.6 (4 – 6)	?	?
?	Hamnavoe (Northmavine)	?	40 – 50	?
?	Stenness (Northmavine)	?	40 – 50	5.9 (10.9)
?	Uyea (Northmavine)	?	40 – 50	?
8	Aithsting & Sandsting fishing from Papa Stour	18 (5.5)	?	4.7 (8.9)
4	Quarff fishing from Noss	18 – 20 (5.5 – 6.1)	50	2.5 (4.6)
	Unst	18-22 (5.5-6.7)		2.5 - 4.2 (4.7 - 7.7)
25	North Yell	17 - 20 (5.2 – 6.1)	?	?

Table 17. *Edmondston (1809: 235); The New Statistical Account of Scotland Vol XV 1845.*

(Fig. 173). Each kappi weighed about 16 lbs (7.25k) and to the kappi a rope riser was fastened, which led to a buoy attached to it on the surface. As well as the kappi stanes each line had its own sinker called a bighter which weighed about 2lbs (91g) (*New Statistical Account* 1845: 131). When the lines were set the boat's crew would wait at the last buoy for about one and three-quarter hours, after which they would haul the kappi, and proceed rowing the boat along the line, whilst one man hauled it, and another took the fish off the hook; whereupon another crewman would gut and behead the fish, which was then stowed in the shott; the heads and the livers being kept in the midrum, and the lines and buoys were then stowed in the headrum of the boat (Fig. 174) (Shirreff 1814: 87; March 1970: 40).

Sixareen rums

The divisional spaces between the bands in Shetland's vernacular boats were called rums (rooms), and each room was given a name, and served a function (Fig. 174). In the sixareen (beginning at the bow of the boat) these rooms were: the headrum which contained the fishing lines and two water breakers; the sail was also stowed there when not in use. Next was the forerum which was the fore-half of the boat, where the ballast was stowed along with the fire kettle, the cooking pot, and fuel for the fire (peat). Food preparation was also undertaken in this section of the boat and the provisions were kept in a sea chest, covered by a tarpaulin, that was secured against the forerum taft. The midrum was used in fine weather for shooting and hauling the fishing lines. The owserum came next, and the tilfers here were slightly higher than elsewhere in the boat so that the shøl (shovel) had a clean sweep from one side of the boat to the other. The shøl was able to hold two gallons (10 litres) of water, so this was hard work for the person bailing. Next to the owserum was the shott, also sometimes called the run or waderum which was where the fish were stowed. To prevent the catch from shifting fore and aft and unbalancing the trim of the boat there were vertical slats fastened between the crossbeam (bekk) and the frame (band) called reabands or fiskavils (Fig. 174). Then finally there was the room variously called the shott-hole, kannie or hurrick which is where the helmsman, who was also the skipper, sat; and as well as steering the boat he also controlled the mainsheet. A pump was fitted to the bulkhead of the shott-hole and this was within easy reach of the skipper. A dry card compass was also fitted here. It was not possible to steer by compass when the weather was bad, so the skipper would take a bearing, and then use the wind as his guide (Fig. 175) (Johnson 1932: 189-196).

Fishermen's garb

An important part of vernacular boat use was the clothing the men wore to protect themselves from the elements. Edward Charlton in 1832 provided a good eye-witness account of the garb worn during that period.

Fig. 173. *Kappi stanes for a fishing long line. Photo: J. Peterson, (1956). Courtesy of Shetland Museum & Archives.*

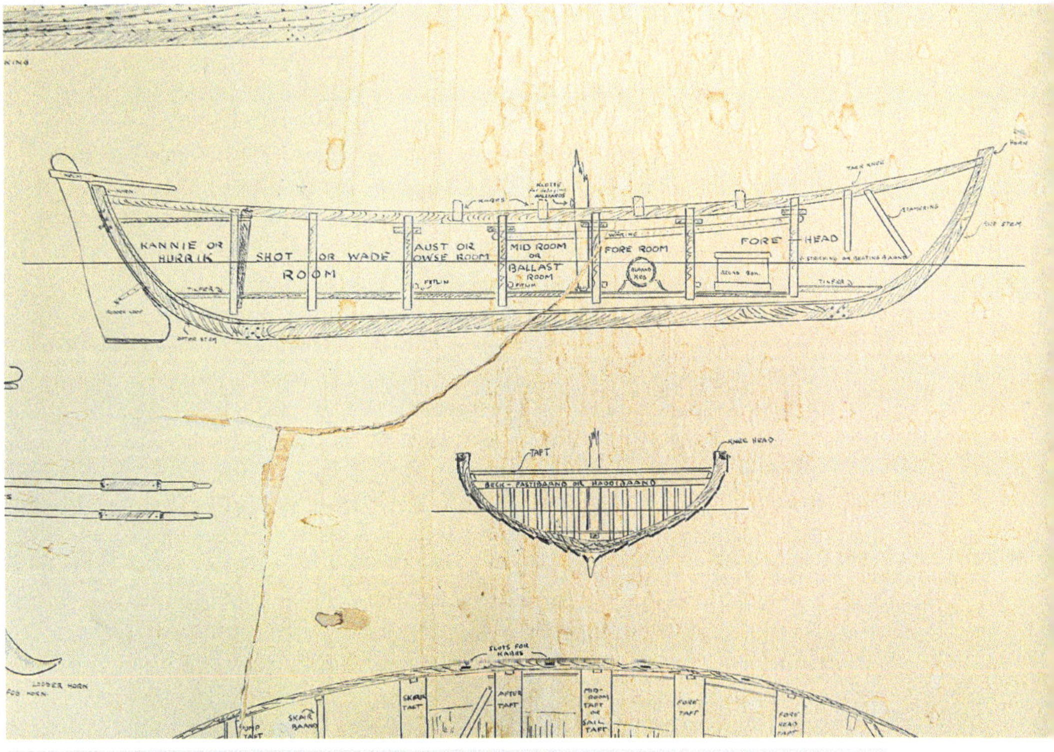

Fig. 174. *Drawing by Arthur Johnson of the general arrangment of a sixareen (c.1930). ART1993.313. Photo: M. Chivers. Courtesy of Shetland Museum & Archives.*

Fig. 175. *Sixareen compass made by David Stalker, Leith. Formerly owned by P. Blance. Shetland Museum & Archives collection FIS. 7874. Photo: M. Chivers.*

... two yawls full of, to me, strange looking mortals broke through the mist, pulled astern of the ship without hailing and disappeared in the driving fog. They were Shetland fishermen, the first I had ever seen, and I shall never forget the impression their strange garb made upon me. Dressed in their skin coats and breeches, with their nether limbs encased in huge boots, they rather resembled the pictures we have seen of some of the Esquimaux tribes ... However, the long fair hair of the Shetlanders, escaping in curls down upon their shoulders from beneath their large pendant caps of variegated worsted, certainly gave a more picturesque appearance than the inhabitants of the more northern clime. Their boats, extremely sharp at both ends, with an extraordinary spring fore and aft, were not the least curiosity about them, and the rapid glance I caught of the whole as they burst suddenly through the fog, and were as quickly reinvested in its heavy canopy ... (Charlton 2007: 5).

Charlton's description is complemented by an observation on haaf fishermen by John T. Reid, in his book *Art Rambles in Shetland*, published in 1869: "... the fishermen commonly appeared in knitted nightcaps, with brilliant strips of colours, or with a tarpaulin 'sou-wester'; a surtout of tanned sheepskin, that covered the arms and overlapped their woollen trousers; and stout seaboots that reached up over their knees" (Reid 1869: 56). By the late nineteenth century, when imports were common, canvas smookies that were waterproofed by being coated with linseed oil replaced the sheepskin type (PI, Tait 2016). This description is further supported by clothing in the collections of the Shetland Museum and Archives (Figs. 176-181). This, although from the early twentieth century, will have been very similar to, if not the same as, that worn by fishermen during the late nineteenth century..

Fig. 176. *Drawing of Shetland fishermen by Samuel Hibbert (1822).*

Fig. 177. *Knitted fishermen's undergarment c.1920s. Shetland Museum & Archives collection. Photo: M. Chivers.*

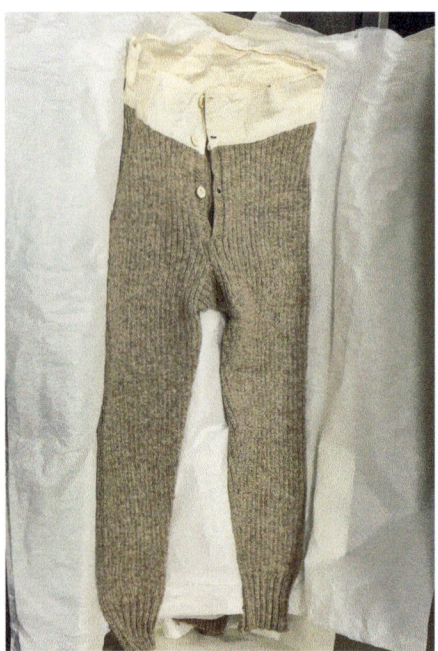

Fig. 178. *Knitted fishermen's undergarment Shetland Museum & Archives collection. Photo: M. Chivers.*

Fig. 179. *Fishermen's froke or "smookie" c.1920s. Garment is made from heavy cotton and coated with linseed oil to make it waterproof. Would have been tacky to touch when warm. Shetland Museum & Archives collection. Photo: M. Chivers.*

Fig. 180. *An atypical haaf hat, Fair Isle 1916. Normally haaf hats had simple geometric patterns. Shetland Museum & Archives collection. Photo: M. Chivers.*

Fig. 181. *Sixareen crew from Ollaberry. Note the knee high fishing boots. Photograph c.1880. Courtesy of Shetland Museum & Archives.*

Competing fisheries

During the 1820s a new cod fishery began to develop. This was a distant offshore enterprise undertaken from much larger fully decked boats, of between 15 and 20 tons, of a non-indigenous type (Fig. 182). These cod sloops, and later cod smacks, operated from the west and southwest coasts of Shetland. The reason for the development of the cod fishery is opaque. Historian Hance D. Smith suggested that its leading proponents, James Hay and John Ross, used it as a cover for smuggling, and even though the cod fishery continued to expand it never superseded the haaf fishery. Indeed, even the 1832 disaster only had a temporary limiting effect on the growth of the haaf which was boosted by high fish prices. This new cod fishing enterprise was not always successful, and there were seasons when the cod did not appear (Smith, H. 1984: 110-112).

Samuel Hibbert described the cod fishery as being of great importance as it provided employment to many seamen who were given the opportunity of purchasing small shares in these vessels. These men, Hibbert explained, had been sailors in the navy or at the Greenland whaling, and they had brought home small amounts of savings with which they brought their fishing shares (Hibbert 1822: 523). These returning seafarers therefore were not tied to any tenancy agreement, in which they were obliged to fish for a landlord or a merchant, but instead were free to fish and trade on their own account.

Fig. 182. *Cod smack* Ida *LK 25. Photograph c.1880. Courtesy of Shetland Museum & Archives.*

Fig. 183. *A rare depiction of a half-decker. Painted by Charles McEwan. Courtesy of Shetland Museum & Archives.*

The rosy picture painted by Hibbert should be tempered slightly, as it is not clear how many men who returned home found themselves in the position of being free from obligations to fish for their land-master or his nominated merchant. Indeed, Hance D. Smith pointed out that the haaf fishery during this period was expanding due to high fish prices, albeit not at the same rate as the cod fishery. But without further evidence, it is not possible to speculate how many men returning home were investing in the cod fishery.

The development of the cod industry was followed during the 1830s by the emergence of a herring fishery, and again, non-indigenous boats of the mainland Scottish half-decked type were commonly used (Fig. 183) (New Statistical Account 1845: 5; Gear 2013: 65). It is clear from the *New Statistical Account* that ling, cod and herring were the main fisheries at that time, and both the cod and the herring industries increasingly took men out of the ling-fishing workforce. By 1840 Hay & Ogilvy owned approximately 100 herring half-deckers, and they built approximately 120 further boats. However, this was a short-lived herring boom that was brought to an abrupt end by several factors: the storm in 1840 (during which many half-decked boats were lost); sub-standard fish curing; the emancipation of slaves in the West Indies (herring was the staple food in the slave colonies and with emancipation this trade ceased); and the collapse of the Shetland Bank in 1842 (which pushed Hay & Ogilvy into bankruptcy). (Nicolson 1982: 32; Gear 2013: 65).

Pløyen, during his visit of 1839, provided a first-hand account of these half-decked boats which shows that they were not a generic type: "Such a boat is 80 to 100 barrels burden, but although alike in size, their build and rigging are extremely variable. Some of them are sharp both fore and aft, some have a flat stern and broad bow, some have one mast with a large spret sail, foresail and jib, others have two masts and a big lug-sail – in short there is the greatest variety" (Pløyen 1896: 170).

It is important to realise that although the herring industry was prosecuted in the main from half-decked boats it was also undertaken from many of the haaf sixareens, after the short three-month ling season had ended (SMA, CE85/11/5: 6, 21, 27, 29-32, 46-47, 54-55, 58, 68, 78, 94). During the 1860s herring fishing from sixareens in the parish of Walls was encouraged by Hay & Company. This venture failed mainly because sixareens were not large enough to carry sufficient nets to make it profitable (Coull 2007: 108, Halcrow 1950: 82, 130, Gear 2013: 65). This failed enterprise resulted in the Walls sixareen crews, along with the Walls shop owner John Lyall, being in debt (Coull 2007: 112). It was not surprising to learn from the fishing boat registers that by 1869 the Walls sixareen crews had abandoned herring fishing (SMA, CE85/11/5: 15, 85, 140, 161, 174, 175, 180, 211-213. CE85/11/6: 15).

From about 1872 mainland Scottish decked boats had begun to visit Shetland and fish at the haaf. These Scottish boats set and hauled longlines under sail, which Shetland fisherman had previously thought was impossible, and by 1880 the haaf fishery was beginning to feel the pressure from these Scottish boats

(Goodlad 1971: 125; Coull 2007: 46-47). This was further exacerbated by the previously mentioned Gloup fishing disaster in 1881 in which 10 boat crews were lost. During this storm there were several decked ling, cod, and herring boats at sea. All these decked boats came though the storm unscathed. They were safer and much more economic to operate. Cost efficiency was the greatest factor, more than any other, that heralded the end of the sixareen (Goodlad 1971: 124). Following the 1881 disaster there ensued a public debate, held in the press, extoling both the virtues and vices of the sixareen. Jesssie Saxby in 1882 wrote that the idea of some people is to do away with this outmoded craft and adopt the "bluff-bood Buckie boat," whereas there are others that wish to extol the merits of the sixareen and encourage the fishermen to continue as their forefathers had done (SMA, D1/134/228). Others went further still and attempted to instruct the men on how to manage these boats in case of any emergency. Saxby herself who was one of these commentators: "This giving of advice to fishermen is often thankless work, as they generally consider themselves better judges than land's men in general and ladies in particular" (SMA, D1/134/228).

By the mid-1880s the fish trade was changing. The herring boom had begun but as well as resources being channelled to meet the demand for herring, another lucrative new market in fresh fish was also beginning. This new demand for fresh cod, haddock, hake, skate and halibut was made possible by the development of the refrigeration process to manufacture ice. The innovation of manufactured ice, along with the new all-year-round steamer contacts between Shetland, Aberdeen and Leith, and the new rail links to the south made the transport of fresh fish commercially viable (Hance Smith 1984: 161; Coull 2007: 55-57).

The fishery board annual report for 1882 stated: "The quantity of ling caught in Shetland during the season was fully equal to the average of recent years; and in the cod and ling fishing, as in the herring fishing, the six-oared open boats, which were formerly so much in use, are gradually being superseded by large decked boats" (SMA, SA4/1199/1: xxxiv). The report for 1884 said that the herring fishing that year was very good and the Shetland fleet had increased from 792 to 932 boats, and of these 45 were old six-oared boats (SMA, SA4/1199/2:xxiv).

In 1886, following the passing of the Crofters Holdings (Scotland) Act, the Lords of the Treasury gave powers to the Fishery Board of Scotland to grant loans to fishermen in crofter parishes that abutted the sea. To bring these new powers into effect parliament passed the Public Works Loans Act. This provided the fishery board with an annual grant of £20,000 for making loans to fishermen to buy boats and equipment. In addition, the Sea Fishing Boats (Scotland) Act 1886 enabled, for the first time, fishing boats to be used as security against which loans could be made. These three acts were very important in enabling the British fishing industry to develop. Parliament recognised that the people of Argyll, Inverness, Ross, Cromarty, Sutherland, Caithness, Orkney and Shetland were "wretchedly poor" and dependent upon the sea for the means of their subsistence (SMA, SA4/1199/2: xxix).

Fig. 184. *Haddock boat sailing in Linga Sound, Whalsay. Rigged with standing lug and jib. Courtesy of Shetland Museum & Archives.*

This new source of funding meant that fishermen could apply for loans and use that capital to build a new boat or buy new fishing gear, and the boat itself was used to guarantee the loan. In 1889 the fisheries board reported that they had received 19 loan applications from Shetland, 16 of which were for boats, and three were for gear; the total amount advanced was £1,816. 18/- (SMA, SA4/199/3: Iiii).

The inshore cod and haddock fishery

The fishing industry was changing rapidly and the traditional haaf fishery, along with the sixareen, was now in decline. However, as previously discussed, there were two new specialised types of indigenous craft – the spring or summer boat (colloquial names for the inshore cod boat) and the haddock boat (Fig. 184). These had developed in response to the demand for fresh fish (Hance Smith 1984: 168). Whilst there was a drive for fishermen to invest in larger boats, in the parts of Shetland where the inshore cod and haddock fishery developed the vernacular forms prevailed until the early twentieth century, when competition from Aberdeen steam trawlers changed the scale of the fishing operation in Shetland (Simpson 2010: 61). The haddock fishery was more widespread, and a much larger operation than the regional inshore cod fishery, which was localised to the area between Scalloway and South Havera.

Fig. 185. *George Henry of Shoreside, Bridge of Walls, baiting a haddock line with mussels (c.1939). Courtesy of Shetland Museum & Archives.*

Technological development in communication aided the growth of the inshore cod and haddock fishery, and in 1884 it was reported by the Fishery Board of Scotland that the extension of the telegraph in Shetland was enabling fast communication between fishermen and fish curers. Good communication was essential to arrange for the prompt collection and shipment of fresh fish. And the telegraph, along with the new steamer link was a very important factor in the development of Shetland's fresh fish industry (SMA, SA4/119/3: lxxxii).

Haddock lines

A haddock boat would commonly set about half a nautical mile (0.9km) of line, with hooks spaced roughly 4.5ft (1.4m) apart (PI, Williamson 2016). Mussels, limpets or piltocks were commonly used as bait, and unlike haaf longlines haddock lines were baited onshore (Simpson 2010: 60) (Fig. 185). The haddock fishery operated in a very different way to the haaf (where the fishermen travelled and lived at a fishing station during the week). The catch was packed in ice and shipped to mainland Scotland, and this obviated the need for drying beaches. The fishing was inshore so the men were able to live at home during the season, their boats hauled up in convenient nearby noosts. Both the haddock and the summer boat were in effect small versions of the sixareen. Haddock boats ranged in keel length from 13-15ft (4-4.6m), whereas the larger cod boat's keel was around 17ft (5.2m). The reason the summer boat was so much bigger was simply to do with the size of fish, the cod being much larger.

Even though the haddock fishery usually operated within three miles from land, it was not immune to tragedy. Seventeen fishermen died in a storm that struck on 9th December 1887 (Simpson 2016: 34). This began at 3pm. The hurricane force wind was accompanied by an exceptionally heavy fall of snow that lasted for four hours. During this time several feet of snow accumulated on the ground, with snow drifts of up to 6ft (1.8m) deep in Lerwick (*The Shetland News*, 1887).

This tragedy did not slow the development of the haddock fishery. The fishery board reported in 1898 that haddock fishing was now being under-taken all year round; and for six months, from the middle of September until the middle of March, it was the only branch of fishing pursued in Shetland. The bulk of fish were caught between January and March which was when haddocks were in their best condition (SMA, SA4/119/3: 212). During the early years of the twentieth century haddock fishing became an important centralised activity in Skerries, Whalsay, Lerwick, Burra and Scalloway (Goodlad 1971: 222-223).

Subsistence boat use

Subsistence boat activity was the most crucial of all, as it was conducted every day, every year, but little is seen in the written record (PI, Tait 2016). Until the 1840s, when the first roads were constructed, a boat was an essential pre-requisite to living in Shetland. Subsistence boat use included: fishing; hunting whales, seals, and birds; moving livestock; flitting peats; flitting cargo; and going to the shop. Most farms were small, and so were the boats, with many activities requiring only one or two people, whilst other activities such as moving livestock, flitting peats, or whale hunting were communal tasks that brought communities together.

Of subsistence fishing, the most abundant catch were piltocks (the young of the saithe, which when smaller were called sillocks), these were available all year round, and caught close to shore. Sillocks and piltocks, were caught by rod and line from small boats and sometimes using a method of fishing, previously described, called pock netting. In the parish of Delting it was noted by the Reverend John Paton that sillocks and piltocks were exten-sively caught, and these fed the population (*New Statistical Account* 1845: 58). The importance of subsistence fishing was noted by Alexander Fenton who stated that during the 1790s the population of Delting was able to sustain itself for three-quarters of the year provided the sillock and piltock fishing did not fail. Sillocks also supplemented grain stocks, as noted by ministers in the parishes of Lerwick, Nothmavine, Unst and Bressay, where fishing for sillocks took place in the winter (Fenton 1978: 529, 530). A brief description of fishing for sillocks was provided by Edward Charlton: "As we swept slowly up the sound we passed many small boats fishing for sillocks, the fry of the coalfish, which forms a good part of the diet of the poorer classes in Lerwick ... I was surprised to see how many of the boats were rowed by women" (Charlton 1832: 6).

Charlton's surprise at seeing so many women rowing is perhaps not that remarkable considering that in Shetland the division of subsistence gender work roles was not separated as it had been in other parts of Britain at that time. This flummoxed the middle class – male – visitors who came to Shetland in the nineteenth century and witnessed women carrying out tasks that elsewhere would have been the preserve of men (Abrams 2005: 57). Artist and author John Reid wrote that "... we met our host-to-be at the paltock fishing. His daughter, a comely lass, rowed skilfully ..." (Reid 1896: 22). Certainly, during the nineteenth century, when increasingly men were away at sea, the task of running the farm fell to the women. Indeed, the ability of women to sail and row boats as well as any man was described by Fothergill who, in his journal *Travels in Shetland*, noted:

> Having obtained a four oared boat with two men and one woman to row us we were glad to embark at an early hour of the morning in the further prosecution of our voyage. Since so many of the men are carried off to the fisheries, to Greenland, to Hudson's Bay and into the navy, women have been obliged to learn the management of boats in many parts of the Zetland Isles, and this day we had a specimen of what could be performed by one of them, for our female rower seemed to pull at her oar quite as steadily as the men. (Fothergill 30th July, 1806).

Lynn Abrams in her book *Myth and Materiality in a Woman's World: Shetland 1800-2000* provides us with ethnological material that illustrates that women were as capable as men in handling boats, and in this respect there was no division in labour. Often it was the women who regularly flitted peats home, or rowed or sailed to reach the nearest merchant to whom they delivered their hosiery or, if left with no option, to catch fish in the voe.

> They could row and they could use heavy lines because they couldn't afford if the men was away and they saw a nice plank of wood that could be made into useful things, they learned to do the heavy [work] ... and they shopped using the boats. The North of voe women at regattas would outrow the Mid Yell women because they rowed every week across the voe and there were always women's rowing races at regattas ... (Abrams 2005: 95).

Mary Ellen Odie who spoke about her great, great, grandmother, whose husband drowned in the 1832 disaster: "... and she took the boat and went to the fishing to catch something to eat just like a man would ..." Another example of subsistence boat use was provided by Agnes Leask whose aunt, a spinster who lived on a distant rural farm with her brother, would think

Fig. 186. Driving Bottle-Nosed Whales, *Carter 1891. Note women rowing in some of the boats. Courtesy of Shetland Museum & Archives.*

nothing of taking the boat, hoisting the sail, and sailing to Scalloway for a drum of paraffin (Abrams 2005: 95-96).

Of all subsistence boat activity the one that involved the whole community with as many boats as possible was whale hunting. Indeed, apart from going to church this was the only other boat activity permitted on a Sunday (PI, Tait 2016). If a pod was spotted everyone would drop what they were doing and take to their boats. Whales were a valuable resource: their blubber, which was rendered down into oil, was highly prized, but surprisingly the flesh of the whale was very rarely eaten and the corpses generally were left to rot on the beach. The largest recorded pod consisted of 1,540 whales that came into Quendale Bay on 22nd September 1845 (Fenton 1978: 549). A painting titled *Driving Bottle-Nose Whales* by Richard Henry Carter, painted in 1891, perhaps portrays that 1845 Quendale Bay whale hunt (Fig. 186). In Carter's painting women wearing happs can clearly be seen rowing with the men. However, other than this painting there is no written record that women took part in whale hunting.

Another painting, this time by Frank Barnard titled *Typical Scene in Lerwick* (1890) depicts a fourareen lying alongside a quay. On the quay an old woman walks towards the boat carrying provisions. In the forerum of the boat a man holds out his hand to assist her. The boat contains three other women one of whom, standing next to the man, is holding a basket, whilst another is making ready to row, and the remaining woman peers into her basket (Fig. 187). Both these artworks are in the nineteenth century romantic

Fig. 187. Typical Scene in Lerwick, *Barnard 1890. Courtesy of Shetland Museum & Archives.*

Fig. 188. The Market Boat, *Barnard 1890. Courtesy of Shetland Museum & Archives.*

Fig. 189. Ann Jane *LK 331 (built in Lerwick in 1903) swimming off cattle from Stenness to Saila for summer grazing. Photo: W. Brown. Courtesy of Shetland Museum & Archives.*

tradition and therefore depict an idealised version of reality. Nevertheless, the subsistence roles depicted in these paintings provide evidence of normal everyday boat use and helps to reassert that women played an equal part with men.

Flitting

A well-known Shetland scene painting titled *The Market Boat* portrays two women, one elderly and the other young, rowing a heavily laden fouraren containing two other women, one of whom is standing whilst she moves a large heavy basket, presumably to better trim the boat. As well as the women, the boat carries ducks and a dog across Bressay Sound to the market in Lerwick (Barnard 1890) (Fig. 188). The relaxed countenance of the boat's occupants illustrates the normal everyday nature of this crossing. The representation of the boat is accurate, the oar visible in the painting is a faithful representation of a Shetland oar, and the details of worn routh and kabe illustrate that this family boat was old and well-used.

Fig. 189 illustrates the regular subsistence boat activity of flitting livestock during the summer months. In this photograph the men are flitting a cow to the island of Saila, now known as the Isle of Stenness, for summer grazing. Sheep and swine, as well as cattle, were also kept on the isles. Large animals such as oxen and horses, used for ploughing and pulling carts, were transported by swimming them alongside the boat whereas smaller animals such as sheep, ponies, and swine could be transported onboard. Boats that moved smaller livestock were adapted for this purpose by having boards fastened

Fig. 190. *Horse in Cullivoe flitboat, Yell. Note the boards inserted to prevent the hooves of the horse stamping the strakes. Photo: Rev. M. Johnston, (c.1930). Courtesy of Shetland Museum & Archives.*

across the bands that prevented animal hooves stamping the boat's strakes (Fig. 190). Landing livestock on a small holm or island was relatively easy as the boat could be beached, and so there was no need for a pier or quay.

Going to the shop was often undertaken by boat, and it is perhaps not surprising that many shops in Shetland were situated in a convenient waterside position, not just for the ease of their customers but because the goods were also brought there by boat. One example of a waterside shop is the one at Altona, in Mid Yell (Fig. 191). A photograph taken in February 1947 shows the residents of Stivla, Mid Yell, digging their fourareens out of the snow so they could get to the shop on the opposite side of the voe (Fig. 192). This was not a long journey, only about one third of a nautical mile, whereas going around the voe was over four times that distance. This was not unusual. Boats were essential to tend crops, to ferry people across a voe and to go to the shop as Brian Wishart recalled:

> My mother talks about, in the 1930s, two gentlemen, both over 80, who regularly sailed their 22ft boat about 13 nautical miles from their home in Scalloway to tend crops at Walls near to where she lived. She recalled that they had boarded their boat at the end of the day

Fig. 191. *Sandison's shop. Altona, Mid Yell, with the old manse on the hill behind. Photo: C. Stout, (c.1920s). Courtesy of Shetland Museum & Archives.*

Fig. 192. *Digging fourareens out from under the snow in Stivla, Nortavoe, to make a trip to the shop in Mid Yell. Photo: J. Peterson, (1947). Courtesy of Shetland Museum & Archives.*

and faced a long and tiring row home since the wind had died completely. She says they undertook it without a second thought. I myself can recall a gentleman of a similar age using a small flat-bottomed rowing/sailing boat in the late 1950s to take himself about a mile and a half to the local shop and back on a regular basis, and not always in the best of weather. Another elderly lady living nearby used to ask me, a 12-year-old would-be sailor in a 17ft traditional boat, to sail her the half-mile across the voe to visit her relations. What strikes me as significant about this is that she was prepared to put her trust in someone so young, based on her wont, rather than out of any ignorance of the risks. This was in the early 1960s, and I cannot but reflect on the rapid change of lifestyle which followed, in so many ways, but almost always taking people away from their inherited experience of waterborne activity (PI, Wishart 2015).

Travel by fourareen was absolutely normal and nobody gave it a second thought. Prior to mass car ownership and the building of the bridges that link some of the islands to Shetland's Mainland, there was no option other than to travel by fourareen, which can be thought of as the family car of its day.

As already discussed, the mail also came by boat. George Peterson described the postal service that ran between the post office in Sandness and Papa Stour. The service was provided by Sandness man, Laurence Sinclair (Laurie postie). Sinclair retired in 1900, at which time Peterson's grandfather (George Frazer) had a fourareen, the *Maggie*, built in Lerwick, and was awarded the postal contract that same year (Fig. 193). Frazer ran the service until he died in 1937, then one of George Frazer's sons, Willie Frazer, flitted the mail until about 1938 when his brother-in-law, Gideon Sinclair took over the contract until 1962, which was when he and his family left the island and moved to Scalloway. The mail was then taken on by John Jamieson (who had been a whaler) and he had a large non-vernacular partly decked boat built in Burray, Orkney. As well as the mail Jamieson used his boat to fish for lobsters. Jamieson's boat was wrecked around 1983 and the mail service was then taken over by Shetland Islands Council (PI, Peterson 2016).

The majority of subsistence boat activities were family organised operations. Although, as with whale hunting, the flitting of peats was another activity that involved the whole community. This activity is probably best exemplified in the district of Walls. Peter Tait described how, as a child, the flitting of the peats was the highlight of his, and his friends', summer (SMA, DVD 2010). The standard crew for the Walls sixareen flitboat *Industry* was four men and two women, although sometimes there would be more than six people onboard. Although the name of the boat was *Industry* she was always known locally as either the *Flit-Boat* or the *Flittie* (PI, Wishart 2015). The *Flittie* carried a small kedge anchor, and as the boat approached the shore the kedge, which had a long warp attached, was dropped from the stern and when she touched the beach the line was made fast. The kedge served two purposes. First, it kept the boat at ninety degrees to the beach, and second,

Fig. 193. *Launching the Papa Stour mailboat,* Maggie, *at the South Sand. Photo: J. D. Rattar, (c.1930). Courtesy of Shetland Museum & Archives.*

it meant that the boat could be hauled-off when the peats had been loaded aboard. The boat was held in position on the beach using two lines that led from the bow at approximately forty-five degrees to one another; securing the boat ashore. There were two trestles on the boat, one with long legs which was positioned aft, as the water was deeper there, and one with short legs which was positioned about the middle of the boat. Once these trestles were in position, gangplanks were set on top. At this point the women would gather-up the kishies (baskets) and go ashore to start filling them with peats (SMA, DVD 2010).

As well as the main stack of peats there was another stack of small and broken peats; these were shovelled into hessian sacks and were used during loading. The boat would be filled until the peats were gunwale high, and then the peat-filled hessian sacks were arranged on top of the gunwale, around the aft-end making a wall, so that more peats could be loaded three or four feet above the height of the gunwale. Forward in the boat the peats were also stacked above the gunwale, but the main bulk of the peats were stacked aft. It was important to occasionally haul the boat off the beach slightly, to ensure it did not become grounded when fully loaded. To haul the boat off an old ship's lifeboat oar, which was called the pokey, was placed under the stem and used to lever the boat slightly off the beach (SMA, DVD 2010).

Normally there were two peat flitting runs per day and there were a lot of people waiting in Walls to help unload the boat and take the peats to where the stack was being built by one of the old men. Each household would need two boat loads of peats to keep the fires burning over the winter (SMA,

Fig. 194. *Flitboat and peat workers, Vadlure, Walls, late 1920s. Photo: William (Baillie) Moffat. Courtesy of Brian Wishart.*

DVD 2010). Fig. 194 illustrates the Walls community's relationship with the *Flittie*. The people gathered for this photograph are all from the Sooth Neuk of Walls (PI, Wishart 2015). This group photograph is an exemplar of the connectedness that people had to their boats, and how such subsistence flitting activities created close bonds that helped glue communities together through a shared common purpose (PI, Scott 2015, PI, Holt 2015).

Changing boat use 1846-1986: Roads and steamers

The movement of people and goods by sea remained constant for centuries and only began to be undermined with the building of the road network during the mid-1800s. This new road network, for the first time, permitted the use of carts drawn by horse or oxen to move goods with relative ease over land. An adjunct to this road network was the introduction during the late 1800s of new passenger and freight steamer services, which made the transport of cargo and people between the larger populated islands easier.

The first road constructed in Shetland was a gun track, built around 1781, that ran from Fort Charlotte to the Battery at the Knab. Then, in 1797, a road was built from Clickimin Inn that ran over Staney Hill and ended at

Windy Grind (O'Dell 1939: 182). This was built by John Ross of Sound and Walter Scott of Scotshall, but unfortunately this road went straight uphill; the builders had not taken into account the gradient that it climbed, which made it too steep for wheeled traffic. This road was extended to Wadbister Voe in 1829, and a road was also built between the Docks and Clickimin Inn, today called Gilbertson Road (Flinn 1989: 229). Between 1840 and 1847 approximately 15 miles (24km) of road was constructed between Lerwick and Scalloway for the alleged primary purpose of supporting the herring industry, as until then, barrels, salt, nets and provisions had to be transported across the hills on the backs of ponies – or on the backs of men and women. During this period the herring industry was not flourishing and the wording used was intended to appeal to the fishery board of Scotland to whom the roads committee had applied for funding. (Smith, H. 1984: 220).

It was the potato famine in 1846 that was the real harbinger of the road network. During the famine monetary and food relief was provided by the Edinburgh Central Committee for the Relief of Destitution in the Highlands and Islands. This relief was terminated in 1848, but that year the potato crop again failed. The committee decided on a new co-operative strategy in which the board, together with a contribution from landowners, would provide cash wages to the destitute for their work on some major project (Flinn 1989: 217). The project decided on was the creation of a system of trunk roads that would provide easy access to a free market in Lerwick, thus enabling the poor to travel more easily to distant work, and also encourage returning sailors and whalers to return home swiftly rather than to dally in Lerwick, and "squander" their wages (Flinn 1989: 217). The government gave the services of Captain Theodosius Webb, Royal Engineers, to survey the road system and supervise its construction, and he had the assistance of six sappers and miners who acted as local overseers. Road construction began in 1849 and the central board set aside £10,000 for the purpose, and also pressed the proprietors to contribute a third to a quarter of the cost for the construction of roads that crossed their lands (Flinn 1989: 217).

After 11 years of work, and at a cost of £19,000, the trunk road system was completed in 1860. One hundred-and-two miles of road and 18 bridges had been constructed on Shetland's mainland, plus an additional 17 miles of road throughout the islands (Flinn 1989: 233). The importance of a road infrastructure with Lerwick was now apparent, and it was agreed that it would provide the outlying, and remote communities, with better routes of communication for the conveyance of livestock and the mail (Lyndsay and Mackenzie 1859: 720-726). This view was affirmed in *The Shetland Advertiser* on 31st March 1862: "It used to be said that the staple produce of Shetland, fish, being always transported by sea, roads were unnecessary for commercial purposes, and would only serve the personal convenience of a few individuals who had occasion to travel. This remark cannot be made now that there is an increasing land traffic in cattle, sheep, eggs and other country produce" (O'Dell 1939: 182).

Fig. 195. *The* Earl of Zetland *prior to being lengthened. Photograph (c.1880). Courtesy of Shetland Museum & Archives.*

Ten years after the completion of the trunk road system horse- or oxen-drawn carts were becoming more commonly used and road traffic slowly began to increase. In 1864 the Zetland Roads Act was passed. This permitted the establishment of road trustees and the appointment of a road surveyor. Although the trunk road system was complete, people living in the countryside were dissatisfied and, in 1890, the newly established county council, was inundated with petitions from residents requesting the network be extended (Hance Smith 1984: 220, 221). This was the beginning of a cultural shift away from travel by sea to road.

Steamers

This was also a time when the transport of people, freight and livestock between Shetland's North Isles evolved with the introduction, in April 1877, of the steamship the *Earl of Zetland* (Fig. 195). This service was run by the Shetland Islands Steam Navigation Company Limited. It is perhaps ironic that the *Earl of Zetland*, whilst providing an important passenger and freight service to Shetland's scattered north isles communities, was itself hampered by the poor peripheral road infrastructure. This made the transport of goods and people to and from the ship difficult as the network was sparse and roads un-metalled. This was compounded by the lack of piers and quays at which the ship was able to dock (Robson 2002: 2).

The issue of poor road infrastructure was highlighted by Andrew O'Dell in his book *Historical Geography of the Shetland Islands* which was published in 1939. O'Dell stated: "The great disability of water transport is the transferring of goods from shore to steamer or vice versa" (O'Dell 1939: 181). In the whole of Shetland there were only four piers or quays suitable for steamer access, and these were at Lerwick, Scalloway, Walls, and Baltasound, where the pier, until 1932, consisted of an old hulk. (O'Dell 1939: 181). The lack of piers necessitated the use of flitboats to ferry passengers, cargo and livestock to and from the ship and, generally, it was old sixareens that were used as flitboats (Fig. 196).

Dr Harry Taylor, who was the medical officer for Fetlar and Yell from 1890 until 1935, provided a description of the flitting process: "When the steamer dropped anchor, these flit boats and other smaller craft came alongside, the owners of the smaller boats taking ashore their friends, relations, and goods for themselves, while other passengers, mails, animals and general cargo for the local shops were deposited in the flit boats" (Taylor 1948: 17). Taylor recalled that he enjoyed watching these proceedings and listening to the banter between the officers of the *Earl* and the skippers of the flitboats. This banter, Taylor reported, was unprintable and would have "made a Thames bargee envious, and astonished a Billingsgate porter" (Taylor 1948: 17). The flitboat skippers usually had the upper-hand, and won these verbal exchanges, as the officers were required, by dint of their authoritative positions, to exercise restraint in the use of offensive language. There were occasions however, when the flitboat skippers met their match, and Taylor recalled one instance when a group of Highland girls were travelling to one of the herring stations, and one of the lasses gave a flitboat skipper a ... "verbal trouncing he would never forget" (Taylor 1948: 17).

The service provided by the *Earl*, although running to a timetable was, retrospectively, leisurely, and to a degree flexible, being dictated by freight and passenger movements and, of course, subject to the vagaries of Shetland's weather (Robson 2002: 3). The steamer's schedule was divided into two passages: The Yell Sound passage, where the ship called at Symbister, Vidlin, Burravoe, Mossbank, Ollaberry, Sullom, Brae, Garth and Swinister. And the Unst passage which called at Symbister, Gossaburgh, Mid-Yell, Cullivoe, Uyeasound, Baltasound, Haroldswick, Aith, Tresta, Fetlar and Skerries (Robson 2002: 10).

The *Earl of Zetland* at that time provided steamer services to the east side of Shetland. However, by 1881 this service had expanded to provide a service to Dunrossness, in south Mainland. In that year the west side service began, linking Leith and Aberdeen with Stromness and Scalloway, and gradually more ports on the west side of Shetland were added to the itinerary (Hance Smith 1984: 218, 258). Then in 1885 another ship, the SS *Lady Ambrosine* was chartered to support the existing service. Competition was introduced in 1887 when the Leith to Aberdeen steamer was also put on to the North Isles run during the summer peak season and in 1890 the Shetland Islands Steam Navigation

Fig. 196. *Sixareen flitboat, Burravoe, offloading from the* Earl of Zetland II, *(c.1940s). Courtesy of Shetland Museum & Archives.*

Company became amalgamated with the North Isles Packet Company, which then effectively had a monopoly over all internal freight and passenger services (Hance Smith 1984: 218).

The logistics of travel

Despite roads and steamer services isles residents who had to journey to Shetland's Mainland had no option but to travel by small boat and then complete their journey on foot. A typical example was provided by George Peterson, whose grandmother, in the late 1800s, was one of a group of Papa Stour knitters who regularly travelled to Lerwick to sell their wares. Their journey began with a sail or row to Melby, and from there they walked to Lerwick, a distance of 28 miles (45km). They broke their journey on reaching Weisdale or Whiteness where they spent the night. Then, the following morning, they walked to Lerwick where they sold or bartered their woollen produce before returning home – their round trip taking four days (Peterson 2016).

By 1890 the road network was expanding on Shetland's Mainland, however this was not the case on the other islands. Dr Harry Taylor recalled that in his early days of practising medicine there were only two roads in Yell. The first ran north to south, and the second ran east to west, whilst in Fetlar there were no roads at all. People went by foot across these islands and seldom did they travel on the back of a Shetland pony. So, when someone in Yell needed the doctor they travelled on foot to fetch him. If the doctor was needed in Fetlar they would row or sail to Yell, and then walk to the doctor's house (Taylor 1948: 50). Taylor described a memorable night when he was woken by his wife, who informed him that a boat had come to take him to Fetlar to tend at a birth. "It was a lovely calm, keen frosty night, the heavens aglow with Aurora Borealis. The men had to row all the way back with me. When crossing Colgrave Sound the reflection of the sky in the water was beautiful … When we landed at the island two men met us at the beach to escort me to my patient, who lived three and a half miles across hills over which we walked through fairly deep snow" (Taylor 1948: 51-52). This was on a calm night, but such journeys had to be undertaken in all weathers, and it must have been particularly difficult when medical assistance was urgently needed but the weather was simply too bad to fetch the doctor.

During the 1930s people in Burra and Trondra were fortunate to have a regular motorised ferry service. Before the common use of the telephone there was a simple communication system that operated between east and west Burra: "If help was needed a white board or bed sheet would be placed, or hung outside the house, and folk would know that someone had to row across the voe … If the white board was placed on the shed door at Bru, Hous, the ferryman then knew he had to pick folk up from there …" (PI, Herculson, 2015).

It is not known when this system began but its simplicity meant that it was

Fig. 197. *People on ferry on their way from Scalloway to Burra. Photo: H. W. Armstrong, (c.1933-1939). Courtesy of Shetland Museum & Archives.*

Fig. 198. *Car is PS33, 4.5 horsepower Rochet Schneider Voiturette. Registered to Dr Harry Taylor in Reafirth, Yell. Photo: G. Robertson, (1905). Courtesy of Shetland Museum & Archives.*

effective. The ferry ran from Blacksness, Scalloway, and called at the following places in Burra: Easterdale, Brough, Toogs, New Grunnasound, Bridge End, the Kirk, the Dock, Freefield, Newtown, Houss and Papil. Two main ferries provided this service, the *Madge* and the *Dove*. Motor boats continued to run this service until the bridges were built connecting Burra to Trondra and Trondra to the Mainland in 1974 (Fig. 197) (PI, Herculson 2015).

The beginning of road dependence

With the advent of improved roads and the introduction of the motor car Shetland began to turn its back on the sea as a means of communication (Fig. 198) (Donaldson 1958: 44). Cars were luxury items, and they did not begin to gain a foothold in Shetland until the 1920s (Pedersen 2013: 23-24). However, by the late nineteenth century the bicycle had become very popular as shown by the photograph of the Shetland Cycling Club taken in 1897 (Fig. 199). Although cars remained out of the financial reach of most people in the early part of the twentieth century, by the 1920s and 30s the motorbike had become an affordable and practical alternative mode as the photograph of motorbikes outside the Westside shop at Uyeasound in Unst illustrates (Fig. 200).

The popularity of two-wheeled, over four-wheeled transport is perhaps best demonstrated by the construction of the bridge that joined Muckle Roe to Mainland in 1905. Unfortunately, four-wheeled vehicles were unable to manoeuvre to the bridge, and it was proposed that a turntable should be built to permit their access. However, merchant James Inkster opposed the building of a turntable, as this would have permitted his rival, T.M. Adie & Sons' van to cross the bridge and nothing was done to permit vehicle access until the early 1920s when the Inkster business was sold and the turntable was finally built (PI, Peterson, 2016, PI, Tait 2016).

By 1935 there were 10 motorcars in Yell and, once the road in Fetlar had been constructed, Dr Taylor was given permission by Sir Arthur Nicolson to keep a motorbike in a shed near to Brough Lodge which was the nearest landing place to Yell. As well as the car in Yell and the motorbike in Fetlar the doctor also had a motorboat, and from then on he was able to convey himself with relative ease between the islands (Taylor 1948: 58-59). The example provided by Taylor helps illustrate the changes in transport that had taken place in little over 80 years.

During the 1930s an innovative island-hopping service came into existence – "the overland". The new service had an advantage over the *Earl* being faster, more frequent, and more convenient. Passengers, parcels and bicycles were taken by bus from Lerwick to Mossbank (later Tofts Voe). From there a boat was taken across Yell Sound to Ulsta, and from there a bus to Mid Yell where passengers and cargo transferred to another bus for Gutcher. From Gutcher a boat was taken across Blue Mull Sound to Belmont where yet another bus took passengers and parcels to the other Unst communities (Pedersen 2013: 24).

Fig. 199. *The Shetland Cycling Club at the Huxter Inn, Weisdale. Photo: R. Ramsay, (1897). Courtesy of Shetland Museum & Archives.*

Fig. 200. *Motorcycle group outside the Westside shop, Uyeasound, Unst (c.1933). Courtesy of Shetland Museum & Archives.*

Fig. 201. *Motor boat newly built by Jimmy Smith and Attie Williamson. Boat built for the Shetland Bus operation and fitted with a 1½ Stuart Turner engine. Photo: J. Peterson, (c.1940). Courtesy of Shetland Museum & Archives.*

Motorised boats

Although road transport in Shetland was beginning to revolutionise travel most families, in the rural parts of the county at least, still relied upon the family fourareen. By the 1930s both the inboard and outboard petrol engine had been developed. The most popular were the 1½ horsepower Stuart Turner inboard, and the Seagull and Atco outboard, but the use of these engines in Shetland's vernacular boats only became popular from the early 1950s (Scalloway Museum 2015). However, during the Second World War boatbuilders such as Johnie Bruce, Walter Duncan junior, Jimmy Smith and Attie Williamson were building vernacular boats with inboard engines for the Norwegian resistance (Fig. 201). These boats were transported upon the decks of Norwegian fishing boats as part of the covert Shetland Bus operations (SMA, D62/1/20, 36, 37). This was an important service that was invaluable to the war effort. Anecdotally, Shetland boats looked different to the boats from western Norway, but the Germans, unfamiliar with these different boatbuilding traditions, were unable to tell the boats apart and so these resistance boats were able to operate without detection (PC, Økland 2014).

Evidence for the continued popularity of the fourareen was provided by Stewart Williamson, who was originally from Skerries. Stewart described his family's boat, which was built by Johnie Bruce (Skaw, Whalsay) towards the end of 1922. Stewart's father collected the boat and took her back to Skerries in January 1923. This boat was simply called the *house boat* (the boat belonging to the house) and was used for subsistence fishing for the table, and catching bait for the haddock and halibut lines. The boat was also used for fetching home the peats that the family cast each year in Whalsay. Stewart's father also did the odd hire in her, taking folk from Skerries to Billister in Nesting, a distance of 12.4 nautical miles or 23km. This boat, in her early years, was sailed and rowed but later, probably just after the Second World War, a 1½hp Stuart Turner inboard engine was installed. This engine remained in use until it became unreliable and was replaced by Stewart with an outboard engine at some time during the 1980s (PI, Williamson 2016).

Malcolm Hutchison explained that the most well-known boatbuilders from Whalsay during this period were Johnie Bruce (1882-1961) and Davie Bruce (1904-1977) and both men lived and worked in the tiny settlement at Skaw (PI, Hutchison 2015). Like the aforementioned Walter Duncan and Jimmy Smith, some of the boats they built were intended for either inboard or outboard engine use. These adaptations took various forms and were very similar to those made to west Norwegian boats.

In Norway, as in Shetland, the outboard engine during this period outweighed the use of sail and oar for the simple reason that the engine made the boat faster enabling journeys to be completed in less time and with less effort (Djupedal 1986: 334). No doubt the use of engines in Shetland became popular for the same reason. However, an important factor to consider is that Shetlanders during the 1950s were able to afford boats with engines, indicating a rise in living standards.

The installation of an outboard engine required boats to be adapted, which in my opinion spoiled the appearance of the boat. The fact that people were happy to "spoil their boat's appearance" further illustrates that the benefit of the engine outweighed any disadvantages. Vernacular boat adaptations to permit outboard engines to be used comprised the following: making and fitting a bracket on which the outboard could be mounted (Fig. 202); the construction of an external metal or wooden bracket, fitted around the stern stem-post, on which the outboard was mounted (Fig. 203); slicing-off of the stern and fitting a transom (Fig. 204); and the construction of a well within the boat, into which the engine could be fitted (Fig. 205).

Each method had advantages and disadvantages that affected the performance of the engine or the boat, or both. Mounting the engine bracket on the side of the boat was a relatively easy task, and whilst it preserved the boat's aesthetics, the engine was less efficient because when operated it was not in line with the keel (Djupedal 1986: 335).

The mounting of the engine on an aft-bracket also preserved the appearance of the boat, and because the engine operated in line with the keel it was more efficient. However, one of the main problems with mounting the engine aft was the tendency for the stern of the boat to be pushed down by the combined

Fig. 202. *Fouareen moored in Hay's Dock, Lerwick, belonging to Jack Duncan. Note the engine mounting bracket which is easy to remove. Photo: M. Chivers.*

Fig. 203. *Metal and wooden outboard bracket on the halv yoal* Kelpie. *Boat belongs to Davy Johnson, Sandwick. Photo: M. Chivers.*

Fig. 204. *Transom sterned fouareen built by Davie Bruce, Skaw, Whalsay. Photo: M. Chivers.*

Fig. 205. *Haddock boat* Water Lilly *built by William Isbister, Haroldswick, Unst in 1910. Outboard well added after 1972.*

weight and force of the engine, which in turn lifted the bow (Djupedal 1986: 340). This effect was magnified when the person operating the engine was seated towards the boat's stern. This uneven trim was dangerous. To solve this problem ballast was placed forward to prevent the bow from lifting. Alternatively, the steering arm of the engine could be extended, allowing the operator to sit towards the centre of the boat, thus correcting the boat's trim (Djupedal 1986: 340). A good Shetland example of fitting an aft-stem bracket was provided by Duncan Smith (PC, Johnson 2015) who recalled the halv yoal, *Kelpie* which was fitted with this type of bracket in the late 1950s, on which a small Seagull outboard engine was installed (Fig. 203). The making and fastening of this bracket was undertaken by boatbuilder John Irvine, who moved to Leebiton, Sandwick from Skerries in the 1950s, and who worked out of an old wartime Nissen hut, known as the Green Store, where he repaired and built boats (PC, Johnson 2015). The Whalsay boatbuilder Davie Bruce built some transom stern boats intended for outboard use (Fig. 204) as did prolific Lerwick boatbuilder Jimmy Smith who, after the Second World War, specialised in the leisure boat market.

Another method of attaching an outboard engine that preserved the boat's double-ended aesthetic, and provided good engine performance, was the fitting of a well. The major downside to the well was that the engine could not be tilted (Fig. 205) (Djupedal 1986: 340-341). A more superior resolution to the outboard well was the installation of an inboard engine. This, however, required structural modification to the aft stem in order to accommodate a stern tube and a cut-out for the propeller (Fig. 206). Engine beds also had to be made and fitted, and an engine box constructed. These modifications however did preserve the above waterline aesthetics of the boat. Inboard engines were installed towards the centre of the boat, so trim would not be affected. The introduction of small diesel engines also made engine operation safer, should fuel be spilled or a leak occur, as diesel is much less inflammable than petrol.

The motorised fourareen was more convenient to use but the necessary structural modifications required to fit an engine to a double ended craft created their own complications and boat handling compromises. An unforeseen consequence ultimately has been the loss of sail and oar boat-handling skills, diminished further by the decline in the subsistence use of the family fourareen.

The car becomes dominant

By the late 1930s transport by road, instead of sea, had become more common. Letter evidence from Burra boatbuilder John Laurenson illustrates that by this period even boats were being transported by road. In 1938 he wrote to Mr Johnson of Catwell, Eshaness: "Your boat is now ready but I don't know what way you will get her. The weather in the first place is so bad. There is

Fig. 206. *Boat built by Davie Bruce, Skaw, Whalsay. Note the stern mounted wooden outboard bracket. Boat also modified to accommodate a 1½ horsepower Stuart Turner inboard engine. Note the sterntube and cutout for the propeller. Photo: M. Chivers.*

a motor lorry belonging to the North of Scotland Company at Scalloway that runs all over and I understand goes at times to Hillswick. It carries 5 tons and your boat with everything in her will not be 5cwt" (PC, Herculson 2015).

Further evidence of increasing road dependence is found in a photograph that illustrates the racing boat *Menevea*, which was built by Walter Shewan (Fetlar), being transported by road tied onto the back of a Model T Ford in 1937 (note the metalled road) (Fig. 207). The number of photographs of lorries, cars and motorbikes in the Shetland Museum and Archives illustrates the dominance of the motor vehicle over the boat, indeed by this period peat flitting was increasingly by road rather than by sea (PC, Tait 2016).

During the 1930s almost every family had a fouareen, a common size of which was 11 to 12 feet (3.3m to 3.6m) of keel, with an asymmetric dipping square sail. It was common for boats to be able to be rigged with a fore and aft sailing configuration too, and it was this type of rig that was generally used at the regattas (PI, Isbister 2015). By the 1930s the demand for new boats was in decline. "Aald Walter Duncan died before the war and Thomas Walter Scott he died in the 30s too, but even then boat building was starting to fall away you ken, cos there were a lot of boats, and they lasted a long time if they were looked after, and so folk did not need to buy new boats;

Fig. 207. *Peter Duncan supporting his racing boat* Menevea *which is tied to a Model T Ford truck. Photo: J. Peterson, (1938). Courtesy of Shetland Museum & Archives.*

it was supply and demand" (PI, Isbister 2015). The reason boats were not being replaced as frequently was because their use had changed. Commercial fishing was taking place on a large scale, and vernacular boats were no longer used for that purpose (Simpson 2010: 61). After the Second World War boats were mainly being used as taxis, going to and from places, rather than being used, as previously, for commercial and subsistence fishing (PI, Isbister 2015).

Roll-on-roll-off ferries

The introduction of the roll-on-roll-off (ro-ro) ferries to Shetland in the mid-1970s caused a significant change to road communication between the main inhabited islands (Fig. 208). For the first time it was possible to go from Sumburgh, the southern tip of Shetland's Mainland, to Skaw in the north of Unst, by car. This, along with the construction of the bridges linking Burra and Trondra to the Shetland Mainland, was the final blow to vernacular boat use.

Bressay had its own ferry, the *Brenda*, used for transporting food, fuel, livestock and people (Fig. 209). John Scott recalled that when timber was needed people would go by small boat to Hay's at Freefield and the timber would be dropped in the water and then towed back to Bressay. Indeed, before the invention of the tractor this was how plough horses were brought across to the island; they swam alongside the boat. Scott reflected on the intro-

Fig. 208. *Roll-on-roll-off ferry at Gutcher ferry terminal, Yell. This ferry links Yell with Unst. Photo: M. Chivers.*

Fig. 209. *The Bressay ferry* Brenda *arriving at the entrance to the small boat harbour, Lerwick, on a stormy day. Photo: J. Angus, (c.1950s-1960s). Courtesy of Shetland Museum & Archives.*

duction of the ro-ro service which made small island living so much easier, for example, lorries could bring building supplies directly to where they were needed. In hindsight, this convenience came at a price, as part of the island's community spirit was lost. Before the ro-ro ferry came there were activities such as transporting large consignments of fuel, building materials, or livestock that brought the whole community together (PI, Bressay History Group, 2016). A similar sentiment was echoed by Andy Holt, a long-time inhabitant of Papa Stour, who explained that once the Papa Stour residents lost the control of their own ferry a part of island community life was lost (PI, Holt 2016).

John Scott recalled life during the 1960s, and how travelling the short crossing from Bressay to Lerwick for a night out could become quite an adventure:

> The *Brenda* would stop running at 5.15pm and so small boats were used quite a lot at night. So, if you were going out to Lerwick in the evening you would take your own boat, which was ok in summer of course, but in winter it had its moments. I remember one time, Wendy and I were newly married, and John Graham who was the head teacher at the school and his wife had asked us over for a meal, this was in early December, and it was not a particularly good night. The wind was south westerly, and it was very dark. We set off at 7pm and got across to Lerwick ok, and we went up to their house, and we had only had two courses served, and we could hear the wind absolutely howling in the chimney; so we plucked-up our courage and said, I am sorry but we are going to have to go … I said could we use the phone first, and so I phoned Geordie at the cottage at Gardie and asked him if he could go down to the end of the pier with a torch to give us something to aim at. So he did that, and we got to the small boat harbour and we went up to the Knab and came back before the wind, … occasionally we could see this little blink, so we knew what to aim at, but we should never have been in a boat that night, there was a big sea, and we came with a big whoosh beside the pier, we just managed to grab the pier before the next big wave came (PI, Scott, 2016).

Scott emphasised that Lerwick at night during this period was dark, unlike today when at night the harbour is well lit. So much has changed in just over a generation, the ro-ro ferry runs between Lerwick and Bressay until 11.45pm on a Saturday night, permitting people to travel in reasonable comfort and safety.

The redundant fourareen

John Scott recalled a fourareen that they still own, but no longer use, in which they used to flit sheep between Bressay and Noss (Fig. 210). This boat, the *Bressay Lass*, was a replacement for the original one owned by Willie Hardie of Kirkabister which was run down by the Burra fishing boat *Children's Trust* in Bressay Sound in September 1910. The replacement *Bressay Lass* was built in Whalsay by Laurence Simpson of Vevoe (1876-1935) who during his lifetime built 19 boats (PC, Irvine 2015). Simpson's boats were a good comprise between sail, oar and load carrying capacity and were generally considered fine boats (SMA, D62/1/177). *Bressay Lass* was sold in the 1920s by Hardie to Lowrie Anderson of Ham, and Henderson Anderson of Roadside for £6. The boat was then sold in the late 1940s by Henderson Anderson's widow for £30 to George and Laurence Sutherland at Gunnista. The Sutherland's held the tenancy at Noss and they used *Bressay Lass* to flit lambs every September. Then in 1969 John and Wendy Scott of Gardie took over from the Sutherland's. The Scott's continued to use *Bressay Lass* for flitting up to 25 lambs per crossing; the lambs were prevented from jumping overboard by being covered by a net. In due course *Bressay Lass* was replaced by a large rigid inflatable boat whose outboard engine made the flitting of lambs much less onerous (PI, Scott 2016, PI, Irvine 2015). The replacement of the Shetland vernacular boat by a modern fibreglass or aluminium flitboat with an engine has been common across Shetland. Indeed, the flitting of sheep to small islands, such as South Havera, continues to this day but the boats used bear no resemblance to their forebears.

Marinas

Boat culture in Shetland changed again with the coming of the oil money in the 1980s. This led to the building of marinas which is an epilogue to the development of the road and symbolises the dominance of the car over the boat, as Ian Tait pointed out: "... everyone wants to drive to their front door, and drive to their boat, any place a boat is kept is unviable if there is no road to it" (PC, Tait 2017). The marina provides comfort: boats can be safely kept afloat, and instead of walking down to the beach to haul the boat off, people can now drive to the marina, walk along the finger pontoon and step onto their boat. In some cases these boats are of the modified Shetland vernacular type being partly decked, with an inboard engine and a wheelhouse (Fig. 211). As well as the clinker vernacular boats, there are other various boat types constructed from glass-fibre reinforced plastic or aluminium, with transom sterns, and many of these, particularly the GRP mass produced boats, are the same as those found in every other part of the world.

Fig. 210. Bressay Lass *is a fourareen modified to a two-oared boat, presumably because the distance between Bressay and Noss is very short. Photo: M. Chivers.*

Fig. 211. *Shetland Model boats and a modern GRP fishing boat. Bridge End marina, Burra. Photo: M. Chivers.*

Chapter 11

Vernacular racing boats

By the middle of the twentieth century vernacular subsistence boat use was all but dead. But the story of the indigenous boat doesn't end there – it continues with the late nineteenth century development of competitive rowing and sailing. This was a period of major societal change that provided roads, the means for road transport, better inter-island connection, modest disposable income and leisure time. The latter, particularly, precipitated the founding of boating clubs to organise competitive sailing and rowing events.

Pleasure boating amongst the better-off in late nineteenth century Shetland society became increasingly popular, as demonstrated by the establishment in 1880 of the Lerwick Boating Club (LBC). This followed an advert in *The Shetland Times*: "A meeting of the owners of pleasure boats and others who may be interested is requested in the Commissioners of Police Office, Queens Lane, on Wednesday, August 4th, at 8.30pm to consider the advisability of having a Sailing Regatta before the end of the season" (LBC 1980: 1).

Lerwick's inaugural regatta, the first in Shetland, was held on 20th August 1880. The regatta was managed by the committee from on-board HM cruiser *Eagle*; from there the races were started, timed, and finished (LBC 1980: 1). Seven races were scheduled and four of these were sailing events for boats fore-and-aft rigged. It is of note that there were no square sail races (dipping lug) that day, and there is meagre evidence for the types of fore-and-aft rigs used.

Photographic evidence suggests that a standing-lug mainsail and bowsprit-rigged jib was the preferred configuration of the larger yachts; whilst the smaller vernacular boats were gunter rigged (Figs. 212-213). The popularity of this event was captured in the photograph illustrated in Fig. 213. Spectating took place along the quay and onboard various sized vernacular boats. Clearly, this was predominantly a gentlemen's sailing competition, and it was not until the following year that fishing boats were permitted entry (LBC 1980: 2). The organisation was aimed at the better-off; those who could afford boats designed primarily with racing in mind. As can be seen in Figs. 214 and 215 these gentlemen's yachts were either fully or partially decked. The boat on the far right in Fig. 212 is not vernacular, and neither are the boats under sail in the middle of the photograph in Fig. 213, nor is the partly decked boat in Fig. 215: this boat is double ended, but it has side decks with coamings, a mainsheet horse, benches fitted around the aft end, called sternsheets, and other fittings not associated with Shetland vernacular boats.

Fig. 212. *Lerwick regatta pre-1907. Note the standing lug rigged boats. The sailing boat on the far right is not of the Shetland Model type. Photo: J.D. Rattar. Courtesy of Shetland Museum & Archives.*

Fig. 213. *Tub race, Lerwick. Note the rig of these sailing boats are standing lug rigged with the exception of the boat nearest the pier which is gaff cutter rigged. Photo: J.D. Rattar, (c.1900). Courtesy of Shetland Museum & Archives.*

Fig. 214. *On board the yacht* Queen Mab. *Left to right, John Irvine (ship broker), Dan Mitchell, John McWatt, Alexander Mitchell (solicitor). Photo: J. Irvine, (c.1889). Courtesy of Shetland Museum & Archives.*

Fig. 215. *James Hunter at the helm of a racing boat. Photo: J. Irvine, (c.1890). Courtesy of Shetland Museum & Archives.*

Fig. 216. *Two women's rowing teams at Lerwick regatta. Photo: J.D. Rattar, (c.1890s). Courtesy of Shetland Museum & Archives.*

The cost of entering races, the names of the winning boats and their skippers, and the prizes they won are presented in Table 18. Race six of this inaugural regatta was advertised in the event programme as a "females' pulling race" which was open to four-oared boats under 15ft (4.6m) of keel, entry was one shilling and the distance to be rowed was half a mile. The first prize was £1.10 shillings and the second prize15 shillings (LBC 1980: 22, programme insert).

Three young women from Trondra wished to compete in this race, and so on the morning of the regatta they rowed to Scalloway, where their boat was lifted onto a horse-drawn cart and taken by road to Lerwick. When they arrived they went to register their entry to the race, only to discover that they were the only entrant; consequently, the race was to be cancelled. Of course this was a disappointment to the Trondra team and Sherriff Thoms, on hearing this, intervened, arranging for the girls to race against two male crewmen from HM cruiser *Eagle*. Thoms then volunteered himself to be the girls' helm, and the Trondra rowers trounced the naval team. The Trondra women competed for many years at the Lerwick regatta and Thoms continued as their helm until 1893, when the women decided that he had become too heavy (Sutherland 2013: 8-9) (Fig. 216).

Other clubs, such as Unst Boating and Swimming Club (UBC) were now being founded. The first Unst regatta, held in August 1891, became the

Lerwick Regatta, 20th August 1880

Event & entry fee	Boat name	Skipper	Prize
Class 1			
For boats 14-22 feet of keel (4.3m - 6.7m) 7 shillings	*Yacht Lizzie Hay*	A.J. Hay	Silver cross of the club & £2
Class 2			
For boats 11-14 feet (3.4m - 4.3m) of keel 5 shillings	*Bluebell*	L. Goudie	Silver cross of the club & £2
Class 3			
For boats under 11 feet (3.4m) of keel 2 shillings	*Sunbeam*	A. Irvine	Silver cross of the club & £2

Table 18. *Class race winners (Henderson, Irvine & Burgess et al 1980:1).*

template upon which all proceeding events, until just before the First World War, were based. All the fore-and-aft rigged boats came from Baltasound, and the dipping square sail fourareens and rowing competitors all came from north Unst (Robertson 1991: 2). In 1892 the committee organised a more ambitious programme that included an open handicap sailing race, a dipping lug race, two men's pulling races, a sailing canoe race, and a swimming race. The handicap was set at quarter of a minute per foot per mile and the canoes had a handicap of half a minute per foot per mile. In 1901 Jessie M.E. Saxby reported that boats were being built locally, specifically to compete at the regatta (Robertson 1991:2-8). This further illustrates that the role of vernacular boats was changing; no longer were they being used purely for subsistence or commercial work – they also had a recreation function.

The development of vernacular boats built specifically for racing is illustrated by Fig. 217. Note the strakes have become narrower and increased in number. Presumably the reason for this was so that hull shape could be better controlled. Also note that both boats have sternsheets that will have made sailing more comfortable for the helmsman. Of interest are the double knees fitted to *Iris*, the smaller of the two boats. These permanently secured the tafts in position. The fitting of non-removable tafts is a significant departure from the vernacular tradition, making the boat stiffer, which is advantageous for sailing, and also more robust when coming alongside other boats or piers (Chapelle 1994: 458-459; Røssel 1998: 194). Looking closely at Fig. 217 it is apparent that no kabes are fitted, even though there are oars lying inside each boat. This photograph, along with the report by Saxby, further demonstrates the departure from the vernacular working boat, to a type built primarily for recreational use. The form of these boats, whilst outwardly maintaining the appearance of the Shetland vernacular, was changing, no doubt as a consequence of outside influences. Although these boats were primarily built for racing, fore-and-aft rigged boats such as *Katie*, built by Walter Shewan in 1921, were also used for haddock and dorro fishing (PC, Tait 2016).

In 1909 the Unst club organised a single-handed race for a small class of boat, the race took place on the Monday prior to the main regatta. The rules for the race were:

1. That boats be of Shetland Model of size of keel not exceeding 10.5 feet [3.2m].
2. That only one sail be used, that of the standing lug pattern.
3. That the mast be no longer than can lie within the boat.
4. That the yard (or gaff) be no longer than three fourths of the total length of the mast.
5. That the length of the foot of the sail be no longer than from the mast to the inmost part of the sternpost on top of the Hinniespot and if a boom be used it must be able to swing clear forward of the sternpost.
6. That only one man sail the boat unless otherwise arranged on the day of the race.
7. That the handicap be on the waterline at the rate of quarter of a minute per ft. per mile.
8. That no side decks or false keel be allowed.
9. That a boat may be trimmed in ballast in any way before or during the race.
10. That except as amended by the foregoing the Club rules and conditions are binding on all competitors.

The race was won by *Rotchie*, skippered by L. Edmondston, in second place was *Daisy* skippered by William Gray, and in third place was *Peril*, skippered by James Johnson (Robertson 1991: 12-13). It is important to note that in the rules, the term "Shetland Model" was used to describe a vernacular racing boat. This is the earliest known use of this amorphous term, which Osler described: "... within Shetland itself there is a ready distinction between what is called the Shetland Model of boat and all other types of boats, the Shetland Model is not easily defined in objective terms" (Osler 1983: 20). Indeed, Osler suggested that the term originated in regards to racing and this supports his claim; although today the term is applied to a wide range of vernacular boats, even those with a transom stern to accommodate an outboard engine (Osler 1983: 20).

By 1909 there were at least two other boating clubs in Shetland, which further illustrates the growing popularity of competitive water sports. Sandwick Boating Club (SBC) was founded in 1896 following a protracted debate about organising an annual regatta. Eventually it was the minister, the

Fig. 217. *Two new-built racing fourareens in a noost at Mary Park, Baltasound. Boat on left is* Iris, *boat on right* Caroline. *Both boats built by Magnie Johnson. Photo: J.J. Sutherland, (c.1900). Courtesy of Shetland Museum & Archives.*

Reverend Nairne Baldie, who invited a select group of Sandwick gentlemen to the manse for the purpose of forming a regatta committee (Irvine 1996: 1). The first meeting took place on 9th September and the first regatta was due to be held on 17th September, but the event was postponed until the 22nd due to the sudden death of James Smith.

Sandwick's programme consisted of two sailing races, the first was a fore-and-aft rig race, whilst the second was for dipping lug rigged boats. There were also pulling races for men, youths 16 to 20, boys under 16, and young ladies. Sandwick adopted a sail racing programme similar to that developed by LBC. The fore-and-aft race was for first class boats, and these, at that time, as in Lerwick, were partly-decked yachts. In 1900 the regatta programme consisted of racing for sailing first class boats, for dipping lug rigged boats and for quillies (whillies) (Irvine 1996: 5).

Whalsay Boating and Sports Club (WBSC) was established in 1903, and its first regatta took place at the beginning of October that year. There were two principal sailing races; one for lugsail rigged boats and another for square sail rigged boats (WBSC 1991: 2-3). There was also a boys' and a men's pulling race. Then, in 1904, an advertisement was placed in *The Shetland Times*: "The Harrison Challenge Cup for boats of Shetland model open to all comers will be competed for at the regatta to be held as early as possible after the close of the Herring Fishing. Particulars on applying to R.H. Bell, Symbister." (WBSC 1991: 4).

In a public notice in 1906 it was stated that there were to be no boats entered with lead keels, and that the depth of the keel should not exceed six inches when measured from the lower edge of the garboard (WBSC 1991: 5). This notice lends weight to the fact that people were adapting boats to the limit of the rules in order to gain a competitive advantage. As previously described, the class one yachts were not of Shetland design, and this outside influence no doubt spread to the class two and three boats; so the term "Shetland Model" was used to clarify that racing boats should be vernacular in origin. In 1908 there was another restriction included in the public notices that stated that no decks were to be allowed, and that the boats' crews must be from the district to which the boat belonged (WBSC 1991: 6). As well as the boating clubs previously discussed, it seems that by this period there were numerous boating clubs throughout Shetland. Evidence for the existence of the North Isles clubs is provided in 1923, when the clubs from Unst and Yell met and formed the North Isles Yachting Association (NIYA). During this meeting the dates for the following year's North Isles regattas were agreed, and a proposal presented by Charles Sandison to standardise the rules regarding the measurement of boats was also approved (Robertson 1991: 33).

Racing boatbuilders

It is evident that whilst the first class yachts were the preserve of Shetland's wealthy elite, the other racing classes were principally the family fourareen. However, as previously stated, there is clear evidence that by this time even the fourareen was beginning to be built with racing in mind, a good example of this is the fourareen *Spindrift* built by Lowrie Smith from Bressay. Lowrie was a time-served shipwright who worked for the Malakoff boatyard and chandlers in Lerwick, where he repaired and maintained fishing boats. However, work at the
Malakoff was seasonal, and during the depression there were long periods with no employment. Even so, it seems that there was still a demand for Shetland Models, which Lowrie built for several customers. Then, in 1936 Lowrie built the *Spindrift* for his family's use, in the cowshed next to Twageos House (PI, Wills 2015). *Spindrift* was raced by Lowrie in the 1938 Lerwick regatta where he came first in the utility class which were boats of 8-11ft (2.4m - 3.4m) of keel (Fig. 218) (LBC 1980: 10).
The most prominent racing boatbuilders in the 1920s were Jimmy Smith and Walter Shewan (LBC 1980: 33). Notable boats built during this period by Jimmy Smith were *Foam*, built in 1923, which competed in the 1924 Lerwick regatta, and *Ripple*, which competed in the 1925 regatta (Figs. 219, 220). *Foam* was later sold and taken to Chicago by John Leask, where he regularly sailed on a freshwater lake. Unfortunately the boat succumbed to rot. *Foam* was finally burned as a galley on the lake (SMA, D62/1/6). Among Walter Shewan's well known boats were *Bella, Still* and *Smugga* (Figs. 221, 222).

Fig. 218. Spindrift *under sail c.1938. Courtesy of Jonathan Wills.*

Fig. 219. Ripple *racing at Cullivoe, Yell. Photo: J. Peterson, (C.1940s). Courtesy of Shetland Museum & Archives.*

Fig. 220. Ripple *on a trailer in Lerwick. Note the deep double garboard that gave the boat good windward sailing ability. Courtesy of Shetland Museum & Archives.*

Fig. 221. *A copy made in 1978 of an original photograph of Still sailing. Photo: J.A. Hughson, (c.1930s). Courtesy of Shetland Museum & Archives.*

Fig. 222. Smugga *lying alongside the head of Victoria Pier. Photo: J. Peterson, (c.1950). Courtesy of Shetland Museum & Archives.*

Perhaps the best known of all Shewan's boats was *Miss Gadabout* (Fig. 223). *Miss Gadabout*, built in 1925, was first raced in the Baltasound regatta when *The Shetland Times* reported: "Considerable interest was centred in the race for the Club Shield, for which there were six entries. One of the boats was new – *Miss Gadabout* – and another, the *Juanita* had recently been purchased from Lerwick, while the *Jemima*, owned and sailed by Mr. J. Hughson, Burrafirth, thirty years ago was used as a saithe boat, and no one ever thought at that time that this humble saithe boat would be running our modern racers hard for premier place at our regattas" (Robertson 1991: 33).

It is interesting to note the comment in *The Shetland Times* that an old saithe boat was as competitive as the newer designed and built racing boats. This demonstrates the fairness of the linear rating rule, which had a handicap of 15 seconds per foot per mile, and illustrates that people did not need the newest design to be competitive (Charles Sandison 1954: 39, 44, PI, Duncan Sandison 2016). This view was not shared by all, and during the 1930s controversy arose as boats were increasingly being built purely for racing, and this was felt by some to be unfair. The rating rule handicap system was still successfully used during the early part of the 1950s, when it was noted that the boats that were successful were those with a waterline of 16 to 17ft (4.9m to 5.2m). The boats of this period had internal ballast of between five to seven hundredweight (250 to 350kg). This ballast was made from lead, some of which was shifted to the windward side by the third member of the crew when the boat was sailing close to the wind (PI, Duncan Sandison, 2016).

Inter-club

In 1928 the Lerwick Boating Club suggested that a competition should take place between it and the clubs from the North Isles, and it was suggested that the racing should take place in Lerwick under LBC rules. However, after discussion between Lerwick and the North Isles Yachting Association it was agreed that the competition would take place at Uyeasound in Unst. This event took place on 28th and 29th of August, and Lerwick won with its boats *Ripple*, skippered by W. Robertson, and *Surf*, which won both the races, skippered by Andrew Nicolson (Fig. 224) (LBC 1980: 11). Conflicting opinion followed regarding the course of events that took place in trying to organise the following year's competition. This may have been in part due to incomplete minutes of meetings, or simply the consequence of a misunderstanding between the NIYA and LBC.

The Lerwick club met in September 1928 and a lengthy debate ensued about where the next inter-district race should take place. The aim was to find a central venue that would enable all Shetland's boating clubs to take part. It was eventually agreed that Sullom Voe should be the venue. All boating clubs were notified and invited to forward their views on the subject (Burgess et al 1997: 3). This view, presented by the Shetland Inter-Club

Fig. 223. Miss Gadabout *at the first Burravoe regatta (Yell) after the Second World War. Willie Nicolson, Norman Jamieson, John Stewart (skipper). Photograph (c.1946). Courtesy of Shetland Museum & Archives.*

Fig. 224. Surf *racing at Walls regatta in 1939. Photo: J. Peterson. Courtesy of Shetland Museum & Archives.*

Yachting Association (SIYA), differs to that presented by the UBC who stated that in December 1928 their committee held a meeting to discuss the possibility of having an inter-district race that had been proposed by the North Yell Club (Robertson 1991: 36). This idea was warmly received, and UBC proposed that there should be three teams of four boats representing the North Isles, Lerwick and the West Side.

It was proposed that the race should take place in Lerwick and it was noted that only Shetland Model boats should be permitted to compete, and that the rule defining a Shetland Model should permit all boats currently racing to be classed as such. No spinnakers were permitted, and the jib was not to be detached from the end of the jib boom. The boats were to be rated with their largest suit of sails at the time of registering. Only internal ballast was to be permitted, and only boats without decks allowed to be classed as a Shetland Model. Then, the following February, a meeting of the NIYA was convened, and it was proposed by Charles Sandison that the event should be held at Sullom Voe or some other similar central venue. The North and Mid Yell delegates disagreed and argued that the suggested venue would be difficult to get to, and proposed that races should be sailed on alternate years in Lerwick and the North Isles. A letter was written to LBC but apparently no response was ever received (Robertson 1991: 36). These conflicting views suggests disagreement between the North Isles and Lerwick but evidence to ascertain the true course of events is lacking.

There was no inter-district race in 1929 and LBC held a special general meeting in September that year where the correspondence received from the interested clubs was discussed, these being; the NIYA, Walls Regatta Club, Brae Sailing Club, Aith Boating Club, and Bridge of Walls Sailing Club. A conference was arranged for 11th November, that date being the most convenient for the NIYA. The following rules were proposed at the meeting:

1. **Fixed** ballast.
2. **Rating** $\underline{\text{L.W.L. plus beam plus .75 of the girth, plus .5 } \sqrt{\text{Sail Area.}}}$
$$2$$
3. **Class** open Shetland boats.
4. **Entry** fee to be 20/ per boat.
5. **Number** the number of boats to be restricted to two from each club.
6. **Venue** Sullom Voe.
7. **Handicap** 10 seconds per foot per mile.
8. If decked boats used, the girth measurement to be taken from the coaming.
(Burgess et al 1997: 3).

It was agreed that *Surf* and *Ripple* should represent Lerwick in the July inter-district race. However, for an unknown reason, possibly because agreement could not be met between Lerwick and the North Isles, the event did not take place (IYA 1997: 4). There was no further attempt to hold an inter-district race until after the Second World War and between 1939 and 1945 there was no racing in Shetland, with most boats being laid-up (LBC 1980: 33). This use of the phrase "laid-up" demonstrates that by now many of the Lerwick boats were used solely for recreation and racing.

Following the war, competitive sailing recommenced in 1946 and then, in 1948, the first Inter-Club Regatta was held in Lerwick. Following the success of this event the Zetland Inter-Club Yachting Association (ZIYA) was formed (Burgess et al 1997: 4). The Inter-Club Regatta since 1946 has always been hosted by Lerwick and was held in the first week of September. The main trophy was the Memorial Cup (in memory of the men who gave their lives during the Second World War). As well as this cup, there have been numerous other trophies commemorating worthy individuals presented over the years (Burgess et al 1997: 6).

The rating of boats was defined as being the Froude Rating:

$$\frac{\text{Length} + \text{Beam} + \frac{3}{4}\text{ Net Girth}, + \frac{1}{2}\sqrt{\text{Sail Area.}}}{2}$$

Edmund Froude was a member of the International Yacht Racing Union – later its president – and he developed this rating in 1906 in an attempt to address a problem that still exists today: that a winning racing yacht owes its success to its measurement-cheating advantages rather than its general speed qualities. Froude's rating ensured that racing yachts also had good sea-keeping ability, an important consideration for boats competing in the waters surrounding Shetland (Brown 2006: 234).

Maid Class

Duncan Sandison said of the development of the Maid Class "... that looking back it was pure chance ...". After the Second World War his father's boatbuilding firm, Alex Sandison & Sons Ltd in Baltasound, Unst were building loch fishing boats that Duncan had designed: "... it was just a whillie, a pretty wee boat, and then we built the second one." The first boat took too long to build and so was uneconomic. Duncan sought to speed-up the construction process by building the boat upside down "...putting the bands in first, because I knew exactly where they were going to go, and she was built, but she was a bit of a disaster for technical reasons." The boat developed a shoulder about where the mast was, and this was caused by the way the boards were bent. "They [the builders] didn't follow my plan, they went their own way, so she was a bit straighter and so you got this knuckle on the boat, and not only that, but the wood was appalling, so I decided that we couldn't sell her" (PI, Sandison, 2016).

Sandison had been racing the first-class ballasted boat *Laughing Water* (Fig. 225), but then he married, and his wife, who was keen on sailing "... couldn't shift ballast, and this boat [*Maid of Thule*] had been lying in the shed doing nothing, so I said, we'll put a sail on her and try her out, so I rigged some kind of old sail on her, and she went very well, which rather surprised me" (Fig. 226). The following year Sandison acquired a newer sail, and the *Maid of Thule* performed even better "... and I started competing with the first class ballasted boats, and she still did well, and in due course, we were picked with *Flying Cloud* to sail in the inter-club" (PI, Sandison, 2016). Sandison recalled:

> This was in 1955 and the boat performed quite well, and then in 1956, *Maid of Thule* won the Challenge Cup, and along with *Flying Cloud* we won the inter-club. It was an appalling day, there might have been about 30 boats that started and we were one of the few boats that finished ... the *Maid of Thule* came through. People couldn't understand it, but the reason for it was that the ratings rules were designed for ballasted boats [displacement boats] and the *Maid of Thule* was benefitting by this rating, because being a lighter boat she sailed faster against the rating. We started way, way ahead of everyone else, and ok, we lost out a bit going to windward against the bigger boats, but nothing drastic. And that was really what set it off [the development of the Maid Class] and boats began to be built, some to the original plans I had, and some started building on their own ... and built very good boats, that worked fine, but of course, when plywood came in the boats got lighter and performed better, and the *Maid of Thule* and the other heavier boats lost out. And from there on it just took off. It was a pity in a way, because if they had stuck to the original boats, which had to be the same size and weight [larch built] it would have made better racing. But, when they started building plywood boats the shapes altered and they found they could make them lighter and faster, and that was it" (PI, Sandison, 2016).

The big ballasted boats, which had a large sail area, really had to be built by a boatbuilder, and so were expensive, whereas the unballasted Maid Class, being smaller, were cheaper to build and could be built by an amateur handyman if they had a set of plans or knew what they were doing. As Sandison pointed out, it was a very interesting period in competitive sailing, and this was when the sailing rig was changed from the sliding gunter to Bermudan rig. Many owners began to use sails from other classes of racing boat, such as the Flying Fifteen, Flying Dutchman, 505, or Wayfarer. Others had bespoke sails made from measurements or a template. Sandison recalled the making of a sail for the *Maid of Thule* by the Norfolk sail-making firm Jeckells. Mistakenly, Jeckells had thought that Sandison had specified that the sail should be red. Sandison refused this red sail so Jeckells tried to remove the dye and in so doing the sail became pink. By that time, it was too late to make a new sail, as the sailing season was about to begin, so Sandison reluctantly agreed to take the sail (which turned-out to be excellent) on condition that Jeckells agreed to accept half the price (PI, Sandison, 2016).

This was the period when Duncan Sandison, along with other leading regatta sailors, had tried to get agreement on a standard Shetland Maid hull and rig which would have created a one-design boat that would have been affordable (Burgess et al 1997: 13). Disappointingly no agreement was reached, and the Maid

Fig. 225. Laughing Water
in foreground, racing at the
Inter-club regatta, Lerwick,
in 1953. Photo: J. Peterson.
Courtesy of Shetland Museum &
Archives.

Fig. 226. The Maid of Thule *(pink sail and green hull) at Uyeasound regatta, Unst, in 1958. Courtesy of Shetland Museum & Archives.*

Class became a development class, which meant that hull and rig design changed almost annually as new innovations in sailing race technology were adopted. As Sandison mentioned, it was the use of plywood and epoxy resin in the mid-1970s that revolutionised the Maid Class. The first plywood Maid was built by Willie Mouat in Unst for Albert Priest. Priest wanted a boat that could compete against the two new Yell boats, *Sundance*, and *Moonwind*, which were both based on the astonishingly successful *Arctic Mist* built and skippered by former Jimmy Smith apprentice Robbie Tait (Lerwick). So Willie built *Telstar* out of Thames Marine ply which was the best plywood that could be bought at that time. Priest was very successful in *Telstar* and its successor boats (PI, Mouat, 2016).

Willie Mouat recalls that he began his apprenticeship in 1963 with Sandison's in Unst. He had always been interested in boatbuilding, and he described the first boat he built when he was just nine years old; "... it was just a square boat, made from sheet metal, with a stem and a transom." This boat he sailed on the burn near where he lived, when it flooded the adjacent land, turning it into a small loch: "... the sail was made from an old hessian sack, and the boat could only sail before the wind; the important thing was to miss the fencing posts that stuck out of the water". In the winter of 1959 there was a boatbuilding night class in Unst, and they built a boat called *Maid of Unst*, and then in 1962 Willie managed to attend the boatbuilding night class, and that winter they built a pramm tender. Willie is still building boats, and the most recent of these is the construction of a replica of *Still* which, as previously discussed, was built by Walter Shewan in 1920. *Still* was owned by Willie's father, Duncan Mouat, but the boat was originally built for a family in Uyeasound and was to be used by the children. The boat however was deemed to be rank – unstable – and she was sold to someone in Yell.

In the late 1940s *Still* was bought by Duncan Mouat of Haroldswick and converted to a sailing boat. She was the first vernacular boat to successfully adopt the Bermudan rig, using an old aluminium dinghy mast. *Still* competed in many regattas and at the inter-club where she won many prizes. The boat competed regularly in regattas until the 1980s, by which time people were willing to commit ever increasing amounts of money and time into competitive sailing. During this period there were some notable individual enthusiasts who dedicated their time to teaching maritime skills and navigation. Prominent among these were Bertie Mowat in northwest Shetland, Tammie Moncrieff in Lerwick, and more recently, Brian Wishart in Walls, Sandwick and Lerwick.

Jimmy Smith and his apprentices

Jimmy Smith was born on 16th September 1902, at Point-a-Taing, Walls, to Thomas and Mary Smith. He became one of Shetland's most highly regarded racing boatbuilders of the pre- and post-Second World War era (SMA, D62/1/6, LBC 1980: 7). During his career Jimmy built at least 70 boats and trained many apprentices. Among these were latter-day boatbuilders Jack Duncan, Robbie Tait and Alan Moncrieff. Jimmy began his apprenticeship at the Malakoff in 1917, and built *Spray*, his first boat, in 1920. After the Second World War Jimmy and Attie Williamson began Allcraft Company in a Nissen hut at the West Dock in Lerwick (SMA, D62/1/6).

The business gradually expanded, and another Nissen hut was acquired, followed by a large shed. The Allcraft Company workshop stood near to where Lerwick's Toll Clock shopping centre is situated today, and Jimmy soon after became the sole owner of the business. Jimmy was a perfectionist – his boats remain highly revered and his eye for detail and aesthetics has passed down to his apprentices.

Employment opportunities in Shetland during the early 1960s were scarce, as Jack Duncan pointed out: "... there were no jobs, I had a choice of [boatbuilding], or being a baker, and I wasn't interested in baking." Robbie Tait was given the choice of boatbuilding or going to sea, and it was the boatbuilding apprenticeship that came-up first, and so he embarked on that path (PI, Duncan and Tait, 2015).

Alan Moncrieff's story was similar to that of Jack and Robbie's and, as Alan pointed out, Jimmy would not accept just anyone as an apprentice, you had to go and spend a day with him so he could see if you had any potential, and what sort of person you were. Alan recalled "... the day I spent with him he was sewing-up a sail. Jimmy worked Monday to Saturday lunchtime, the hours we worked were 7.30am until 5pm. The only power tool used in the workshop was the big band saw and the apprentices would often make their own tools (PI, Moncrieff, 2015). Jimmy's perfectionism was illustrated by Robbie Tait who described the making of a hinnispot: "... there used to be two points that used to go in around the stem, that you had to cut out, and those two points was cross grained, and if your chisel wasn't really sharp and you broke one of them he made you make a whole new hinnispot just because of the two points" (PI, Tait 2015).

Jimmy's setting of high standards was reinforced by his emphasis on not rushing, but working steadily. He was a good teacher and had the ability to pass on information in his quiet way (PI, Moncrieff 2015). Every now and again Jimmy would set a test for one of his apprentices, as Alan Moncrieff recalled:

> ... he was to make a rudder which involved joining two pieces of wood together to form the rudder blade, joined by long bolts, and you had to bore the holes through both pieces of wood and bolt them together. These wood pieces were 3/4 inches thick, and once they were bolted together Jimmy would say to take them to the mill and get them thicknessed to 5/8 of an inch thick. Now if the bolts were not perfectly centred then this would damage the knives on the thicknesser, Jimmy always gave you the opportunity to back out. I asked the guy at the mill to take less off one side and more off the other (PI, Moncrieff 2015).

Following completion of his apprenticeship Alan Moncrieff continued boatbuilding and built many of the modern Maid Class boats. Alan is an innovator and he pushed the design boundaries of the Maid Class. However, during the 70s and 80s, as remains the situation today, there were insufficient orders to make a full-time living from boatbuilding. Alan's main income was derived from fencing and construction, working with his brother Jim. Jack Duncan spent most of his working life at Malakoff, and then as slipway foreman at Moore's in Scalloway, while Robbie Tait worked in the construction industry and was one of the founding directors of the Shetland construction firm DITT. Tait, who built and sailed the very successful *Arctic Mist* continued to sail, but unlike Duncan he did not actually repair or build any boats until they retired, when they were persuaded by then Shetland Museum and Archives curator Tommy Watt to build the sixareen *Vaila Mae* in 2008. However, since 2010 they have restored around 20 boats belonging to the Shetland Museum. Shetland Museum and Archives Curator, Dr Ian Tait explained that restoring museum collection boats requires a very high level of skill which is far more exacting than repairing or building a new boat (PI, Tait 2016).

Decline in competitive sailing

During the 1970s and 1980s regatta sailing and the inter-club were extremely popular events. Willie Mouat recalled that the Unst regatta attracted hundreds of people who came to watch the sailing and rowing (PI, Mouat, 2016). Alan Moncrieff described how in the 1970s he sailed every weekend at the regattas: "It was brilliant, and was a big social occasion. There was nothing else to do, everyone did it. It was very competitive on the water but once ashore everyone was the best of friends, there was always parties and dances in the evenings" (PI, Moncrieff 2015). By the late 1990s the new Maid Class boats had become extremely technical racing machines that required a high level of skill to sail them well. As well as being difficult to sail, the boats themselves were always evolving. So every couple of years boats were having to be updated in order to remain competitive. This was, and remains, expensive sailing, and this has been widely attributed as the main factor for the rapid decline in sailing in Shetland.

During the mid-1980s Sandwick Boating Club adopted a different approach to other clubs by opting to build a fleet of four identical clinker epoxy-plywood boats based on the lines of two of the most successful boats of that time, *Vilparina* (Fig. 228) designed and built by Alan Moncrieff and *Wild Wind*. It was agreed that these new boats were to be 17ft 9 inches overall length on a waterline of 15ft 6 inches, with a beam of 5ft 1 inch. In view of the fact that the boats were to be sailed on open water they were built slightly fuller in the ends to make them more seaworthy. The stems were laminated, and the boats were built in a production-line manner (the boats were only allocated an owner on the completion of all four boats). The building took place over the winter of 1987/1988 and they were launched in May that year.

The project was successful and two more boats were built the following winter. The success of this project however was short-lived due to a relaxation of the building rules for new boats, which permitted changes to beam, depth, and underwater profile. This marked a step-change in the evolution of the Maid Class which in effect made all the older boats obsolete (Irvine 1996:

65-79). The Maid Class had become a development class and this fundamentally transformed an egalitarian recreational activity, open to anyone with a fourareen, into an elitist sport. It seems that following these rule changes in 1988 interest in sailing, and the district regattas, rapidly faded and is now nothing more than a fond memory in the minds of those who took part in those hugely popular summer events.

Indeed, some people have suggested that it was not just the rule changes to the Maid Class that ruined sailing, but the coming of the oil money in the 1980s, and the subsequent building of Shetland's numerous sports centres. Prior to the sports centres there was only sailing in the summer and football in the winter, there were few other activities and now people have a far greater choice (PI, Hutchison 2015).

Fig. 227. Vilparina's *launch day, 1987. Designed and built by Alan Moncrieff. Courtesy of Alan Moncrieff.*

Fig. 228. Vilparina's *maiden sail in 1987. Courtesy of Alan Moncrieff.*

Chapter 12
Epilogue

I t would be easy to think that this is the end of Shetland's maritime heritage but of course it is not. Instead of using traditional boats people now use modern boats with engines for recreation and commercial fishing. Although traditional boat use is at an all-time low there are some positive actions being taken to ensure the skills of traditional boat handling are preserved and passed on to future generations. For example, competitive yoal rowing has been popular since the 1990s, and there are several clubs that regularly train and compete at local rowing regattas during the summer. There are also youth sail training opportunities which take place onboard the Fifie fishing boat *Swan*, LK 243, which was built by Hay & Company in Lerwick in 1900, and is now operated by the Swan Trust.

Shetland Amenity Trust's sixareen, *Vaila Mae*, which was built in 2008 by Jack Duncan and Robbie Tait, is used to teach traditional open boat dipping lug sailing and rowing skills. And, thanks to the efforts of Brian Wishart, Jim Tait and Robert Wishart, there is a growing band of enthusiastic volunteers who have been trained to crew and skipper *Vaila Mae*. Shetland also has an annual maritime festival, Shetland Boat Week. This event, which began in 2016, is the highlight of the year for *Vaila Mae's* crew who take members of the public out for sailing trips around Lerwick harbour. For many this is the first time they have been on a sailing boat and it is gratifying to see the obvious enjoyment people get from this experience. During Boat Week 2019 *Vaila Mae* was joined by the Unst sixareen Far Haaf, and it was wonderful to have two sixareens sailing in company, which of course also meant that twice as many members of the public could savour the experience of going for a sail in a sixareen while learning about the lives of past generations of Shetland seafarers. (Fig. 229)

As well as these on the water activities there is also a new community interest company, Moder Dy, which was founded by myself and Dr Esther Renwick in 2018 to help shelter and secure Shetland's maritime heritage for future generations. Moder Dy provides workshops, outreach school programmes and community maritime archaeology projects that are geared to building a more complete narrative of life in Shetland before roads, bridges, ro-ro ferries and cars.

So, although traditional boat use is in a bit of lull at present, there is a growing band of enthusiasts determined to keep these environmentally friendly boats and traditional boat handling skills alive for future generations to enjoy.

Fig. 229. Vaila Mae *sailing during boat week. Photo: M. Chivers.*

Appendix A

Eighteenth and nineteenth century Shetland boat builders

Name	Date of birth	Place born	Place worked & listed occupations	Types of boats known to have built	Died
Donald Anderson	27th June 1779	Braehoulland, Eshaness, Northmavine.	Scarff, Northmavine. Blacksmith and boat builder.	Six-oared boats 1826-1828 Priced at £1.5 shillings.	30th August 1853, Scarff.
Matthew Anderson	1790	Northmavine	Boat builder	?	19th March 1865, Cru Green, Ollaberry
John Anderson	9th July 1847	Sandwick, Whalsay.	Crofter, fisherman, boat builder.	Whillie or eela boats akin to Walter Shewan	23rd June 1917, Lerwick.
Laurence Bolt (Brother to Robert)	1831	Lerwick	Ships carpenter Garthspool	?	20th Nov 1870
Robert Bolt	1833	Lerwick	Carpenter, Garthspool	?	13th March 1915
Malcolm Brown	?	? Lerwick	Served under Davey Leask, Hay & Co.	?	?
Thomas Bruce (Father of Laurence and Thomas)	25th Sept 1811	Skaw, Whalsay.	Fisherman, crofter, carpenter.	Whillie or eela boats.	23rd March 1894, Skaw.
Laurence Bruce (White Lowrie)	20th May 1839	Westhouse, Skaw, Whalsay.	Skaw. Boat builder, crofter, fisherman.	Fourareens and Sixareens.	29th Jan 1919, Westhouse, Skaw.
Thomas Bruce (Brother to White Lowrie and father to John)	10th Sept 1848	Skaw, Whalsay.	Skaw. Crofter, fisherman, boat builder.	Whillie or eela boats	7th March 1927, Skaw.
Walter Colvin	19th Nov 1801	The Mull, Sandwick	Ship's carpenter	Hay & Co head carpenter	27th April 1879, Freefield, Lerwick
? Donaldson	?	? Lerwick	Served under Davey Leask, Hay & Co.	?	?
George Dalziel (Father of Jeremiah)	1818	Aith, Aithsting	Boat builder	Built and altered sixareens.	8th Jan 1904, Mark, Aith.

Jeremiah Dalziel *(Jerry a Stiva)*	18th March 1840	Northness, Aithsting	Boat carpenter, shoe maker	?	4th Aug 1920, Stiva, Aith.
John Duncan	?	? Lerwick	Served under Davey Leask, Hay & Co.	?	?
Charles Duncan	17th Sept 1876	Greenmow, Cunningsburgh	Carpenter	?	2nd Dec 1942, Greenmow.
Walter Duncan	20th May 1869	Branchiclate, Burra	Boatbuilder, carpenter. Served his time with Hay & Co, Blackness, Scalloway. Started his own business in 1887 or 88.	Fouareens, haddock boats etc. During the Second World War he built small boats for the covert Shetland Bus operations.	6th Jan 1944
William Eunson	?	Fair Isle	Boat Builder Took over Thomas Stove's workshop following his death in 1873.	?	?
John Eunson	8th Feb 1836	Glen Dunrossness	Boat builder, carpenter. Punds of Eastshore	Yoals.	8th March 1894, Punds of Eastshore.
William Gilbertson	13th Nov 1799	Geosetter, Dunrossness	Boat carpenter	?	27th Dec 1888, the Mails, Dunrossness.
Gilbert Gilbertson	1815	Whalsay	?	?	1880
Laurence Goodlad	23rd Oct 1836	Lerwick	Boat builder Lerwick. Served his time with Laurence Arcus. Founded the Malakoff.		20th Aug 1910. St. Olaf Street, Lerwick.
Gavin Harper	?	?Lerwick	Served under Davey Leask, Hay & Co.	?	?
John Henderson of Bothin	1700s	?	Boat builder	Norwegian boats in boards	?
John Henry	?	? Lerwick	Served under Davey Leask, Hay & Co.	?	?
Peter Hunter	1810	Bressay	Joiner, boat carpenter	?	30th Jan 1880, Nestigarth, Bressay
James Hunter	16th Oct 1827	Strome, Whiteness	Boat builder, crofter	?	8th Dec 1902, Brugarth, Whiteness
Laurence Inkster *(Uncle to John)*	1785	Houlls, Burra	Boat carpenter North Houlls banks	?	27th Jan 1866. Booth at Houss
John Inkster *(da Houllsie)*	27th Oct 1828	Houlls, Burra	Boat builder, carpenter North Houlls banks	?	12th May 1912, Houlls.

Thomas Isbister	24th Feb 1868	Leraback, Foula	Blacksmith, boat builder	?	24th May 1933.
Laurence Jamieson	1839	Cunningsburgh	Boat builder	?	4th Jan 1894
Robert Thomas Jamieson	19th May 1869	Veister, Sandwick	Carpenter, fisherman. Served his time with Walter Sinclair	?	24th July 1930, Sandwick.
William Johnson	1700s	?	Boat builder	Norwegian boats in boards	?
George Johnson	26th Aug 1859	Ireland, Bigton	Master joiner	Built Yoals	10th Nov 1941, Skelberry, Dunrossness
Robert J. Laing	23rd July 1855	Lerwick	Boat builder, shipwright Hay & Co	All types of Shetland boats	Unknown
Adam Henry Laurenson *(Brother to Maikie & Uncle to Harry)*	28th May 1826	Lochend, Sandwick	Carpenter at Hay & Co, Blackness, Scalloway.	All types of Shetland boats	19th July 1895, Scalloway
Malcolm *(Maikie)* **Laurenson** *(Brother to Adam and uncle to Harry)*	1833	Lochend, Sandwick	Foreman carpenter Hay & Co, Blackness, Scalloway	All types of Shetland boats	8th May 1904, Scalloway
Harry Peter Laurenson *(Nephew to Adam and Maikie)*	14th May 1860	Dunrossness	Carpenter	All types of Shetland boats	31st May 1919, Skeld, Sandsting
Magnus Laurenson *(Father of Dempster)*	1772	Quoys, Catfirth, Nesting	Boat carpenter		3rd Jan 1851, Quoys.
Dempster Laurenson *(Father of John)*	6th Sept 1802	Quoys, Catfirth, Nesting	Carpenter, built over 400 boats	All types of Shetland boats	20th Sept 1892, Quoys.
John Laurenson *(Son of Dempster & father of Dempster)*	20th Aug 1846	Quoys, Catfirth, Nesting	Boat builder, learned from his father	All types of Shetland boats	16th Sept 1917, Quoys
Dempster Laurenson *(Son of John)*	22nd Aug 1878	Quoys, Catfirth, Nesting	Ship's carpenter	?	Died before 1959. ?1947.
David Leask	1st Jan 1836	Kirkabister, Mid Yell	Foreman boat builder, carpenter, Hay & Co	Fourareens, sixareens, haddock boats, carvel boats, pleasure boats.	23rd Feb 1903, Lerwick.
Gilbert Linna	1700s	?	?	Norwegian boats in boards	?
John Mouat *(Brother to Laurence)*	18th Oct 1820	Midgarth, Unst	Boat builder	?	31st Jan 1896, Liverpool

Laurence Mouat	?	?	Served time under Walter Colvin. Ships carpenter, head carpenter T.M. Aidie & Sons, Voe. Started his own business at North Ness (saw mill at Skibbadock). Walter and his brother, James, owned the first bandsaw in Shetland (1883).	?	?
Robert Nicolson	1850	Gardie, Haraldswick, Unst	Boat builder Haraldswick	Built at least 100 boats	1922, Gardie Haraldswick
James Ollason	?	?Lerwick	Served under Davie Leask, Hay & Co.	?	?
Robert James Laing	23rd July 1855	Lerwick	Boat builder, shipwright	?	1901, Govan
John Sandison	23rd August 1832	Burn, Hillswick, Northmavine	Fisherman, boat builder	?	15th Jan 1917
Francis Sandison	?	? Lerwick	Served time under Davey Leask, Hay & Co.	?	?
Thomas Walter Scott	4th Jan 1859	Scalloway	Joiner, boat carpenter Manager, Hay & Co Blackness, Scalloway.	Built 215 boats over 37 years.	8th April 1929
Thomas Shewan *(Father of John and Alexander)*	2nd May 1834	Scatness, Dunrossness	Boat carpenter, fisherman Served his time under Lowrie Arcus.		18th Dec 1908, Garthspool, Lerwick
John *(Jack)* **Shewan**	29th Oct 1865	Dunrossness	Boat Carpenter. Apprenticed to Hay & Co, Under Davie Leask. Later became foreman	All types of Shetland boats and other vessels.	17th May 1958, Lerwick
Alexander Shewan	1st March 1871	Dunrossness	Carpenter, boat builder	?	20th July 1911, Skibbadock, Lerwick
Laurence Simpson *(Lowrie a' Vevoe)*	18th July 1876	Vevoe, Whalsay	Fisherman, crofter, boat builder.	Built about 20 fine examples of Shetland boats.	9th Feb 1935, Vevoe.
Thomas Smith	1700s?	?	Boat builder	Norwegian boats in boards	?
William Stout	2nd Aug 1864	Taft, Fair Isle	Crofter, fisherman, boat builder	Yoals.	20th April 1948.
Thomas Stove	18th Nov 1808	Liverpool	Ships carpenter. Served time under Peter Smith at Freefield. Set-up a saw mill		16th June 1873 Lerwick.
Samuel Taylor	?	?Lerwick	Hay & Co served under Davie Leask	?	?

Christopher Tulloch	Before 1730	Leascol, Northmavine	Boat builder	Norwegian boats in boards	Unknown
John Yates	1801	Kirkabister, Bressay	Sailor, fisherman, crofter, boat carpenter	?	25th Nov 1881, Ham, Bressay.

Appendix B

Probable saithe boats operating in Unst in 1869.

No.	Archive reference	Boat name	Location	Owner	Skipper	Keel Length feet	Oars	Rig	No. Crew	Remarks
984	CE85/11/6	*Joan*	Skaw	William Clark	William Clark	14	6	No sail	4 men 1 boy	Cancelled 1878
1457	CE85/11/5	*Joan*	Skaw	Andrew Clark	Andrew Clark	14	6	Square sail	4	Cancelled 1873. New owner William Clark new No. 984
1458	CE85/11/5	*Barbara*	Norwick	Laurence Laurenson	Laurence Laurenson	13.5	6	Square sail	5	Cancelled 1878. Boat condemned.
737	CE85/11/6	*Anne*	Haroldswick	John Johnson	John Thomson	13	6	No sail	5	Cancelled 1875. Boat useless
744	CE85/11/6	*Active*	Haroldswick	James Spence	James Spence	14	6	No sail	5	Cancelled 1885. Boat useless
745	CE85/11/6	*Willie*	Haroldswick	Magnus Bruce	Magnus Bruce	13	6	No sail	5	Cancelled 1875. Boat condemned.
749	CE85/11/6	*Laura*	Norwick	Spence & Co	James Thomson	13	6	No sail	4	Cancelled 1875. New owner John Spence.
751	CE85/11/6	*Betsey*	Haroldswick	Henry Edmonston	Henry Edmonston	14	6	No sail	4	1871. Cancelled, owner left the Islands.
1548	CE85/11/6	*May*	Newgord	William Fraser	William Fraser	13	6	Square sail	3	Cancelled 1886. Unfit for sea.
746	CE85/11/6	*Mary*	Norwick	Duncan Thomson	Duncan Thomson	12.5	6	No sail	4	1878. Fishes only inshore.
847	CE85/11/6	*Mary*	Haroldswick	Spence & Co	John Sutherland	14	6	No sail	4	Cancelled 1875. New owner John Spence.
848	CE85/11/6	*Nancy*	Haroldswick	Thomas Clark	Thomas Clark	14.5	6	No sail	4	Cancelled 1878. Fishes only inshore.
735	CE85/11/5	*William*	Burrafirth	William Mathewson	William Mathewson	15	6	Square sail	6	1886. Boat condemned.
849	CE85/11/6	*William*	Norwick	William Harper	William Harper	14	6	No sail	4	1872. Cancelled. Boat sold: William Anderson No. 979

850	CE85/11/6	*Brothers*	Norwick	James Harper	James Harper	14	6	No sail	4	Cancelled 1875. New owner Gilbert Gray.
851	CE85/11/6	*Janet*	Norwick	William Robert Henderson	William Robert Henderson	14	6	No sail	6	1872. Cancelled. Boat sold to James Sinclair now No. 974.
866	CE85/11/6	*Emma*	Westing	Andrew Thomas Harper & others	Andrew Thomas Harper	13	6	No sail	4	Cancelled 1878. Fishes only inshore.
848	CE85/11/6	*Nancy*	Haroldswick	Thomas Clark	Thomas Clark	14.5	6	No sail	4	Cancelled 1878. Fishes only inshore.
905	CE85/11/6	*Nancy*	Haroldswick	William Nicholson & others	William Nicholson	13	6	No sail	4	Cancelled 1886. Out of existence. [Last entry 06:06:1874.]
743	CE85/11/6	*Margaret*	Burrafirth	Mathew Mathewson	Mathew Mathewson	13	6	No sail	4	Cancelled 1886. Boat condemned.
752	CE85/11/6	*Goldfinch*	Burrafirth	Magnus Manson	Magnus Manson	12.5	6	No sail	4	Cancelled 1878. Boat done.
1455	CE85/11/5	*Margaret*	Haroldswick	Andrew Thomson	Andrew Thomson	13	6	Square sail	5	Cancelled 1878. Fishes inshore only.

HM Customs Fishing Boat Register. Shetland Museum and Archives CE85/11/5, CE85/11/6

References

Published

Abrams, L. (2005) *Myth and Materialty in a Woman's World: Shetland 1800-2000.* Manchester: Manchester University Press.

Ballin, T.B. (2011) "The Post-Glacial Colonization of Shetland – integration or isolation?" *In Farming on the Edge: Cultural Landsacpes of the North.* ed. by Mahler D.L., Andersen C., Copenhagen: The National Museum of Denmark, 32-43.

Ballantyne, J.H., Smith, B. (eds.) (1994) *Shetland Documents 1580-1611.* Lerwick: The Shetland Times Ltd.

Ballantyne, J.H., Smith, B. (eds.) (1999) *Shetland Documents 1159-1579.* Lerwick: The Shetland Times Ltd.

Ballantyne, J.H. (ed.) (2014) *Naught but Trouble - The Hays in Yell 1775-1824.* Lerwick: The Shetland Times Ltd.

Ballantyne, J.H. (ed.) (2016) *Shetland Documents 1612-1637.* Lerwick: The Shetland Times Ltd.

Barnes, M. (1998) *The Norn Language of Orkney and Shetland.*

Barrett, J.H. (2008) *What Caused the Viking Age?* Antiquity, 82, 671-685.

Batey, C.E. (2016) "Viking Boat Burials in Scotland: Two New Boat Burial Finds." In *Shetland and the Viking World, Papers from the Proceedings of the Seventeenth Viking Congress, Lerwick.* ed. by Turner, V.E., Owen, O.A., Waugh, D.J. Lerwick: Shetland Heritage Publications 39-45.

Brand, Rev. J. (1701) *A Brief Description of Orkney, Zetland, Pightland, Firth and Caithness.* Edinburgh: George Mosman.

Brown, C.G. (1998) *Up-helly-aa: Custom, Culture and Community in Shetland.* Manchester: Manchester University Press.

Brown, D.K. (2006) *The Way of a Ship in the Midst of the Sea: The Life and Work of William Froude.* Penzance: Periscope.

Bruce, R.S. (1914) "The Sixern of Shetland." *The Mariner's Mirror* 4 (9), 289-300.

Bruce, R.S. (1932) "More about the Sixerns." *The Mariner's Mirror* 20 (3), 312-322.

Burgess, G., Smith, I., Robertson, l, Smith, B., Sandison, A., Moncrieff, L., Wishart, B., Reid, C., Abernethy, J., Smith, B., Manson, M., Leask, B. (eds.) (1997) *50 Shetland Inter-club Regattas.* Lerwick: Shetland Inter-club Yachting Association.

Candow, J. (2009) "The Organisation and Conduct of European and Domestic Fisheries in Northeast North America, 1502-1854." *In A History of the North Atlantic Fisheries Volume 1: from Early Times to the Mid-Nineteenth Century.* ed. by Starkey, D.J., Thór, J, Th., Heidbrink, I. Bremen: Deutsche Schiffahrtsmuseum, 387- 415

Charlton, W. (2007) *Travels in Shetland 1832-52: Edward Charlton.* Lerwick: The Shetland Times Ltd.

Chapelle, H.I. (1994) *Boatbuilding a Complete Handbook of Wooden Boat Construction.* New York: W.W. Norton & Company.

Chivers, M. (2016) "A Similar but Different Boat Tradition: The Import of Boats from Norway to Shetland 1700-1872." In *Beyond Borealism: New perspectives on the North.* ed. by Giles, I., Chapot, L., Coojimans, C., Foster, R., Tesio, B. Edinburgh: Norvic Press, 56-77.

Chivers, M., Stratigos, M., Tait, I. (2019) "An Ethnography of Shetland's Oldest Boat, the Sixareen Mary LK 981." *The Mariner's Mirror* 105 (4), 442-460.

Christensen, A, E. (ed.) (1968). *Boats of the North a History of Boatbuilding in Norway.* Oslo: Det Smaleget.

Christensen, A, E. (1972) "Boatbuilding Tools and the Process of Learning." In *Ships and Shipyards Sailors and Fishermen: Introduction to Maritime Ethnology.* ed. by Hasslöf, O., Henningsen, H., Christensen, A.E. Copenhagen: Rosenkilde and Bagger.

Christensen, A.E., Morrison, I. (1976) "Experimental Archaeology and Boats." *International Journal of Nautical Archaeology and Underwater Exploration* 5 (4), 275-284.

Christensen, A.E. (ed.) (1979) *Inshore Craft of Norway. From a Manuscript by Bernhard and Øystein Færoyvik.* Oslo: Grøndahl & Son.

Clark, A. (1837) *The Miscellaneous Works of Adam Clark, LL.D., F.A.S., VolXIII.* London: T. Tegg & Son.

Coull, J.R. (2007) *Fishing, Fishermen, Fish Merchants and Curers in Shetland: Episodes in fishing and Curing Herring and White Fish.* Lerwick: Shetland Amenity Trust.

Cowie, R. (1874) *Shetland descriptive and historical; being a graduation thesis, on the inhabitants of the Shetland Islands.* Edinburgh: John Menzies & Co.

Davis, G. (2011) (second edition) *Vikings in America.* Edinburgh: Birlinn.

Djupedal, K. (1986) "The Nordfjordfæring of Western Norway: Changes in an Ancient Small Boat Design in Response to New Technology." *The Mariner's Mirror* 72 (3), 329-350.

Doe, H. (2009) *Enterprising Women and Shipping in the Nineteenth Century.* Woodbridge: The Boydell Press

Donaldson, G. (ed.) (1958) *Shetland Life Under Earl Patrick.* Edinburgh: Oliver & Boyd.

Donaldson, G. (ed.) (1991) *Court Book of Shetland 1615-1629.* Lerwick: Shetland Library.

Edmondston, A. (1809) *A View of the Ancient and Present State of the Zetland Islands; Including their Civil, Commerce, and the State of the Society and Manners Vol. I.* Edinburgh: John Ballantyne & Co.

Eunson, J. (1976) *Words, phrases and recollections from Fair Isle.* Lerwick: The Shetland Times Ltd.

Fenton, A. (1978) *The Northern Isles: Orkney and Shetland.* Edinburgh: John Donaldson.

Flinn, D. (1989) *Travellers in a Bygone Shetland: an Anthology.* Edinburgh: Scottish Academic Press

Gear, R.W. (2013) "Re-assessing Shetland's Herring Industry before the 1870s." *Journal of the North Atlantic.* Special volume 4, 61-68.

Gifford, T. (1786) *An Historical Description of the Zetland Islands.* London: J. Nichols, printer to the Society of Antiquaries.

Gjellestad, J. A. (1969) "Lit om Oselverbåter." *Norsk Sjøfartsmuseum Årbok 18-29.*

Goodlad, C.A. (1971) *Shetland Fishing Saga.* Lerwick: The Shetland Times Ltd.

Greenhill, B. (ed.) (1959) *Out of Appledore. The Autobiography of a Coasting Shipmaster and Shipowner in the last days of Wooden Sailing Ships.* London: Percival Marshall & Co. Ltd.

Greenhill, B. (1976) *Archaeology and the Boat.* London: A&C Black.

Gwilt, J. (1867) *An Encyclopedia of Architecture: Historical, Theoretical and Practical.* London.

Halcrow, A. (1950) *The Sail Fishermen of Shetland, and their Norse and Dutch Forerunners.* Lerwick: T.&J. Manson.

Hall, R. (2007) *Exploring the World of the Vikings.* London: Thames & Hudson.

Hamilton, J.R.C. (1957) "Jarlshof, a Prehistoric and Viking Settlement in Shetland." In *Recent Archaeological Excavations in Britain.* ed. by Bruce-Mitford, R, L, S. London: Routledge & Kegan Paul.

Henderson, T. (1978) "Shetland Boats and their Origins." *In Scandinavian Shetland. An ongoing Tradition?* ed. by Baldwin, J, R. Edinburgh: Scottish Society for Northern Studies.

Hibbert, S. (1822) *A Description of the Shetland Comprising an Account of their Geology, Scenery, Antiquities, and Superstitions.* Edinburgh: Archibald Constable & Co.

Irvine, B. (ed.) (1996) *Sailing at Sandwick: The Story of a Shetland Sailing Club.* Sandwick: Sandwick Boating Club.

Isbister, T. (1995) "The Active (story of a boat, her builders and her crew)." *The New Shetlander* 194, 17-18.

Jakobsen, J. (1928) *An etymological dictionary of the Norn language in Shetland.* London: David Nutt (A.G. Berry).

Johnson, C. (1932) "Experiences of a Northmavine Survivor, told by Himself Fifty Years Later." In *Manson's Shetland Almanac.* ed. Manson, I. Lerwick: Manson (Shetland Museum & Archives SA4/2461/41)

Johnston, A., Johnston, A. (ed.) (1913) *Orkney and Shetland Records Volume I.* London: University of London: King's College.

Johnston, A. (1932) "The Shetland Sixern." The Model Yachtsman and Marine Model Magazine 5, 9-12 & 29-32.

Joensen, J.P. (2009) "Fishing in the 'Traditional' Society of the Faroe Islands." In *A History of the North Atlantic Fisheries Volume 1: from Early Times to the Mid-Nineteenth Century.* ed. by Starkey, D, J., Thór, J, Th., Heidbrink, I. Bremen: Deutsche Schiffahrtsmuseum, 312-322.

Johnston, A., Johnston, A. (ed.) (1913) *Orkney and Shetland Records Volume I.* London: University of London: King's College.

Kerr, A. (1831) "A Narrative of the Disaster Among the Shetland Fishermen in June and July 1830." *Christian Herald X,* 189-194.

Kinnaird, T.C., Sanderson, D.C.W., Preston, J., Dugmore, A.J., Newton, A.J. (2017) *Luminescence dating of sediments from Underhoull and Lund, Unst, Shetland.* Glasgow: Scottish Universities Environmental Research Centre.

Knooihuizen, R. (2008) "Fishing for Words: the Taboo Language of Shetland Fishermen and the Dating of Norn Language Death." *Transactions of the Philological Society.* 106 (1) 100-113.

Laurenson, J.J. (1963) "The Sixern Days: Some Odds and Ends Part III." *The New Shetlander,* 65, 22-23.

Lerwick Boating Club (1980) *The First Hundred Years.* Lerwick: Lerwick Boating Club.

Lillehammer, A. (1990) "Boards, Beams and Barrel-Hoops: Contacts between Scotland and the Stavanger area in the Seventeenth Century." *In the Mackie Monographs I: Scotland and Scandinavia.* ed. by Simpson, G.G. Edinburgh: John Donald Publishers Ltd

Low, Rev. G. (1879) *A Tour through the Islands of Orkney and Shetland in 1774.* Edinburgh.

Lyndsay, J.H., Mackenzie, J.H. (1859) *Report of the Commissioners for Inquiring into Matters relating to Public Roads in Scotland Volume I.* London: Her Majesty's Stationery Office.

MacPolin, D. (2008) "The Drontheim: Typical Norway Yawls of the North-East Coasts." In *Traditional Boats of Ireland: History, Folklore and Construction* (ÁrmBáid Dúchais). ed. by Mac Cárthaigh, C. Doughcloyne: The Collins Press.

Manson, T. (1923) *Lerwick during the last half century (1867-1917)*. Lerwick: T.&J. Manson.

March, E. (1970) *Inshore Craft of Britain in the Days of Sail and Oar*. Volume I. Newton Abbot: David & Charles.

McKee, E. (1983) *Working Boats of Britain: their Shape and Purpose*. London: Conway Marine Press Ltd.

Megaw, B., Megaw, E. (1941) "Early Manx Fishing Craft." *The Mariner's Mirror*. 27 (2), 91-105

Monteith, R. (1845) *Description of the islands of Orkney and Zetland, by Robert Monteith, of Englisha and Gairsa, 1633, reprinted from the edition of 1711*. Published under the superintendence of Sir Robert Sibbald, Knt. M.D. Edinburgh: Thomas G. Stevenson.

Morrison, I. (1973) *The North Sea Earls. The Shetland/Viking Archaeological Expedition*. London: Gentry Books.

Mortenson, A. (2000) *Hin føroyski róðrarbáturin. Sjómentir føroyinga í eldri tíð*. Tórshavn: Annales Societatis Scientiarum XXVI.

Munro, A. (2012) *Small Boats of Shetland*. Lerwick: Centre for Nordic Studies, (University of the Highlands & Islands) and the Unst Heritage Trust.

Neill, P. (1806) *Tour through some of the Islands of Orkney and Shetland with a View Chiefly to Objects of Natural History, but Including also Occasional Remarks on the State of the Inhabitants, their Husbandry, and Fisheries*. Edinburgh: A. Constable & Company.

Nicolson, J.R. (1981) *Shetland's Fishing Vessels*. Lerwick: The Shetland Times Ltd.

Nicolson, J.R. (1982) *Hay & Company Merchants in Shetland*. Lerwick: The Shetland Times Ltd.

O'Dell, A.C. (1939) *The Historical Geography of the Shetland Islands*. Lerwick: T.&J. Manson.

Osler, A.G. (1978) "Boatbuilding by the Duncans of Hamnavoe." In *Scandinavian Shetland an Ongoing Tradition?* Ed. Baldwin, J.R., Edinburgh, Scottish Society for Northern Studies.

Osler, A.G. (1983) *The Shetland Boat: South Mainland and Fair Isle*. Greenwich: The Trustees of the National Maritime Museum.

Økland, K.M. (2016) *Oselvar den Levande Båten*. Leikanger: Skald.

Pålsson, H. and Edwards, P. (1978) *Orkneyinga Saga: The history of the earls of Orkney*. London, Penguin Books.

Pedersen, R. (2013) *Who Pays the Ferryman? The great Scottish Ferries Swindle*. Edinburgh: Birlinn.

Pløyen, C. (1896) *Reminiscenes of a Voyage to Shetland, Orkney and Scotland in the Summer of 1839*. Lerwick: T.&J. Manson.

Power, R. (1990) "Scotland in the Norse Sagas." In *Scotland and Scandinavia 800-1800*. ed. by Simpson, G.C. Edinburgh: John Donald.

Rampini, C. (1884) *Shetland and the Shetlanders. Two Lectures Delivered before the Philosophical Institution, Edinburgh on the 5th and 8th February,1884*. Kirkwall: William Peace & Son.

Reid, J.T. (1869) *Art Rambles in Shetland*. Edinburgh: Edmonston & Douglas.

Reid, K., Zimmermann, R. (2000) *A History of Private Law in Scotland Volume II: Obligations*. Oxford: Oxford University Press.

Robertson, L.B. (1991) *Unst Boating & Swimming Club: A Hundred Years of Sailing*. Unst: Unst Boating & Swimming Club.

Robinson, R. (2009) "The Fisheries of Northwest Europe, c.1100-1850." In *A History of the North Atlantic Fisheries 1. From Early Times to the mid-nineteenth Century*. ed. by Starkey, D.J. Thór, J, Th., Heidbrink, I. Bremen: Deutsche Schiffahrtsmuseum, 127-171.

Robinson, R., Starkey, D.J. (1996) "The Sea Fisheries of the British Isles, 1376-1976: A Preliminary Survey." In *The North Atlantic Fisheries, 1100-1976 National Perspectives on a common resource*. ed. by Holm, P., Starkey, D.J., Thór, J, Th. Esbjerg: Studia Atlantica 121-144.

Robson, A. (2002) *The Saga of the Earls. A pictorial history of two ships*. Lerwick: The Shetland Times Ltd.

Rössel, G. (1998) Building Small Boats. Brooklin: Wooden Boat Publications.

Sandison, C. (1954) *The Sixareen and Her Racing Descendants*. Lerwick: T. & J. Manson.

Sandison, C., Sandison, D. (1954) "The Shetland Boat." In *the Viking Congress Lerwick*, July 1950. ed. by Simpson, W.D. Edinburgh: Oliver & Boyd.

Shaw, F.J. (1980) *The Northern and Western Islands of Scotland: Their Economy and Society in the Seventeenth Century*. Edinburgh: John Donald Publishers Ltd.

Shirreff, J. (1814) *General View of the Orkney Islands; with Observations on the Means of their Improvement; drawn up for the Consideration of the Board of Agriculture*. Edinburgh: Archibald Constable & Co.

Simpson, C. (2010) *Water in Burgidale: Shetland Fisheries in a Pre-Electronic Age*. Lerwick: Shetland Amenity Trust.

Simpson, C. (2011) *Shetland's Heritage of Sail*. Lerwick: The Shetland Times Ltd.

Simpson, C. (2011) *Shetland's Heritage of Sail*. Lerwick: The Shetland Times Ltd.

Simpson, C. (2016) "The Night that Mouat (and Sixteen Others) were lost: an Analysis." *The New Shetlander*. 276, 34-40

Simpson, C. (ed.) (2017) *Shetland's Open Boat Days: Tales of the Fishing Under Sail and Oar*. Lerwick: The Shetland Times Ltd.

Small, A. (1968) "The Distribution of Settlement in Shetland and Faroe in Viking Times." *Saga-Book of the Viking Society*, 17, 145-155.

Smith, B. (1980) "Stock-Stove Houses." In *The Shetland Folk Book*. ed. by Graham, J.J., Tait, J. Lerwick: The Shetland Times Ltd.

Smith, B. (1986) "Shetland and the Crofters Act." In Shetland Crofters a Hundred years of Island Crofting. ed. by Graham, L. Lerwick: Shetland Branch, Scottish Crofters Union.

Smith, B. (1990) "Shetland, Scandinavia, Scotland, 1300-1700: the Changing Nature of Contact." In *The Mackie Monographs I Scotland and Scandinavia 800-1800*. ed. by Simpson, G, G. Edinburgh: John Donald Publishers Ltd.

Smith, H.D. (1984) *Shetland Life and Trade 1550-1914*. Edinburgh: John Donaldson.

Smith, L., Preece, A. (1994). *Sailpower: the Science of Speed*. Arundel: Fernhurst Books

Smout, T.C. (1963) *Scottish Trade on the eve of Union 1660-1707*. Edinburgh: Oliver & Boyd.

Starkey, D.J. (2009) "Introduction: Diverse Waters, Common Themes." In *A History of the North Atlantic Fisheries Volume 1: from Early Times to the Mid-Nineteenth Century*. ed. by Starkey, D.J., Thór, J, Th., Heidbrink, I. Bremen: Deutsche Schiffahrtsmuseum, 13-35.

Storm, G., Bugge, A. (1914) *Norges Kongesagær. Utgaven, Sverres Saga bind III*. Kristiania: Stenersens.

Sunde, J, Ø. (2010) "Not a Stick of Wood: Trade Relations as the Core of Shetland-Norwegian Connections up to the Mid-Nineteenth Century." *New Shetlander*, 253, 18-20.

Sunde, J.Ø. (2010) *Vegen Over Havet frå Mowatane på Shetland til Baroniet Rosendal*. Bergen: Barionet Rosendal.

Tait, I. (2012) *Shetland Vernacular Buildings 1600-1900*. Lerwick: The Shetland Times Ltd.

Tait, I. (2014) "Our Smallest Boat of all." *The New Shetlander*, 268, 20-24.

Taylor, H. P. (1948) *A Shetland Parish Doctor*. Lerwick: T. & J. Manson.

The Ministers of the respective parishes, under the superintendence of a committee of the society for the benefit of the sons and daughters of the clergy. (1845) *The New Statistical account of Scotland Vol XV*. William Blackwood and Sons, Edinburgh.

Tompson, P. (1978) *The Voice of the Past Oral History*. Oxford: Oxford University Press.

Thowsen, A. (1969) "The Norwegian Export of Boats to Shetland, and its Influence Upon Shetland Boat Building and Usage." In *Norwegian Year Book of Maritime History*. ed. by Peterson, L., Thowsen, A. Bergen: Sjøartshistrisk Årbok.

Thór, J, Th. (2009) "Icelandic Fisheries, c.900-1900." In *A History of the North Atlantic Fisheries Volume 1: from Early Times to the Mid-Nineteenth Century*. ed. by Starkey, D, J., Thór, J, Th., Heidbrink, I. Bremen: Deutsche Schiffahrtsmuseum, 323-349.

Turner, V.E., Bond, M., Larsen, A. (2013) *Excavation and Survey in Northern Shetland 2006-2010: Viking Unst*: Lerwick: Shetland Heritage Publications.

Whalsay Boating & Sports Club (2003) *Whalsay Boating & Sports Club: The Sailing Years 1903-2003*. Lerwick: The Shetland Times Ltd.

Williams, G. (2014) *The Viking Ship*. London: British Museum.

Wilson, J. (1842) *A Voyage Round the coasts of Scotland and the Isles*. Edinburgh: Adam and Charles Black.

Withrington, D.J., Grant, I.R., Sinclair, J. (Sir). (eds). (1978) *The Statistical Account of Scotland 1791-1799 Volume XIX Orkney and Shetland*. Ilkley: E.P. Publishing Ltd.

Zickermann, K. (2011) 'Shetland's Trade with Northwest German Territories During the Seventeenth and Early Eighteenth Centuries.' *Journal of the North Atlantic*, 4, 43-51

Unpublished

Barrett, J.H. (1995) *Fish Middens and the Economy of the Viking Age and Late Norse Earldoms of Orkney and Caithness, Northern Scotland*. University of Glasgow [unpublished PhD thesis].

Lamb, D. (2010) *Modelling an Island Landscape in the North Atlantic Iron Age: the Interpretation of Monuments and Resources in Order to Understand Local Factors Influencing Settlement and Social Organisation*. University of Bradford [unpublished PhD thesis].

MacGregor, L. (1987) *The Norse Settlement of Shetland and Faroe, c.800-1500: a Comparative Study*. University of St. Andrews [unpublished PhD thesis].

Munro, A. (2011) *More Similarity than Difference? Physical and Cultural Connections in the Open Boats of the Northern Isles*. University of the Highlands & Islands, Centre for Nordic Studies [unpublished MLitt dissertation].

Newland, K. (2010) *The Acquisition and use of Norwegian Timber in Seventeenth Century Scotland, with reference to the Principal Building Works of James Baine, His Majesty's Master Wright*. University of Dundee [unpublished PhD thesis].

Smith, B. (2003) *Shetland and her German Merchants, c.1450-c.1710*. Avaldsnes, Norway [unpublished lecture notes].

Smith, R.J. (1986) *Shetland in the world economy: a sociological history of the eighteenth and nineteenth centuries*. University of Edinburgh [unpublished PhD thesis].

Thomson, A. (1991) *The Scottish Timber Trade, 1680 to 1800*. University of St. Andrews [unpublished PhD thesis].

Watt, A. (2012) *The Implications of Cultural Interchange in Scalloway, Shetland, with Reference to a Perceived Nordic Based Heritage.* University of Aberdeen [unpublished PhD thesis].

Wills, J.W.G. (1974) *Of Laird and Tennant – a Study of the Social and Economic Geography of Shetland in the Eighteenth and Early Nineteenth Centuries, Based on the Garth and Gardie House Estate Manuscripts.* Edinburgh University [unpublished PhD thesis].

Conference proceedings

Christensen, A, E. (2014) Boat Building in Western Norway Tradition and Innovation. [Key note speech] Second St Magnus Conference [9 April 2014].

DVD

Shetland Museum & Archives (2010) *Vaila Mae, the Making of a Sixareen.* [DVD] UK: Shetland Museum & Archives.

Online

Canmore (2002) *Balta, stone settings Late Iron Age or Norse in origin* [online]. Available from https://canmore.org.uk/site/216006/balta [25 January 2016].

Christensen, A, E. (2014) *Trebåten to Tusen år Gammel Håndverkskunst.* Grind [online]. Available from https://grind.no/naering-handverk/trebaten [17 January 2020].

Crofters Holdings (Scotland) Act (1886) [online]. Available from http://www.legislation.gov.uk/ukpga/1886/29/pdfs/ukpga_18860029_en.pdf [16 February 2015]

Denton, J. (2015) "Price of a loaf of bread rises by 11,000% in the past 100 years thanks to inflation – and will hit £150 by 2115 if prices rise at the same rate." *This is Money* [online]. Available from http://www.thisismoney.co.uk/money/news/article-2950798/Price-loaf-breadrises-11-000-past-100-years-thanks-inflation-says-Lloyds.html [20 February 2017].

Dictionary of the Scots Language [online]. Available from https://dsl.ac.uk/results/yoal [3 January 2016].

Grydehøj, A. (2013) "Ethnicity and the origins of Local identity in Shetland, Uk-Part I: Picts, Vikings, Fairies, Finns, and Aryans." *Journal of Marine and Island Cultures* [online]. Available from http://www.sciencedirect.com/science/article/pii/S2212682113000164 2, 39-48 [26 November 2016].

Guthrie, W. (1872) *Second Shetland Truck System Report* [online]. Available from https://www.gutenberg.org [1 May 2016].

Heide, E. (2012) *The Early Viking Ship Types.* Særtykk fra sjøfortshistorisk Årbok [online]. Available from https://www.academia.edu/6944485/The_early_Viking_ship_types [27 March 2014].

Litwin, J. (2016) *Shipbuilding Techniques from the Medieval Age Onwards* [online] http://www.nmm.pl/1stCHFpdf/pdf_articles/6.1_Litwin.pdf [1 February 2020].

Lythgoe, D. (2016) *North Isles Family History* [online]. Available from http://www.bayanne.info/Shetland [29 December 2016].

Morrison, I. (1978) 'The Potential for Shetland-Model Hulls for High Speeds Under Sail and Oar.' *Scottish Society for Northern Studies* [Online]. Available from http://ssns.org.uk/resources/Documents/NorthernStudies/Vol12/Morrison_1978_Vol_12_pp-15_19.pdf [17 December 2013].

Osler, A. (2019) *Ruminations on Rudders ...* [online]. Available from https://www.moderdy.org/post/ruminations-on-rudders> [16 November 2020].

Osler, A. (2020) *Ness Yoal Builders: Chips and Shavings* [online]. Available from https://www.moderdy.org/post/ness-yoal-builders-chips-and-shavings [16 November 2020] Oxford English Dictionary (2016) *Timber boards* [online]. Available from https://www.oed.com/ [7 May 2016].

William Pole (1872) *Pole, Hoeseason & Co* [online]. Available from https://www.bayanne.info/Shetland/getperson.php?personID=I8118&tree=ID1 [16 November 2020].

Scotland's People (2016) *Census* [online]. Available from https://www.scotlandspeople.gov.uk/?gclid=CjwKEAjw3KDIBRCz0Kv-ZlJ7k4TgSJABDqOK7oNKybEHOQ9_y53S8p_tnrNcIZ5Tg4Zqy3gKZIzTs9xoC1-Pw_wcB [21 June 2016].

Sea Fisheries Act (1868) Order in Council regarding lettering Numbering and Registering of British Sea Fishing Boats [online]. Available from http://www.legislation.gov.uk/ukpga/1868/45/pdfs/ukpga_18680045_en.pdf [17 May 2016].

Smith, B. (1988) "Shetland in saga-time: re-reading the Orkneyinga Saga." *Scottish Society for Northern Studies* [online]. Available from http://ssns.org.uk/resources/Documents/NorthernStudies/Vol25/Smith_1988_Vol_25_pp_21_41.pdf [23 May 2016].

Smith, Captain, J. (1673) *England's Improvement Revived Digested into Six Books.* [online]. Available from http://name.umdl.umich.edu/A60464.0001.001 [23 July 2015]

Shetland Museum & Archives (2016) *The Shetland Times Saturday, July 30, 1881* [online]. Available from file:///Users/marc/Google%20Drive/Marc's%20PhD/Archive%20research%20documents/Shetland%20Museum%20archive/Maritime/1881st.htm [22 May 2016]

The Shetland News (1887) Fearful Gale and Snowstorm, Disaster to Fishing Fleet, SAD LOSS OF LIFE, December 10th, 1887 [online]. Available from file:///Users/marc/Google%20Drive/Marc's%20PhD/Archive%20research%20documents/Shetland%20Museum%20archive/Maritime/1887SN.htm [13 November 2020].

Newspaper Sources

Gorman, S.O. (1885) "My First Year at the Haaf." *The Shetland Times*, Friday, 3rd October, 1885: 5-6

Gardie House Archive, Bressay, Shetland

Amended ferry freights GHA.292.1733.

Thomas Mouat Ledger (1788) Gilbt Henderson of Liverpool, Sellar & Henderson, 1788, "goods pr my big boat consigned to his disposal" L33:61.

Thomas Mouat Ledger (1794-1796) John Johnson carpenter Oganess. L49.

Thomas Mouat Ledger (1783-94) John Henderson of Bothin. L49:12.

Thomas Mouat Ledger (1783-1787) William Johnson carpenter. L49:20.

Thomas Moaut Ledger (1801) Edward Thomason, Pund at Lochend. L48:103.

John Mouat of Garth (1822) "... am a frequent importer of boats in boards from Norway (proven by experience to be the fittest for our purposes) ... GA/1822

National Library of Scotland

Hay of Hayfield papers (1818) Letter to His Majesty's Customs. Acc. 3250, Folder 4, box 85.

Hay of Hayfield papers (1818) Letter from Thomas Winwick to William Hay regarding American logs. Acc. 3250, box 108.

Hay of Hayfield papers (1824) Letter from George Henderson to William Hay. Acc. 3250, Folder 1, box 31.

Hay of Hayfield papers (1824) Letter from George Henderson to William Hay. Acc. 3250, Folder 1, box 31.

Hay of Hayfield papers (1825) Letter from Arthur Nicolson. Acc. 3250, Folder 1, box 32.

National Records Office Scotland

E41/3 The rental of Shetland crops 1611 and 1612 with account of the denunciations of land, 1613.

E72/17/1 Accounts of the Customs & Excise of Orkney Caithness and Zetland from the 1 November, 1668 to the first of November, 1669.

E72/17/2 Importation an account of this customs and excise Orkney, Zetland and Caithness from the 1 November, 1671 to the 1August, 1672.

E72/17/3 An account of the customs and excise Orkney, Zetland & Caithness from the 1August, 1672 to the 1 August, 1673.

Orkney Archive Library & Archive

OASC11/5/1628/1 Disposition James Magnusson to Thomas Chesser.

Shetland Museum & Archives

Bruce of Symbister Papers (1708) Note between Andrew Sinclair and Unknown. GD144/34/17.

Bruce of Symbister Papers (1728) Accnt current between Thomas Gifford and James Harrower. GD144/40/32.

Bruce of Symbister Papers (1733) Cash to Mr John Harrower. GD144/10/11.

Bruce of Symbister Papers (1736) Instructions. GD144/97/2.

Bruce of Symbister Papers (1741) Timber from Hamburg. GD144/111/3.

Bruce of Symbister Papers (1742) Instructions from Lady Margaret Bruce. GD144/15/14.

Bruce of Symbister Papers (1743) Correspondence between Henry Sinclair to unknown. GD144/105/13.

Bruce of Symbister Papers (1745) Cash disbursed purchasing our cargo at Norway. GD144/100/3.

Bruce of Symbister Papers (1745) Timber from Hamburg. GD144/174/22.

Bruce of Symbister Papers (1748) Letter to Gifford from Davidson Regarding a Delivery of Boats. GD144/12/12.

Bruce of Symbister Papers (1748) Letter to Gifford from Davidson Regarding a Delivery of Boats to Mavis Grind. GD144/41/18.

Bruce of Symbister Papers (1748) Norway Cargo. GD144/4/1.

Bruce of Symbister Papers (1754) Invoice to Thomas Gifford. GD144/100/3.

Bruce of Symbister Papers (1756) Letter form Thomas Sanderson to unknown. GD144/240/31.

Bruce of Symbister Papers (1769) Goods shipped on Dolphin. GD144/112/22.

Bruce of Symbister Papers (1769) Goods shipped on Diligence. GD144/59/12/2.

Bruce of Symbister Papers (1770) Timber from Hamburg. GD144/94/15.

Bruce of Symbister Papers (1771) Patrick Torrie to unknown. GD144/11/25.

Bruce of Symbister Papers (1771) Timber from Hamburg. GD144/104/3.

Bruce of Symbister Papers (1771) Letter from John Mitchell to unknown. GD144/237/64.

Bruce of Symbister Papers (1772) Robert Robertson to Unknown. GD144/54/19.

Bruce of Symbister Papers (1774) Correspondence between Gideon Gifford and Alexander Wallace – East Sea boat. GD144/104/19.

Bruce of Symbister Papers (1783) Correspondence between Gideon Gifford and Alexander Wallace - building an uncommonly large boat. GD144/57/25.

Bruce of Symbister Papers (1807) Thomas Mouat to unknown. GD144/217/12.

Bruce, R, S. (undated) Incomplete letter correspondence between Bruce and Henderson, T. D25/95/50.

Catalogue, CUR 8020 Silver medal awarded by Danish Government for saving lives to John Anderson.

Catalogue, FIS 2011.54 *Mary* LK981.

Catalogue, SEA 2007.19 *Industry* LK 718.

Fishery Board Report (1882) SA4/119/1: xxxiv.

Fishery Board Report (1884) SA4/119/2: xxiv.

Fishery Board Report (1889) SA4/119/3: liii.

Fishing Boat Register (1869) CE85/11/5-6.

Fothergill, C. (1806) Journal Anent: Travels in Shetland. D.1/379.

Shetland Customs Quarterly Accounts 1742-1772 SA.1/7/1.

Thomas Gifford accounts book D17/6/10.

T.M.Y Manson papers (1950) "... the haaf boats sails had a slight peak ..." Uncatalogued Box 21/1.

T.M.Y Manson papers (1953) Letter from Charles Sandison to Manson. D37/1/85/81/1.

T.M.Y Manson papers (1966) Letter from Manson to Charles Sandison. D37/1/85/81/4/1.

T.M.Y Manson papers (1966) Letter from Manson to Charles Sandison. D37/1/85/81/4/2.

T.M.Y Manson papers (1966) Letter from Charles Sandison to Manson. D37/1/85/81/5.

T.M.Y Manson papers (1970) Tom Henderson writing to Manson- There is first a sleek of swiftly moving water ... Uncatalogued.

T.M.Y Manson papers (1978) Øyvind Dössland to Manson - Hjalta-skantar. 6th February. Uncatalogued.

T.M.Y Manson papers (1978) Øyvind Dössland to Manson - Hjalta-skantar. 26th September. Uncatalogued.

Moncrieff, T. (undated) Alphabetical List of Boat Builders. D62/1/1-177.

Nicolson Papers (1762) Arthur Nicolson letter book Feb 1761 - June 1764. D24.

Norski document page 5 John Harrower in his sloop Mary of Yorry to Hamburg then Norway.

Noski document page 6 Harrower ... take non but good large four-oared boats ...

Norski document page 7 Correspondence between Thomas Gifford and William Irvine 1753.

Papers of Hay & Co. (1844) Letter from Hay & Co to Alexander Grieg & Son. D31/1/2: 846.

Papers of Hay & Co. (1844) Letter from Hay & Co to Alexander Grieg & Son. D31/1/4: 425.

Papers of Hay & Co. (1846) Letter from Hay & Co to Alexander Grieg & Son. D31/1/7.

Papers of Hay & Co. (1852) Letter from Hay & Co to Alexander Grieg & Son. D31/1/20.

Papers of Hay & Co. (1855) Letter from Hay & Co to Alexander Grieg & Son. D31/1/25.

Papers of Hay & Co. (1860) Letter from Hay & Co to Alexander Grieg & Son. D31/1/36.

Papers of Hay & Co. (1872) Letter from Hay & Co to Alexander Grieg & Son. D31/1/58: 261.

Papers of Hay & Co. (1811) Cost of setting-up a boat-in-boards. D40/181/85/1.

Papers of Hay & Co. (1815) Instructions. D40/243/3/1.

Saxby, J. (1882) The Shetland Sixern. Shand, J. [Broughty Ferry] D1/134/228.

Saxby, J (1882) Leisure Hour Jottings – The Shetland Sixern. Shand, J. [Broughty Ferry] D1/134/226.

Shetland Court Book 1773 page 179. SC12/53/5.

Shetland Customs Quarterly Accounts 1742-1772 SA.1/7/1.

Shetland Customs Quarterly Accounts 1773-1830 SA.1/7/2.

30 September, 1648 Shetland Commissariat Register

Personal Communication

Bjørnevik, H, F.; Christensen, A, E.; Økland, K, M. (2014) Informal discussion forward facing scarph on Oselvar. [meeting in Oslo] with Chivers [17 July 2014].

Bjørnevik, H, F. (2015) Snikk [email] to Chivers [20 March 2015].

Christensen, A.E. (2014) Documenting boats [email] to Chivers [14 June 2014].

Christensen, A.E. (2014) Boat fastenings [tutorial Oslo] to Chivers [17 July 2014].

Christensen, A.E. (2014) Boats [email] to Chivers [22 October 2013].

Christensen, A.E. (2015) Boat snikk [tutorial Oslo] to Chivers [10 March 2015].

Christensen, A.E. (2015) Looks like Norwegian bete [email] to Chivers [9 November 2015].

Christensen, A.E. (2016) Boats from Gothenberg [email] to Chivers [14 March 2016].

Irivine, M. (2015) Bressay Lass [email] to Chivers [06 June 2015].

Johnson, D. (2015) Sandlodge boats by Duncan Smith, Sandwick. [email] to
Wishart, B. Chivers [07 December 2015]

Osler, A.G. (2016) yoal oars [email] to Chivers [27 June 2016].

Osler, A.G. (2020) Galvanised boat fastenings [email] with Chivers [2 February 2020].

Smith, B., Tait, I. (2015) Skuda [informal discussion] with Chivers [17 March 2015].

Smith, B. (2016) Fares [email] to Chivers [03 March 2016].

Smith, B. (2015) Norwegian Trade [email] to Chivers [1 June 2015].

Tait, I. (2015) bekk [email] to Chivers [11 November 2015].

Tait, I. (2016) Fastenings & rudder hangings [email] to Chivers [14 July 2016].

Tait, I. (2016) yoal [email] to Chivers [3 January 2016].

Tait, I. (2016) Eight-oared boat noost [email] to Chivers [03 February 2016].

Tait, I. (2016) Kalliness [email] to Chivers [14 June 2016].

Tait, I. (2016) Viking myth [email] to Chivers [13 July 2016].

Økland, K.M. (2015) Brugdebåt [skype] with Chivers [16 February 2015].

Interviews

Duncan, J. (2015) Boat Builder, Boat User [Interview by M. Chivers] Boat Shed, Shetland Museum, Lerwick [08 December 2015].

Duncan, W. (2015) Boat User [Interview by M. Chivers] Boat Shed, Hamnavoe, Burra [2 May 2015].

Holt, A. (2016) Boat User [Interview by M. Chivers] Northouse, Papa Stour [24 February 2016].

Hutchison, M., Mc Neil, A. (2015) Sailors / Boat Builders [Interview by M. Chivers] Yell [7 February 2015].

Hutchison, M., McNeil, A. (2015) Sailors / Boat Builders [Interview by M. Chivers] Whalsay, 14 March 2015.

Hurculson, L. (2016) Descendant of Boat Builder, John Inkster. [Interview by M. Chivers] Houlls, East Burra Isle, 28 January 2016.

Isbister, T. (2015) Boat Builder / Sailor [Interview by M. Chivers] Burland, Trondra, 12 February 2016.

Isbister, T. (2016) Boat Builder / Sailor [Interview by M. Chivers] Burland, Trondra, 4 March 2016.

Jacobson, G. (2020) Descendent of boat builder John Eunson. [Interview by M. Chivers] Virkie, Dunrossness, 8 February 2020.

Moncrieff, A. (2015) Sailor / Boat Builder [Interview by M. Chivers] Tumblin, Aith, 11 November 2015.

Moncrieff, L., Wishart, B. (2015) Sailors [Interview by M. Chivers] Sandwick, 6 April 2015.

Mouat, W. (2016) Boat Builder / Sailor [Interview by M. Chivers] Northwick, Unst, 24 May 2016.

Peterson, G. (2016) Boat User [Interview by M. Chivers] Brettadal, Brae, 3 March 2016.

Rendall, A., Wishart, B. (2016) Boat User [Interview by M. Chivers] East Voe, Scalloway, 4 February 2016

Sandison, D. (2016) Sailor / Boat Designer [Interview by M. Chivers] Haroldswick, Unst, 24 May 2016

Scott, J. (2016) Boat User [Interview by M. Chivers] Bressay Heritage Centre, Bressay, 23 March 2016

Tait, R. (2015) Boat Builder / Sailor [Interview by M. Chivers] Boat Shed, Shetland Museum, Lerwick, 8 December 2015.

Williamson, S. (2016) Boat Builder, Boat User [Interview by M. Chivers] Brae, 16 February 2016.

Wills, J. (2015) Boat user [Interview by M. Chivers] Bressay, 9 September 2015.

Wishart, B. (2015) Sailor [Interview by M. Chivers] Sandwick, 9 November 2015.

Index

Boats and their furniture, related items, and regattas